The Wisdom of Solomon

Paul Solomon

Compiled and Edited by Grace de Rond

The Paul Solomon Foundation
PO Box 7
Swinford
Co Mayo
Ireland
http://www.paulsolomon.com

Printed in the USA.

ISBN: 1453634738
Library of Congress Control Number: 2010935330

Cover design and interior design by Grace de Rond.

Photo on page 469, courtesy of William G. Thomas.

For further information on Paul Solomon:
http://www.paulsolomon.com
http://www.wisdomofsolomon.com

Immeasurable thanks to Paul Solomon
for making so many things possible.
And to Ron, Gabriel, Michael, Joseph,
Zosha, Paul and my mom.

EDITOR'S NOTE

When I was fifteen, my mom gave me my first book on Edgar Cayce: *There is a River* by Thomas Sugrue. Eight years later, she gave me a book on Paul Solomon's work as a spiritual teacher and a psychic channel: *Excerpts from the Paul Solomon Tapes* compiled by Daniel Emmanuel and Tom Johnson.

Within a year of reading the book about Paul, I made my way to Virginia Beach, VA and showed up at the door of his organization to volunteer. This was 1975, and I was assigned the task of indexing Paul's trance readings low-tech style, using a cassette tape player, enormous old-fashioned headphones on a spiral cord, and a notepad and pencil.

From the first audible word, I fell in love. More than three decades later, much of who I am is a result of my study of Paul's work and my experience of him as a personal teacher.

In 1977, I received a personal reading from Paul that described my role with his work. "Let your direction be in cataloging, indexing and making of value the information that is set before you. Through the categorizing, become an authority on what is given and said. Spare no moment in sharing it. Be of assistance in every way, in allowing the facts, ideas and concepts that are here to become more and better known. Be constantly a force behind gathering, assembling and disseminating the material from these records. The time is upon you, and you must be about it. Apply your energies to it, and let that be a form of your service."

Over the years, I worked on many writing projects involving Paul's lectures and readings. He told me to always make the text understandable while safeguarding the message. If the reader could not grasp the message, what good was the publication? At first, I refused to change a word. Eventually, I followed his instructions. And I always prayed before I began.

Following Paul's death in 1994, I wanted to create a book from his work. I began compiling *The Wisdom of Solomon* in 1996. I spent six years sifting through as many versions of a single concept as possible, using cassette tapes as well as hardcopies of his recorded lectures. I compiled each chapter from dozens of lectures on various complementary topics, which at times was mind-boggling. For example, I used 24 versions of his lecture on How to Evaluate a Psychic Reading to create the chapter of that title – sitting on the floor surrounded by printed copies of all the versions, initially editing with scissors and tape. In editing his spoken words into written form, the challenge was to cover topics as thoroughly and effectively as he did, while keeping repetition to a minimum. And of course, to make him sound as good on paper as he did in person!

In 2002, I submitted the completed manuscript to the Paul Solomon Foundation for permission to publish, which they authorized, sharing equally in any profits. I spent the last eight years running up and down various avenues of publication.

Finally, in 2010, it is finished.

Every man beareth the whole stamp of the human condition.
Michel de Montaigne 1533-1592

Clasp the hands and know the thoughts of men in other lands.
John Masefield 1878-1967

In days to come, it will be more and more possible for men
to experience what Paul experienced at Damascus.
Rudolf Steiner (1861-1925)

CONTENTS

INTRODUCTION
By Grace de Rond

Paul Solomon was an extraordinary man. His wisdom and abilities surpassed what is considered common, or even normal. He was known internationally as a teacher, prophet, healer, minister and humanitarian. Yet like many great spiritual leaders, Paul's journey toward wisdom and mastery over his powers was not uncomplicated.

Paul was the son of a Southern Baptist minister, born into a family where the ministry was presupposed as a vocation. To the non-Southern Baptist, a mental image arises of a narrowly defined religious lifestyle and a fundamental conservatism dictated by a literal interpretation of the Bible. Often missed or misunderstood by outsiders is the powerful constancy of support that exists in the home of a Southern Baptist family.

The security stems from an indisputable belief that it is possible to talk to God and receive answers. God exists as an active member of the household, and two-way communication is a daily occurrence. In his own home, Paul was powerfully affected. He watched as his parents sought daily guidance and noted how they based decisions on the silent replies they received. God was accessible, and the Holy Spirit was an active participant in everyday life.

Growing up in a fundamentalist Christian home, a child trusts that God is always available for guidance and support and is comforted by that knowledge. However, as the child grows into a Baptist teenager, normal tendencies arise that he would rather God not notice. A dilemma evolves: How to be good all the time, and what in the world to do with all that guilt.

The Baptist doctrine provided no answer for Paul as he moved into puberty. Burdened by orthodox views on morality and what defines appropriate behavior, he began to discover tendencies that were enjoyable but forbidden. Paul believed what he had been taught from an early age – that God was always present, always watching, and always keeping records. The result was an overwhelming obsession with sin and guilt. When he could no longer stop himself from committing "transgressions against God," Paul would turn his framed picture of Jesus facedown on his bedside table, hoping for a moment's privacy from his savior.

Paul also exhibited uncommon abilities, which compounded his dilemma of trying to be a good Baptist. From an early age, he could see colors around individuals and called them "good lights" and "bad lights," depending on how he perceived the person's character. As a young child, he would point at a person and sound the alarm, "He's bad!" His embarrassed parents would scold him for being rude, so eventually he learned to keep quiet. He could also read minds. He knew what people were thinking and discovered early that people regularly say the opposite. He also knew what was going to happen and could predict the future, which only undermined his efforts to be just like everyone else. While these psychic experiences were natural for Paul, obviously they were not "normal." Paul's growing sense that he was abnormal and the resulting isolation were becoming excruciating for him.

Paul could also "absorb" the information in his schoolbooks if he carried them in front of his body with his arms folded over them. This was particularly useful to him since traditional methods of learning were proving difficult. However, chaos broke out one day when he was dared by his classmates to "read" what was written in their notebooks. The kids taunted him, not believing he could actually do it. As Paul began to reveal the private scribbled notes of one of the girls, the group fell silent, first shocked and then frightened. Word of his disturbing demonstration spread through the school, and he ended up in the office, listening to the principal tell his mother, "We don't know what he's doing, but he'd better stop!"

Sitting at the kitchen table with his mother later that afternoon, the mood was grave as Paul waited for her to speak. For his mother, it was the culmination of years of confusion and worry. His strange skills were incomprehensible to her. For years, she had watched him struggle to manage his mysterious abilities, feeling helpless to provide him answers. Were his abilities a blessing, or were they a curse? She hoped for the first, while fearing the latter.

Paul felt humiliated. He could still see the shock and betrayal in the girl's eyes, followed by fear and repulsion on the kids' faces. He was a freak. The principal threatened to throw him out of the school. And now, what was his mother going to say?

"Your father and I have been aware of these unusual abilities of yours for a long time," she began slowly. "We've known since you were little that you're different. You have abilities that most people don't have."

Yes, he was different from other people. That was becoming increasingly more apparent to everyone. He was definitely strange, but there was more. For a Baptist boy, strange implied wrong, and wrong was sinful. It was sinful to do these things. Worse, it was sinful to be able to do these things.

"We know these things are possible because sometimes certain people are given powers that others don't have," his mother continued. "These powers can come from only two sources. They can come from God, or they can come from the devil."

There was more, but by now Paul was sobbing. He already suspected what she would say next. He was certain that an evil force was at work in him. He had long been consumed by dread of his own powers. For years, he had apologized to God, begged for forgiveness, pleaded that the terrible powers be taken away. He just wanted to be normal, like the other kids at school.

"If you were using these abilities of yours to help people, we would know that they came from God...."

She had said enough. For young Paul, the message was clear. He was evil, a tool of the devil. He was sure his mother had confirmed his worst fears. He might even be the anti-Christ. His terror of who he might be and the hatred he felt for himself were unbearable. That night, after everyone had gone to bed, Paul tried to kill himself.

The effort was more messy than effective. With a dull knife and halfhearted attempts, suicide was hardly possible, though he scared himself and his family badly.

A dash to the emergency room and a subsequent session with a psychiatrist only compounded Paul's misery. Not only was he a failure at living, he was a failure at dying. The psychiatrist assured him that, at age fourteen, his fascination with sexual things was normal and that the other "unusual behavior" was probably just his imagination. However, since the doctor was not a Baptist, his opinion did not count.

Paul's only recourse was prayer, and lots of it. Over the next year, he prayed constantly, hoping to cleanse himself of the evil that apparently drove him. He deliberately disciplined his thoughts, memorizing and silently reciting Bible passages constantly to keep his mind occupied. He learned to turn off the psychic abilities that had become a curse, by changing channels in his head whenever his thoughts went in an unwanted direction. He understood that stopping a habit is more difficult than replacing one, so he kept his thoughts on God, hoping there would be no space left for evil to trespass.

His sexual interests were not as easily managed. No Baptist came forward to tell him that it might be hormones or that it was normal, so he struggled along. According to his tormented conscience, there was only one way to right the wrongs that he could or would not relinquish. He would turn his life completely over to God, hoping the ministry would redeem him.

Feeling some confidence from his new decision, Paul lay in bed one night listening to the familiar, reassuring sounds of a prayer meeting lead by his father in the living room. The group assembled regularly for an animated study of the Bible. They were young Baptist ministerial students, ardent and fiery. They prayed loud and hard. Long, impassioned invocations filled the air with zealous euphoria until in the end each of them fell exhausted to the floor, laughing and crying uncontrollably. The atmosphere was simultaneously electric and comforting to Paul.

Eventually, the house and the people, and the bed where Paul lay, no longer existed. He found himself walking along a dirt road with fields of tall grass stretching to the horizon on either side. A warm breeze blew, and the air was fresh and cool, sweetened with the aroma of damp soil. He felt peaceful in this setting for the first time in memory, moving forward toward something unknown.

Far in the distance, he could see an enormous light filling the horizon. Out of that light arose a being bigger than the world itself. It was an image of Jesus. Jesus, as Paul imagined he might appear, only more beautiful. The being reached out to Paul, causing something deep within him to respond. In that second, something transformed and Paul's life would be forever altered.

What he experienced was a change in perspective. For months, he had been praying to be "fixed," as if sin is God's exclusive domain and hard-sought rewards like redemption, rescue and salvation are his to hand out when motivated by whim. In that moment of experiencing an image of God face-to-face, an image that sprung from within rather than from the writings or sermons of others, Paul for the first time decided to take responsibility for himself and for his personal relationship with God.

"You're *my* God now!" he shouted as he ran into the embrace of this irresistible being formed of light. "You're really my God, and nothing can change that or take that away from me!" Instantly, the years-long schism seemed healed.

Just as suddenly, Paul found himself back in his bedroom. He had been shouting and crying, delirious yet happy. He woke, certain that he had disturbed everyone, but instead the house was quiet. The prayer meeting had adjourned long ago, and his family was asleep. He knew it had not been a dream. He could only assume that the experience had occurred in some distant place, far from his bedroom and far from his waking consciousness.

In the years following this experience, Paul's God remained a Baptist and existed most of the time in a box labeled, "Guilt, Condemnation and Disapproval." But never again would Paul feel unacceptable or separated.

The obvious next step for him was to answer the calling. At age fourteen, Paul became an ordained, licensed minister. Young but wiser than his years, he instinctively shared with his congregation what he had always accepted as truth.

"If you have a problem, you can talk to God, and you'll receive answers," he told them. "You'll receive guidance and instructions, and you'll be comforted."

Paul was taught from infancy that two-way communication with God was possible, yet he never received specific instructions for how that could or would take place. He had experienced a personal, direct encounter with God, his personal calling. However, no words had been shared. The being of light had not actually said anything.

He wanted his congregation to maintain the possibility, even an expectation, that they could have a direct conversation with God. But in truth, Paul believed that if any member of his congregation suddenly heard an unexplained voice coming from out of nowhere, he would be frightened out of his wits and probably believe himself crazy. And so would his family and friends.

So how would guidance come? What form would God's voice take? Was he relegated to inspiring hunches or feelings, or could the all-powerful God make himself heard with the physical ear?

It would be eighteen turbulent years before Paul would discover the answers. Through an extraordinary experience in 1972, he would discover that his source and creator could literally speak to him, and through him, in precise and understandable terms. Eventually, that discovery would completely alter the course of his life.

As a minister, Paul's course of direction was clear and fixed, and he was eager to be on his way. Following high school, he completed a tour of duty with the army, during which time he married. Soon the young couple gave birth to a daughter. After his release from the army, he immediately enrolled in a Baptist seminary, following the path of his father, his grandfather and his uncles.

Feeling at home for the first time, Paul thrived in the religious academic setting. He developed a reputation, first as someone who could hold his own in classroom debates. He reveled in challenging the professors whom he believed dogmatic, born and schooled deep in the Bible Belt. Secondly, he developed as a speaker with sought-after talents of his own. He inspired congregations in the surrounding churches and eventually traveled as a guest preacher to churches throughout the state. And through his night job with the police department, he initiated a much-needed prison ministry.

Gradually, Paul managed to leave behind the strange and troublesome powers of his youth. By the end of his senior year of seminary, he was well on his way to a successful career as a skilled and respected pastor. Then the bottom fell out of his world.

In competition with full-time studies, two jobs, a speaking schedule, and Paul's new popularity, his marriage had suffered. Fed-up with feeling abandoned, his wife left with their baby to visit her parents and never came back. Paul's appeals by phone and mail went unanswered, so he went to plead with her in person. But by that time, she had fallen in love with someone else.

In 1967, divorce was rare. Among southern Baptist ministers, it was nearly nonexistent because it was unconditionally unacceptable. Devastated and depressed, his dreams shattered for the second time, Paul considered his plight from a bed in a psychiatric hospital.

He agonized over why God would call him to preach as a minister, lead him into the seminary, allow him to come so close to his goal by experiencing a taste of the joy and respect of a ministerial calling fulfilled, and then pull the rug out from under him. Instead of guilt, this time he felt rage. Again, this punishing unreasonable God who ruled impulsively through fear and havoc had betrayed him, bringing more personal crisis to his life.

This time, he was determined to rid himself of the deceiver completely. He decided to spurn everything religious, so he left the seminary only weeks away from graduation. In defiance, he bought a pack of cigarettes. For a well-behaved pastor's son, who never smoked, drank, swore, danced or went to movies, this was decisively rebellious. He smoked the whole pack and made himself sick, but he felt consoled because now God knew he was angry. Next he bought a beer, and another, and another. And so began five long years of addicted chaos and numbed pain.

Paul's goal was to break every rule that had so far defined his life. In a relentless pursuit of time and experiences missed, he maintained a drugged and drunken existence while he explored sexual experiences that he had never even imagined. As his anger eventually sank into despair, he stayed on the move. He traveled the country, holding dozens of jobs from bartender to beautician, hospital orderly to restaurant manager. Through it all, he attempted to assure himself that he was having a good time. After all, he had finally outsmarted God.

Sitting alone in his apartment one day, Paul watched his pet hamsters racing on their spinning treadmill, their legs pumping furiously yet going nowhere. Just like him, they probably thought they would arrive somewhere shortly, blind to the pointlessness of their efforts and their situation. Watching despondently, Paul recognized his own predicament – running faster and faster, intensely heading no place.

Disheartened, he turned away. Then he bolted the door of his apartment, pulled all the shades, took the phone off the hook, and sat in the dark to wait. A debilitating depression descended. Work was necessary for survival, but nothing else could get him out of the self-made asylum of his dark apartment. He refused to speak to anyone. Even drugs and alcohol finally lost their appeal and their stranglehold. The constant parade of lost souls like him, which had filed in and out of his apartment for years, gradually disappeared.

Paul was thirty-three years old, had accomplished nothing, had failed at everything, and was going nowhere. As his estrangement from life increased, he sank further and further into depression. He had no one. He had spent the last five years accumulating meaningless relationships with people who were also searching for escape and were generally worse off than he was. He had no friends and no confidants.

His parents cared, but he knew their solution and refused it: "Go to church, pray and read your Bible." Paul still wanted nothing to do with God. Yet deep inside himself he knew an answer had to come quickly.

Many years earlier, Paul had trained as a hypnotherapist while stationed at Brooke Army Medical Center. Under the supervision of doctors, he had used hypnosis to help soldiers with a variety of personal problems, including depression. Remembering the success of that program, he thought that a good hypnotherapist would be helpful. He found a hypnosis clinic in the yellow pages, called and made an appointment. The therapist seemed confident that Paul's problem was a deep-seated guilt complex brought on by his strict religious upbringing and was sure that successful treatment was possible. However, when Paul heard the exorbitant price of the twice-weekly sessions, he left feeling more miserable than ever. Even when he sought help, it remained just out of his reach. His state of mind was at a crisis point.

Paul went to work that night feeling incensed and bitter, but at least he was finally talking. He angrily described his predicament to a familiar customer at the bar. "How in the world am I supposed to afford hypnosis at those prices?" he protested.

"I hypnotized someone once," Harry offered, his voice trailing off as Paul continued to rant about the unfairness of life. Suddenly comprehending what Harry had said, Paul stared at him in disbelief.

"You hypnotized someone once?" he echoed.

There was a dubious confidence in Harry's hopeful expression, and Paul supposed "once" would have to do. "Let's go, then!" And off they went to Paul's apartment where he lay down and closed his eyes, submitting himself apprehensively to Harry's novice attempt at hypnosis. Paul's last conscious thought was, "This'll never work. This guy has no idea what he's doing. If anything happens, it'll be because he bored me to sleep."

The night was February 15, 1972. *"You have not attained sufficient growth or spiritual awareness to understand contact with these records,"* spoke a powerful voice, not dissimilar from Paul's, as he lay unconscious on the couch. *"That which you perform is a foolish experiment, for you attempt to harness powers you do not understand and to contact sources, records and intelligences you are not familiar with. How will you try the spirits should you attain that you seek? Would you recognize him whom you do not know, have not been familiar with?"*

This was not what Harry expected. He wrestled himself out of his shocked state and groped for something intelligent to ask, "Who are you? Are you a familiar spirit or a guide? Do you have a name?"

"Neither familiar spirit nor guide is necessary for the reading of these records," the voice continued. *"It is rather in yourselves, in your own development, that understanding and guidance will come. Not from a lesser spirit, but from the throne of grace itself. It is through your development that you may come before these records and read what you will, for the instruction and development of those*

on your plane who would know more of the divine. Then go and study, with prayer and meditation. Develop the self and your own spiritual understanding, so that you may return. Being familiar with these planes, you will be welcomed and may read and rejoice."

Just as suddenly as it had begun, the extraordinary session ended. Paul awoke, remembering nothing. He felt like someone had hit him hard in the stomach, and his body was doubled over in pain. On top of that, he still felt depressed. Harry, on the other hand, was practically jumping up and down with excitement.

"Some kind of spirit spoke through you!" He could hardly get the words out. "It talked about spiritual awareness and prayer and records!" Still in pain, Paul could not care less.

"Well, what do you expect when you hypnotize an ex-Baptist preacher?" he demanded. Not waiting for an answer and still clutching his stomach, he led Harry to the door, wanting to be done with it.

Over the next days, each man's determination grew, though in opposite directions. Harry could hardly wait for another opportunity to talk to the voice. On the other hand, Paul threw himself into his work, determined not to get involved in another dead-end venture where God was bound to be lurking.

Harry returned every day, insistent that they had stumbled onto something fantastic. He bought a book about the medium Arthur Ford and brought it over for Paul to read. But Paul was implacable. He was definitely intrigued, though a little frightened, but he was not interested in going any further with the experiment. He still believed the information had spewed out of his Baptist-saturated subconscious.

In the end, Harry finally won Paul over. His argument was, "It couldn't have been you talking. You're not that smart." That finally made sense to Paul. When Harry showed up with a tape recorder, Paul agreed to try it again, but only on his terms.

There was one way to prove the validity of Harry's claims. Paul needed a test question concerning information that neither of them knew, yet something verifiable. Only then would Paul be assured that the voice was something beyond his own mind.

Paul's great-grandfather had been murdered many years earlier. He died without revealing the hiding place of a large sum of money. The family knew he had been saving it, but could never locate it. Where was the money? This would be an excellent test question. Paul also wanted to know the cause of the abdominal pain he felt when he woke the first time, and how it could be prevented. A third question would concern the preparation needed to approach "these records." The fourth: "Who are you?" Not necessarily in order of importance, Paul would recall years later.

As Harry prepared his tape recorder, Paul lay down again and closed his eyes. In response to Harry's bland attempts at hypnotism, Paul's body suddenly jerked upward, then gently relaxed as if asleep.

I am approaching the entrance to a tunnel. It is similar to the mouth of a cornucopia because it seems to spiral inward and upward. I can see two figures at the opening. They seem to be waiting for me. One is Merle who was my girlfriend in high school until she died in our senior year. The other is my young friend, Jaida, who remained my secret companion for years following his death when we were seven. They each take me by the hand and lead me through the tunnel. We come out the other side onto a grassy hill. As we begin to climb, I see that we are approaching a temple at the top of the hill....

Paul awoke from his dreamlike vision of former friends to Harry's excited shouts. This time, Harry had captured the voice on tape. Paul sat in stunned silence as he listened to a more potent version of his own voice pinpointing the location of the lost money. It could be found in the chimney of the old family home. The circumstances of his great-grandfather's death were also described.

"Your consciousness is disengaging itself from the physical body," the voice explained concerning the abdominal pains. *"When the physical body feels consciousness leaving, it associates that with death. It will do anything in its power to hold consciousness in the body. For that reason, those muscles are cramping in an attempt to sustain life. As soon as the body becomes accustomed to the procedure and realizes that the cramping is not necessary or even effective, the reaction will cease."*

Concerning preparation, the voice provided several suggestions, including meditation, sacred scripture study, a set of physical exercises, and an approach to diet. Prayer was also suggested, though something quite different from what Paul had been doing for years and calling prayer. He was certain that this information had not come from his own mind.

"This is not a spirit," said the voice in answer to the question concerning identity. *"This is not a personality. You are not talking with someone else. You are talking with the rest of your mind."*

The voice explained that beyond our conscious and subconscious minds is a greater portion, which contains all knowledge and intelligence. This superconscious mind could draw information from records that only it could access, records written on the skein of time and space. *"They are the records of the universe – past, present and future – and they are available to all individuals."*

Paul had never encountered anything like this before. In one sense, hypnosis had been successful because he was too amazed to be depressed anymore. His previous associations had never included psychics, readings, spirits, superconscious minds or records of the universe. There had only been God or the devil.

In the Baptist seminary, Carl Jung was discounted as a lunatic. To mention a psychic would have been blasphemy. Paul's earlier participation in the army's hypnosis project had brought warnings from his friends, and his parents had begged him to leave it alone.

This amazing phenomenon of a voice that spoke of spirits was frightening, yet it was too intriguing to ignore. So the two men went on to contact the voice repeatedly in the next few weeks.

The two figures are waiting to take me through the tunnel. As I come out the other side, I find myself in a meadow of wild flowers where a soft breeze blows, and I can hear the sound of a brook. Ahead of me is a mountain. As I climb, I pass through seven terraced gardens of glorious color. At the top, I enter a temple. The air is rich with music, though I see no one. I see rows and rows of books with names on the bindings. I am in an enormous library....

A collection of profound and insightful information accumulated as the two men returned to read daily from the records. Additionally,

Paul and Harry's conscious awareness expanded as they continued their new disciplines and studied every related book they could find.

The Source, the term eventually introduced by the Readings themselves, provided information that often felt familiar to Paul, like an innate recognition. However, many ideas were completely new. He was comfortable with the language used, including religious concepts and Bible quotations, but he rejected the growing references to reincarnation.

Paul and Harry were in an extraordinary and unfamiliar realm. There were "the records" to consider and fathom, records that contained the history of the world and even its prehistory. Then there were masters, angels, spirit guides, the Great Cloud of Witnesses, the Great White Brotherhood, and discarnate souls who in previous lifetimes had mastered certain areas of knowledge. The Source described itself as a collective consciousness that included all these and more – a *"group of beings with a single consciousness, who follow in the light of Christ... communicating from the mind of God, the Throne of Grace itself."*

"The voice that you are talking with is the source of your mind, which gave birth to your mind. It pre-existed your physical body and created your physical body. Its relationship to God might best be described as the child of God, the only son of God."

The Readings explained that the "Christ" they referred to has expressed through many religions and cultures from the beginning of time, including the historical figure, Jesus. They clarified that a person does not have to be religious to speak with the source of his or her being. That source can be called by any name, because unlike man there is no ego involved.

Paul's Baptist God, who ruled through fear and punishment, was breaking down day by day. The God he had worshiped for thirty years, even grudgingly during his time of rebellion, was reducing to a fantasy figure of his own design. The Source described that God as the one *"created by man in his own image."*

Paul was thrilled with the possibility of firsthand confirmation of a creator who could speak. Could it be true that God was not mute, was not relegated to a long ago burned out bush or an ancient talking donkey? After all the years of hearing, from the front of the sanctuary, that communication was possible – could it be as simple as listening to a voice inside ourselves?

One dilemma remained for Paul. In the first communication, the voice had said, *"It must be obvious to you, even at this point, that these things do not come from the mind of man."* It was obvious to Paul, and it was becoming increasingly clear with every successive Reading. The process as well as much of the content went against what Paul believed to be "righteous." What if it was from the devil? He could almost hear his mother's concerned voice, "There are only two powers in the world that can produce this kind of ability...."

Here was the same unresolved issue again, almost two decades later. Since the night of his attempted suicide, he had managed to successfully suppress these strange abilities. Was this new phenomenon simply evidence of some evil force residing within? Was he really just a tool of the devil?

There was only one person to whom Paul felt confident to turn. Paul's father was a formidable man, quick to call a backslider by name. He was a stalwart Baptist pastor whose love for his family never confused his priorities. God and the church always came first. Paul turned to his father for help, knowing he would receive a wise and honest answer. He was certain his father would think it was the devil at work, but possibly he could offer some form of protection since the work seemed valuable.

Paul was shocked by his father's response after listening to the recorded voice detailing discarnates, past lives and the living-God within each person.

"It is of God," he stated matter-of-factly, without hesitation.

"How can you say that?" exclaimed Paul, so shocked that he seized the opposite argument. "It doesn't sound at all Baptist to me!"

"On the contrary," his father explained, citing the Bible as evidence. "Daniel needed to know what King Nebuchadnezzar's dream was, along with its interpretation. So what did he do? He went into his room with his friends, lay down to sleep and received the information that would save their lives. It sounds like you're doing the same kind of thing.

"There is a verse in scripture that says, 'Which one of you, if your child asks for a piece of bread, will give him a stone? Or if he asks for a fish will give him a scorpion?' Your mother and I have been praying for you every day for the past five years, since you left the ministry. Praying that something would happen that would get you back on track. I knew that it would have to be something dramatic. I never doubted that it would happen, and I believe this is it. I asked God to bring you back, and I know he didn't give me a stone or a scorpion. That's how I know it is of God. You are communicating with the Holy Spirit. You go back and get to work," he directed. "You do what that voice tells you to do. It's your life work."

I am walking into the tunnel, which is now very familiar. I look for my two friends, but this time there is no one waiting for me. I hesitate, since this has never happened before. Finally, I walk through the tunnel alone. As I come out the other side, there on a distant hill are Merle and Jaida, waving goodbye. They turn and begin to walk away, toward something that I cannot see. I know that I will never see them again. They have completed their work in opening the way for me to approach these records. They have pointed me in a direction beyond themselves and into a communication with the source of all there is to know....

Following the encounter with his father, Paul began his new work in earnest. The Readings took precedence over everything else in his life. As he accumulated more information each day, he grew in his own understanding of what was happening and what was being given. He also continued to investigate the identity of the Source.

"This is not a spirit or another person. You are talking with the rest of your mind. The mind that you think with is minute. There is much more to your thinking ability than what you experience. The mind that you ordinarily think with is a result of your external senses, observing the world around you and making judgments about what it sees, hears and feels, gathering information and making logical conclusions. It is the sum of your intelligence. It is external, a body phenomenon, a result of the brain functioning."

The Source added, *"There is also an intelligence that is inherent within you, that is not the result of the brain functioning. The voice that you are talking with is that higher consciousness – the greater consciousness within you."*

15

The obvious question arose: Was the ability to access this consciousness of information unique to Paul, or could anyone do it? The Source explained that Paul had been successful because he could silence his conscious mind long enough to listen to a consciousness greater than his own.

"The phenomenon of the rest of your mind, the superconscious, the greater intelligence, is not peculiar to one person. In this moment, cells in your body are actively dying. Simultaneously, another phenomenon is occurring. You are replacing those dying cells with new cells, new life. The intelligence within you that knows how to make new life, knows how to cause your heart to beat, knows how to heal your body, that is coexisting in the body with you – it is that intelligence that made you. It is the creator of your brain, your consciousness, your body. If that intelligence created your ability to communicate, surely it can hear you and knows how to communicate with you directly. That same intelligence is available to everyone."

Paul had been successful in reaching the unconscious state, not primarily because he was hypnotized, but because he had been desperate to escape consciousness. The Source explained that anyone could enter a subtler reality or altered awareness. Losing total consciousness was not necessary. And in that place, anyone could ask questions and receive answers from the source of life.

As word spread of Paul's work, people began to flock to his home, many of them desperate for answers to life's challenges. The demand grew daily, so he asked the Source what to do. The Source cited a familiar allegory: Give a hungry man a fish, and you have fed him once; teach him to fish, and you have fed him for a lifetime.

"Teach people how to receive their own answers instead of providing them the answers they seek. Teach others to discover the answers within themselves."

Following this directive, Paul gathered the guidelines that the Source had offered him personally, to prepare himself to read the records. These included instructions for diet, exercise, meditation and prayer. There were also specific exercises for enhancing personal growth, developing intuitive abilities and gaining a comprehensive understanding of the impartial laws by which this universe operates.

Paul combined these as the cornerstone of Inner Light Consciousness, a guided experience in spiritual evolution. He offered the course to tens of thousands of people throughout the world until his death in 1994. He also trained many individuals to be teachers themselves, so this wealth of wisdom remains available today.

Paul made available instruction on virtually every phase of human existence. He did this through thousands of hours of trance readings, published writings, residential programs, and seminars and lectures before worldwide audiences.

The Fellowship of the Inner Light, the nondenominational interfaith church that Paul founded in 1972, has united people of diverse nations, races, religions, faiths, disciplines and viewpoints under one roof. The common ground has been the belief that every individual has a gift to give to those who have ears to hear, and that through perfect love we can literally cast out fear and its effects.

From the moment of his first trance experience, the focus of Paul's life became the empowerment of others. His dream – his ministerial calling fulfilled – was to inspire others in their pursuit toward their full potential. He believed that pursuit could be enhanced in no better way than through a direct, experiential relationship with one's creator.

Like other great spiritual leaders, prophets and teachers throughout time, Paul sought to emphasize not his own unique abilities, but rather the message itself. He never lost his childhood devotion to his Father. Though he was considered one of the foremost international teachers of human potential and spiritual wisdom, in everything he did, he always pointed toward the greater teacher, the God within.

SLEEPING GODS
FROM THE PAUL SOLOMON SOURCE

L   *ook about you and see that all those about you are as sleeping gods. And your purpose is to cry them awake for the time that is at hand. Awaken God in the heart of every man and woman you see. Not placing him there as some have claimed to do, not lighting the light – but rather point to, bring attention to, cause consciousness of that light that is innate within each one.*

Awaken the gods on this plane that they may rejoice as the sons of morning, even as they rushed in, in that time when the morning stars sang together, when this plane was perfect. These were the sons of God, now only captured in sleep, only sleeping Gods lying about this plane.

Cause these to awaken to themselves, and to shake off the dust of the earth, to shake off these physical bodies that are the dust of the earth, and to rejoice, crying out. Cause these to return to their Father.

These all are a portion of the same family, and in coming together, a portion of the same body. So will that giant body of God arise, and in shaking the dust of the earth from itself, will rise up in glory, in power, in might and in light upon this plane. So then will this plane be shaken, and this earth will be changed and transmuted to a plane of light that would be as the footstool of God.

THE PLANETARY MYSTERY SCHOOL
You have never been without a teacher.

Hidden in secluded and forgotten forests, where only narrow footpaths snake through impenetrable tracts of scrub and thicket, or high atop distant veiled mountains where only the intrepid dare venture up perilous pathways, there exist shrouded schools of the ancient mysteries. Only those rare individuals who have set aside all earthly considerations in order to pursue enlightenment at any cost will find these sequestered schools. Only the most venerated initiates can teach there – those who have surrendered to, and gone beyond, the laws of this physical plane.

No one can make application to a mystery school. The spiritual seeker can only attempt to meet the normal challenges of daily life with inviolate skill and wisdom. In time, a master whose influence can prepare a way of entrance into a mystery school may notice him. Once there, through a series of devised initiations, the applicant's consciousness is molded. He is presented the opportunity to progress as rapidly as humanly possible. He journeys through the hierarchical stages of soul development, as he subdues the challenges and masters the lessons, which have been carefully and specifically designed by an inscrutable master teacher.

...or so I imagined.

In 1972, I suddenly detoured off the mainstream thoroughfare of Baptist fundamentalism, onto the lesser-known spiritual path. Unsurprisingly, I was like a starving man let loose at a banquet. I read every metaphysical book I could find. I attended dozens of seminars and classes. I formed my own study group. I was eager to try every herb, potion and appliance. Eventually, I studied astrology, the Tarot, the I Ching and Qabalah.

19

Of all my discoveries in those early days, nothing fascinated me more than the concept of the existence of present-day mystery schools. I could hardly wait to enroll in one. I wanted nothing more than to purify myself, master all my lessons, and quickly get to a mystery school.

I was determined. Never mind that the related literature referred only to ancient times when Hermes-Toth was High Priest and Initiator to Egypt, or when Pythagoras wrote his esoteric doctrine in secret symbols rather than words. In my search for information, I had stumbled upon an obscure teaching: "There are still mystery schools operating in this day. They are hidden and impossible to find, however they do exist. When the student is ready, the teacher will appear. Only then will entrance to the mystery school be possible."

So I did everything I could to make myself ready. I continued my disciplines, read my books and practiced what I believed were appropriate responses to my daily challenges. But how would I know when I was ready? How would *they* know when I was ready? How could I be sure that the talent scout would find me? It was not easy to leave it all to blind faith.

As I was studying and meditating, working to prepare myself, I discovered a law of telepathic communication in the writings of Dion Fortune, who was a spiritual teacher, author and occultist in the early 1900's. The law states, "If you focus on someone, whether in the flesh or not, by picturing his or her image in your mind and by calling his or her name repeatedly, the individual's consciousness will be attracted to you."

Why shouldn't that work for a mystery school, I wondered? At least they would find me. They would know I exist and take a look to see if I'm ready. Maybe I could convince them, if I could just make contact with them.

So I decided to try it. I had no idea on which mystery school I should focus. I only had the models as they appeared in the literature. From those descriptions, I formed what I thought was a connection with the ancient tradition of the mystery schools. As I sat in meditation one day, I held an image in my mind and repeated what seemed like an appropriate mantra.

Eventually, I experienced a sensation, as if I were touring another dimension, another reality, a world separated from this one. Suddenly, the room where I had been sitting no longer existed, and I was somewhere else. I felt as though I were floating through space.

What happened next was the most frightening experience of my life. I could see a procession of beings coming toward me, dressed in long black robes with hoods that shrouded their faces. As this line of beings began to form a circle around me, I could hear a drumming sound coming from all directions. As the sound grew louder, the beings came closer and closer. Apparently, I was the object of their processional, and I was not sure their intentions were good.

At the same time, I realized that I could not stop what was happening. How was I going to get back to my room? I had no idea how to separate myself from this scene or from these dark beings. What had I gotten myself into?

All I knew to do was pray, so I prayed like I have never prayed before. Never mind New Age affirmations, or supplications to the popularized Universal-Father-Mother-God-Goddess, whoever that is! I turned to what I knew best! I reverted right back to the old-time religious prayers of my childhood – the ones I learned in Sunday School class. I knew I had better get hold of Jesus and beg him to get me out of there.

Then it occurred to me that if I could contact these individuals by imaging them and by calling to them, I could probably contact myself by calling my own name. So I did exactly that. I began to call my name and to focus on the room where I had been sitting before the experience began. As a result, I quickly re-associated with my body, meaning I got back in it, and I was suddenly back in my room. I awakened, sweating, physically uncomfortable, dizzy, scared and very relieved. I felt thankful it was over.

Once I calmed down, I read further in the book by Dion Fortune and discovered that mystery schools maintain and enforce psychic and occult protection. Entrance or invasion on a psychic level is apparently not allowed. So I assumed that I had encountered some sort of cosmic cops.

My next step was to lie low. I had had enough of mystery schools for a while. I had probably made my presence known. They would discover me soon enough. Unless, of course, I had flunked the entry exam, which seemed more likely.

So I went about my business, which was the continuation of the trance readings and exploration of the amazing information coming from the Source. Word of our experiences spread quickly, and a small group of interested individuals began to form. As more people showed up daily to share the discoveries coming through the Readings, it became necessary to organize ourselves in some way. The demand for our services grew as fast as the enormous amount of information that was accumulating.

Out of a need to handle all of it, the Fellowship of the Inner Light was born as a nonprofit interfaith educational organization. By this time, we were offering a basic workshop in guided spiritual growth, since many people wanted to learn the techniques given to us through the Readings. In addition, we established an interfaith worship service Sunday mornings, which we called Joy in Worship.

Although our schedule was full and still expanding, I had no idea then that we would grow into a worldwide organization. It was inconceivable that Fellowship Centers would eventually exist around the world offering seminars, residential programs, counseling services and Joy in Worship services.

One day, soon after my experience with the Cosmic Cops, I passed a woman in the doorway of our little building as she was hurrying out. "I have to go make love to some trees," she said as she rushed past. Curious, I asked what she meant. She told me that she was enrolled in a bonsai class and that I really should get to know her teacher because he was a Zen Master.

"Master?" My ears instinctively perked up at the word. Eager to meet him, I decided to visit the Sho-K-In School of Bonsai.

Finding it was not easy. I passed the narrow dirt drive tucked away in the hedges several times before seeing it. Leaving my car, I wandered a narrow path into the woods until I found an unremarkable wooden building that blended with the surrounding trees. I knocked on the door, got no response, and decided to check behind the building.

There, I discovered an outdoor classroom of people who appeared to be intensely involved in torturing miniature trees. They were like gentle giants in a Lilliputian world. Everywhere were tiny pine trees in various stages of transformation. They resembled the gnarled trees that hug the side of a windswept cliff overlooking the ocean, with one side bare of branches because of the wind and salt spray. There were also tiny flowering wisteria trellises and groves of diminutive orange trees.

Each tree appeared to have grown naturally, defying its trainer whose hands had carefully molded its shape over months, perhaps years. The tiny forests sometimes included a lake, a mountain or a cliff, adding to the authenticity and quaint beauty.

I found it fascinating. Something unusual was happening here. I was certain that the person behind all this must be a master, and I grew excited.

Eventually, a slight, unassuming man appeared and greeted me as if he already knew me. Walking together through his gardens, I noticed distinctive things about him. In contrast to me, he never hurried. I was so excited that I asked three questions before he answered one, whereas he moved slowly and purposefully. As I became impatient, he moved even more slowly, and I became more impatient. Not that it seemed to matter to him. His attention was fixed on the living world around him. He communicated with his trees, as you and I would speak to each other. Our manners were in such contrast that, by the end of our tour, I was certain he was apologizing to the garden for my presence.

This man was teaching me something, but not through wise words, not even by pointing anything out. Apparently, I had the option of not even noticing.

We sat talking about his bonsai school. He spoke as slowly as he moved, while he sipped green tea from a tiny cup. I was in mid-sentence when suddenly he was no longer there.

There he was across the yard, gently touching the hand of a student as he spoke. "You must warn the tree before you cut, or it will bleed. Speak to the tree. It must know your intention, or it will think you mean to harm it with those clippers."

"You must realize that this is a living being," he explained to another student. "Do not think of it as a plant. Think of it as a soul. This soul needs to be molded in a particular direction. These training wires are like karmic experiences that mold its nature into a more beautiful expression.

"Do you see that if you place a rock here," he asked another, "it will conflict with the direction of this branch? And you will create conflict in this plant. Conflict cannot be created in the plant if you have no conflict within you. Before you touch the plant, be still and resolve your inner conflict."

This bonsai master was providing more than instruction. He was not just teaching horticulture, or botany, or bonsai. He was illustrating spiritual truths and laws of the universe. A real sage! So slow and understated – acting as if he were not brilliant.

When he returned to his seat beside me, I said, "I know that you won't admit to being a teacher of spiritual growth. But I can see that you are. I want to learn from you. Will you teach me?"

He appeared to steel himself against what must have seemed an accusation. In a voice almost hurt, he answered, "I am not a spiritual teacher. I do not teach spiritual lessons. I do not believe in teaching spiritual lessons."

How peculiar, I thought. I wonder what he does believe in.

"What do you mean?" I asked him. "I know you're teaching more than how to torture these little plants. There's a bigger message here. I can hear that in what you're saying. What do you mean you're not a spiritual teacher?"

"You are accusing me of separating life from its essence," he responded, seeming incensed. "What I teach is life, a relationship to the universe. I do not separate spiritual lessons from the lessons of life. There is only one law. Spiritual growth is growth. That is all. There is no such thing as a spiritual teacher because such a person would be attempting to separate spirit from life and life from growth, which is not possible. And it would be an error to try. Spirit and life are one."

Now I was really impressed. I asked again, "Will you teach me?"

In answer, he set before me a pitiful-looking pine that I suspected had already died and been thrown out by some inept student. He gave me some tweezers and told me to pick out the brown needles. There were hundreds! Obviously, my first lesson would be about patience. But I was determined to get on with it.

I'm going to do this if it kills me, I thought as I began to pick out the tiny brown needles, one by one. As I plucked and plucked, I thought of all the other things I should be doing. The more I plucked, the more my thoughts raced.

He should be over here talking to me, I reasoned. Instead, he went on an errand. He could be here teaching me fantastic lessons. Instead, here I sit plucking these damned little needles.

It seemed like hours before he finally returned and approached my table. The brown needles were gone now, but my little tree still looked scruffy and unkempt. At last he sat with me and began to comment on my work.

"If you were going to mold this tree into a more beautiful shape, how would you do that?" he asked.

I looked at the beautiful, perfectly shaped trees of his students surrounding my scraggly one and suspected that nothing could help it. "I don't see any way that this tree can look better," I told him.

He stared silently at the poor little tree, so I grasped for anything to say. "Maybe I could bend this branch this way, and I could cut this off." I picked up the shears to begin.

"Don't cut that yet!" he cried in the most agitated voice I had heard yet. "You did not ask permission."

"What do you mean?" I asked, dropping the shears.

"You have to talk to the life that is in that plant so that it understands your intentions. In that way, the tree's spirit will cooperate with you. That is how you will find out what direction it wants to go."

This is great, I thought. He's going to teach me to talk to devas!

"How do I do it?" I asked.

"Just talk to it," he said, his voice displaying the first sign of impatience, his eyes narrowing.

I drew a blank. I had never talked to a tree, and I had certainly never heard a tree speak. But he was watching me, and I was still determined. For the first time, I sensed that behind that calm demeanor, he was laughing at my discomfort.

While I searched for something to say that would not sound too ridiculous, he finally added, "If you could see that tree as a human being, what would that being look like?"

25

Now that was easier. A particular image had been in my mind all morning. I began to describe a sad little girl, dirty and unkempt, skinny little legs sticking out of combat boots, scraggly uncombed hair. A lost and unloved waif.

"Close your eyes," he said. "See the little girl standing before you." I closed my eyes and could see the little girl.

Then the bonsai master leaned close to me and whispered, "Now talk to her. Do not talk to the plant. Talk to the little girl. Ask her what she wants."

With my eyes closed, I saw the little girl, and I heard her say, "You've already washed my face. Now comb my hair."

I opened my eyes and looked down at my little tree. It had changed, viewed through a different perspective now. I felt the tree's excitement. It no longer feared my touch. Just like the little girl, it was excited at the prospect of looking more beautiful.

Without knowing specifically how, I began to communicate with the spirit within that plant. By the end of the afternoon, I had transformed my little tree into a gently leaning, windswept pine, the branches and bark missing on one side. I painted the bare trunk with lime so it looked like the sun had bleached it. Looking at it, you could almost smell the salt spray of the ocean. I was thrilled. I felt as if I had seen the transformation of a soul. I had taken something wild and discarded and had created living art, as if made more beautiful by nature itself.

What I learned from this man in those few hours affected me profoundly. Afterwards, I said to the teacher, "For a long time, I've wanted to be a student in a mystery school. I want to grow spiritually, as fast as I possibly can. I believe that you could teach me more than I could possibly learn from my little study group. I could learn more in one year with you than I could learn in many years on my own.

"Will you take me as a project and shape my consciousness like yours? Will you work with me and mold my life like the masters did in the ancient mystery schools?"

He listened to me thoughtfully. Then at last he spoke. "Paul, could you leave the Fellowship? Close its doors, and come here as my servant? Wash my teacups, make my bed, sweep my floors, and pick the dead needles off tiny pines? Could you do all these things even if I never said anything wise to you?"

The question stunned me. The Fellowship was my child, like a living being. I loved it more than anything. To close its doors would be like closing a part of my life, like cutting off a limb. It was an impossible choice.

I weighed the options for a moment and realized that there really was no choice. The life of the Fellowship was not confined to a small building or a particular group of people. The Fellowship was bigger and greater than all of that. It would continue, even if the doors were closed. As for me, there was nothing more important than finding a teacher. "Yes," I offered. "I will come and be your servant."

Looking away, he said, "That being true, I cannot teach you."

I was astonished. That was not the reply I expected. What did he mean? I was sure I was in. I knew I had made the right choice and given the right answer. And my answer had been authentic. Learning from a teacher was the most important thing in the world to me. I felt hurt and could feel the tears welling up as I asked, "Why not?"

"For one thing," he answered, "you are too emotional.

"Secondly, if you could close your Fellowship and come here, then I have need to learn from you, because I could not close this school to study at your Fellowship. In that case, you have much to teach me."

For a moment, there was nothing to say. I learned more in that single exchange than I thought I could learn in a lifetime. It was an unacceptable answer though. Here I was, knocking at the door of my mystery school. I had finally found it, and I was being turned away. I refused to accept it. I was determined to get in somehow.

"If you won't take me as a student," I asked, "will you at least introduce me to your teacher?" For years following this exchange, I marveled at my own boldness.

"No," was his answer.

I refused to let him deter or discourage me, though I felt tears welling up again. Fighting to control them, I repeated the question, "Why not?"

"Because you are too emotional," he answered.

This was apparently going to be a substantial obstacle. Trying my best to sound emotionless, I asked if he would monitor my progress in the future and perhaps make the introduction to his teacher someday when I was ready.

"Only the teacher can make that decision," he said. "If he wants to meet you, he will."

I finally gave up and left. I felt dejected, leaving with nothing more tangible than an intimation that someday, something might happen. I went back to my Fellowship and tried again to set aside my hunger for a mystery school.

That evening, I read the story of Annie Besant's apprenticeship to Madame Helena Blavatsky who founded the Theosophical Society in 1875. Annie's preliminary steps to actually becoming a student were a tale of torture. Until her emotions no longer denied her the lessons, she continued to blunder through each experience, refusing to take no as an answer from the great teacher. I decided to follow her example.

The next morning, I returned to the bonsai school at dawn, planning to have tea prepared when the teacher awoke. I would not take no for an answer. There was no way he would get rid of me.

To my surprise, the back door was unlocked when I arrived, and waiting for me on the kitchen counter was a list of instructions. He had fully expected me to show up. Thus began my initial experience as a student of the mysteries.

Over the next months, I arrived daily at the bonsai school. And daily, I was bent in ways I did not know I could manage. I became the teacher's assistant, caring for his clothes, washing his dishes, running errands for him, helping in his classes, traveling with him to speaking engagements.

My greatest challenge? Becoming responsible for my thoughts, words, actions and emotions. If I could not control myself, how could I ever master anything else? The teacher set up every conceivable situation that would irritate or confound me. It often seemed like I could do nothing right. I made mistake after mistake – from making bad tea and ruining his clothes, to causing him to miss his plane and important speaking engagements.

His response? Calm reserve. Nothing was ever explained. There were no wise teachings. What had he said? "Could you do all these things even if I never said anything wise to you?"

I read Annie Besant's story repeatedly. The first challenge, the first step of a spiritual student is to learn to be serene in the face of any situation of life, to learn to manage thoughts and emotions. Week after week, I willed myself to remain calm, no matter what mess I had created around me. I grew stronger at choosing how to respond rather than simply reacting without thought or choice.

After six months, the teacher finally dismissed me. He reminded me that he was not my teacher, had never been my teacher, and would never be my teacher in the future. He told me to go back to the Fellowship. This time, I did as he said.

Over the next few years, the Fellowship grew from a small group of interested followers in Atlanta, Georgia, to an organization headquartered in Virginia Beach, Virginia with more than a dozen satellite centers around the world. My days were filled with the business of lecture tours, seminars, residential programs, the development of Fellowship programs and trainers, the operation of the Fellowship Church, counseling sessions, and the never-ending requests for trance readings.

Life was very full when one day I received a call from a man at the Norfolk Virginia Botanical Gardens. He said that he knew the bonsai teacher and asked if he could show me a tree he had been tending. He hoped that I could make suggestions for its care. We agreed to meet that afternoon.

Later that day, a slight elderly man of Oriental descent arrived carrying a beautiful bonsai still in its training wires. We sat together and looked at the tree. We talked a few minutes about bonsai techniques. Then he left, asking that I keep the tree and care for it. Thinking that the tree was a gift from the bonsai teacher, I called him to thank him.

"I did not give the tree to you," he said.

"Well, then who did?" I asked.

"He did."

"What? Why should one of your students want to give me a tree?" I asked.

"That was not my student," he said almost indignantly. "That was my teacher."

My heart sank. What had I done? For years, I had waited, hoping that someday I might have the opportunity to meet this master teacher. I had sat right there in the chair next to him, without even recognizing him. It had not even occurred to me who he was. I had not asked him a single question. I could not believe my own ignorance. Obviously, mystery schools were still a mystery for me.

I immediately phoned the Botanical Gardens to speak to the man. I hid my eagerness, not wanting to reveal that I now knew who he was. And the last thing I wanted was to appear emotional. Instead, I stressed that I was not sure how to care for the plant. Could I please see him again? Graciously, he offered to return.

Again, I found myself sitting with this gentle man, peering at the little tree. This time, I was captivated by every word and gesture from him. How could I have missed the signs? The slow and purposeful movements, the strength of presence. I could hardly contain myself, but I knew I must.

As we sat there, he began to refer to the tree sitting before us. "As I was training this branch, instead of bending in a new and beautiful direction, it was stiff and ready to break," he explained softly. "That was the period when you decided to teach instead of publish your work."

"What do you mean? How do you know that?" I stammered.

He quietly replied, "This tree was put in training wires at the time that my student told me of you. Since then, I have watched you in the branches of this tree. Everything that you have done has been reflected in this image of you. If I met resistance in a branch, I knew that you were experiencing resistance in what you were doing, in your work or in your personal life."

I was astonished by what I was hearing. This teacher of teachers, who I had never even met, had been participating in every experience of my life for the past three years.

Looking at the little tree differently now, I realized that every branch had been a point of communication between him and me. He had been teaching me through the tree. He never forced me to learn anything. He never manipulated me by bending the branches in ways they did not want to go. He only made gentle suggestions to the tree, and to me through the tree, that I shape myself in more beautiful, harmonious directions.

I knew that I had come very, very close, and had somehow been allowed to touch the periphery of a genuine mystery school. A tangible, present-day school of the ancient mysteries. I asked the question that persisted in my mind. "Are there places, perhaps in China or Japan, where priests and priestesses provide instruction? Where an individual can learn how to respond to every situation of life, how to master life?"

"There may be such a place," he answered, "but you are already enrolled in the highest possible form of mystery school on this earthly plane. You have never been without a teacher. You study at the feet of a perfect teacher who has put the necessary lessons before you perfectly, throughout your life. Why would you go in search of something less than what you already have?"

Then he told me the story of another young man who had gone in search of a mystery school. This young man found himself enrolled in a Pythagorean School of the Mysteries and waited for the classes to start. As he left his room and walked down the long hallway to the dining room, he noticed a broom leaning against the wall and some dust nearby on the floor. Someone has not finished his work, he thought. This place is a mess. This is no way to run a mystery school. The young man had his meal and came back along the same hallway. He noticed that the dust and the broom were still there. He went back to his room and meditated, still waiting for the classes to start. After his afternoon meditation, he went again to the dining room for dinner. The broom and the dust remained, and now a mop and a bucket sat a little further down the hallway. How careless, he thought. This school was supposed to be the best available. Irritated, he went to eat. When he returned, the mess in the hallway remained. "I'm going to tell someone about this," he muttered. "In fact, I'm not sure I want to stay here. If the masters of this school can't manage things better than this, they can't teach me very much." And there the young man sits, even to this day, still waiting for the lessons to begin – still ignoring the mop and the bucket.

Following this encounter with the master teacher, I dropped my search for a school hidden on some distant mountaintop. I accepted his advice and decided to concentrate on the mystery school hidden within me, within each of us.

Each of us is enrolled in a school that I call the Planetary Mystery School. We entered this school the day we were born. Since our birth, a master teacher has been carefully designing and presenting the perfect lessons that we need in order to strengthen our ability to master life on earth – our ability to respond appropriately, with compassion, kindness and wisdom, to every situation that arises. Through this school of life, we are being shaped daily in more beautiful and harmonious directions.

Not all mystery school teachers are slight, gentle men bearing tiny trees. Teachers come in many disguises. The training wires in this school can come in all shapes, sizes and personalities.

No waiter or waitress was ever rude to me in a restaurant for no reason. No cashier was ever impatient for no purpose. No family member ever created trauma for me when I did not have something to learn from it.

In this school of life, it is impossible to need a particular lesson without that lesson appearing. It is impossible for a lesson to appear without my needing it. The next lesson is always ready and waiting. The mop and the bucket are always out in the hallway. The teacher has placed them there so we will stumble over them if necessary. Each time we walk by without seeing them, the teacher's purpose is to move them a little closer to the middle of our path.

Whatever the lesson we face, we have two choices: Pick up the mop and start scrubbing, or push it out of the way and say, "Isn't it ridiculous that somebody left this here?"

Enrollment in this mystery school of life is mandatory. The only elective is whether we do it consciously or not. Some people are sleeping through their classes. Others are awake, paying attention, taking notes, studying old tests, learning the correct answers for when the teacher calls on them. Guess who gets better scores and passes to the next grade?

When we make the decision to pay attention and to participate in our lessons on purpose, life takes on new meaning. We feel less victimized when the plumber overcharges, the car breaks down or the promotion falls through. We feel less defeated if our marriage struggles. We feel less alone if we become ill.

We move from feeling like a victim toward becoming a master of our own lives.

When we live consciously, we recognize the presence of a teacher, a guide and a partner in our personal growth. No external teacher can ever teach us more about ourselves, the mysteries of life or our creator than is already garnered within our own hearts.

We are students in the school of life, learning to accept, to love and to serve one another. None of us is perfect yet. None of us has graduated from this great Planetary Mystery School. We are still children – child-Gods growing up to be what our Father is.

RELIGION: MAN'S ATTEMPT TO CREATE GOD IN HIS OWN IMAGE

It is not helpful or appropriate to pass religious doctrine to a person who is hungry for his source and say, "This is who God is, and these are the rules for how you must relate to him." It is impossible to reveal God through doctrine. It is only possible to reveal God by becoming that expression.

A wise man once walked among God's people. The people wanted to know God and to grow spiritually, so they said to the man, "Master, give us rules by which to live." He consented and began to list some rules that, if followed, might lift the people's consciousness to the level of God-realization.

He said, "One day a week should be holy. Let it be a time when you set yourself apart and forget everything else. You should spend a seventh of your time doing absolutely nothing except sitting still, listening and worshiping, thus making your creator and source most important in your consciousness."

"Yes, we will do that. Now, tell us more," said the people. They wanted to know exactly how they should worship. How should they prove that their creator was most important?

So the wise man said, "On the seventh day, you may go only a few yards from home. That is how precious this holy day is. You cannot travel, and you cannot buy or sell on that day."

"Yes, we will do that. Tell us more."

One rule led to another, and the list grew and grew. Soon the rules extended into the personal and private lives of the people. The wise man said, "Your body is precious because it is the temple of God that lives within you. Thus you should have rules about diet and rules about exercise." He set up a program of nutrition for the health of the body, and the people believed that they must eat according to these rules to grow toward God.

On and on grew the list. There were rules regarding cleanliness, and rules regarding fair exchange, and rules regarding marriage. There needed to be an official name, so the rules were called "laws and commandments." For every rule, there were a dozen guidelines for its application. The rules extended into every area of life as they became more complex.

By now, the wise man was gone and could no longer interpret the rules for the people or help them in the application. So the elders of the community pondered the importance of the rules. A university was established where the rules could be studied and wise interpretations of the meanings behind the meanings could be determined. Churches evolved around the rules, and some leaders of the churches said, "The rules mean this," while others said, "The rules mean that." The rules became points of contention. The differences in thought engendered hate, and wars broke out.

God was no longer most important in the people's consciousness. The rules had become most important.

Eventually, another wise man came and walked among God's people. This new wise man saw that the rules had become the people's god. He said, "Understand this. It is not through following rules that you will come to know God. You may believe that you seek him through your rules, but you will not find him there. It is only through a transformation, which occurs within you, that you will come to know God."

So the second wise man instituted a new form. He said, "Come with me to the river, and there I will put you under the water and bring you up again. It will be as if the old you who is fascinated with rules, the old self, will be dead. A new self will come up out of the water. Think of it as a burial and resurrection. The new self will live life in a new way because a transformation has occurred within you."

He led the people to the river and taught them about the futility of their rules. Many were baptized and experienced burial and resurrection. But soon, the people turned baptism into the new rule.

Everyone had to be baptized to be saved, to become new, to know God. The people had discovered another rule to worship.

Over time, another wise man came and walked among God's people. This new wise man saw that the people had complicated God with rules. Worship was no longer joyous for it was burdened with restrictions. He said to the people, "All these rules and laws and commandments can be summed up in one simple statement. It is not a new commandment, but a fulfillment of the old. *Love one another.* Love your neighbor as you love yourself, and love God most of all. That is my only teaching. Having mastered this one thing, you can then do all other things. With love, you can accomplish anything."

The wise man taught the people on the hillsides and in the town squares. The people listened, and they were astounded by his words, which were so simple. The wise man taught that if the people would simply love one another without condition or restraint, all the rules would prove unnecessary. There would be no need for the old laws in an environment of love.

The wise man used his life to demonstrate this truth. He was love personified. At times, he deliberately broke the old laws to reveal their impotence. The people saw that he was a holy man, yet the old laws had no bearing on his holiness. He was God-like, not because of the rules, but because of what lay beyond the rules. Because he lived the purpose of the laws, the laws had no power over him.

Then he was gone. So his followers taught the people and said, "You only need to experience within yourself a living presence. There is no need for laws of worship. The only sin is selfishness. If you insist on your selfish ways to the exclusion of others, and their way, and their happiness, it is wrong. There is nothing else that is wrong, so you do not need rules."

But the people said, "We understand about love, and we will be loving. We understand about listening within, and we will do that, too. But give us rules. Life is simpler when we have rules to tell us what to do. Should we be vegetarian?"

The wise followers said, "It is not what goes in your mouth that defiles you, but what comes out."

"Well then, should we keep the Sabbath?" the people asked.

"Make every day holy," replied the wise followers.

"Should we wear certain clothes?" they asked. "How often should we pray? Must we have steeples on our churches? Is it better to laugh or be somber? Give us some rules. We must have rules!"

"You must find the soul behind the laws, beyond dos and don'ts and shoulds and shouldn'ts. You must look past the practice to the essence of the law, beyond the regulation to the spirit of the law. When you know the spirit of the law, you will know the creator of the law, the Initiator. You will be one with the law, and it will be for you a way of life, not a dictate. Then you will know that there are no rules."

But the people dismissed their words and made rules anyway. They divided into groups and built structures and jurisdictions around their rules. They established hierarchies and granted the leaders of their churches piety and the right to know God, while they deemed themselves unable and unworthy. They formed judgments of others who practiced a different set of rules. Judgment often turned to persecution, and persecution sometimes turned to war. But they were only following the rules and so were justified. They did it all for the glory of God, and they called their handiwork "religion."

DOES RELIGION WORK?

Religions have existed from the beginning of time. Humankind has always felt a need to acknowledge something outside and separate from itself – a superior creator of the created. It was humankind that invented religion. God had nothing to do with it. We invented religion as a means to appease our feelings of guilt and to provide a forum for socializing that would also satisfy our need for ritual and convention.

Does religion work? Does it do more than satisfy our instinctive need for retribution and socialized ritual? Does it help us know God? Religion claims to help us know more about God, but can it help us know God? Most people have no idea. They have little understanding of whether their religions are working and do not know whether they actually know God.

There is undoubtedly something of gold to be treasured in the practices and doctrines of each of the thousands of religions that exist today. Religions communicate truths. They provide ritual and faith and instill wonder and inspiration. Interestingly, many religions oppose each other in nature. Their beliefs and tenets can sit diametrically opposed – for example, belief in one god versus belief in many.

These opposing tenets have become very important to people. Many individuals believe that "Mine is right, so yours must be wrong. And mine will be even more right if I can get you to convert." Much time, energy and money has been invested in making other religions wrong, as if there were only one path to God. Holy wars are even authorized by doctrine, as if God likes the murdered victims of other faiths scattered along his one path.

THE COMMON POINT

It will be a great day, and a great step in humankind's evolution, when we finally realize that it is neither valuable nor effective to argue which religion is right and which is wrong. If there is any debate, it should be this: Enlightened beings have appeared since the beginning of time in various religions, races, cultures and nations, speaking different languages and expressing different beliefs and faiths. There is not one specific religion that has produced all the masters that the earth has known. What is important when exploring and comparing various religions is to discover and attempt to understand the common point shared by those faiths that caused one or two of their members to evolve into masters.

Throughout history, in all countries, nations, societies, cultures and religions, there has been only a handful of people whose relationship with religion was truly alive. They knew that their faith worked, and how and why it worked. They did not need to give it a particular label or even call it religion. These people have been called saints, mystics, wise men, prophetesses, sometimes psychics, healers and miracle workers. They were people on fire with spiritual power and willing to shed their blood for its sake. They were solitary individuals within spiritual groups who showed the world a source of inspiration. They were people who changed the course of history and added something to the quality of life. They made a difference because they lived.

No single religion can lay exclusive claim to these people. They can be called neither Christians, nor Jews, nor Eastern yogis, nor Muslims, nor pagans, nor Catholics. Yet each of these religious groups can probably claim a prophet as one of its members, perhaps even as its founder.

These were individuals whose spiritual lives worked. They shared a commonality, but it was not religion or even belief. Their faith superseded religion. It is interesting to study the beliefs and practices of their individual religions but not important in understanding the source of their zeal. To understand the source of their zeal is to know what causes religion to work and to come alive.

What set these people on fire? What defined them as masters? What was the source of their wisdom? What distinguished them from the masses?

What all these prophets shared in common was a vibrant, experiential, personal, expressive relationship with their creator. Their experience of God, rather than their belief in God, fueled their devotion, their worship and their lives.

BELIEF WITHOUT EXPERIENCE

The world is full of people who believe in God. Religious teachers and leaders have instructed us to believe in God and to let that be the foundation on which our relationship with God is built. The problem is that belief has little to do with experience.

Many people have a strong religious belief and are satisfied that that is enough. However, they have never had a genuine mystical experience, a direct face-to-face encounter with the source of their existence. They are content and satisfied with their belief. They cannot prove it; they have no experiential evidence of what they believe. But they do not need that because they are satisfied that to believe is enough.

That covers almost all religious people in the world. They have only a belief in God. Several questions arise concerning that. If God does not exist and you believe in him, does it matter? Does it make him exist to believe in him? And if God does exist and you do not believe in him, does that destroy his existence? Or perhaps more to the point, if God exists and you do not believe in him, do you think he will be mad at you?

Most religions will assure you that the answer is yes. God is going to judge you and even condemn you to hell for not believing in him. Nearly six billion people maintain a belief in a god who has an ego problem. His feelings will be hurt and he will react vengefully if you do not believe in him. From a common sense standpoint, that god needs to be fired so that he can go and seek therapy.

These prophets-on-fire were not satisfied with belief. They were people who sought, even demanded, to know God face-to-face. As a result, their spirituality had everything to do with experience and little to do with belief. According to the nature of the initial experience, according to how and when and where it happened, they described God in varying forms. Most of the forms did not fit those extolled by the religious leaders. Since the masses of people had already granted the religious leaders the right to know God while denying themselves the ability, the forms presented by these prophets were often considered offensive. So they were persecuted.

These prophets, saints and mystics provided a valuable lesson, but humankind generally missed it. Humankind consistently found their light a threat and attempted to destroy their fire. Humankind attempted to destroy any individual with the personal power of an experiential relationship with God, believing that it was impossible.

Succeeding in an experiential, powerful relationship with God, even today, is not necessarily a popular, comfortable way of life. If your spiritual fire is lit and roaring, if you are a spiritual power, people around you are often threatened. People are often threatened by others who appear more powerful than they are, even if that power is the power of God.

People also feel less worthy in comparison. "If you are a saint and I am not, what does that make me? How worthwhile is my life compared with yours? If you were not around and I did not have to be compared with your holiness, I might look more saintly."

It is particularly so if the other person has prayed, worshiped, tithed and been faithful to a particular doctrine his whole life, yet nothing has happened. There you were standing in the shower one day, and the rushing, relaxing water took you into an exalted state of experience, and you met God face-to-face. How fair is that?

A STATE BEYOND BELIEF

This is one of the many paradoxes along the spiritual path. Some people spend years studying sacred texts and practicing various spiritual techniques, looking, searching, yearning, begging to know God; and nothing happens. While others live lives that appear useless, perhaps drinking too much or using drugs, seemingly nonreligious lives. Then they have a spontaneous, unexplainable experience and suddenly become enlightened, spiritual leaders.

The point is not whether it is fair, but that it does indeed happen. These spontaneous, sudden, authentic spiritual experiences occur regardless of specific religious beliefs, and sometimes in spite of them. The experience may even change or reverse an individual's religious beliefs and focus.

This prime initiatory experience can take different forms. It can be associated with an altered state of consciousness. It might be initiated simply through physical exertion, going beyond exhaustion to the second wind. A sport enthusiast might reach the second wind and enter an altered state of consciousness resulting in a spontaneous, unsought, genuine experience of God.

Another individual might purposely perform a religious dance, like the circular dances of the whirling dervishes. The body's response to the spinning might produce an altered state of consciousness as the rational, logical mind is overcome by light-headedness. Beliefs about God can be similarly overcome, allowing and even sparking an authentic encounter.

Priests, preachers, spiritual teachers, sensible people tell us, "Believe in God and you will be saved." But what do beliefs about God accomplish? The sports enthusiast and the dancer produce in themselves an altered state of consciousness in which they cannot hang on to their beliefs. Their beliefs no longer matter or have preference. The individuals have reached a state beyond belief, rationality and logic.

Here is a situation that could happen to anyone. Perhaps a person has had a bad day, and later while sitting in a hot steamy bath, he feels exhausted, stressed and emotional. Because of his sensitivity and feelings, he begins to sob. Because of his sobbing, he begins to hyperventilate. Hyperventilation results in a decrease of carbon dioxide in the blood and can knock the socks off anyone's rational, logical belief system. In this case, it could open the door for an enlightening experience. And our bather goes on to become a world-renowned teacher of spiritual truths.

Imagine an instance where an individual finds herself in a life-threatening situation. A boat has capsized and sunk, and she has only a rope to cling to – a rope that is not attached to anything! As she sinks below the water's surface, she believes she may die. By the second dunk, she is unsure what she believes anymore. By the third dunk, the atheist who fell out of the boat prays desperately, "Help me!" to whomever might be listening.

In a life-threatening moment, people become less picky. No one says, "I only want to talk to a Baptist God." No one prays specifying, "I'm a Catholic, and I'm in trouble here. Only the Catholic God can answer my prayer." When logic does not apply, no one cares whether it is a masculine or feminine God, a Jewish or Muslim God, the one-God or a baker's dozen. What an individual says in a life-threatening situation is, "Help! Whoever you are, whatever you are, I need you!"

You could go lifetimes without ever uttering those words. When it finally happens, in that moment, you know that all the human powers you possess – your thinking ability, your talents, your skills at problem-solving, your attractive looks, your endearing personality, your well-placed contacts, your bank account – are not enough. In that state of absolute desperation where beliefs do not matter, an individual becomes a prime subject for a mystical experience.

What about the person who has done everything correctly? He has studied every religious book, gone to every lecture and workshop, followed every leader, practiced every mantra, kept every rule and tenet to know God better, yet nothing has happened. He sits in a meditation group, listening as everyone else relates experiences of celestial music, flashing lights and beings with exotic names. "Nothing ever happens to me," he whines.

What is going to make the difference for him? Why has he never experienced God face-to-face? It is possible that nothing has happened because he has never reached a point of desperation that allowed all the learned religious belief structures to fall away? Is it possible that he is just not empty enough? It is likely that when an individual is doing everything correctly, whether the teachings were supplied by a member of the clergy or the leader of a yoga class, nothing will work.

Though your T'ai Chi form is faultless and your breathing is perfect, it may be only a relaxing rhythmical dance. Your daily scripture reading may be nothing more than a peaceful moment at the beginning of the day. You may be proud of a decade of perfect church attendance – twice on Sunday and Wednesday night too! But have you seen the source of your being, up close and personal, so that your life was changed for all time?

What will make the difference? It is likely that the frustration from ineffective efforts will mount until one day you cannot take it any longer, and from some place deep within you, a scream comes forth, "I can't stand it. I have to know God. What I believe doesn't matter anymore. I admit that I don't know anything. I'm willing to forget all my opinions. I want to know something divine – directly, experientially, outside the bounds of the church and all the rules and beliefs and dogma. I want to know *you*, God, face-to-face!"

A LIFE-CHANGING ENCOUNTER

If the desperation is authentic and all encompassing, an experience of *personal crucifixion* may occur. That means that you die. That means that you become so fed up with who you are and what you believe and what you think and all your dos and don'ts, and shoulds and shouldn'ts, and rules and laws, that you finally say, "This is not enough! I want to know what is greater than this."

This does not mean that the experience will necessarily be negative or painful. The process of burying who and what you were before that moment is a baptism and can occur in the blink of an eye. What rises out of that experience is new life. This new life will spring from a moment when you encounter something unique and previously unfamiliar. That something may be a great light, it may be a voice, it may be a being. It may be an encounter with an unknown part of yourself face-to-face.

What makes this a life-changing encounter is that it will not be something in which you have to believe. It will not be something that someone else has told you is true about God. It will be something that you experience personally. You will know it, so you will not have to choose whether to believe in it.

You can say to yourself, "I know that I know God because I have experienced a personal, intimate, experiential, interactive, two-way encounter with whatever God is." You may not be able to explain to someone else what God is. You may never even be able to make sense of your experience. You may never duplicate the initial encounter. What you will see is the evidence of the encounter in your daily life. Other people in your life will recognize that something is different about you. They will begin to see you differently. They will relate to you differently.

Depending on how secure those people are in their own spiritual lives, they will greet the new you with validation or with fear. Those who are threatened by the new confidence you express will react unkindly. They may make fun of you. They may try to talk you out of your new experience. They may be critical and gossip about you behind your back. They may avoid you. They may persecute you.

People who live and breathe an inner strength and power can be frightening to the rest of the world. These are the rare individuals who know their source first hand. They speak with God daily, hourly, moment to moment. They are never *not* communicating with God. They have a relationship that is experiential, personal and constant.

Individuals who truly know God have had an experience so personal that it was different from any experience that anyone else has written about or talked about in history. The experiences are unique and personal because they belong to individuals. They are like fingerprints. A personal encounter with God is what these individuals share in common, yet no two encounters or relationships are alike.

So it is difficult to describe a specific means to this personal encounter with God. There is no guidebook or road map. The Biblical prophet, Elijah, described his search in this way. "I went to the mountains to find him, and he was not there. I looked on the great cliffs and the high seas, and he was not there. I sought him in the whirlwind and the hurricane, and he was not there. I sought him in every powerful place in which I could look for him, and he was not there. And then, in a moment of quiet, a still, small voice came and spoke – and he was there." (I Kings 19:11-13)

When he stopped doing everything that he was so desperately doing, what he had sought revealed itself in a nondramatic moment. He had looked in every powerful place imaginable. And in a desperate, hopeless, helpless moment, he stopped *doing*. In the vacuum created by his stillness, God spoke, and Elijah heard him and was made a prophet by the experience.

There is not a specific technique for knowing God. However, there is an attribute or an environment for knowing God. You must want to know God more than you want anything else in the world, including life itself. You must want to know God more than you want your family, more than you want prosperity, more than you want health, more than you want to make a contribution, more than you want world peace, more than anything.

When knowing God personally has become more important to you than life, family, health, success, possessions, knowledge, beliefs, religious doctrine, even enlightenment, and you are willing to set those aside for a personal, experiential relationship with who God truly is, whatever that is, you have provided the conditions in which the still, small voice can speak. And you can listen.

There are people who decide to become healers, so they study healing techniques, and as a result they may become effective medical practitioners. There are people who want to become psychics, so they study ways to develop psychically, and they may indeed develop some psychic abilities. There are many areas of service where individuals can develop an expertise to serve humanity. Helping others in need is a noble and worthy pursuit and is the work of God. Yet not everyone in a field of service has had an encounter with God.

An individual who is in a personal, experiential relationship with his or her divine source will be easily recognized, because that person will look for a way to serve, which will also introduce that source to others. That individual may be a healer, or a psychic, or a teacher. Or he may be none of these. What will be obvious is that that individual is in love.

Imagine an adolescent boy who has till now been into personal pursuits exclusively, thinking girls are not interesting and definitely not worth the energy required. Then one day, he meets a particular girl and falls in love. Now he can talk, think and dream of nothing else. He is completely enamored and wants to share his new love with the world. He is so in love that he cannot keep quiet about it.

When an individual encounters his source face-to-face, he immediately falls in love. It is like coming home. It is like everything perfect and loving and wonderful in life. That individual is so full of his newfound love that he cannot contain it. He wants to share what he has found, not so that others will believe as he does, but because he knows that everyone deserves to know God personally, and directly, and to reap the blessings of the creator's love.

You will recognize an individual who has met his source face-to-face because his life will illustrate that there is more to God than belief. He will encourage others to seek a personal relationship. He will not attempt to describe the path or define the parameters of the relationship. He will only point the way, with a joyous enthusiasm that is irresistible.

For individuals full of the experience of God, things that used to be interesting may seem unimportant now. The focus will change. They may never even use the term God, but they will devote their lives, their time, their energy, their attention and their money to helping other people make a similar discovery. They will want others to have a personal, unique experience of the nature of God that lives within, and they will devote the rest of their lives to that goal.

Such people may never be known as psychics, but they will have a unique way of saying just the right thing that others need to hear. God will speak through them to other people. They may never acknowledge that, or even be aware of it, but the listener will be moved unexplainably and wonder, "What made her say that? How did she know I was thinking about that?"

Miracles are natural and commonplace for a person in an interactive relationship with the source of the universe and everything in it. Others may not even notice what is happening. However, to the individual, it will seem as though a guardian angel is handling things, helping situations to work out, causing problems to resolve and relationships to improve. An element of magic is present in the individual's life.

People who have a direct relationship with God have a unique kind of wisdom. It may not be revealed through doctorate degrees or even good communication skills. These people will just be in the right place at the right moment to say just the right word. They will be there to provide an arm to lean on at just the right time. They are the people that save others' relationships, well-being, even lives, by saying or doing just what is needed, often without any knowledge of what they are doing. They have the wisdom to be there because they have become tools of the living presence of the divine. Situations and circumstances are created so that these individuals can be used to make a difference in other people's lives.

Then why are these people not living perfect lives? If individuals who know God personally are so wise, why do they become sick? Why do they experience problems? Why can they not avoid pain, challenge and heartbreak?

THE LEVEL OF COMMITMENT

Dr. Elisabeth Kubler-Ross is one of these individuals. She knows her source personally and has attempted to guide others in discovering a similar relationship. Simultaneously, she has built a life centered on important and controversial issues. In return, the world has repeatedly challenged her. She has been in court repeatedly. Individuals have been irate and ready to torch her house. She has been out of money and sick. Yet through it all, she has exemplified the calm confidence of a consistent, persistent relationship with God that is never challenged by circumstances or conditions. It is the Job-quality, as in Job from the Bible, which allows her to continue her chosen service in spite of health problems, lack of money, people's negative reactions, etc.

She sometimes shares with her audiences a time when she had lost her land, her home, her possessions, and someone had tried to kill her. She felt utterly alone. In desperation one night, she prayed, "God, give me your shoulder to lean on." She unmistakably understood the still, small voice to respond, "No. It will not be given."

So she said, "God, give me an arm to cling to." Again she heard the inner voice say, "No. It will not be given."

"Lord, give me a hand to touch."

"No, it will not be given."

"Lord, just the tip of a finger."

"No."

Her response to that was, "Well then, if I can't even have the tip of a finger, never mind! I'll just do it anyway, by myself." In that split second, she committed to go on with the work, no matter what. In the next moment, she tells her audiences, God was suddenly there, and she received the comfort she sought.

In that flash of an instant when she was prepared to follow God regardless, even if she could not have a fingertip, God was there. She had not pitied herself, had not attempted to strike bargains such as, "I'll serve you if you'll make me healthy. I'll serve you if you'll make me a popular speaker. I'll serve you if you'll just fix everything." She would serve God no matter what, because she was full of the experience of God. She could not *not* serve her divine source.

There can be no conditions or requirements in the service of your creator. Even if there is no mystical experience. Even if there is no evidence of a personal relationship. There can be no reason for doing it more important than doing it.

"Even if you don't respond, God, I will walk with you. Even if I can't tell you're listening, I will talk with you. Even if I don't know whether you're there, I am here."

Not "I will walk with you if you'll give me a blinding light to see." No conditions. Not "I will walk with you if you'll make me a psychic." No conditions. Not "I will walk with you if you'll provide for my financial needs." No conditions.

Knowing God requires absolute innocent and childlike devotion. You must become as a little child to enter the kingdom of heaven. (Matthew 18:3) Knowing God requires that knowing God be the most important thing in your life. Knowing God requires creating an environment for knowing God. Continue to study. Continue to pray. Continue to surround yourself with people who have similar values.

Why? What is the motivation for this level of commitment?

There are billions of souls alive today. Of those, probably 99.9% will spend their entire lives doing something that they call making a living. When they have succeeded in making a living and come to the end of their life experience, they will discover that it is too late to live a life. They will disappear from the earth, and it will not matter that they were here. This means that the earth will be no different for their having been alive. All those people made no contribution that changed the course of history or humankind's consciousness.

PROPHETS ON FIRE

On the other hand, there will be a handful of people in every generation throughout history who cannot live an ordinary life. They will be unable to shake the sense that there is more to life than getting an education, having a job, raising a family, owning things, being popular, feeding and grooming the body. These people will maintain an inner sense that there is more to life than making a living.

There will always be a few people who long to experience a more meaningful life. They long to know who or what is behind it all. They are hungry. They are searching.

It is not their responsibility to find – only to search. It is God's responsibility to be found, discovered and known. It is their responsibility to keep searching, to stay hungry. The hunger of the soul to personally know its creator can keep the consciousness open to knowing God.

These few people will feel that they cannot live without knowing God. They will refuse to take another's word for it. Organized religion of any form will not satisfy them. They will demand a personal experience of knowing. And when they have finally achieved that knowing, they will make sure that it matters that they lived.

That is what life is all about. Will it matter that you lived? Will someone's life be better because you were here, because of the way you live your life, because of the way you express, because of the way you contribute? Does your life make a positive difference in the lives of others? If so, then you have met your destiny as an expression of God on earth. That is your purpose for being here, and it is a purpose that matters. If you can let God express through you, whoever God is, in whatever form, whatever culture, whatever belief system, you can make a difference.

There are people around us all day, every day, who are hurting. There is great pain in the world right now. There are many people who are willing to cause pain, and that includes almost everyone whom you will ever meet. People are frightened because they feel threatened. And frightened people are dangerous people because they are willing to cause harm.

What the world needs is a nucleus of people who have taken responsibility for living consciously, without fear. It matters that the course of history is changed. How many magicians does it take to change the course of history? If you have billions of unconscious people and one conscious person, can that one conscious person change the course of history for the billions who are unconscious? Yes. And this is the reason that it is possible. Unconscious people are like sheep. They follow in whatever direction the current trend takes them. If the current trend takes them toward hate and war, and the politicians and priests instruct that it is patriotic and in the service of God to fight, those sheep will even go to battle and kill each other.

However, one man or woman who knows God personally can anchor the consciousness of humanity and become a voice that will cause the underlying knowledge of God contained within each of us to be awakened.

How can one person make a difference in the lives of billions? One conscious person is more powerful than a billion unconscious people because one conscious person can cause the thought forms that the unconscious people will pick up and act upon. If a person is consciously evil, they can produce disasters of planetary proportions. If one person is consciously, positively effective, the planet can be changed on a global scale, in a way that will make a positive difference in history.

Do not discount the possibilities. It is possible to heal our nations. It is possible to change the course of history. It is possible to create a new world. And it is time for that to happen.

Consider the possibility that you can create a bond of love so strong that it can awaken the consciousness and anchor the knowledge of God in the hearts of all humankind.

HOW RELIGION FAILS US

There are people wandering the streets who are hungry, afraid and unloved. They are not the homeless and downtrodden. They are the average workers in the business place – the cashier and the next door neighbor, the medical technician and the restaurant worker, the lawyer and the construction worker, the politician and the minister. Unfortunately, the downtrodden, afraid and unloved are also the children of the world because they are being raised by frightened parents. People want to defend themselves, even though they are not sure precisely what they fear. They are willing to fight and lash out. They are willing to hurt another to protect themselves.

Underneath their fear and pain is an inherent sense of their source, an inherent longing and hunger to know that source personally. It serves none of these wounded people to teach them a *form* of God. Knowing their source personally has nothing to do with someone else's form, religion, doctrine, dogma, tenets, rules, practices, beliefs or proclamations. It is not helpful or appropriate to pass religious doctrine to a person who is hungry for his source and say, "This is who God is, and these are the rules for how you must relate to him."

It is impossible to reveal God through doctrine – it is only possible to reveal God by becoming that expression. Those who seek will find. It is not anyone's responsibility to make sure that they find. It is not even possible. It is not necessary to reveal God to another person. All one person can really do for another is to stimulate the search and awaken the unconscious desire to know.

People only need to be reassured that each of them can come to know God as a reality. They need to hear that God is alive and well within each of us. They need to hear that it is possible to know God themselves, without intermediaries.

Our religious leaders would do well to stop telling people what God is like and instead encourage people to discover his nature and presence for themselves. Then they should ask those people to share what they have discovered – not what God "is like," but rather, the fact that it is possible to truly know divinity in a direct way.

Instead of building boxes and fences around denominations and faiths and dictating what people should think, our leaders should be encouraging their congregations to search until they find. The search may require passing through many gateways, many paths, many rituals, many religions, many faiths and many forms. Our religious leaders should applaud that search, wherever the journey leads. Even if the journey leads in the direction of another faith. Even if a Christian encounters God face-to-face on a Buddhist path, or a Jew discovers his source within a Muslim mosque.

Those who hunger and search for righteousness will be filled. What difference does it make under what roof that encounter occurs? The responsibility of our religious leaders is to create a vacuum in the hearts of individuals so that God can come in to fill it.

Our responsibility is to be as little children – child-Gods. But that can be difficult. We have been handed rules, beliefs and standards that have imprisoned us and prevented us from doing what we feel like doing. When was the last time you gave yourself totally to something that you knew would make you look foolish but you really wanted to do it anyway? Ten years? Twenty years? When you were five years old?

A misguided teaching handed down in our culture is that being mature equates with being serious, feeling concerned and looking worried. Mature people have furrowed brows, tight lips and sober expressions. They take life seriously; therefore they are responsible.

These same people worship seriously. In a traditional western church, they go to a formal place where they greet each other appropriately. They wear somber faces as organ music begins to play. They sit silently before an altar that is often decorated with symbols of death. What could be more formidable? They begin to sing lofty songs about things they do not necessarily mean and probably do not express in their daily lives. They contemplate their countless sins and beg for forgiveness and mercy. They contemplate their needs and plead for what they do not believe they deserve from a God they have never met and are not absolutely sure exists. They believe their prayers will work best if they feel guilty and fear God, because they have been taught that God feels honored by that.

What does all this have to do with worshiping the divinity who created us?

The truth is that I talked with God this morning, and she said that it is all right for us to enjoy ourselves in church. In fact, she wants us to have a ball – to shout and sing and laugh, because the world is beautiful and spectacular, and she is joyously, absolutely in love with every one of us!

Now that is a God worthy of worship. The God who invented this fascinating masterpiece full of adventure, beauty, joy, humor and play is best worshiped by enjoying the creations. When we are absolutely joyous and loving with one another, we compliment God on the success of creation. That is the highest form of worship humankind can offer.

WHAT IS WORSHIP?

Worship is the act of assuming that God really wants you to enjoy yourself, that God is that generous and loves you that much. The assumption that God wants us to be miserable, or to feel guilty and sorry, or to feel unworthy or sinful while approaching an ominous altar, is left over from a period in history when religious leaders wanted to maintain control of the masses by keeping them poor and uneducated. How could a joyous, loving God be pleased with that?

Worshiping your creator means totally enjoying the abundance of life and having a ball with the gifts provided. The more you laugh because you simply enjoy your divine relationship, the more naturally worshipful the experience will be. Your worship will not be born out of a set of rules and standards for appropriate church behavior. Your worship will not be born out of fear. Your worship will be a natural act of devotion born of a shared love between you and your source.

Authentic reverence for an altar comes from knowing that its instruments are symbols for the abundance of life, given for you to enjoy because you are a loved child of a creator who wants to give you more and more. Your appreciation is best expressed through totally enjoying life and its abundance.

Imagine a father who would create a whole table full of presents and then tell the child, "You can only take one of these presents, but only if you are really sorry for how bad you have been. You can't have more than one because you don't deserve it. The rest are for someone better than you." It is a ridiculous proposition, yet our religious leaders tell us to worship this God.

The generally accepted form for worshiping God seems to be an insult to what God is. We would do better to simply take responsibility for our own mistakes, by going back and correcting them in our daily interactions with people. Let God off the hook and leave him out of all the melodramas that we create. We should take personal responsibility for our lives. And then make church an experience of celebration.

Now and then, in one of life's extraordinary and rare moments, it is possible to look over unnoticed at a *peace-filled* individual sitting next to you, gaze into that person's relaxed countenance, and see what our natural divinity must be like. The heavy lines of concern and worry have relaxed. The manufactured appearance of "I can keep all this under control because I'm seriously responsible," has faded away for the moment. There is freshness, softness, a cleansed look. A light seems to shine from within, glowing and radiating. That individual expresses the wide-eyed, innocent trust of a child, in love with its parent. And looking into a face like that causes you to feel good, because it is the face of God.

THE RADIANCE OF GOD

The best way to see God is to see someone through whom God is radiating for a moment. Sometimes, that is a person who has been working through a lot of intense challenges. That person has been taking responsibility for handling some commonplace problems and is now finished. There is a moment of fulfillment when the creator-self inside radiates out through the eyes and says, "I did a pretty good job of this, didn't I?" That is God inside communicating, radiating, speaking, expressing. In that moment, the source of all life in you gives excitement to others. It causes life and liveliness to spring up in others. When you feel good about your effectiveness, your efforts to maintain healthy relationships, and your attempts to live consciously, you radiate God's goodness from within you.

When you feel good and you look into someone else's eyes, that person is immediately affected by the source of life in you. God in you reaches out and touches that individual. What happens? The God in you calls to the God in that person. Can he or she continue plodding along through life – worrying, hurting, feeling guilty, feeling angry, wanting to hurt someone? Only if he or she is absolutely determined to continue in that way.

Joy is contagious, and in most cases, that other individual, the person opposite you, will catch it. Suddenly, the God in that person will radiate and return your smile. A bridge is built between the two of you, and you share one sense, one feeling, one life, one love, one joy. What occurs is a marriage of communication between two people, and the marriage produces a child. The child's name is joy. The child's name is love. The child's name is life.

THE ABUNDANT TABLE OF LIFE

Every day, there is set before you a table spread with the abundance of life. On that table are all kinds of delicious fruits of life that you can taste and enjoy. There are no forbidden fruits. And you do not have to earn the right to take the fruit. They are all yours.

There are fruits full of joy and excitement and adventure. And you are invited to eat from them till you are filled. There are some fruits that have a bitter taste. There are some that are not sweet. There are some that are rotten. You are welcome to take those as well, but when you do, they will not taste good. The appropriate thing to say at that point is not, "Oh, I'm awful. I feel so bad. I took the wrong fruit," whining and crying over the tragedy of the situation. The appropriate thing to do is to toss that piece of fruit aside. Just drop it and reach for another piece.

Choice is involved in all situations of life. The table is spread abundantly. There is every choice imaginable to be made. The people around you are making choices and enjoying their fruits. Are you going to sit there with your old, rotten, worm-infested plum, feeling jealous of those who got the good fruits? Stop doing that. Throw down your rotten plum and make another choice!

The creator of the banquet is not pleased if you take just a little, or if you take the bad fruits, or if you feel sorry that you picked a rotten one, or if you feel unworthy to pick a good one. The creator is not concerned if you throw the bad one down and reach for another, or even if you take all the good ones. It is not bad manners to take what you want from the table of life. That beautiful, bountiful table of fruit has been set out so that you can enjoy it. There is no point in feeling upset because someone else has better fruit than yours. There is enough fruit for everyone, and all you have to do is reach and take something different.

Most important is to enjoy the party. God is worshiped as his lover finds delight in the banquet. Worshiping God means delighting in God. Worshiping God means complimenting God on the creation by enjoying it.

Undoubtedly, God could use a compliment by now. Millions of ungrateful humans run around on earth every day saying, "This in an awful place. Life is terrible. It's getting worse every day. The world is a mess. I hate it. Everything is awful." With all that crying and moaning and complaining, it must be refreshing for God to find a small pocket of people on the planet saying, "Wow, what a banquet! This is incredible! What wonderful fruit! Oh, I really got a rotten one a while ago, but look at this one. It's beautiful and delicious!"

What is worship? Worship is noticing that there is beauty everywhere and that joy is always available. Worship is being filled with joy every moment. What you receive in return is not only the experience of enjoying the fruit, but the opportunity to make a contribution.

If you can make someone happier, you have made someone better. Happy people do not believe that they must compete with their partners, their neighbors or their colleagues. Happy people do not wish that someone else was hurting or lacking. It is impossible to harbor negative thoughts when you are enjoying yourself and life. You are not tempted to wallow in hurt, pain, misery, selfishness, anger, hate, jealousy or competition when you are joyous.

A NEW WORLD

When you express in a consciously joyous way, it is as if your consciousness moves to a higher place or vantage point. You look around and say, "Oh, I never saw this world before. What a wonderful place to be!" You look back at the other people who are plodding miserably through their awful world, fighting with their families, getting mad at their neighbors, competing for this and that, fearing, dreading, worrying, scraping for survival, tearing at one another. And you say to them, "Hey, come look at this world. It's so beautiful up here." But they are busy in their misery and may not hear you.

You move into this new experience by turning loose of the old one, the old way of thinking. "There's never enough for me. I never get what I want. I don't deserve it. I never get a break. With my luck, this'll never work out. Everyone's out to get me. Everything is awful. I hate life."

It means turning loose of the way you used to be and moving into the way that you can be. It means letting go of false securities.

Your identity and sense of importance have been based on what you think you are, who you think you are. Who are you? "Well, I'm this little person with all these problems. My parents treated me dreadfully, and my siblings treated me worse, and I was potty trained badly, and I had this really bad time throughout school, and I've always been fat, and I have no talents, and all these terrible things happened to me, and that's who I am. I can't turn loose of all that without turning loose of who I am."

Meanwhile, the creator of the bountiful banquet is standing there saying, "Just turn loose. Just release all that. It isn't who you are. There's no benefit in staying the way you've been. Just let go. Let go and fall into a new kind of relationship with yourself and life."

"But what about all the tragedy?" you ask. People who insist on worshiping doom and death and heaviness and hurt can find ample reasons. It is true that life can be unimaginably tragic and painful.

Did you know that each "but what about..." is a creator? You attach yourself to a "but what about..." and you form a cooperative partnership, a marriage, and then you produce a child. The child's name is whatever follows the "but what about...." It is a masterful technique for creating.

You say, "But what about my bank account? I don't have enough money to be constantly joyous." Congratulations, you just gave birth to poverty consciousness. "But what about my partner? She's awful, so my world will never be beautiful." Congratulations, you just gave birth to marital strife. Understand that your fears and negative thoughts have been busy creating and birthing, and you are living with the children.

Forget those. It is a delightful world. Why not enjoy yourself, enjoy life, have a ball, feel loved? What benefit do you receive by doing the opposite? Oh yes, you get to be a member of the rest of the adult world that is mature, concerned, serious, worried and responsible. Is that really a benefit?

Make an assumption that your creator put you here to love you and please you. Make an assumption that your source is incapable of being mad at you or considering you inadequate. Change your belief about your relationship with God. Assume that you are the apple of God's eye and live as if it were true.

The people around you will discover a new, delightful person in you, someone who is having a ball and enjoying life. Now and then, you may notice that they are still complaining and worrying and competing and arguing, but their misery does not affect you anymore. You go on having a ball because that is the way you want to live and because you have made a choice to live differently. They can choose the alternative, too.

How do you help them find the alternative? By living it, being it.

What we are is what we dwell on. What we think about expands. You have the opportunity to build something new, to choose a new piece of fruit. Why not assume that you are all right, that life is good, that people are not out to get you, that God is not mad at you, that you deserve only the best? Assume that you and the world really are totally all right, whatever is going on, whatever the circumstances. Assume that you are not a person who has phobias, health issues, unsolvable problems, troubled relationships with family members, inadequacies, hurts and scars.

Believe the best about yourself. Expect the best from yourself, and others. If they surprise you with the opposite, it does not have to alter your opinion of you or the world. It is not necessary to be in a bad situation and be miserable, too. Make your decision that you are good and the world is a beautiful place to live, and let nothing change your mind.

Step into a new, consistently joyous life that remains stable, smooth and peaceful. If you get a piece of bad fruit now and then, toss it aside. Don't dwell on it. The world is too wonderful to focus on bad fruit.

Life is exciting, joyful, good, abundant and full of beauty. Worship your source by noticing it, by appreciating it, by saying, "Wow! Thank you so much!"

God is not particularly impressed by old English vernacular structured in poetic declarations of thanksgiving. God is impressed by sincerity and delighted when you absolutely, deliriously enjoy the incredible banquet. Who decided that God is an old, masculine, unyielding puritan who hangs out in darkened, silent sanctuaries and gets off on guilt? Who says that God prefers ritual and remorse to ecstatic laughter?

IN HIS OWN IMAGE

There is a living being, a living consciousness, in this universe that gets off on life. Life is passionate, animated, building, growing, developing, expanding, flourishing, thriving, succeeding, prospering and loving. You relate to that being best when you express similarly.

The source of this universe delighted in forming this planet. There is plenty of evidence around us that the universe was created while God was laughing. Did you ever study the aesthetics of a hippopotamus? When God put this little universe together, some ridiculous creatures resulted. It is obvious that God was enjoying the experience. If the divine creator of this fantastic universe had no sense of humor, how did *you* get here?

Imagine God's enjoyment in flinging the stars and planets into the sky and then going on to design whales alongside plankton, dinosaurs alongside gnats, and even you with all your intricacies and peculiarities. Look around you. Life speaks of beauty and fascination, it speaks of fun and irony, it speaks of cleverness and whimsy.

Many people believe that being good, being spiritual, growing to be like God is difficult, an uphill battle. But that is not true. It is natural for you to be God-like because you are made in the image of God. You are the child of God. The God-nature in you is life-generating. The only reason that you cause imbalances is because, in your interactions with others, you have developed the false belief that you have to compete with others who want your share. You believe falsely that you are a separate being and should act accordingly.

Why do you think it should be difficult to live according to your true nature, which is the nature of God? It becomes easier as you realize that you best emulate and honor your source by enjoying life and by making that your purpose for being here.

Discover for yourself what delights your creator. When you have become so intimate with your source – through a direct, personal, experiential, interactive, unceasing relationship – that you know what causes your source delight, your religion will be working effectively. You will need no one to mediate your relationship with God because you will know God face-to-face, heart-to-heart, moment-to-moment. Your body will be the house of God. Your natural expression will be an act of worship and devotion. Your contribution will make a difference. And long after you are gone, it will matter that you lived.

KNOW GOD PERSONALLY
FROM THE PAUL SOLOMON SOURCE

*H*ow would you teach children to know God? You would teach children to know God by, above all else, teaching them to know that they themselves are loved and that they deserve to be loved.

Teach them that they are inherently good. Teach them that that which grows in them, and loves, and is good within them, is the child of God within. And as they come of age, three to seven, allow them to begin to think of, to build in their minds, to draw on paper, to clearly envision and make real, a pleasant, peaceful place within themselves.

A place where God dwells within them and where they can go to visit, to talk and to listen.

As they grow, help them to grow in responsibility, to use their personal tools of prosperity. Teach them that they have the right to live prosperously and whole. That they can live prosperously in spite of outward conditions. In that way, they shall learn to know that God is their prosperity. Avoid any teaching that suggests that money or the desire for money is sinful. Help them rather to see money as a sacred instrument, which symbolizes energy and love, sent forth to accomplish a purpose. Take care not to instill within them poverty consciousness, a belief that there is inherent good in being poor, that it is more spiritual to experience lack and limitation than prosperity and wealth.

As they grow, from seven into early adolescence, teach them a sacred respect for their bodies without shame. Give particular attention to early adolescence, for this is the natural time to begin to express independence. Yet they are unsure of themselves. Teach them confidence, self-confidence, self-worth, self-respect, self-love, so they might have within them the strength to be a leader in a peer group, rather than a victim of peer pressure.

Teach them always to be joyous and happy, in spite of outward conditions. Teach them that it is more important to be joyous than to accomplish certain tasks or marks of approval.

Above all else, teach them to know God personally and experientially, rather than knowing an image of God that has come from someone else's mind, ideas, beliefs, doctrines or dogma.

Allow children a personal relationship and a personal experience of living love within themselves. Help each one to come to know the child of God growing within — for they are all child-Gods growing up to be what their Father is.

THE ORIGINS AND PURPOSES
OF THE HOLY SACRAMENTS

Do you want to know what it is that will surely destroy this planet?
It is for us to entertain the idea that we have enemies in the world
who we do not even know, which will cause us to lock ourselves
away, inside the boundaries of our countries, inside the limits of
our cities, inside the walls of our homes,
inside the prisons of our beliefs.

Jesus gave many instructions to his small school of disciples during the three years he spent with them. He instructed them in many acts that were private, personal exercises. None of these were "holy sacraments."

These practices, which Jesus taught his disciples, involved a personal relationship between man and God, and included forming a personal relationship with the Christ spirit. They included prayer and meditation, and private forms of worship. However, they did not fit the definition of a sacrament.

What makes a particular action a sacrament? Sacraments are community based. They require the participation of a community to fulfill accomplishment. They involve coming together as a group to confirm a *family* relationship with God, which is different from a personal relationship with God. Sacraments cannot be performed privately. They require more than one person, a community.

There is one more thing that makes an action a sacrament. When coming together and assembling for worship, Jesus instructed the people to invoke his presence. He said, "Do this in remembrance of me." (Luke 22:19) Jesus gave this instruction at the initiation of every sacrament. He said, "Do this because I have commanded you to do it. Do it to remember this commandment, to remember our relationship."

Essentially, he meant, "When you do this, you invoke me. It is the most effective, positive form of invocation of my presence. It is a very clear communication. Because you do this, I will be there."

You can certainly invoke Christ through prayer, which builds a personal relationship between you and the Christ spirit. But Jesus specified the worship of more than one. "For where two or three are gathered together in my name, there am I in the midst of them." (Matthew 18:20)

THE SACRAMENT OF MARRIAGE

A wedding is an intensely personal act between two people – so why is it a community sacrament? Why, in fact, was a wedding the first sacrament that Jesus instituted?

Essentially, Jesus said that joining two people together in marriage is the holiest thing a church can do. Consider what that means – holier than communion, holier than baptism, holier than the ordination of ministers.

How important is marriage? Marriage is obviously not necessary for two individuals to live together. And two individuals do not have to be married in order to live together in harmony. People do not even have to be married to have children. They do not have to be married to satisfy the law. They no longer need the church to form a marriage so that they can live together legally. They can simply draw up a contract, attend a civil ceremony, and that is a marriage.

However, it is not a sacrament.

What is the difference between a sacrament and a legal marriage? The difference is esoteric. If you can take the spiritual essence of God, the spirit of God, and apply it to an act on this plane, so that you can see it and feel it and participate in it, then you have made a connection to the spiritual plane. When a real marriage occurs, meaning a holy sacrament, heaven has been married with earth through the act.

According to ancient Judaism, until the time of Jesus, the Sabbath was the bride of God. The Sabbath was the holy day of the week and was celebrated in the home and the synagogue. The doors and the windows of the home were opened to allow for the entrance and the welcoming of the feminine god, the wife of God, the feminine aspect of God. She was ushered in as a bride by the women who lit the home candles and performed wedding dances, rather than the priests in the temple.

However, Jesus identified the bride of God differently. "The Sabbath was made for man, and not man for the Sabbath." (Mark 2:27) What is holy is not the day of the week. Rather, it is the purpose of the day that is holy. The purpose of the Sabbath is to come together. Who comes together? It is the community of people who form a holy unit. This holy unit is a family. And through the coming together of a group in holiness, a sacrament occurs.

Family is the term that Jesus used, from the Latin *ecclesia*. When translated into Greek, the word became church. Over time, the religious authority decided that the church itself was to be the bride, rather than the Sabbath.

However, the true bride of God is the family, the community, the holy unit of people joined together.

Modern society is experiencing extreme difficulty right now because of its abandonment of the tribal system. Under the tribal system, marriage between a man and a woman is a participatory experience of the community.

If weddings were conducted properly in modern society, the entire congregation of community members would be a part of confirming that the two people seeking marriage belong together. Marriage needs to be an act of community. All the people in a community need to be married to one another. In that way, true community can work.

When everyone in a community is married to one another, children born into that union are the responsibility of all the adults. That does not change the fact that the children have a mother and a father. It does not destroy the nuclear family. It places the nuclear family in the nest of a tribe.

Humanity is nearing self-destruction because of the widespread existence of single-parent families that are not actual families, in the definition of the word. Instead, they are struggling, desperate units of people scraping to survive with little support from any kind of tribal unit including a church.

This is where the church is failing today's world. Marriage, as a sacrament of the church and as an extension of the congregation, is not being practiced today.

When a tribe of individuals raises children, the spiritual lives of those children are different. Their financial, material and emotional security is different. Their role models are different.

When children live alone with a single-parent, they are exposed to that parent's strengths and weaknesses and little else. When children are raised by a tribal unit, they are exposed to a gamut of possibilities. Traditionally, this has been aunts and uncles, cousins, grandparents and great grandparents. They all were part of the rearing of the children. And they knew that they were all part of it. It was accepted, normal. The adults affected one another. They shared each other's joys and struggles. They gently helped one another through crisis. They did not abandon a single-parent to his or her own devices, to come unglued in front of the children, teaching them that this world is a threatening place, terrible and frightening – so that the children grew up with fear as their ruler and their god.

Real marriage does not turn into a matriarchy or a patriarchy. Real marriage consists of a tribe or a family.

If there is anything that every individual needs, it is the support of a family. We function best when we are active in a family. We need the love, support and communication that a family can provide. We need the social, economical, moral and educational support a family can provide.

There is one thing that I will preach till I die: Get together, people, and form a family!

Create a local family, an extended family, even if you are a single-parent, *especially* if you are a single-parent. Form a family of individuals who may or may not be related by blood, together on a piece of land if you want. Create a local community of family members, living and working side-by-side, supporting one another.

More importantly, though, if the people in the Soviet Union and China and North Korea and Iraq become your aunts and uncles and sisters and brothers and children, you will not kill them.

So get in touch with them. Write to them. Go there. Visit them. Spend time with them. Invite them here. Have them into your homes.

Do you want to know what it is that will surely destroy this planet? It is for each of us to isolate ourselves in our homes and lock our doors. It is for each of us to send a message that "If you are going to visit me, be sure you call me first. Make an appointment if you want to see me." It is for each of us to place such a priority on order and "my way" that we separate ourselves into little cubicles so that life becomes a regimented prison. It is for each of us to entertain the idea that we have enemies in the world who we do not even know, which will cause us to lock ourselves away, inside the boundaries of our countries, inside the limits of our cities, inside the walls of our homes, inside the prisons of our beliefs. It is for us to live in fear of our fellowman.

The destruction of the tribal unit came as a result of wars. Wars resulted in taking people out of their tribal units, putting them together in new artificial units, and moving them around the world. These individuals witnessed and experienced different cultures, causing expansion of development and progress. At the same time, it caused individuals to lose their roots.

One of the institutions most responsible for destroying the tribal unit and the family is Christianity. Christians spent their time, energy and money, and patted themselves on the back, to send missionaries to Africa to tell the naked heathens to put on clothes, which made them considerably less healthy – physically, mentally, spiritually and morally. Christians then told themselves that what they had done was wonderful, and that God was pleased.

Never mind that individuals were stripped of their beliefs, their Gods, their roots, their national identity, their cultural identity, their tribal identity. They became believers of Christianity, so the goal of the church was met.

The question arises: Through these actions of the church, did these individuals actually gain an understanding of what true Christianity is, as Jesus might have defined it? One wonders if the barter was fair or valuable.

In our modern western culture, we encourage independence, sometimes to a fault. Yes, we must all be responsible for self – for our thoughts, words and actions – because that is the ultimate relationship with God. However, responsibility for self includes responsibility for each other, for humanity as a whole and as single individuals. Independently-minded people who place a high premium on independence, above responsibility for others, are refusing to recognize responsibility for their own need to join with others.

It appears that our creator did an interesting thing when we decided to enter this level of existence. God was so exceptionally loving that he gave us the greatest gift of all – the gift of free will. As much as God loved and trusted us, though, he did something additional to steer that free will. He took half of us away, and he created from that half someone else. Then he released that other entity somewhere else in the universe and said, "Now go find your other half. Go ahead. Take your time. Spend eons if you want. When you become whole again, you and I will become whole again as well. We'll become family again, and the universe will be in harmony." So we have been running around looking for our soulmates ever since.

This division, which our source masterminded, guaranteed that we would always feel a need to bond with another being. The natural need to bond exists in everyone. We need to bond with family, we need to bond with community, we need to bond with humankind. We need to know that if anything is in my best interest, it is in everyone's best interest. We need to know that we are all one on this planet.

There has long been a belief that a person has to sacrifice individual needs to meet community needs. That is not quite accurate. A person has to sacrifice selfishness. That is different from sacrificing self-interest.

An individual's self-interest is the interest of the community. An individual's self-interest is the interest of the tribal unit. An individual's self-interest is the interest of every other individual. If we do not recognize that, our selfishness has gotten in the way.

Originally, women were linked integrally to the family unit, the tribe. It was their responsibility to bear and care for the children. The men, by nature of their function and responsibility, had opportunities to go off with bands of other men to hunt or fish, whatever they needed to do to support the society.

At some point, the dynamic began to change. It may be that the matriarchy herself expressed her independent views and communicated to the men, "We don't really need you. One man in the community is enough to produce all the children we need. We have the children. We have the home. You have nothing. Scoot!"

Or perhaps it was the selfishness of just one man who left that hunting party, went out on his own, discovered that he could survive on his own, had some adventures, came back and told some stories, and incited other people to become independent and individualistic. Perhaps at that point, men began to abandon the community.

We do not know which happened first, or if either happened at all. The point is that independence became appealing. And beyond that point, war and power became more important than the ability to bear children.

Originally, the matriarchy, including the high priestess, came into power because of the ability to give life. It was the ultimate magic. Additionally, women had another ability valued in ancient times. They tended to be more intuitive. Women were more intuitive because they protected their children in a different way than men. Men had the responsibility for responding physically to defend the children. Women had to sense the children's needs and therefore developed psychically. Because women were more psychically developed, they were more inclined to be in touch with spirit, with source. Thus they had more ability as a prophet/prophetess than men did.

As society changed and as war became the focus of the community, protection of the fortress became more important than childbearing or prophecy. Over time, the patriarchy took power. And we continue to live with the consequences today.

There was a period in prehistory when all people were contented living on earth because they were confident of a particular truth. Profound, yet simple, here is the truth by which they lived: If there were not freely available on this planet everything needed to survive, humankind would have never appeared and developed on the planet.

This planet is productive and bountiful enough to provide for all our needs. We did not need to manipulate the environment of earth to supply our needs. We did not need to work, to organize, to build fences or fortresses to protect our communities. We did not need to practice imperialism by conquering foreign lands, looting stores and taking slaves.

What happened to change that period of contentment and plenty? At some point in this Eden, two people reached for the same piece of fruit at the same moment. When those two people reached for that same piece of fruit, there was an ensuing perception that "Your interest is in conflict with mine."

The perception was not true. Your interest does not conflict with mine, according to the bountiful supply of this planet. There is plenty of fruit. We could not stop the fruit from reproducing if we tried. It is the natural state of this planet to be abundant.

Our interests cannot conflict. All I have to do is reach in a different direction, while knowing that my reaching in another direction in support of you is in my own interest and that it assures my wellbeing as well as yours.

That original misperception of conflicting interests, occurring between those two beings, meant that bees developed stingers and roses developed thorns. Everything that was manifesting on the globe took up a means of self-protection. It was the birth of fear on earth. It was the "fall of man." Humankind has yet to re-establish the knowledge that we are all one and that there can be no conflict of interest within a unit of one.

In the tribal unit, marriage is a coming together of families. Two different families or tribes will come together and become married to each other. Two families become one.

In modern society, that dynamic occurs to some extent when in-laws and also friends join as a group in support of a couple. If the two married individuals seek divorce, all the members of a family are devastated. Grandparents and grandchildren are torn apart. Individuals lose not only partners but also mothers-, fathers-, sisters-, and brothers-in-law. In second divorces, parents lose stepchildren whom they loved and raised as their own. Yesterday, all these people formed a family – but today, it is gone.

Marriage is a community experience. Two young people coming together need our energy, our support, our blessing of their union. In that way, everyone is moved and affected by the experience. It becomes a spiritual experience for the community.

The entire community should be committed to the marriage of those two young people. They should not be left alone to either get along or not get along, with the option of abandoning one another when there is trouble in the marriage.

Did we abandon them first? What happened to the community coming together and playing the role of mediator, helping each of them to understand their responsibilities? Our abandonment of community has allowed the abandonment of marriage, and has caused marriage to abandon its own sacredness.

Let each of us be committed to our children, and to their marriages, and to their children – so that divorce does not take my children or my grandchildren away from me. They remain a part of my family, no matter what. My ex-daughter-in-law should remain a part of my family, as much as if she were born into my family. Separation and divorce should not change everything.

Never let it be said that people were too busy to get involved. In a community marriage, everyone is involved. We cannot abandon these children. It is a part of our spiritual commitment to be a part of the solution, to be there for them, no matter what – till death parts us.

THE SACRAMENT OF BAPTISM

Perhaps the second most important holy sacrament is baptism. There are several types of baptism, at least four.

The first baptism is of earth, which is a material baptism or immersion in matter, beginning with physical birth and continuing on as one of the biggest challenges humankind faces. The second baptism is of water, which is immersion in the stream of life, through spirit and emotion. The third baptism is of fire, which is a commitment to spiritual direction and life purpose. The fourth baptism is of air, which occurs at physical death.

The baptism into earth. The challenge of baptism into earth occurs as we avoid being totally in our body during any present moment – as we avoid being who we are, where we are, doing what we are doing, right now.

Instead of being alive in our bodies in this moment, we try to be dead right now and alive yesterday or tomorrow. We remember something that we accomplished in the past, keeping that in mind, and thus forget to notice what is going on in the present.

"I feel the way that I feel right now because of something that happened earlier."

"I feel the way that I feel right now because I did this wonderful thing in the past, and I need to make sure you find out about it because I'm not important unless people know that I accomplished it."

"I feel upset right now because an hour ago my boss yelled at me. I am dead to this pleasant present because my consciousness is still there in the office being yelled at. I am so concerned with trying to be alive an hour ago when something terrible happened that I am dead right now."

We are capable of keeping the terrible past alive to the extent that we can produce disease in our bodies. We can live a tormented present because we were misused twenty years ago.

"My potty-training was traumatic, so now I am neurotic." "I was abused as a child, so I will never be able to succeed at anything." "I suffered a business failure, so I can't think differently about money." "I was molested when I was younger, so I will never feel right again." "I was betrayed in the past, so I will never trust anyone again." "I had a nervous breakdown, so I'll never be able to handle this."

Yes, tragedy happens. No one gets through life without experiencing tragedy. Allowing past tragedies to determine the present multiplies the tragedy.

It is also called being dead in the present by trying to be alive in the past. Are you having a nervous breakdown right now? Are you being abused today? Are you addicted to drugs right now? Are you failing this very moment? If you are, get some help immediately. If not, stop letting the past control your present.

Being alive in the future also means being dead in the present. If you are waiting to live – until you make a fortune, until you get your degree, until you get married, until you become a parent, until you get out of debt, until you get thin, until you get sober, until you get your act together, until you become enlightened – you are trying to be alive in the future.

When do you plan to be totally alive? What will it take? When do you plan to be totally participatory, totally all right with yourself, totally accepting of this moment just as it is, without wishing it were different?

Those of you who are dead, please just lie down so the rest of us will know how to relate to you. Have the courtesy to go ahead and fall over on the floor if you are going to be dead now.

If the way I am feeling right now is a result of what I am experiencing right now – if I am making a choice to be conscious right now, and I am in charge of myself and how I feel right now, and I am totally alive right now, and none of that is dependent on anything other than my participation in this present moment – then I am alive and I have accomplished the baptism into earth. The baptism into earth means being here now.

The baptism into water. Baptism into water is a personal, experiential involvement in the movement of spirit. Jesus described it this way: "When you experience the earth baptism, you acquire some physical senses, and with them you perceive the physical environment. In order to have the second birth, which is the water baptism, you need to give birth to a new set of senses that are beyond the physical. When you see the leaves move on the trees, you know that the wind is moving among them and causing them to move. You know that there is wind even though you cannot see it. The baptism into water or spirit requires that you develop a sight that sees the wind." (John 3:5-8)

The man to whom Jesus was talking said, "Lord, we know that you are a master, otherwise you could not have healed these people. You could not have changed their symptoms."

Jesus replied, "You saw symptoms change, and you thought that was what I did. The change in the physical symptoms was like the movement of the leaves on the trees. What actually happened to the leaves was caused by the wind. You did not see the wind that moved the leaves, nor did you see the movement of spirit that changed the symptoms. The change in the symptoms was not the result of what I did, it was the result of who I am, who lives in me. You must give birth to a new set of senses so you can perceive in a new way, so you can see who lives in me."

The baptism into water is the birth of love. It is the birth of your ability to perceive what another understands without using your eyes or your reasoning deduction. It is the birth of your ability to experience a heart-bond with another, beyond compassion and empathy. It is the birth of your ability to experience another's feelings, another's nature, another's individual expression, to be one with others on a new level, to open yourself to communication with the spiritual world, to live in the world of spirit.

The baptism into fire. Baptism into fire means commitment – total commitment to spiritual direction and life purpose. You pull out all the stops. There is nothing that can hold you back from giving yourself to your soul's purpose. Total transformation occurs. Because of total commitment, you have all the energy needed to accomplish what you came to accomplish.

We witness such people and call them geniuses. They simply allow no distractions. They have given themselves over totally. They have married their purpose. They have experienced the release of the fire baptism. They are the movers and the shakers. They transform the world in their lifetimes.

The baptism into air. At the end of the life experience comes baptism into air. The body dies, and the spirit, which we are, is released. The spirit goes on to the next graduatory experience, or the next cycle of entering and passing through the cycle of baptisms – the cycle of earth, water, fire and air. These are the four baptisms that comprise the holy sacraments.

THE SACRAMENT OF THE MARRIAGE OF ELEMENTS

The next sacrament is called by various names. Some call the taking of bread and wine the Lord's Last Supper. Some call it the Holy Eucharist. Others call it Holy Communion. If we look at the origins and evolution of this ritual, we find that it did not originate with Jesus or Judaism. It was practiced in ancient Egypt and probably in other ancient cultures as well.

The practice was a recognition of energy meeting matter. In these ancient ceremonies, matter was reduced to a very simple form, which was ground grain combined with water. Leavening was not added, nothing to make it more palatable. There was just the dry wafer of earth. As they introduced water to the dry grain, they wanted to invoke a greater symbolism. The intention was to create a marriage of earth, air, fire and water. It was believed that the coming together of these four elements produced a dynamic result. The sum of the parts would be greater than the whole.

There was another element in the ritual. That pivotal element says, "Whatever I am thinking when I bring these elements together dictates the nature of the power released when they meet each other within me. So I take the bread and the wine, knowing that I am introducing within myself the four elements simultaneously – earth, air, fire and water – knowing that they will meet together in an expansion of energy."

The objective of the ceremony was to commit that energy to a specific purpose. The moment was made holy through the release of the energy within toward a higher purpose, with holy intent.

On at least two recorded occasions when this ritual was practiced, the teacher or the one introducing the practice said, "When you do this, you can literally transform yourself to work miracles." Melchizedek said it to Abraham, claiming him to be "possessor of heaven and earth." (Genesis 14:18-19) Jesus told his disciples when he served the sacramental meal, "He that believeth on me, the works that I do, shall he do also; and greater works than these shall he do." (John 14:12) He said, "You are capable of doing anything that I have done. There are things greater than this that you can do. And the power to do it is released in this experience."

In today's churches, we have a ritual celebration occurring, which Jesus did not institute or practice, generally called communion. Communion is the taking of bread and wine within a community for cementing a congregation as a church. It is not a sacrament.

The sacrament aspect of this ritual is the sacred meal that is taken as a communion with God, involving the holy marriage of the elements for transformation.

Jesus said, "My flesh is meat and my blood is drink." (Luke 22:19-20) What did he mean? His message was not esoteric. It was made crystal clear in the fourteenth chapter of John. Jesus said, "The things that you have seen me do, which you consider miracles, really did happen. They are miracles in that they are expressions of laws that you do not understand. They did happen. I really did do them. The reason that I can do these miracles is not because of myself, as this body or this flesh. The reason I can do them is because my Father is in me."

The word father should be examined. The word would have been better interpreted as *source* – not necessarily father or mother, not necessarily masculine or feminine.

Jesus said that "The source of myself is in me, the source of life itself is in me. And that source of life gives life, heals life, creates laws, transcends laws and creates miracles, because it is in me. Because I am not in competition with it, I can produce these miracles. When you look at me, because I am not in competition with my source, you can see my source when you see me. My source and I are one. You have come to know me. If you have come to know me, you have come to know my source, because my source and I are one. If through knowing what I am – at harmony with my source – if you have that same harmony inside you, if you have me in you as I have God in me, then everything that I do, you can do and greater things than these."

The next step was for Jesus to say, "Let's just illustrate this. Let's say this piece of bread is my body. Take it into your body. Now you have me inside you. Because you have me inside you, you can do what I have done. This wine is my blood. Drink it. My source that is in me is now in you, and you can do whatever I have done and more."

Then Jesus said, "Now take it one step further. Every time you drink or eat anything, from now on, for the rest of your life, make it a holy experience. Take me into your body and release within yourself all the power that I have had."

That was the original intent and purpose of this holy sacrament – nothing short of personal transformation.

THE SACRAMENT OF ORDINATION

Ordination is the next holy sacrament. There is a particular misconception about ordination. Many people believe that to ordain a person as a minister, a pastor, a spiritual leader under any name, in a church, makes that person different, special, perhaps more holy than others.

Using the same logic, is it also true that licensing someone as a dietician, or a boat captain, or a plumber makes that person different, special, perhaps more holy than others?

The point is that there are people within any community who have particular talents. Those talents should be recognized and licensed. People should be licensed as artists, musicians, builders, gardeners, chefs, healers, ministers, psychics, teachers, whatever the talent.

When a person's vocation, competence, expertise becomes his or her life purpose and commitment, that talent has then become a holy ministry, something sacred to that person. It is appropriate then that that person be ordained to that ministry by the community and receive a *laying-on-of-hands* by each member present. That means that that person is blessed to that particular service and is held responsible by a supportive community for carrying out that service to the highest degree.

Every one of us needs recognition, confirmation, affirmation and validation of what we do. Any one of us may have an incredible talent, yet without receiving recognition for it, we may lack the confidence and the courage to explore it. That talent can go undeveloped without the support of a community that provides consistent validation.

We all need positive feedback from one another. That is what the sacrament of ordination offers. We as a community should ordain all individuals who approach their passion with fervor and hard work, as a ministry and mission, whatever form it takes. That should be an individual's measure for ordination.

THE SACRAMENT OF INITIATION

Initiation is a very important, yet neglected, holy sacrament in our modern society. Initiation happens on two levels. The first level of initiation occurs within an individual. The second level occurs through confirmation by a community.

The first, inner level says this: When you have run up against a lesson so hard that it smashes your face, and bloodies your nose, and bruises your backside and your head and whatever else you used to run up against it, when it has slapped you down over and over and over – till one day, at last, you gain a certain insight that had probably been staring you in the face all along, but you had not realized it previously – and finally, in that moment, you absolutely *know*, "I'm over this. This will never slap me down again. It just can't happen. It doesn't have the ability to do it to me anymore. It doesn't have the power." On that day, with that realization, with that step in growth, you have *begun* the process of initiation. You were not actually initiated yet, but you started the process.

Initiation occurs in two parts. You initiate the graduation from the lesson, meaning you set it in motion. And then you graduate. Each initiation has a beginning and an end. The amount of time between the beginning and the end is relatively short. Initiation and graduation happen within twenty-four hours of each other, or else they do not happen, this time around.

Graduation is not always guaranteed. When you initiate the graduation experience, the catalyst – whatever has been repeatedly smacking you in the head, perhaps for lifetimes – will appear again within twenty-four hours. With it comes your opportunity to graduate from the lesson. If you really did arrive at the initiation point and the lesson has no more power to upset you, the encounter will not bloody you this time. It will not affect you. It will slide right by, and you will say, "You know, if that had happened last week, it would have killed me!" You step over it like a greasy spot on the pavement, and you go on to live your life. That is the first level of initiation. That is the personal experience of initiation.

What is the community's experience with initiation? What is the church's role in initiation? What is the tribal unit's responsibility for initiation? If we are wise as a community, and as a fellowship and church, we will pay attention and notice when individuals have broken old patterns and ended age-old struggles, when they have won a long-fought battle with a seemingly insurmountable foe.

When we witness the graduation of our friends, when they have claimed it and we see that it is so, we should bring them before the entire community and create a ritual that exalts them to the heavens. We should congratulate them with our hearts and our beings. We should validate their victory and their mastery over self.

The community's responsibility in the holy sacrament of initiation involves reward, validation, affirmation, confirmation, support, faith, love and perhaps a special ceremony. Any completed initiation is a cause for the whole community's celebration, because the growth of one nurtures and enhances the growth of all.

THE SACRAMENT OF FOOTWASHING

The final holy sacrament is called footwashing. It is not included among the sacraments of most churches. Footwashing says, "I am confident enough in myself and feel good enough about myself to be able to get down on my knees and be your servant," at least for a few minutes and hopefully for a lifetime.

Performed as a symbolic or theoretical act, footwashing does not qualify as a holy sacrament. Footwashing as a sacrament is humility with confidence. "I feel good about me. I am not subjecting myself to you. I am not being servile. However, I am *serving*. And I bow in reverence and service to you and your divinity."

The sacrament of footwashing is an electrical experience, both sensorially and literally. It is a sharing of vitality between two bodies. It essentially says, "May you be as healthy as I am. Let's make an electrical contact through a power point of your body, your feet with my hands, so that I can charge you. In that way, let us be charged with energy together."

During the time of Christ, the disciples washed Jesus' feet because he was their master. He was the classical guru, meaning they did everything for him. They prepared his meals, arranged his lodging, took care of his finances, his clothes, his hair. They related to him as a servant.

One day toward the end of their study period with him, Jesus brought them together and said, "For the last few years, you have called me master. And I have called you my servants or chelas. That was appropriate. But I want to change that relationship now. I am no longer your master, and you are no longer my servants. Instead, I will call you friends. You are my friends. You have graduated, and I want to mark this graduation in a particular way." (John 13:17)

He took a basin of water, knelt before them and began to wash their feet. Before long, Peter raised a raucous. "Thou shalt never wash my feet!" (John 13:8) Jesus responded to him by saying, "Peter, you have been a good servant. But if you cannot learn the role of master and let me serve you, you cannot live with me in the kingdom of heaven."

Almost anyone can be a good servant. It requires first getting your ego in place, and then everything else, including the clothes, the dishes, the closets and drawers, the flowerbeds, the cars, the accounting books, the scheduling, the public relations.

It is not difficult to be a good servant. It is not even difficult to be a good student. It is very difficult to be a master.

It is difficult to be held responsible for being the perfection that you suggest is possible. It is difficult, when you absolutely know that perfection is possible, but you are still working on expressing it perfectly during all twenty-four hours of the day. It is difficult when you absolutely know that there is a living Christ within you, but so far, you have only managed to touch the hem of the garment.

Being a master means being willing to help shape another's ability to express the living Christ within and recognizing that as the greatest form of service. If there are those who are willing to take on that responsibility, if there are those who can serve simultaneously with humility and confidence, then let the community come together for the holy sacrament of footwashing and bow in reverence to the divinity in each person.

HOW TO EVALUATE
A PSYCHIC READING

*The best evidence of the existence of a greater intelligence than
your conscious self is the fact that you are sitting there in that
body while it remains alive.*

P sychic readings have become popular, even normal, resources
for information and understanding. Psychics and channels
have come mainstream as individuals turn to sources other
than religion and science for answers.

Yet specific guidelines for obtaining readings are muddled or
nonexistent. Many seekers lack a clear understanding and command
of the process and mistakenly assume that it is the psychic's
responsibility to generate a good reading. They neglect to take charge
of the experience and often accept platitudes in place of an
opportunity for real advancement. Psychic readings have become
commonplace, however a solid understanding of the process
generally remains a mystery.

When is it appropriate to get a psychic reading? How should you
prepare for a reading? What questions are important to ask? How can
you tell if a person is a good psychic or not? How do you know if the
information is valid and legitimate? Which information should be
thrown out, especially if the reading concerns health issues? How
should the information be put to work?

BEGINNING THE PROCESS

Most people seeking psychic readings believe that everything
depends on finding a first-rate psychic because he or she is
responsible for the reading's content, validity and applicability. "If I

can just find a good psychic, I know I'll get the answers I'm looking for." Placing the responsibility on the psychic is the first mistake in the process, because the results of any psychic reading are primarily dependent on the seeker, not the channel.

When faced with a problem, most people instinctively search themselves for an answer. Even individuals considering a psychic reading will look for the answer within themselves first. Unfortunately, many do not look long enough or listen attentively enough to hear the answer when it comes. Listening within should always be the first step in seeking a psychic reading.

Imagine that you have a serious need for information. Your relationship with your partner is steadily deteriorating, or you have a chronic illness, or you cannot find a crucial document. You want a solution immediately. So what is the first thing you do?

You begin thinking about what the answer *might* be. In other words, you ask yourself for the answer. Call it calculated logic, call it reasoned investigation, call it prayer, or call it desperate hope. In any case, you have formulated a question, and you hope the answer will come. You can also call this self-directed activity *asking your source for an answer*.

Your source, who created you and has infinite knowledge of you, has every answer you could possibly seek. Even more interesting is that, after asking your source for the answer, you can then go to almost anyone, even someone with no obvious talent for channeling, and the exact words you need to hear can be put into his or her mouth. Have you ever had the experience where someone said exactly what you needed to know without even knowing that you had a problem?

The most important occurrence of a psychic reading takes place in the heart of the seeker. It usually takes place before he approaches the location of the reading and certainly before the channel opens his or her mouth. This stage of the process is called attunement. It simply means doing the necessary homework ahead of time.

How have you prepared for the reading? Do you have a genuine need for the information? What is your state of mind as you anticipate the reading and during the process itself? Are you depending solely on the channel for answers? Or are you really asking your source for information, believing that the channel is only an instrument? Do you anticipate that the channel is nothing more than a way for God to put into words an answer that already exists within you?

An important way to prepare for receiving answers, whether internally or through a psychic, is to take the experience seriously. Say to yourself, "This may be an opportunity to talk with my source of life, my source of wisdom, my source of guidance. This may be an opportunity for my source to speak to me in a direct, experiential way."

THE SOURCE OF YOUR MIND

Your mind has a source. You do not assume that you grew that thing by yourself, do you? Your mind originated somewhere, somehow. The source of your conscious mind is a greater intelligence that pre-existed both your mind and your body. This greater intelligence knew how to create functioning glands, cells, organs and tissues, and it designed and assembled your body into a fine-tuned working system.

This intelligence that built your body knows it inside out – how your body functions, what it needs to run, everything that has happened to it since birth. This intelligence has remained a part of the action from the beginning.

At this moment, your source is carrying on impressive activities within your body, which you could not perform without help. Your source is creating new cells, maintaining heartbeat and breathing, regulating relationships between different organs and systems. It is a massive job. Did you think you were running that show alone? The best evidence of the existence of a greater intelligence than your conscious self is the fact that you are sitting there in that body while it remains alive!

This supreme intelligence is the creative nature within you. You can call it by many names: God, higher consciousness, the superconscious mind, the source of you, the creator-you, the Divine-aspect of who you are, the spark of divinity that animates you.

It was you before your body, mind and personality came into existence. It remains closely connected to you. It is so close that it shares the thoughts you think, the words you speak, every decision you make, every action you take.

Consider this: Is it likely that this supreme intelligence that gave you the ability to think, and a body with ears to hear, and a mouth to speak, is incapable of hearing and responding when you use those tools to attempt communication with it?

Any intelligence that can give you the ability to think, to speak and to hear can undoubtedly hear what you have to say and respond to it. Choosing to depend on external channels, whatever their level of development – rather than talking with the source of your own mind, your own body, your own ability to think and speak and hear – seems misguided. Why not go right to the one that made the product?

Imagine the information accessible if you can learn to communicate with that greater intelligence within you. Skilled communication with this limitless source of personal information should be a goal of every individual on this planet. Whatever the measure of your intelligence, whether you are learning-disabled or genius, if you can transcend what you know as your conscious mind and tap its source, your knowledge and your thinking ability will expand. This internal source is the first place to turn when information on any issue is needed.

ACCESSING AN INTERNAL SOURCE OF INFORMATION

Accessing information within you has variables. Without directed effort and regular practice, the process can become as muddled as consulting external sources. So how should we seek a psychic reading from ourselves?

There are several levels within you from which information can come. There is the sensory consciousness, which is the conscious mind. All that this level of consciousness knows – its wisdom, the things that it has learned and contemplates – comes through the five external senses. The sensory mind is limited to what you have seen, heard, felt, tasted or smelled.

Generally this rule holds true, but there are exceptions. Once, I was riding in a car with a friend who was a doctor. A particular phrase had been running through my mind for quite a while. It was incessant, like a TV jingle that refuses to go away. This phrase was a strange collection of words that I was sure I had never heard before. I asked my friend, "What is the irradiated ergosterol steambop process?" Naturally, he looked at me strangely and said he had never heard of it. As it turned out, I did a diagnostic reading for one of his patients that evening, and the Source of the readings used the term "the irradiated ergosterol steambop process." I never learned exactly what it meant, as my attention was more focused on why those words kept coming back to me. In the end, I reasoned that it was necessary to plant that phrase in my mind so that I could pronounce it when necessary for the reading. The phrase was made available to my conscious mind though I had never heard or seen it. This was an unusual phenomenon because the information did not come to my conscious mind through my senses. Such things do occur sometimes.

The five senses are hard at work twenty-four hours a day. You receive information through these five sensory sources continuously. In fact, you take in more information than you can use at any given moment, including the temperature, the smells and fixtures of the room, and even the characteristics and movements of everyone in the room with you.

Of course, the conscious mind cannot deal with all that input. Information that does not need immediate attention is stored. Rather than be distracted by all those details, you send them to another place and shut the door tight saying, "Now stay down there!" That memory storage bank is called the subconscious mind.

The contents of the subconscious arrive through the senses as impressions rather than thoughts. For example, when you experience trauma in your life, you may symbolize or characterize it. By the time it arrives in the subconscious, it may have evolved to the image of a monster. When these monsters periodically surface in the conscious mind, you may experience nightmares or imagine dreadful scenarios. These originated as actual traumatic events, hurts or fears that you assigned a visual, sensory form and stored in the subconscious mind as symbols.

People seeking psychic readings often ask about recurring dreams. These dreams usually originate as specific events that occurred early in life. For years, the memories of these traumas could only exist as dream symbols, until sometime in the future when the person was ready to explore and attempt to resolve the feelings around the earlier actions.

By becoming familiar with your personal dictionary of dream symbolism and how you assign specific associations, you can better understand the personal fears and anxieties that arise in daily life. Imaging or dreaming of a monster is not necessarily the result of the horror film you saw that evening and almost certainly does not mean that you are going to see a monster tomorrow. It is more likely a representation of some aspect of you, perhaps one difficult to face.

Taking the time to examine the image opens a door to not only facing, but also understanding and integrating, that frightening part of self. Symbols are actually gifts from the subconscious mind, even the frightening ones. They are purposeful communications, sent to help you deal more effectively with your daily experiences. Dreams and images are the subconscious' effort to tell you something that you need to know. Exploring these symbols is never a waste of time.

A third level of consciousness, the superconscious mind, contains information that did not arrive through the five senses and did not originate through the symbols of the subconscious mind. However, subconscious symbols may be borrowed by the superconscious mind to communicate its message. The superconscious mind is unlimited in the sources and the methods it can use for communicating.

THE SUPERCONSCIOUS AND THE CONSCIOUS MINDS

The relationship between the superconscious mind and the conscious mind can be better understood if compared to scuba diving. When scuba diving, you first travel by boat out beyond the surf to a distance where the sea is less rough and the boat rolls steadily up and down the waves. The setting is absolutely beautiful. Behind you, palm trees wave in unison as the breakers rush to shore. Along the distant horizon, the sky and water compete in a dazzling array of blue and turquoise. Billowy clouds pass before a bright sun, while a steady breeze freshens the air.

The setting is perfect – a solid world, unquestionably real. But you have decided to make a dive. You put on some heavy, cumbersome equipment. You strap a bulky tank to your back. It is uncomfortable and unwieldy in the boat, but you will need it where you are going. You put a mask over your face that limits your vision considerably. You put a tube in your mouth so you can breathe where you are going. You put flippers on your feet, making it nearly impossible to maneuver in this perfect setting. No turning back now. You position yourself on the edge of the boat. Then you fall backwards into the water, tumbling, plummeting deep into another world. From that moment, the world left behind no longer exists. The palm trees, the warm sun, the boat and the mainland all fade like the trail of tiny, extraneous air bubbles disappearing toward the surface.

In this new world, your experience is limited to the equipment you are using. In fact, the equipment defines the experience. Your vision has been narrowed and shortened. Your ability to survive in this world is dependent upon the tank on your back. Mobility is affected by the flippers on your feet, which made you immobile in the previous world.

You have entered a foreign dimension, one that is not your natural habitat and definitely not home. Yet the longer you remain in this foreign world, the less aware and more disconnected you become to the previous one. This new world requires and elicits your full attention for the duration of the experience. There are so many wonderful and fascinating things to see that you want to linger when it is time to leave. When the equipment has performed to its limit, you reluctantly return to the surface and the boat. You talk excitedly with your friends about your dive and what you saw, the stunning coral, the curious anemones, the dangerous moray eels, the menacing barracudas. Without these exciting things along the way, it might have been a boring dive.

Being born is a lot like scuba diving. You put on some heavy, cumbersome equipment that is absolutely useless in your native world. But you need to master it quickly if you want to move freely and effectively in the new world that is coming up soon. The new world is amazing and summons your full attention. You can delegate some responsibilities. Air supply is automatically monitored thanks to good pre-planning. But life in the new world is something of a struggle. In fact, staying alive can occupy the mind so completely that the palm trees and crashing waves are long forgotten.

Pre-planning for the dive also included various desired accomplishments, such as looking for certain life forms, exploring new areas, practicing new skills, becoming familiar with new equipment. While in the water, the you that planned the dive takes a back seat to the you that is busy with the experience. However, that part of you remains present, still remembers the dive-purpose, knows what you intended when you tumbled backwards into the unknown, recalls the plan of how far to go and what to explore. Surfacing means returning to what is normal and natural when the dive is complete. In retrospect, surrounded by the familiarity and comfort of the steadily rocking boat, you are fascinated by the unusual encounters, the dangers, the new information and skills you acquired through the adventure. You immediately begin to anticipate your next dive.

In life, the you that planned the dive is the superconscious mind, responsible for remembering life-purpose, soul-intentions and the previous world. The you that planned the life takes a back seat to the you that is busy with the experience. What does this superconscious mind know about you? In a nutshell, everything.

YOU ARE A CREATOR

In his books, *Fields of Life* and *Blueprint for Immortality*, Harold Saxon Burr describes the superconscious mind as a creative intelligence that knows how to make a body. According to his theory, this field of intelligent life pre-existed the physical body and helped in its design, dictating the strengths, weaknesses, dexterity, talents, abilities, color of hair and eyes, appearance, genetic makeup, everything that comprised the design of your body.

Your body was made according to a specific and unique design. There is not another one like it in the universe. Your design was constructed to meet particular karmic needs and lessons.

Understand that karma is not punishment. Karma is a series of opportunities to learn, which are provided through the weaknesses designed into your body. Your weaknesses are just as important as your strengths are, concerning fulfilling life purpose. Weaknesses that are specifically designed for a teaching purpose are not problems or mistakes in the blueprint. There is not something wrong with the body.

Weaknesses were strategically planned and designed to guide you in a specific direction, so that you could find personal, appropriate responses to those weaknesses and master them. It is something right with the body. Only right things happen. The only way they can become wrong things is through a wrong response to them. They are important opportunities, in every case.

Having designed and constructed these strengths and weaknesses so perfectly, this superconscious mind certainly knows your soul's purpose. This intelligence that knows how to regulate your heartbeat and your lungs, knows how to create new cells, knows how to keep you up and running, undoubtedly knows why you are here. It knows what you should do with your life and the direction that you should take. Through observation, it knows why things have gone amiss. If you have disease, it knows how that situation evolved, and what is missing from your life, and what to do about it. In short, it has all the answers you could possibly need.

Then how can you communicate with this creative intelligence to take advantage of its vast knowledge that is personal to you? One way is to establish a direct, experiential relationship based on familiarity and daily, two-way communication. The place to begin is by addressing it.

COMMUNICATION WITH THE SUPERCONSCIOUS

When beginning a conversation with the superconscious, we are at a disadvantage because we are more comfortable addressing things that we can observe through the senses and through experience. Talking to things that we cannot see or feel can get us into trouble, unless of course we call it "God" and locate it outside ourselves. If we insist on talking to something unfamiliar and indefinable within ourselves, people might think we are crazy. However, that is exactly what we must do. Addressing the superconscious requires communicating with something beyond the senses for which we have no point of reference.

How do you talk with something that you cannot see or hear? When communicating with the superconscious, most people at least want to be able to feel it. They want phenomena. They want lights, heavenly music, vibrations, voices. But the superconscious is not about phenomena. It is not visual, audible or tangible. Then how in the world can you talk with it?

The Bible provides an answer. Jesus instructed Nicodemus to give birth to a new body with a new set of senses to communicate with the unseen kingdom of spirit. (John 3:5-7) His old body could not see spirit. It could only see the result of spirit. Therefore, it could not understand spiritual things. It could only respond to the result of spiritual things. Living and communicating in the world of spirit would require speaking and listening in a new way. It means going beyond simply living life, to personally knowing the one who created life.

To develop a new way of speaking and listening, you need to begin with an assumption that there is a creative intelligence beyond what you can perceive. Begin a conversation and keep talking, even if you get no response at first.

"I'm talking with the source of my mind, my body, my spirit. Whatever you are, whoever you are, I'm talking with you. And I assume that you are listening. Since you gave me ears, I'm going to assume that you can hear me. Since you gave me the ability to think, I'm going to assume that you understand me. I want to get to know you better. So I'm going to look for you in many different ways. I'm going to listen to you speaking to me through the words of the people I live with, the people I work with, the people I encounter throughout the day. I'm going to listen for your voice in my dreams and in the incidents that happen in my life."

The next step is to begin to look for evidence of a response. "I'm going to build a familiarity with you by talking with you and by looking for your active presence in my daily life. I'm going to acknowledge your presence by discovering what you do. This way, I'm going to get to know you better."

You may be surprised how clearly and effectively your higher self can reveal itself and its knowledge to you. The important thing is to start talking and start listening. Expect answers, in every form imaginable and unimaginable. And they will come!

SEEKING BEYOND OURSELVES

It is unnecessary to go beyond ourselves for the information we need to solve our problems or meet our challenges. Yet people generally prefer interaction with something external. Unfortunately, traditional religion has taught us that we must contact an external force that is more evolved than we are, to be taught something that we cannot possibly already know.

Many people turn within themselves hoping to encounter masters, teachers, guides, elder brethren, angels. Yes, these do exist, and you can experience them. However, there is one central truth that is more important than all these. And through this truth, all these beings will be put in their proper place relative to you.

There is no soul in the universe that is older than you are. You came straight from the heart of God. You are a cell in the body of God. Therefore, you are as old as God. All things that are known to God are known to an innate awareness that exists within you. There is no external force that is, ever has been, or ever can be, closer to God than you are, because God lives within you. All that you can ever know of God already exists within you.

The purpose of masters, teachers and guides, whether incarnate on this plane or discarnate on other planes, is not to teach you or to remake you. Their purpose is to awaken you to the God that lives within you. The best way they can do that is by providing a point of reference for, and a reflection of, God within you.

Any teacher or master that causes you to feel inferior by making himself superior is not a master or a guide, and is not good for you. He is distracting you from the truth that is within you.

On the other hand, any being that causes you to be more reliant on the truth within you and teaches you discernment within yourself is truly a master and a guide. A true master will instruct you to turn within to find your divine source.

The nature of God is your true, inherent nature. Therefore, it is not appropriate for you to externalize your allegiance to a supposedly greater master. However, if you discover that everything is within you, and you say, "I don't need teachers. I don't need any master. It's all within me, and I don't need anyone to tell me what I should do," you have given birth to a gigantic ego.

Genuine truth will come through the marriage of this paradox: "God is within me, yet I will recognize God through the point of reference others provide."

If you fail to see God in others, the God that you found in yourself is really the god of ego. On the other hand, if the only God you recognize is the God within others, you have overlooked the divinity that lives within you. You can go no further in your growth until you recognize and acknowledge that God lives within everyone.

"I know God when I see him in you, when I recognize him in my reflection in your eyes."

True teachers, masters and guides will affect you in subtle ways. As you pray and meditate, you may never receive beautiful communications, flashes of light or celestial music. To your frustration, your friends may be experiencing all sorts of wonderful and amazing things, while you see and hear nothing. However, in response to your prayers and meditations, you may begin to notice unusual things happening around you. You will begin to observe little miracles. Things begin to fall into place without effort. Situations resolve themselves more easily. You begin to respond to people and incidents more effectively, in ways you never could. You gain new insights from daily events. Situations that would have provoked frustration in you earlier draw a calmer response now. You meet a difficult situation head-on and say, "OK, this is an opportunity to respond in a better way than I have in the past." As you witness your life changing in response to your prayers and meditations, you can trust that your internal teacher is doing a good job, even without lights and music.

The master of all masters is the master who can teach you without attracting attention to himself. A true master can be an intercessor between you and God, without allowing you to know that he is even there.

The one who gives you an exotic name and channels beautiful images of himself that you can paint in delicate pastels on a canvas is elevating himself and expressing his own ego. He says he is an "ancient master," but more likely he was Joe-average in his past life. Now he prefers exotic names, and he even found a turban thought-form that he could wrap around his head to impress you. He may be genuine, and he may have beautiful, wise things to say to you that he learned from a genuine guru on inner planes. But remember this: From whatever level he comes, however valid the communication, by attracting attention to himself he is taking your attention away from God within you.

If you find yourself calling on your spirit guide one day instead of God, you are in trouble. He has come between you and your divine-self, and you can go no further than him. He has become a distraction from what should be his purpose. When a master becomes your God, when a spirit guide becomes the answer to your problems, you have diverted from your true path.

A real teacher or guide will direct you to the origin of yourself, within yourself.

RECOGNIZING GOD

When you turn within and discover something that wants to do right, that wants to help others, that wants to become one with all that is good, that expresses love and supports life, you have found that part of you that is the true nature of God. Let that be your guide. Fasten on to it and do not let go. When you find that element within you that longs to be like God, that knows itself to be God-like, hang on to it. Recognize it as the still, small voice. Know that that is your teacher and listen only to that.

If you want to build a learning relationship with an external teacher, look for one who can cause that part of you that is the nature of God to respond. Look for a teacher whose words cause you to say, "Yes! Yes, that is it! That is God in me!" That external teacher and that internal aspect of you will be vibrating on the same frequency. Therefore, that teacher will have given expression to the God within you, and he will have caused a greater awareness in you of your true nature. You will be learning and growing. Your inner, spiritual teacher will be teaching you through the services of an external teacher, whether incarnate or discarnate.

If you receive a beautiful communication in your meditation or your dreams, ask, "Who are you?" If that external force says to you, "We are all one here. I am not one that you can identify. I am only one attempting to serve God like you," hang on to him. Attempt to communicate with that being now and then. But consider him merely a friend along the path. He is not a master, not one that you should worship, not one you should ever call upon. If you should ever discover his name and call on him in prayer instead of God, you have done him a disservice because his purpose is not to become a distraction between you and God. He simply wants to grow with you on the path, and his intercession with you, through meditation or whatever, is his means of growth and service to God.

Ascended masters, spirit guides, archangels or even wise teachers are not necessary to help you grow spiritually. There is nothing outside yourself that is essential to your development. This is not to say that you should never communicate with any of these. Someday, you may experience direct communication with an angel, and that would be wonderful. However, that angel should not become a substitute for direct communication with your creator. Always seek the highest within you.

The Qabalah, which is a form of ancient Hebrew wisdom, maintains that God cannot be named. When we think we have reached God – as soon as we name him, describe him, label him, decide he's a he or a she, get our hands on him and seal him up in a little, brown box labeled "Buddhist" or "Christian" or "Muslim" – we have misjudged the mark and missed our goal.

We have to go beyond what we know, strive higher than our last realization. And there we have another paradox of God: We must strive unceasingly to know God, never assuming that we know all there is of that power, yet there is nothing of God we do not know within ourselves.

Fortunately, the idea that we can receive guidance and answers from within is becoming more commonly accepted than ever before. What a great step for humankind to learn to effectively use our innate capacity to know what is good for us, and then to act on that knowledge purposefully!

WHEN ARE PSYCHIC READINGS APPROPRIATE?

With practice, anyone can learn to receive specific information and interpret that information in ways that are useful and practical. Guidance from the superconscious mind comes in many forms, including feelings, hunches, ideas, impressions, insights, dreams and external experiences and conversations.

This variable of possibilities is where the stumbling block occurs for most people as interpretation becomes subjective. Does my dream mean this, or does it mean that? Was the feeling I had about that person accurate, or did I misinterpret because of bias?

At this point, it sometimes helps to seek the advice of an external source for confirmation of your interpretations. This is the point where psychic readings become appropriate, *after* you have sought and received your own inner guidance.

You may want someone else to replace vague generalizations with pragmatic, down-to-earth statements. When a person seeks a psychic reading, he needs to look for someone who can put into clear, precise words the feelings and visions that he has been receiving but not necessarily understanding. In that way, he can look at the information logically. He transfers the messages from the right side of the brain to the left, through the experience of working with a channel.

When using external sources, it is helpful to think of a psychic reading, not as brand new information coming from another person, but as an opportunity for the feelings and impressions that you have been receiving to be worded for you. That is the ideal way to use a channel. In these cases, the seeker often says afterwards, "I feel like I always knew that, and yet I suppose I never thought of it before. It was like hearing something and remembering it. It sounded like the channel was reminding me of something that I had already known but had just forgotten."

This is the first key to the legitimacy of a psychic reading: Recognition establishes validity. You find yourself listening to the information with a feeling of recollection, as if you have heard it before or thought it previously. You are recognizing truth.

On the other hand, if channeled information lacks that familiar tone and nothing inside you responds to it, it does not necessarily mean that you should disbelieve it. Take time to examine it. Test it by living with it.

The most important test of any information's authenticity, no matter how it is received, is its applicability. Is it practical? Will it work? Will the results be beneficial? Did you hear something that you can put to the test, which improves the quality of your living?

Psychics are often judged by their ability to sound good, which generally means to sound "psychic." Especially popular are psychics who state things in a stiff, old-English style and who throw in a few pious thees and thous. Or they use convoluted sentence structure so it sounds like someone from another world has arrived and is just learning the language. Or better yet, they use a voice that is different from their own, meaning they have left the body and attracted someone truly evolved.

Again, the conscious mind is looking for something tangible to grab hold of, some sort of phenomenon. However, phenomena are not the most valid evidence of the subtler world. Experiencing the subtler world requires that you listen in a new way. Turn off your senses and forget phenomena.

Psychic readings are often judged by whether the channel reported something previously unknown. "How did she know that? There's no way she could have known that about me! She's good!" Such phenomena can be impressive and may prove that information can be psychically received, perhaps demonstrating that the reader is telepathic. However, the fact that information is psychically received does not necessarily mean that it is valid. Information can be psychically received and still be totally inaccurate.

Accuracy derives from applicability, whether the information is applicable, workable, valuable and meaningful in the seeker's life. It cannot be repeated too often: Applicability proves legitimacy.

THE SOURCE OF THE INFORMATION

Selectivity is the key when choosing a psychic. It is most important to choose someone who has already developed his own clear channel of communication with the superconscious mind. If you have established a direct, experiential relationship with your superconscious, and the psychic you choose has done the same with his own superconscious, you cannot miss hitting the mark, which would be the highest level from which information can come.

If your psychic manages to turn off his five senses but gets no further than the subconscious mind, he will only receive symbols.

And the symbols coming from his subconscious will be his symbols, categorized and stored carefully according to his experiences, not yours. However, if he can reach his superconscious mind, something like this might happen. His superconscious mind will have a little conversation with your superconscious, saying, "OK, what's happening to your human?" And your superconscious will answer, "I'm so glad you asked! I've been trying to communicate directly with him for years, but he hasn't heard me. So I'm going to ask you to say to him in words what I can't get through to him in any other way. And by all means, while you're talking to him, tell him to listen to me."

People giving psychic readings often claim to channel ascended masters, spirit guides, even archangels. These are no more important coming from a psychic than they would be if they showed up in your private meditation. Keep in mind that in order for you to receive psychic information from some sort of presence, entity, being, spirit, personality or any other secondary source, you first have to bypass the source of your being, the source of life itself. How sensible is it to stumble over the president of the company to have a word with the errand boy?

The president of the company, who in this case would be the creator of the universe, has a direct link with your mini-universe. Why not talk with the source of it all, especially when that source is easier to contact, always available, free of charge and undoubtedly more accurate? If the president wants to send an archangel as his messenger boy, great. Let that be God's choice.

When making the decision to seek a psychic reading, always begin by examining yourself. Pray and listen within yourself. Ask your source whether you should seek a reading. Ask whether this or that psychic is a good choice. The first source of guidance you should address is the still, small voice that naturally guides your decisions and choices. If you feel hesitant about the reading, then set it aside until something in you feels very strongly that it is appropriate to do. At that point, examine yourself again and ask, "What do I really need to know? Are there problems that I need to work out? Are there things that I need to understand about myself?"

FORMULATING QUESTIONS

Just as important as choosing a psychic is deciding what questions to ask. Formulating questions is usually a process of self-discovery. As you examine the possibilities, endless topics arise and compete to be first, including issues you wrestle with and topics you simply wonder about.

Setting priorities will clarify what is really important in your life. Sometimes, this process by itself can result in answers. By the time you have a list of questions on paper, you may have a list of answers in your mind. In that case, the reading has already taken place without the aid of the channel, through examining yourself, asking questions and searching for the answers within.

Sometimes, the questions become part of the reading process. On one occasion, a woman requested a reading from me, and a date was set for one week later. She spent the week examining herself and her life. She let everyone around her know that she considered this a very special opportunity to talk with God. She was excited and expectant, and she wanted to ask only the most important questions. Early on the morning of the reading, she retreated to the beach where she could sit quietly. Eventually, five "perfect questions" arrived in her mind, and she put them down on paper. When we finally began the reading that evening, the Source of the readings started speaking immediately, without ever waiting to hear a single question. Yet every question was addressed thoroughly and effectively. The woman said afterwards that she believed the content of the reading had already been selected and prepared, perhaps long before that evening, and that the appropriate questions had been "given" to her that morning on the beach by the same source that provided the answers.

A popular question asked by individuals is, "Who was I in a past life?" as if that information has relevance to their current issues. Why be concerned with fanciful stories of a past life that might or might not be true?

Before you ask such a question, look at your present-day weaknesses, challenges, strong points, inclinations, likes, dislikes, talents and peculiarities. Look at those and ask instead, "Where do these abilities come from? What is the source of this weakness in me? What is the source of this strength in me? How did I acquire this natural talent?" Then if you still want to ask about past lives, you will have a link connecting you to the past and a clearer purpose for asking about it. If the information about a past life is linked directly to something in your present experience that you need to understand better, you will have a valid reason for asking the question, and you will get a sensible answer.

Curiosity breeds fantasy, while necessity results in truth. If you ask about past lives out of curiosity, the answer will be a response to your curiosity, more likely a fanciful story. It may have meaning, or it may not. It may have applicability, or it may not. You probably will never know whether it was a valid past life experience, so how will that information benefit you?

However, if you need to understand some facet of yourself better and you ask the question based on that need, the information given will probably add to your understanding of yourself in the present. Past life information provided under those conditions will relate to the present. It may even draw to the surface of your conscious mind a memory that will help you understand yourself better. Whether you were that person will not matter because the model or archetype will have meaning for you in the present regardless. The information will be personally beneficial to you.

For instance, a young man came to me for a reading with a question about his "intense anger" and his "need to control others." The Source of the readings described several lifetimes in the military, positions of significant power and authority on battlegrounds familiar to us today. In this present lifetime, he was still carrying the internal message of, "All right, who is my enemy? It could be anyone! I have to be careful!" He still carried the pain of watching comrades die and losing the cause. Some part of him still believed that he was at war. Going back and revisiting those experiences by examining certain past lives allowed him to better understand the present. His message to himself needed to be, "The war is over. I am learning to trust." In that case, knowledge of a past life was beneficial to the present.

THE MOST IMPORTANT QUESTIONS TO ASK

The first important question to ask when seeking a psychic reading is: "What are the things about me that I am hiding and that would be helpful to know?"

That information is vital to each individual. Yet it is the last thing most people want to hear. "What do I most need to know? What are the things that I'm really hiding from myself? What are the communications from my higher self that I have refused to hear? I want to know because that is what is producing conflict. I want to know even if it's painful. I want to use this reading to finally get past that pain." In asking, of course, you need to be prepared for the truth because the information can sometimes seem critical or even harsh.

When seekers approach me with the attitude of, "I have to know the truth. I cannot live without it," the Source will reveal powerful information. But an interesting dynamic happens in those instances. When people will settle for nothing less, they welcome the information because they know they can use it to their advantage. They may be startled, but they bounce back quickly.

Once, a man came to me seeking psychic advice. He had a master's degree in guidance and counseling, yet he had settled into a routine of low output. He had accomplished nothing in several years, and he was living off welfare and using soft drugs as an escape. In his questions to the Source, he asked about reincarnation, specifically Atlantis. The immediate response from the Source was that he had been in Atlantis, and had been a "dropout" then also. Bam! No sugarcoating. As it turned out, these words were just the thing to snap this man out of his present meaningless existence. Following that experience, he liked to tell people that the Source is "so diplomatic that it can tell a person to go to hell in such a way that they will look forward to the trip."

In those instances where truth is sought, the resulting directness is usually recognized as supportive. When a person truly wants to know what is in his or her best interest, a good source of guidance will provide the naked truth and will also include supportive, helpful ways to overcome the challenges described. When formulating questions for a psychic reading, never be afraid to ask about the parts that you are hiding from yourself.

The second question to ask: "Do I have particular abilities that I haven't recognized or that I have taken for granted, so that I am not using them as well as I might?"

Individuals often have talents and abilities that seem ordinary, so they are taken for granted. These abilities go unnoticed and undeveloped. It could be an undervalued ability to create poetry or music. Or it could be a less concrete talent such as an ability to communicate effectively with people, to cause people to feel good about themselves, to make people feel comfortable and happy. Uncovering hidden abilities is important.

The third question might be: "What important next step is before me, immediately, right now?"

Not: "What should I do with my life?" This type of long-term question is not necessarily valuable, though often asked. If you focus on what you might ultimately do with your life, rather than the step that is right in front of you at this moment, you will never get to what you are supposed to do because the groundwork was overlooked.

"What is the most important immediate next step in my life toward accomplishing my soul purpose?" With that question, you have the necessary information to assure the future.

Next question: It is important to know about relationships with family, friends and colleagues. No one exists in your life without reason. Your particular family structure was not accidental. So it is valuable to examine the relationships with people to whom you have been drawn karmically. Why is a particular relationship necessary?

The question should not be: "Where did those people and situations come from? What did I do to them in a past life to deserve this?" Rather, ask: "What influence, coming from people in my immediate circle, is shaping me for the task that I have to do in the future?"

The situations you encounter in your family life are needed in order to respond appropriately to the present and the future. It is helpful to understand how these people, with their traits and peculiarities, were chosen as faculty for the Planetary Mystery School in which you enrolled this lifetime.

When seeking a physical or health-related reading, there are two questions to include. Identify the specific symptoms that you are experiencing. Then ask: "Where in consciousness or activity did this come from?"

Again, this is not a reference to karma. Information concerning karma might come if you need to know what happened in a past life to produce the current situation. More important is: "What am I doing right now, in my conversations, my communications, my relationships, my emotional expressions, my lifestyle management, that contribute to this situation? What are the factors that produced this condition?"

Go beyond the physical level. Ask, "What are the factors in my current lifestyle or my current way of thinking, my belief system, my attitudes, that produced these symptoms? What are the dynamics of the way that it was produced? How did it evolve from a lifestyle problem to a physical symptom?" With that understanding, you can restructure your lifestyle to affect your body in a different way to create a healing of the situation.

For example, something that you are thinking or doing might be harmfully affecting your kidneys. You need to know, "How did that get from my thinking to my kidneys?" The reading might describe a battle that went on between two muscles in your back that caused a subluxation in your spine that affected a particular nerve to your kidney and caused it to break down. You need to know what you have been doing or thinking that resulted in the battle between the muscles. You need to understand the dynamic of how the process evolved, from your lifestyle or your thoughts, into a physical manifestation.

The next issue becomes: "How can I best correct it in my lifestyle?" Furthermore: "How can I best support the result of it in my body, physically?"

So you want two sets of instructions, each dealing with a different level. "How do I restructure my thinking and my lifestyle?" and "What can I do physically, medically, herbally, etc.? What treatments can be helpful? What can I do physically to correct the symptoms?"

When asking health-related questions, do your homework first. If something is malfunctioning in your kidneys, study the kidneys to know how they ought to function ideally. Take responsibility for using the faculties that you already have. Have a mental picture of what the proper function would look like. Then the information that comes in the reading will address the knowledge that you already have. If you have not done your homework by informing yourself and taking the steps already available to you, you may not be able to put the information to work in the most sensible way.

A responsible channel will study a subject before attempting to provide psychic information. Remember the irradiated ergosterol steambop process? The more information each person involved has on a subject, the better the filter will be. The more extensive the vocabulary is, the easier the pronunciation will be, and the greater the understanding will be.

The suggestion that a psychic who reads up on a subject before a reading is cheating is naïve and foolish. When attempting to give words to the wordless, when bringing something without form into the dimension of form, we need all the help we can get, including well-informed seekers and psychics.

CHOOSING A PSYCHIC

At last, with the appropriate questions in hand, the next step is to choose the psychic. There are specific considerations to help you in your choice. First, look for someone whose life shows the effectiveness of his or her communication. "Believe not every spirit, but try the spirits whether they are of God, because many false prophets are going out into the world." (I John 4:1)

Anyone who has been leading an average life, unconscious and unaware, and who suddenly contacts his superconscious, is going to be a person whose life is turned completely around. Such a person will be extraordinary in many ways.

Look for that, beyond psychic ability. Look for what the discovery of a direct, experiential relationship with the source of all life did to that person's daily existence. Has that new relationship produced a sense of joy and prosperity? Has it made that person a consistently loving person? Is that person valuable as an advisor while awake? Is it someone you trust and admire?

Look for someone who is loving and who can genuinely care about you personally. Find a wise person, someone whose words and life suggest wisdom at work. Find someone whose life is clearly working effectively, someone who is going in a direction that you might like to go.

The psychic ability of the individual should be a secondary consideration. A person who is loving, has some wisdom, and has created a life that is moving effectively in a direction that you would like to follow will make a good counselor. That is the person whose information you will naturally respect. A loving nature attuned to God will always prevail over someone with a shingle claiming "Psychic." Optimum is the psychic with the professional shingle, who is also loving and attuned to God.

You can be assured that if a person cares about you, your source can put into that person's mouth the words that you need to hear. You may even save the price of a psychic reading by sharing with a loving friend. Receiving information through someone in an altered state of consciousness does not make the information more valid for you.

There are many ways to prove whether a person is psychic and to establish the depth of trance that the person is using. Such indicators are impressive and perhaps important, if you are a researcher in parapsychology and need that evidence for your work. On the other hand, if you are simply trying to get some direction in your life, use all the sources around you, particularly the caring, loving people in your life. Seek the advice of your friends who are attuned to God within themselves.

THE PSYCHIC'S SOURCE

If you are intent on using a psychic channel, attempt to find out what the psychic's personal belief is about his source of information. Remember, there are many levels to approach for information in altered states of consciousness. The same guidelines and pitfalls apply to external psychics as when you seek the information within yourself. You can learn a lot about the channel by discovering where he goes for the information.

Many psychic channels contact spirit guides to attain information. Generally, a spirit guide is a disembodied person who has lived on earth previously, has left the body, and probably has the same interests as when incarnate. There is no indication that a spirit guide becomes wiser by leaving the body.

There is nothing wrong with listening to the advice of a wise, disembodied person. However, it is puzzling and even comical to watch people pay a medium a good sum of money to ask Aunt Mary for spiritual advice, when they never would have listened to her when she was still in the flesh. It is popular to believe that the Aunt Mary's of the world become smarter when they get out of the body, especially if they are now using an exotic name. Death does not necessarily signify spiritual advancement.

The same is true of spirit doctors. Unfortunately, you cannot examine their credentials now that they have left the earth plane. Would you go to a physical doctor whose credentials, expertise and credibility were not verifiable? If you want a doctor, go to one whose credentials you can examine.

Spirit guides do exist, and they can be helpful. You have friends right now in the flesh whose advice you consider meaningful. Sometimes, they die and go to another plane, and their advice remains valuable. However, it is important to know that nothing about the process of death makes their advice more valuable. The advice of a discarnate friend is valuable in the same way as the advice of close, living friends and should be evaluated in the same way.

The most important factor in seeking guidance is that it is never necessary to go beyond the boundaries of you. The link between yourself and your source is like an umbilicus. A good psychic will use that umbilicus to retrieve the information that you need and will help you interpret and understand what your source is already telling you. Your source of life and wisdom rules out the need for a go-between. Spirit guides are not necessary.

When choosing a psychic, always ask for an explanation of what happens during a reading. Where does the channel believe his consciousness goes to retrieve the information? What happens when he turns off his senses? Ask the channel where he believes the information comes from and listen very carefully to the answer. How does he tune in to the source of his readings? Does he use prayer and attunement? Does he know whom he is addressing? Is it the subconscious, or the superconscious, or is it a discarnate being? If the channel does not use terms that are recognizable to you, ask for explanations. Get clear. You are primarily responsible for the results of your reading, so you need to examine all these factors carefully.

Removing sensory awareness and input, turning off the senses, is not all that is required to contact the higher mind or superconscious. There is another requirement that has to do with intent. It has to do with directing the consciousness. It has to do with familiarity with the source of all there is.

A good psychic or channel is a person whose conversation, feelings, emotions, activities, thoughts, time and energy is absolutely devoted to his source. There will be nothing more important. Of course, there will be the normal activities of daily life. At the same time, there will be a continuous undercurrent of dedication and devotion to his source.

Edgar Cayce was a good example. Who was Edgar Cayce? He was the most documented psychic of the 20th century, having provided more than 14,000 readings before his death in 1945. What was the nature of his devotion to his source? Cayce read chapters of the Bible every day of his life, not because the Bible was his only source of information or wisdom, but because it was related to his source. His interest in his source was a consuming thing. It was where he spent his time and energy. You could say that his source was his closest friend. He maintained a direct, experiential relationship.

Look for evidence of that kind of relationship when searching for a psychic. If the person talks about his source, thinks about it, consults it, acts according to it, lives and breathes it, then you can be certain that when he "loses" consciousness, he does not *lose* it. Rather, he specifically directs it.

Hopefully, the psychic says a prayer or invocation aloud as he attunes, so you can hear the words, so you can know where his consciousness is being directed. How does he word his attunement? Who is he calling upon? Is he talking with a spirit guide? If so, you know the level he will reach. You know that he is not approaching the highest source. He is settling for an errand boy. The information may be correct, but it will be third-hand. Perhaps he is calling on an archangel. Why is he not contacting the archangel's boss, the source of the archangel?

Look for a psychic reader who calls upon the source of life and asks, "God, will you take charge of the information? Send anyone you want to deliver the information. I only ask that you, the source of all there is, take control of what we hear. Not only what we hear, but how we hear it. Give us perfect understanding of what you send."

The prayer of attunement used by the channel provides a clear indication of where his consciousness goes when the lights go out. Ask yourself, "When he closes his eyes, where does his mind go?" Ask him the same question.

Find a psychic who seeks information from God. Then do the same thing yourself, joining with the psychic's effort. Attune yourself to the same source.

Remember the conversation that his superconscious will have with your superconscious: "OK, what's happening to your human?" The information that a good psychic will provide will come from within you. The information will come from your superconscious, through the superconscious of the channel.

In that process of going through the superconscious of the channel, the tenor of the information will take on some peculiarities of the channel. In other words, your reading will bear some resemblance to every other reading that particular channel does. At the same time, habitual phrases and figures of speech that you use may also be picked up by the channel from your language patterns. For instance, specific technical terms that are unfamiliar to the channel may appear in a reading for a scientist. Some aspects of the reading will reflect the channel, while others will be peculiar to the seeker.

A psychic might tell you, "This is what you should do next." That sort of statement should immediately raise a red flag because your source will rarely put information in those terms. If a reading tells you, "This is what you are supposed to do with your life," or "This is the organization that you should join," or "This is what you should do with your money," be suspicious.

Look at some prior readings given by the psychic. The information provided in a psychic reading should include the projected results of various choices. "If you do this, this will be the result. If you do this instead, then this will be the result. Now you choose." Or "You could do this – it is an opportunity, and the result will work well for you in this way."

Valid psychic information does not say, "Do this." It says, "There is this opportunity, and the outcome would probably look like this." You are provided with indications, possibilities and guidance. You do not receive orders. Decisions are not made for you. You will not receive ultimatums, nor will you be left without options. You will receive parameters in which a decision can be made.

When examining a sample reading to form an opinion of a psychic, look for whether the reading instructed the seeker to do something specifically. If so, a prerogative of the seeker's mind was taken away, which is an indication of the wrong kind of guidance. The channel that gives that kind of reading wants to do the seeker's thinking for him. That is not the purpose of a psychic reading.

The role of the channel is to provide the specifics necessary to make a wise decision. That is the purpose of a psychic reading.

Do as much research as possible into the channel's prior readings. Find out what happened when other people attempted to put the guidance to work. Did it work for them in practical ways? Did they even use it? The percentage of people who get psychic readings and actually apply the information is low. People rarely follow the suggestions provided in their readings. Instead, people usually talk about the reading to their friends, sharing the wonderful things the reading said about them, and then they put it away in a drawer.

Sometimes, the information provided is so overwhelming and all-consuming that it feels better to keep it in a drawer. The information is great for discussion with the study group, and at the same time looks impossible to accomplish.

Keep in mind that your source's design for your life is something that would take all your time, energy, talents, dedication, commitment, strength and vitality. Predicted accomplishments probably mean, "This is what you could accomplish if you gave every ounce of yourself to it for the rest of your life." If the source tells you that you are going to build another pyramid, expect that it can be accomplished if you give every ounce of your thought, your time, your energy, your attention and your commitment to this act, every minute of the day, for the rest of your life. When a reading says, "You are going to write a book," or "You are going to become famous," or "You are going to do something wonderful," it means, "If you give it all you've got, unceasingly, that is your potential."

Events are not automatically going to happen as stated. This is a common misunderstanding of prophecies. Predictions are challenges and opportunities that are available to you. You will only receive the benefits of them if you can take the necessary steps to assure their success. That requires living up to your potential, which you probably have never even comprehended. Keep in mind that a psychic reading is usually referring to the outer limits of your ability and the complete commitment of yourself to the task. Taken seriously, the challenge can be discouraging. So be sure that is what you want before you ask.

INTERPRETATION AND APPLICATION
After receiving your psychic reading, there comes another vital step in the process. You have to interpret the information that you have received. One of the first things to do is to listen to the reading several times. You may be surprised to hear new things or experience new insights each time you listen.

The best way to take in the whole reading is to transcribe it, assuming the reading has been recorded on a cassette tape. Always make sure the experience is recorded even if you have to bring your own recorder. Transcribing the reading allows you to absorb individual insights and provides you with a format that can be easily accessed and studied.

The next step is to find two or three other people whom you trust, and who are not necessarily inclined to flatter you. Share the reading with them. Then let them tell you what they think the reading is telling you, without hearing your thoughts first.

If possible, go back and ask the channel that gave you the reading to read it and tell you what he believes it is saying to you. Discuss it with the channel while he is in a conscious state to discover his personal insights.

Then read it again yourself. This time, listen to the reading simultaneously as you read it and underline which statements seem to be emphasized by the source. Listen for voice inflection of the channel as an indication of where the source placed emphasis. Underline those statements. Isolate the specific things said, apart from the explanations that followed.

Most readings make a few important statements, and the rest of the reading repeats those statements in different ways, with different coloration, explanations and emphasis. There will be primary themes reappearing throughout the reading. What were those emphasized themes? What are the themes running through your life? Why were those particular things emphasized for you? What is the message being conveyed to you about the central areas of your life?

Then consider how that information can be applied in your daily life. What can you do with the information in your relationships and in your daily activities? How can you use the information to live differently, more effectively? This is where the validity of the information proves itself, making the whole process of a psychic reading worthwhile.

Then put the reading away for a few weeks. After a time, start over. Listen to the reading as if you have never heard it. Look for new understandings and insights. How can you apply these additional insights in your life?

Do the same thing again after a year. Let the information come alive repeatedly as you apply the enduring guidance to new situations.

A good psychic reading never becomes outdated. You can pick it up ten or fifteen years later and be amazed by its relevancy. There you have verifiable confirmation that the information came from your source. Your source knows today what you will need to hear a decade from now and knows how to say it so it will be timely.

BACK TO THE BEGINNING

The irony of a psychic reading is that, when the process is over and the printed pages lie on your desktop or bedside table, you find yourself right back where you started.

Your first step was to examine yourself for the guidance that you needed. While examining the issues, you came up with a list of important questions. Then you did your homework and found a psychic in whom you believed. When you went for the reading, you attuned right along with the psychic, calling on the highest within you to speak through the channel. When the reading was complete, you worked with it in various ways to understand its message. Now the remaining task is to decide whether the information is valid. You have to decide whether it is applicable and whether you want to follow it. You are back where you started.

Again, you must begin by examining yourself. You must pray and listen within. You need to contact your higher consciousness and ask for an answer concerning the reading's validity. No one can help you with this decision because it has to be made within you. Even someone who received a reading from the same psychic and is absolutely convinced that his reading was authentic cannot tell you that your information is also valid. Only you can know if your information is valid for you. By all means, avoid the trap of getting another psychic reading to know if you should follow your first psychic reading's instructions. Second psychic opinions are not a good idea.

Eventually, within the process, you must depend on your own inner guidance to tell you what to do. Ultimately, something within you must respond to the information, to analyze it, and to accept or reject it.

In the end, the reading will force you to call upon that personal inner knowing that is available to guide you, that greater intelligence within you that was available to you all along. You cannot get away from it. Having consulted an external source, in the end you are back at the beginning, with only your inner guidance to inform you.

That internal support that you call upon, to respond to your need for an answer, is the source of guidance that you need to relate with profoundly, habitually and intimately. It is the source of guidance with whom you need to build a direct, experiential, personal relationship.

The most important thing a psychic reading can do is not to make suggestions for what you should do with your life, your job, your marriage or your health. The most valuable thing a psychic reading can do is to cause you to interact directly with your source, by forcing you to ask within, "Is this right, or isn't it?"

When properly carried out, the process of a psychic reading will re-introduce you to that greater part of yourself that gave you life, that part of you that remembers your life's purpose and intention, that part of you that waits to be sought, ever available and able *to bring to your heart's remembrance all things whatsoever you have need of.*

CONCERN YOURSELF WITH SPIRIT
FROM THE PAUL SOLOMON SOURCE

T *hose who come asking about spirit guides need concern themselves, not with spirit guides, but with spirit. All that is needed from inner planes is given to every person on your plane. And when anyone seeks development concerning spirituality, teachers or influences are sent.*

Realize that if a beautiful star in the heavens has influenced your thoughts, and thus brought a little beauty into your life, the star itself was a teacher and a spirit guide. If a tree impressed you with the beauty of its form, and in it you saw something of God revealed in nature, this tree was for you a spirit guide.

Broaden your realization to know that if one who has failed in this lifetime and rests in the gutter crosses your attention and teaches a lesson, he is in that moment a master and was set there for a purpose. As you learn from seeing his failure, his fault, even his sin, has he not taught well the lesson that he was set there to teach?

The star, the tree, even the one who has failed, were all used by spirit as teachers. Thus be aware that such indications in your life are often the teachings of masters from inner planes. Though you hear no voice, though you see no presence, though you remain unaware of that which leads and causes things to fall in place the way they do, even so, the lessons are provided.

It is a credit to those who provide guidance from inner planes that you are often not aware of their presence and never aware of their identity, for in being aware of the presence or identity, would you not be distracted from the lesson provided? Rather than identify those with a name or an individual personality, learn what they would have you know, which is always provided in perfect lessons.

Seek not an entity or a personality, someone who may be labeled spirit guide or spirit teacher. These things so often are discarnate spirits and are not of the nature of those that would come to you from inner planes as true spiritual guides.

If you would know the true guide, if you would know true spirit, realize that within you is a spark of the divine creator. This spark of light is the you of you, the true identity of you. This is the light that came into the world, came into darkness, yet darkness knew it not. This light, this true spirit, is in your life, and yet you know it not.

Recognize and realize this spark of God, and see God himself as your spirit guide. Seek to turn inward and fan this spark into a flame, and follow its indications. All that you may know of God is written on the tablet of your own heart. Seek not from outside sources, but from deep within yourself for those things that would be of God.

Realize that all influences that come into your life, indicating this direction or that, are spiritual guides and teachers. When the masters, who have gone on before, send this indication or that to teach you, they seek not to draw attention to themselves, but away from themselves and toward that spark that is your divine self. Those true spirit guides, teachers and masters who influence your life seek to turn you away from realizing, identifying or knowing them. They seek rather to turn you inward. This is the purpose of a spirit guide, to detract attention from himself, to point attention instead to the God-force or life force that is within you. These guides are only given as indicators, as markers along the way. It is not the signpost that you seek, but that to which the sign points.

You may encounter one who speaks with the tongue of the gods or as an angel, or he may appear as a minister of mercy or a prophet or a sage, or he may be a healer or a worker of miracles. But if that one calls himself a master, a teacher or a guide and calls you to be his student or to follow him in his teachings and methods, is your attention not focused on the master, the teacher, the method, the tool? And is this not a subtle diversion from truth? Seek not to worship these, for truth itself lies one step beyond the tool, the master, the teacher and even the spirit guide.

Know that there is no one on your plane or on inner planes who is a master who would call himself a master. There is no one who is a servant of the divine that would attract attention to himself and in so doing become a stumbling block or divert attention from that perfection that is you.

If you want to attain cosmic consciousness in this lifetime, it will not come through a teacher, either on earth or on these inner planes. It will not come through a tool such as scripture, or a technique for meditation, discipline or development of any kind.

Then what would bring cosmic consciousness? It would come only through awakening and realizing that all that is needed, all that there is, lies within you and not in the voice of another. Anyone on your plane who would speak the words of God can only divert your attention from that voice within you that is the true teacher.

Truth lies in the quiet stillness. And it will well up naturally when that quietness becomes prime central stillness. It is there that you will find him who is not only the expression of the Almighty, but also the expression of yourself. As he is born and begins to live in your body, so will you attain cosmic consciousness, for his identity is the consciousness of God.

There is available to you a spirit. It is the spirit that that one who was the Christ promised and left to be available to you. It is the Comforter. It is the spirit with whom you should communicate within. There is no greater, no closer, no superior, no more personal spirit guide than this one.

If others would seek to assist from inner planes, they should be taken only as servants and messengers, never as guides or superior beings that would show to you the will of the Father. Is the Father incapable of direct communication? Does not that Holy Spirit of the Father himself live within your heart? Could another, either incarnate or discarnate, be closer and know his will in a closer way than you within your own heart? Attune yourself to the will of the Father and claim the blessing and the presence of that divine spirit that lives within, for this is your spirit guide.

There are those who would seek from inner planes to bring you a little closer to God, who would teach you the path and the means of developing toward God. It should be realized, however, that whether one of the archangels or simply one from past incarnations would speak to you as a spirit guide, this one would not become known to you by name.

He who would be seen as your true guide, as the light in your life, as the one who would lead you closer to God, would be the Christ. And there will be no other between him, there will be no other beside him, there will be no other equal to him. If the names of these others were revealed, would that not distract you from him who is your true guide, him who is your light, him who became the Christ and showed the way?

Realize that there is none closer than the Christ. It is not possible that one could become closer within the heart than the light itself. If there would be one inclined from this plane to act as a teacher, a master or a guide, would not this one want you to realize that he is one with God and one with the Christ? Therefore, he would want no other affinity, which would separate him from God. There need be no other name given. And no other name will be given from these inner planes, from these sources.

If there are names that come in the night, if a name is whispered, if a name is realized as it is repeated again and again in the mind, then this one would be a spirit guide. Know this force to be one from the inner planes and one who seeks to help, teach and guide. Only in this manner would the name of the spirit guide be given. Do not accept those names that are given from outside sources, from these that would speak as psychics and mediums.

The name of a spirit guide would always come from within you. But never should these be confused with or put before him who is the Christ and who would lift you to Christ-consciousness.

You have met masters in this lifetime, but you have not recognized them. There have been spirit guides who came to teach, but you have not realized them. It is to their credit that this is so, for a master who would allow himself to be recognized as a master has failed in his mission, and would no longer be a master.

Know whom you will serve. And know that, as the spirit of the Christ is expressed in all men on your planet and in all those on inner planes, he is not expressed in anyone. In that paradox, you will find truth, for those about you are only statements of him. He himself dwells in your own heart. It is here that you will find him.

In recognizing the Christ-force that dwells within you, you will realize that the one you consider a teacher on your plane is by his very existence a limitation. When you have gone beyond his limitation, his identity, his wisdom and teaching, you will see that what he has failed to attain, to express and to understand, and what he is not capable of giving to you, already exists within your own heart. Then you will awaken with the realization that you have surpassed all the teachings and all the expressions of the teachers on your plane, on all planes.

In the moment that you recognize the Christ-force within you, even the angels in heaven will rejoice and gather about to worship their teacher and master. In that moment, you will realize that you and he are one. And you will know that all that impeded your realization of who he is was that which you know as ego, personality or self. As long as you value identity, personality or self, you will find that barrier between self and the expression of the divine.

Be aware of the necessity to know and recognize the Christ-force. Look not for a master or a spiritual guide, but for understanding of the power of the Christ that is available to all, even in this day. Know that you are surrounded by that presence and that all you need to learn will be placed in your path. Learn from such things each time they occur. Recognize that stimulated within your heart and conscience as truth. Accept it as gold and apply it in your daily life.

Realize God attempting to manifest through you and to shine his light into the world. See yourself as a container of that light that wants to shine forth from inside you, out into the world. Seek to be a light in the midst of darkness. Seek to use your tiny flame as a candle in this world of darkness. And seek that everyone who comes in contact with you would be lifted a little closer to God.

EFFECTIVE PRAYER

Your ability to identify the effects of a divine creative power in your life will empower your prayers beyond any other factor.

Traditional religion has shaped and perpetuated a particular misconception concerning prayer. And that misconception is exactly what keeps prayer from working.

In this modern age, we have come to believe that prayer is the act of begging a God who does not hear well to do something that he does not want to do for someone who does not deserve it anyway.

That concept has destroyed prayer's potency. What makes prayer effective is our ability to combine expectancy with belief in our own causal nature.

Restructuring prayer to effectiveness requires relinquishing the concept of pleading with some external personality – the process of talking someone into doing something. Prayer must be taken out of the realm of personality and disposition, and looked at instead from a scientific perspective.

We live in a universe that is run by universal law. If prayer works, it is because there is a law regarding prayer. By discovering the law and setting it in motion, the determined effect should be produced every time, without fail. Prayer is a matter of cause and effect. As a cause is set in motion, the effect is produced.

Prayer is not a matter of begging someone to do something – as if trying to talk some external being into having a relationship with you, hoping he will like you in spite of your sins, and hoping he is having a good day and will give you what you want. Think about it reasonably. In a universe where everything is so incomprehensibly yet perfectly ordered, is it even logical and rational to consider that

117

the intelligence who created that order then listens to prayers and decides "yes, no, maybe" according to whim?

Prayer is the act of setting a cause in motion.

We are surrounded by power. And that power is so real, so observable, that science has begun to notice its presence. The air around you, the atmosphere around you, is alive with energy and power to cause effects. We know, for example, that the air has electricity in it, and under certain conditions we can harness that electricity and move it in a particular direction.

Simultaneously, there are energies beyond electricity. This power or energy, which surrounds us in the atmosphere, was called "prana" by ancient teachers. The word literally means "the breath of God." They were talking about a force that can cause things to happen, and when taken within, it is a healing, building force. This same force can be called by many names.

The atmosphere, the air, the ether that surrounds you – what appears to be empty space – is alive with energy. That energy is available, and it is obedient. Your mind, your thinking ability, is a cause factor. And the energy that surrounds you is obedient to that cause factor.

When you begin to fantasize fear, for example, the energy that surrounds you begins to vibrate and is set in motion to the tune of that fear, and physical changes occur in your body. The image that you fantasize becomes more and more potent and powerful, until you begin to experience the effects that you fear. Your physical body changes according to the fear your mind is experiencing. If you hold the image in mind long enough, that energy will actually create the incident that you are fantasizing, and you will experience it. If you fear it long enough, if you image it long enough, with enough expectancy, you will cause that result.

Worrying, which puts the energy of fear in motion, is a form of prayer. It is the negative form of prayer. By holding an image of something you fear, and by believing in it to the extent that the energy around you – which is just free energy, available to do anything you tell it to do – begins to undulate to the rate of the vibration of your thoughts, you are praying for what you fear. The energy is obeying you. It is creating what you are fantasizing, and it is causing the potential of it. What prevents it from actually occurring is that you eventually get control of yourself and stop holding the image. You cancel it by thinking about something else.

An important aspect of our ability as creators is that we can change our minds. We can place an order for something, even something fearful – we can imagine it, set the energies in motion, create the atmosphere, tell the universe to begin creation – and then we can simply change our mind and cancel the order. All unconsciously.

Of course, a lot of our orders are canceled. That is fortunate in regard to the fearful things we dwell on, but not in regard to the things from which we would actually benefit if we had them. The same rules apply in either case.

Imagine that there is a car that I want – a beautiful, new, silver Mercedes. I have a definitive image of the car, and I see it clearly. I imagine what it feels like to sit in the driver's seat. I can smell the new leather. I can hear the hum of the motor when I turn the key. I can feel the steering wheel in my hands. I begin to drive the car, and I experience the motion of it as it cruises along. I imagine how it feels to own a Mercedes. I see myself in the car. I feel myself in the car. I know how it feels to own the car. I enjoy owning the car. And the universe immediately begins to respond to my image. As I am driving my new car in my daydream, the car is becoming mine. Eventually though, I wake up from my daydream and I think, "Oh, I can't afford that! It's out of the question." And my image changes to one where I cannot afford the car, I do not have enough money, I cannot drive it, own it or enjoy it. The impossibility of it is my new image. And my previous order is canceled.

Negative imaging works according to the same laws as positive imaging, whether considering material objects or less tangible things. Imagine that someone you love has a catastrophic disease, and you think, "Wouldn't it be wonderful if he were whole, and strong, and well." You begin to imagine that, and you believe it, and you experience the joy of it as a reality. You hold a wonderful, healthy image of that person. And the universe immediately begins to respond to your image. If that person is accepting and holding the same image, something remarkable begins to happen in the cells of his body. But then suddenly, you remember what the medical people said: "Cancer is terminal." And you think, "Oh, this is not just a headache – this is *cancer*. I can't do anything about cancer. I'm not a real healer!" And your image changes to one where you cannot do anything about cancer. And the sparks of energy about you, which are obedient, begin immediately to fulfill your image. In other words, the message is passed from spark to spark that you are not a real healer. And something remarkable stops happening in the cells of the person's body.

Regardless of what you say, regardless of the wonderful words you string together, your prayer cannot cancel out what you believe and expect within. Prayer is the inner supplication of your heart in this very moment. What exists as expectancy in your life right now is your prayer right now. And prayer is always answered – *always*. It always brings forth its result, unless it is canceled by an alternative, which neutralizes the old prayer and establishes a new one.

Your health right now, from your self-esteem to your hangnails, is a direct result of your constant prayer. There is no imbalance in your body that you did not pray for, negatively or positively. Your health at every level is a direct result of your prayer, because prayer is the sincere expectation of the heart. *Effective prayer* is deciding what that expectation will be.

WHAT PRAYER IS NOT

In order to pray effectively, you must understand that you are literally a spark of God – a portion of what God is. That means that you are a creative being. Creating effectively requires more than mouthing the words of a traditional prayer.

Words are nothing more than sounds being forced over vibratory faculties in your throat, which set the air in motion around you. So you are making little waves of warm air. And when those waves become still again, and the air around you returns to normal, the words no longer exist.

The verbalization is not the prayer. Prayer is the creative energy behind the words. It is the expectancy. Verbalization without belief and expectancy is just movement of warm air.

Prayer is anticipation. Prayer is intent. It is not wishing or hoping for something. Wishing and hoping suggest that there is a possibility that something will not occur. Prayer does not allow for impossibility. Prayer requires confident expectation, which affects the energy-potential of the atmosphere and causes results.

The energy-potential is obedient and is always doing what it is told to do. However, arriving at specific results, intentionally and consciously, is not easy for most people. It requires intention, belief, focus and discipline. People are constantly applying the universal laws that govern cause and effect, but they are not doing it in a conscious, disciplined manner.

YOU PRAY CONSTANTLY

Prayer does not have to be religious to work. Spiritual laws are universal laws. If applied, they work whether the application is intentional or not. There is nothing in the universe more powerful than prayer. Whatever you expect, you will produce. And it is not possible to go through life without praying. You are praying constantly.

In the beginning, as sparks of God, we had a desire to experience materiality, and so we projected ourselves into materiality. What was the technique for getting into this plane of matter? Prayer. By expecting to experience sensation, we precipitated sensations. We precipitated matter. By creating the expectation in our consciousness, it manifested in our sphere of existence. And we began to experience the entrapment of matter. Everything that exists is a result of expectancy and precipitated experience. We have created it and drawn it to ourselves. And it is all a result of prayer.

It is not possible to go through life without praying. However, it is possible, and most common, to pray without conscious knowledge.

Everything we think, expecting it to produce results, is a prayer. But fortunately, not every thought is a prayer. Wishes are not a prayer and are ineffective, because of the absence of expectancy. If you wish God would do something for you, but in reality you do not expect it to happen, then you have had a thought, but not a prayer.

You are capable of thinking what you do not expect or believe. You are capable of creating in your mind what you do not expect to out-manifest. And you are capable of fooling yourself as to what you really expect. Many people pray at length to get well from serious long-term illnesses. But when faced with the prospect of building a new identity, one based on wellness rather than the lifestyle the illness has produced, they cannot make the shift and continue to expect a continuation of the illness.

HARMONIZING WITH GOD'S WILL

Traditional prayer is a means of asking God for what we want. "Our Father, please do this because it's what I want." But if that thing is not already occurring, then the actual request is to ask an all-wise God to change his mind and do it our way instead – to conform his will to our will. Is that appropriate? If not, then we must ask ourselves the more important question: "Is it possible and appropriate to ask God for anything in prayer and receive it?"

Effective prayer is the act of introducing power into an act that needs to be performed – putting creative power behind a concept, which gives it creative force.

Imagine that you have a need. Now you must change that need, or that have-not, into a have. How can you put power into that have-not, to cause it to manifest as a have? By tapping a reservoir of power. And that essentially is what prayer is.

There is a great resource of power that is called by many names, including God. That great resource of power has intelligence, and it has will. And the best way to use that power is to use it to do something that it wills, to use the power in its own nature. By using the nature of the power to do what it wills, you do not ask God to change his mind and conform his will to yours. You do the opposite. You conform your will to the will of God. You live and express "in the name of the Father," or in the nature of the Father.

Many people involved in pursuits of spiritual growth are afraid to discover God's will for them because they believe it might be less than what they are already experiencing. God's will is often associated with sacrifice, giving things up, putting things on the altar. And people recoil at the idea of losing things. They accept that the center of God's will by definition has to be the most perfect, peaceful, productive place in the universe, yet they resist arriving there. They cling to the lesser because they do not recognize the greater. It is absurd, because there is no such thing as deprivation for the purpose of greater gain.

Prayer is the act of letting go of what we hang onto, in order to accept what was already available. It is similar to a small child who climbs to the top of a tree and cannot get down. He clings to a limb in terror, just inches away from his father's hands, while his father says, "Turn lose, and I'll catch you." But the child refuses to turn lose until his father has already caught him. That is the portal into prayer – crossing the fine line between clinging to false safety and turning loose – falling into real security.

Then is prayer only effective when asking for what is already God's will? Frankly, I hope so, because "God's will" is the divine order of this universe, and anything else could get us all into a lot of trouble. Prayer works by meshing wills. Then the question is "How do I know if I am asking for what God wants?"

First, look at what God has defined as his will. Many sacred scriptures provide a consistent message of what God wants for humankind. For example, it is not God's will that anyone should perish but that all should come to repentance. It is not God's will that any should suffer. It is not God's will that any should be out of harmony. It is not God's will that any should be impoverished.

Then all these things that we witness as manifesting a lack or a limitation are subject to the laws of prayer and divine re-creation. It would be difficult to find an imbalance that exists and then wonder whether it is God's will to correct it or not. How absurd to even wonder. It is God's will that the universe be in harmony. And limitless opportunities have been provided to bring it into harmony.

Only one thing imprisons this universe in disharmony. During creation, in the realization of man, God gave him free will, that he not remain a puppet. God said, "I will provide opportunity so that you can go one way or the other."

Man was given the gift of free will, which essentially means that you have two alternatives. One is to return the love of God and live in harmony. The other is to satisfy false desires – that means desires that are temporary, desires that are not good for you – and participate in the opposite, the shadow, the reflection of God.

There are only two choices. Where imbalance and disharmony exist, it is because man's will has manifest. The correction of any imbalance in the universe only depends upon solving that problem, correcting the imbalance of the two wills at odds.

In other words, whatever you want to pray for, whatever you recognize as an imbalance that would precipitate a need for prayer, is corrected by the action of effective prayer itself. Because the only imbalance that exists is the separation of man's will from divine will.

Effective prayer is by definition the joining of the wills, so that the prayer is already answered in the action of the prayer itself. The disharmony can no longer exist when the wills are one. Then by tapping that great reservoir of power, which has intelligence and will and can manifest anything, you also can manifest anything. But only if your will is in harmony with the creative power. Effective prayer is the act of aligning your expectancy to harmonize with God's will.

THE FIRST STEP

The first step in effective prayer is the assumption that a higher intelligence exists within you and that you do not have to go outside yourself to have a meaningful communication with that consciousness. Then you only need to pause several times a day to acknowledge that consciousness, forgetting about every other influence. Close yourself off from all other input so that there are no distractions, and focus only on the one fact: Your mind has a source. The source of your mind is more intelligent than your mind. It is the source of your body and knows how your body functions. It is the source of your lessons in life and knows why the particular lessons that you face today are coming to you.

That may be your only point of contact with it – just knowing that it exists. You do not know *what* it is, or *who* it is, but you have an idea or a sense that it exists. That is your point of contact – a belief, an assumption, a faith that it does exist.

You cannot prove it yet, but you assume it is true. Your mind and body have a source, and that source is some form of intelligence. You assume that this intelligence can communicate because it gave you communication abilities. It obviously knows how communication works and how your mind works, therefore it probably knows what you think. And your thoughts can form communication with it.

Then deliberately speak to that being, whatever and whoever it is, by saying, "I know there are many voices, but I do not want to talk with any of those. I am not talking to my ego, to selfishness, to the voice of my appetites, to the voice of my beliefs and prejudices. I am not talking to other people's opinions. What I am focusing my thoughts on in this moment is the fact that my mind and body have a source. That source is an intelligence, and whatever that intelligence is – whoever you are, whatever you are – I am speaking to you. And I'm assuming that you can hear me, whether I can hear you yet or not. I don't know what to call you – God, or Jehovah, or Krishna, or Allah – words are inadequate, just trappings. I am talking to the power and the intelligence that created me, and I understand that you live in the quietest, most peaceful, most still part of me. I am assuming that you can hear me. Whoever you are, whatever you are, what I want to say to you is that I want to get to know you better."

That is the first step.

Then you must listen. You must eliminate all other thoughts and input. You must focus your listening by sensing and feeling the presence of that intelligence, that being, in order to establish a communication. That process is the beginning of effective prayer – the invocation of a divine consciousness. And prayer is not possible without that as the first step.

A FORMULA FOR EFFECTIVE PRAYER

The Christian Bible provides us a specific formula for prayer (Matthew 6:9-13), which is simple, complete and effective when used properly. What we refer to as "The Lord's Prayer" is a comprehensive course in metaphysics and spiritual law. And the principles Jesus incorporated are applicable to any religious belief system because they exist beyond dogma and doctrine.

By law, effective prayer requires attunement. It cannot exist apart from meditation because meditation properly accomplished is like punching in a number on the telephone. One of the ways to know who you have on the other end of the call is to know whose number you used. Jesus gave specific instructions for calling the right number.

In providing a formula for prayer, Jesus essentially taught his apostles how to successfully fill out an order form for what they wanted to manifest, beginning with the name and address of the company from which they would place their orders. In this case, the company was God, and Jesus called it "Our Father."

OUR FATHER

The first word *Our* is a personal, possessive, plural pronoun. Why plural? It seems like a contradiction of Jesus' instructions to enter into a closet for prayer (Matthew 6:6), for an intensely intimate and personal experience – *Our* makes it sound like a crowded closet. Why did Jesus not say *My* Father?

Most people compartmentalize their relationship with God. They pray to him for their spiritual needs, but doubt his genuine interest in their practical concerns, which would include their bank accounts and their romantic lives. They feel separate from God and believe they must solve their everyday problems themselves. They may pray for more money or to marry a wonderful person, but they lack the faith that would produce those results, because their deeper belief is that God is only interested in the "religious" aspects of life. Anything else, and they're on their own.

Jesus taught that the relationship with source is much broader than that. God is a spiritual, mental and physical source. In that way, there are three of you in the closet, three levels of self. A spirit, a mind and a body. And each one is communicating with its source. Jesus' instruction was to make prayer practical by involving all aspects of yourself and your existence. *Our* encompasses all that you are, a multifaceted being. And each of these three aspects of you needs to relate with the source of life. In that way, your spiritual father is more than just a holy ghost, as in dead. Your source is alive and well, has reality on this material plane, and is active on all levels and in all aspects of your life.

Why *Father*? Why not Lord or King? Lord and King certainly conform to the more popularized version of God – elevated, superior, separate. Father, on the other hand, has an almost opposite meaning. Father means progenitor, precursor, creator, originator – one of us.

Why *Father* instead of Mother? What about God's feminine side? When you pray, you are after results, you are creating manifestation. And for that, you need the co-creative participation of the active, masculine-oriented, make-it-happen aspect of your creative source, rather than the feminine, receptive, potential, provide-space-for-it-to-happen aspect of that same being.

Here is the most important thing to know about this teacher's specific choice of the word *Father*: It is absolutely impossible for your divine creator to be of a different species than you are. There ends the dichotomy that man is man, and God is God. If God is your father, what God *is* cannot be different from what you *are*. If God is your father, what are you? You are a child-God growing up to be what your Father is.

In order for your prayers to be effective, you must relinquish the concept that the God to which you pray is different or separate from what you are. For some people, that will require a transformation in thought structures, in belief systems, in self-esteem. But if you cannot make that shift, your prayers will not achieve your desired results.

This is a specific prayer formula based on universal law, and the wording is perfect. It does not matter what name you use. It does not even matter whether you are religious. If you are religious, the name of your denomination is irrelevant, except that if you pray to the God of the Baptists, he will be limited to doing what the Baptists believe God can do. And if you pray to Lord Krishna, you will have to keep your expectations within the realm of what Krishna is believed to do.

If, on the other hand, you can discard all the religious names and concepts, and simply pray to the power and intelligence that created you in the beginning, this formula can work effectively. In the end, it may become a religious experience, but it will not fit the confines of traditional religion. Such a prayer, which is essentially nonreligious, is greater than any religious prayer because it does not put a box around the possibilities of what God is. So discard form, doctrine, dogma, pre-formed ideas, and address yourself to whatever power it was that originated you – the active, creative source of your being, your Father.

WHICH ART IN HEAVEN

The next step in the formula is to direct the prayer to a particular place, an address for God. *Heaven.*

Where is Heaven? Heaven has been described as a beautiful place, a peaceful place, a distant place, a creative place, a limitless place. Throughout scripture, heaven is described as a higher plane of existence. Then Jesus came along and gave heaven a tangible location. He said, "The kingdom of heaven is within you." (Luke 17:21) With that, he negated the concept that God is out there in some lofty place beyond the clouds, apart and unreachable. Instead, he described the dwelling place of God as a quiet, beautiful, peaceful, holy place within each of us.

All that exists of heaven is already within you. Then your prayer becomes a communion with the presence, the power, the origin of you. And the communion takes place on all three levels, physical, mental and spiritual, in a beautiful, creative place called heaven within you. And your prayer goes to the place where God lives within.

HALLOWED BE THY NAME

Here, Jesus further clarified the company – a specific power at a specific address. He described that power. *Hallowed be thy name.* How holy is your expression. How holy is my recognition of you. And where is that power? Within you.

When you pray, begin by saying, "I am talking to the source of my spirit, mind and body that lives within me and is the best part of me." Effective prayer is the act of calling on the part of you that always looks out for your best interest, that cares whether you succeed, that inspires you to greatness, that expresses in positive, supportive ways. *Hallowed be thy name* refers to the creator-you rather than the created-you. It says, "I have reverence for you, I recognize your presence in me, and I hold you most holy." It recognizes that power as most important in your life.

At this point in the prayer formula, the name and address of the company have been clearly stated, and communication is established. Now the prayer moves on to consider what is to be ordered.

THY KINGDOM COME

The next step in the formula is to specify the first request – to list the item and its description. *Thy kingdom come, thy will be done, on earth as it is in heaven.*

Thy kingdom come establishes that the power being addressed is a king who rules a kingdom. Where is that kingdom? It is that still, beautiful, peaceful place of love and greatness within you. This being rules that highest aspect of you. "Yours is the kingdom of heaven within me. Because you are in charge there, it is perfect."

The first request is: *Thy will be done on earth as it is in heaven.* This is not a reference to a time in the future when the kingdom of heaven will descend to earth and all will be transformed in the twinkling of an eye. This is a very practical invocation of the consciousness of God in the daily affairs of life, right now. Jesus was not referring to a distant future of light and love. He was providing a specific means for harmonizing the inner with the outer existence of man in the present moment.

"I want your kingdom to come and your will to be done on earth as it is in heaven." There is no more important request that you can make in all your life.

If you could truly make that request, it would manifest like this: First thing in the morning, before you do anything else, you begin your day by turning off the input of everything around you. You shut your eyes, turn inside, and go to a peaceful place, isolated from everything else. And in that closet, in that quiet place, you say, "I'm talking to you, the source of my being. Today, I will have to make some decisions. I have the option of making those decisions based on my appetites, my ego, my selfishness, my prejudices and my beliefs. If I make those decisions from any of those spaces, I will make a mess, and I will definitely be living in the kingdom of earth. But if you take over as ruler, over the decisions that I make today – if you take over and run my environment, my bank account, my career, my relationships with my spouse and my parents and my children and my co-workers – then my life will change. I want you to rule my everyday life, my earth, as you already rule my heaven within."

The intelligence that created you is available to make your decisions, but does not and will not, unless you request that the decisions come from that level. You can make your life decisions from an emotional space – most people do. You can make your decisions from the standards set by society – look out for yourself, make sure no one takes advantage of you, compete to be the best, and fight to have the most. In every situation, your life will reflect the space from which you make your decisions.

If every day you ask the source of your heaven to make the decisions in your earth, then the kingdom of heaven will come on earth, your earth. The result will be a new harmony in your daily life.

"Take over. Run my life. Be my master." That is the request.

If that quiet place within you, that closet space, is so familiar and so real, that you can go there in an instant, it is possible to be there even while you are experiencing difficult situations. If someone becomes angry with you and is pouring that emotion out, it is possible to say to the king of your heaven, "Please take care of this. Just let me be an empty shell through which you can respond to this person. I don't want to be here. I'll stay in heaven while you take care of earth." You can just step out of the way.

I explained that to an audience of psychiatrists once, and one of them said to me, "I have a number of patients who seem to do that. It sounds like you are suggesting stepping out of unpleasant situations to be in an unreal world and let something else handle reality. What's the difference between what you're suggesting and psychosis?" I did not know the answer to that. So I quickly said to the Source, "Quick, tell him the answer to that." And the Source answered, "The difference in that and psychosis is that it is a conscious decision. When you step out of an unpleasant situation on purpose, to let the source of your being respond, you are doing it because you want to, with control. When a psychotic does it, he does it as escape because he cannot face the situation. There is an enormous difference."

Bringing heaven on earth means being able to step into a serene space, no matter what space people are in around you. It means not giving like for like. You do not need to lash out at people who are upset, even making accusations against you. They already have a foot in hell. Why step into it with them? Let the source of your being respond to the challenges.

One thing to remember is that this source that responds through you in those situations is never motivated to get even or cause hurt. No sarcastic comebacks from the king of heaven. It is usually a kind, supportive, even disarming response that comes through you.

Thy will be done on earth as it is in heaven. "You originated me. You know my nature, my needs, my expression. In the past, I have usurped your authority. I have taken over, and I've had my own way. My life here in this earth is a series of challenges, problems, messes that I have created, because I have acted separately from you. I am requesting that you take over and become the absolute ruler in my daily life and my external affairs on earth, as you already are in the inner planes of spirit. I would like the same thing that makes heaven perfect to be in charge of my life on earth." That is the request of this step in the formula.

Baptists call it the "plan of salvation." It is the way to "get saved." Ask the power that originated you to take over and run your life. But it becomes very narrow when placed in the context of doctrine and religion. Essentially though, we are talking about the same thing.

If you take the power that is in charge of heaven and put it in charge of earth, the result is heaven on earth. The alternative is hell on earth, which comes from putting others in charge of your earth. Whether you are happy or unhappy depends on who is in charge of your life. If other people determine how you feel, they are in charge of your life, and you will experience hell on earth.

You can decide at any point, in any situation of life, to be happy or unhappy. How you feel is your decision, and no other consideration is important – unless you give the power of that decision to someone else. If the highest within you is in charge of how you feel, heaven is already assured. There is no question. And that has nothing to do with the surrounding circumstances. It only has to do with the decision of who is in charge.

GIVE US THIS DAY

The next step in the formula is to ask to be fed. *Give us this day our daily bread.* Feed all three of us, on three levels: physically, mentally and spiritually.

We are required to manage three bodies on this earth plane. And the dominant body always gets fed first because it makes the most noise. It expresses the loudest hunger.

Most people are physically dominant, meaning they let their physical appetites and emotions run their lives. Some people are mentally dominant, analyzing their way through life. Throughout history, there have been only a handful of spiritually dominant people. In those rare cases, the spiritual body could tell the other two what to do, and perform miracles by transcending universal law.

Feed me today on all three levels. Jesus did not say, "Feed my physical and mental bodies daily and my spiritual body once a week." His specific choice of words was *us* and *daily.*

Every prayer will elicit a response. It is universal law that when you pray a force is set in motion that will produce a result. If you say, "Exercise me spiritually, every day," your teacher will provide opportunity. The spiritual body is fed by prayer, meditation and practice-exercises known as life's little lessons – challenges that strengthen character and initiate transformation. So know what you invoke by asking to be fed on that level.

A person grows to spiritual power and effectiveness, and effectiveness of prayer, through practice. He has developed expectancy because he has accumulated repeated evidence that his prayers work. He stops every day, over and over and over, to recognize and acknowledge, "This world around me, this physical world is not all there is. There is a greater world within me. And in this moment, even if I only have a few seconds, I stop to remember that there's more to reality than I perceive by my senses. I have a source. I have a divine teacher within me. All of this means something. These people are coming into my life for a reason. I want to be receptive to the fact that my teacher is here. I want to pause and feel that I am not alone. I want to be aware of a presence that can communicate with me, can fill me with inspiration, can help me in all situations."

Most people say, "I do not have time to meditate three times a day." How many times do you stop for a snack or meal? Stopping to meditate means stopping to feed the spiritual body. The poor thing is probably so starved that it can hardly muster the strength to eat when you do feed it. But if you begin to feed it regularly, if you start feeding your spiritual body a full-sized, healthy meal three times a day, it will soon develop an appetite for more. And if you skip a meditation, your spiritual self will cry out in hunger. And you will know that something important is missing.

If you will begin to stop, two or three times a day, every day of your life, at least that many times, to remember your source within you, you will build a familiarity and a comfort and a dependence on that presence. By feeding the spiritual part of your being, over and over and over, until you learn that the spiritual side of your nature is powerful and effective, that side of your nature will become the dominant being, and the physical and mental bodies will become submissive to it. And extraordinary things will begin to happen.

You are a creative being, and your expectancy affects the atmosphere around you. The atmosphere responds to what you set in motion. Know that you are a co-creator with God. Take responsibility for your part. Prayer is not only asking that something be accomplished – prayer means making it happen. That realization can transform your concept and your experience of prayer.

When you pray, do whatever you can to cause a result, and then expect it to be accomplished. Exercise your prayer effectiveness daily, over and over. Practice. Become an expert pray-er, with documented results. *Feed us daily* means claiming the opportunity to grow and using it for its intended purpose.

FORGIVE US OUR TRESPASSES

The next step in the formula deals with forgiveness. *Forgive us our trespasses as we forgive those who have trespassed against us.* To understand this teaching, we only need to insert the word *exactly*. "Forgive me exactly as I forgive others, because what I give to others is exactly what will come back to me."

What is forgiveness? Forgiveness is the act of giving up forever any claim to revenge, giving up forever the right to make someone wrong about a situation, no matter what. If you forgive a person, you have given up the right to make them wrong, to place blame, to accuse, to be vengeful – now or later. Forgiveness is unconditional. It does not say, "I'll forgive you for that if you promise never to do it again." That is the voice of self-righteousness.

People mistakenly think that forgiveness is something you do for someone else, as if you are doing them a favor, as if they are going to feel better if you forgive them. It is seldom true. People who have done us wrong very seldom care whether we forgive them or not.

People tend to hold back forgiveness until warranted, as if people who are not duly contrite do not deserve the favor. "I would forgive you, except that you don't deserve it. You don't even seem remorseful. Plus, you've shown no inclination to stop. So I refuse to forgive you."

It is for ourselves that we forgive, not for the other person. Until we forgive another person, there is a process going on inside that damages our health and prevents our growth.

For example, you say something that makes another person angry, so she reacts by throwing a book at you and actually hitting you. She feels better because she expressed herself. She walks away feeling fine and does not care whether you forgive her. Of course, you do not hit her back because you are a nice person, and spiritual. You do not take action, but you think about it, for days, maybe years. When you pray or meditate, the incident pops back in your head. You tense up. You cannot go further because there is something inside that needs to be taken care of first. All you can think about is the nerve of that person! She still does not care whether you forgive her, but you need to forgive her for your own peace of mind and growth.

It is impossible for you to think without moving muscles. Every time you think of taking an action, you send electrical energy to the muscles that you would use, and the action takes place in your mind. You might as well have hit the person who hit you if you continue to hold a grudge. You have sent enough energy into your hand with your thoughts to have done so.

The muscle contractions are caused by tiny particles of free-floating calcium at the tips. When you send electricity to them, the free floating particles of calcium bond and stimulate movement.

When you think about moving a muscle, even if you do not contract the muscle, you still send the electricity that bonds the calcium. The projection of unresolved anger at those muscles creates arthritis. The point is: You either must hit – or forgive and forget.

Whether a person deserves forgiveness is not important and irrelevant. Forgiveness will end your karmic relationship with someone who has done you wrong.

A common belief among people in metaphysics is that, when you come back in subsequent lives, you choose your parents. That does not mean you get to view a group of candidates and make a selection based on how appealing they are. You do not necessarily get the parents you want.

You are making your selection right now, by how you relate to people in this lifetime. Guess how you got your domineering parent or your meddling sibling? If you do not want to come back as the son or daughter of your worst enemies, forgive them now so you do not have anything to carry forward. Lack of forgiveness builds karmic bonds.

Whether you believe in reincarnation or not, you build Akashic, karmic cords between yourself and the object of any unforgiven act. And you will continue reacting to that bond throughout this lifetime. Avoiding that person will not dismiss the bond. Any unforgiven act will keep repeating, with that person or with other people in your life. Lack of forgiveness sustains an unpaid debt.

Forgiveness is the act of making a situation as if it never occurred. There is no such thing as forgiving without forgetting. You must erase the incident to end the karmic bond. To do that, you must reconstruct it as if it never happened in the first place.

Forgiveness means that you no longer hold the other person responsible. You no longer recognize them as the same person who built the bond with you. Forgiveness is not something that you do for the other person. Forgiveness is something that you do for yourself in order to end an imbalance in a relationship in your life.

The quality of your relationships will define the quality of your existence. If you have relationships where forgiveness is necessary, but you are avoiding it, the quality of your life will be affected by unresolved, unbalanced relationships. When you forgive, you release that entire imbalance that is eating away at your experience of life. And you release tension as you give up the need for revenge.

What makes revenge appealing? You try unsuccessfully to give worth back to yourself. You feel that a value has been taken away by the action of another, so you attempt to put that person down in order to bring yourself back up. It is a game. A person with self-worth does not play that game. Any desire in you for revenge suggests that you are not valuing yourself.

Forgive others first. Then forgive yourself. All you have to do to forgive yourself is notice things. At the end of each day, every day, go back and explore each time you released negative energies, emotions, images and feelings toward anyone or anything. Is there anything for which you want to feel cleansed? To be forgiven, all you have to do is name it. In that moment of release, you understand why forgiveness is doing you a favor.

Naming the name is an important tool of occultists, mystics and even priests. Naming the name means this: You cannot stop doing what you do not know you are doing. You cannot be forgiven for what you are not aware of having done. You cannot be forgiven for what you are not willing to admit you have done. And you cannot identify what you have done, or what you are presently doing, unless you can recognize and label it.

The name itself is not important. You can call an energy grief, hurt, anger, jealousy, defiance, bitchiness – anything you want to call it. The one requirement is that you be honest in identifying it. If you are honest, and if you are willing to release yourself and others from any uncomfortable energy in your life, you can attain purity. If you can attain purity with high purpose, what you have then is courage.

Courage comes to anyone who feels good about self. When you feel good about yourself, when you feel loved, when you feel accepted and approved of by your source, when you know that you have high purpose, the result is confidence.

Forgive us our trespasses, or "Cause me to see with exact clarity the mistakes that I make." By seeing clearly the mistakes you have made, they change in character, from something imbalanced to something constructive. It is called spiritual alchemy. The moment that you recognize a mistake, it becomes of value because you have learned what not to do in order to produce a right result. What was a problem becomes a lesson, a positive revelation, and no longer a source for self-blame.

Forgive me as I forgive simply says, "Let me see, and let me reveal to others, the lesson, the beauty, the progress in what has occurred between us. If I forgive you, I see what is productive in our relationship and offer to you the opportunity to see it as well." That is what forgiveness is all about. "Let me see and reveal." Forget the words *forgive, guilt* and *sin*, and say instead, "Let me see and reveal the truth of the lessons that are coming into my life."

LEAD US NOT INTO TEMPTATION

The next step in the formula refers to spiritual exercise. *Lead us not into temptation but deliver us from evil.* Theologians have been debating for centuries why God would want to tempt us with evil. The teaching is more accurately worded as "Make me strong in temptation so that I overcome evil. Help me feed all three bodies to become strong, not just the physical and the mental."

Most people think that temptation is an opportunity to sin – it is rather an opportunity not to sin. Temptation is spiritual exercise, just as meditation is spiritual food. It means developing the ability to recognize good without evil as a point of reference, growing into being all that God is.

People in metaphysics today want to pretend that sin, evil and hell do not exist. But they do exist. We all sin, we all make mistakes, and we will continue to do so. Sin, however, is not something to be used as an opportunity to debase yourself and feel guilty. Sin is nothing more than something that happened, an incident that has occurred within your life that made it clearer what you ought to be doing – a marker or a signpost. And that is different from something bad that you have done, for which you must pay.

The word sin originated in ancient martial arts, particularly those related to bow and arrow skills. Sin means to miss the mark, to miss the bull's-eye. The negative emotional attachments to the word sin are our creation. They have nothing to do with the actual meaning: When you miss the mark, you try again, until you get it right.

When sin and evil become a point of reference, they have served you. That is their intended purpose.

Spiritual exercise means finding opportunities to make a spiritual choice, and choosing spiritually. Choosing what is in harmony with the highest strengthens the spiritual body. So spiritual exercise supplements the spiritual diet of prayer and meditation, and makes you stronger. "Make me strong in temptation and cause me to make right decisions. Put before me opportunities for exercise. And at the same time, give me the strength and the inclination to make the right choices, so that I exercise my spiritual muscles and become strong." That is the definition of spiritual growth.

THE FOUR REQUESTS

At this point in the formula, you have completed listing the items and their descriptions on the order form. You have made four requests. One: Establish your kingdom – take over and run my earthly life. Two: Feed me – so that I grow spiritually. Three: Forgive me – reveal to me what I need to know about my mistakes and help me turn them to my advantage. Four: Make me strong – give me strength to make the right decisions, the right choices, which will make me stronger for having made them. Those are the four requests. Having made these four, all other requests are superfluous.

FAITH IN THE ORDER FORM

It is likely that if you had as much faith in God's shipping department as you have in most stores from which you order items, you would receive interesting results, because your prayer would naturally fulfill its intended cause-effect relationship. Unfortunately, it is more likely that you have less confidence, or faith.

When you order something from a store, you include the name and the address of the company, you list the items that you want, you enclose payment, and you sign it with your name, which gives them authorization to act upon your request. Then you put it in an envelope and mail it. Once.

Having mailed it, you do not assume that you need to immediately fill out another order blank to the same company with the same list of items, put it in another envelope, and stick it in the mail again. And again. And again.

You assume that, having done it once, the company will receive the order, the payment and the authorization. You assume that the order will be fulfilled. In due course, you assume that the items are on the way and that they will arrive within a reasonable amount of time. And if they do not, by golly, you will phone the company and say, "Where the heck are my items?"

You would not fill out a second order form listing the items again, sign it, enclose another payment, and mail the whole thing a second time along with a note that says, "Please, please, please, would you send me what I asked for in the first place?" You would not mail a third order form, and a fourth, and a fifth, and on and on – filling out a repeat order form every night before you go to bed and several times a day whenever you think of it.

Then why would you pray that way?

Instead you would say, "Sir, I ordered these items, and I enclosed my payment. Now I would like to know: One, did you lose my order form? Two, are you out of the item? Three, is the post office responsible? I want to know what happened because I set a cause in motion and I am expecting an effect."

Imagine having such a relationship with God and his shipping department. "Look, I addressed the envelope correctly: *God, and Company.* And I sent it to the right place: *Heaven.* I requested the items, and I described them in detail. There wasn't any lack of clarity about what I wanted. Uh-oh, maybe I forgot to include the payment."

PAYMENT

Did you think you could get something from God for nothing? Payment for things requested of God takes the form of a right relationship with source. In that case, your will is not separated from divine will. Your will is in harmony with the divine creative power, and you can manifest anything. If you have not established a right relationship with your source in the areas of your life, your time, your money, your relationships and your interests, you will have a problem with this prayer technique. And you will always wonder if the items you requested are coming.

A right relationship in those areas means essentially this. According to ancient laws, the requirement is one seventh of your time and one tenth of your money. In order for you to have a right relationship with your spiritual source, you need to devote a seventh of your time to receiving – not doing, but receiving, opening up to your spiritual source, which is your spiritual nature.

What is most important to you – your spiritual life, your physical life, or your mental development? What is the most important aspect of your life? Most people will answer, "My spiritual life, of course," because they think that is what they are supposed to say.

The real answer will come from your money. Money is a fantastic barometer of value, and it cannot be induced to lie. Your money symbolizes where your value is. Where does most of your money go? Is survival most important? Comfort? Entertainment? Illness? Protection from other people? Protection against the future?

Your time also cannot lie. What do you spend your time doing? You spend most of your time making sure that your physical body survives? Our physical existence is more important than anything else in the world. We give it more of our time, money and attention than anything else. Who are we trying to kid when we say we are spiritual beings? In truth, our spiritual side usually gets the leftovers.

You did not come to earth to make a living. You probably perfected that task in at least a hundred other lifetimes. This time, you came to make a life. So take your life and invest it in what is meaningful to you – what you feel that you most need to do in this time, what you most want to do, what you most enjoy doing. If you invest your life in that, making a living will take care of itself.

If you will drop what you are doing to make a living, and start what you ought to be doing to make a life, making a living will take care of itself. Give your time, your energy, your money and your attention to doing what ought to be done, what will matter to the well-being of others, what ought to happen on this earth. Put your time and your energy and your life into that.

You can pray till you are blue in the face, you can even follow this particular formulaic prayer every Sunday in church, but if you omit this universal law that says you must have a right relationship with your divine source – financially, time-wise and energy-wise – your prayers will just be warm air, dispersing in seconds.

It will be like sending in an order form without enclosing the payment. You can use credit, of course. You can promise God that you will give your time and energy and money. Sometimes, credit will be extended. But God has the most resourceful credit investigators. He always seems to know your true intention and whether you will fulfill your promises. It takes a lot of foolhardy nerve to make requests of God – even virtuous requests like spiritual growth, healing ability, enlightenment – without fulfilling these two laws: The Law of the Tenth and the Law of the Seventh.

The universe turns on these two laws: A seventh of your time and a tenth of your money devoted to your divine origin, your divine nature. If you are fulfilling those two laws, then ask! Ask and ye shall receive. Knowing that you have done your part, knowing that the debt is paid, knowing that your affairs are in order and your relationship with your source is right and balanced, ask! Ask with total confidence, expecting to receive. In that state, whatever you ask, expecting to receive, it's yours!

STATEMENTS OF POWER

At this point in the prayer formula come three vital statements of power. These statements cause the energy of the universe around you to respond.

So far in this prayer, you have carried out a process of invocation. You have invoked the source of your being. This source of you originally took the raw energy of the atmosphere and created a body out of it. This same brilliant, powerful energy, which is at this very moment filling and animating and energizing the atmosphere around you, has a predisposition to respond to your creativity.

It works like this. If you begin to think about another person for an extended period of time, with a disciplined mind that does not wander, you will direct your thought to that person. It may be a thought of anger or of healing. The law will work in either case. The universe, the universal energy that surrounds you, will immediately begin to move. As you direct your thought in a particular direction, energy begins to move in that direction. And the energy will take on the character of your thought. What prevents that person from being healed or hurt is his own resilience, the fact that he is also a creator. If he is disciplined enough, he may take that energy and change its character through his own creative thought.

The act of using creative thought to tell the atmosphere around you what to do is the act of prayer. As you apply the formula of this particular prayer, you invoke the source of your being and tell the energy of the universe what to do – to create heaven on earth, to feed you, to cause you to grow, to guide you in right directions, to cause you to see what you are resisting and to help you respond to those things in constructive ways, to give you strength. Having done that, you can add other requests.

In the last three statements of the formula is the power that causes the prayer to work, the power that will bring all your requests into manifestation.

THINE IS THE KINGDOM

Thine is the kingdom. "I recognize your authority to do what I just asked you to do." In order to achieve results, you must recognize that the source that you have invoked has the authority and the right to do what you have asked it to do.

Many people wonder why they are not effective with healing while asking questions like, "Supposing this thing is karmic, do I have a right?" By doubting their right to send healing energy to another person, they cancel the request of healing. By leaving out this power-statement of designated authority, the prayer is canceled.

Most people who pray say that God has the right to give them absolutely anything. But what they really believe is that God has the right to give them absolutely anything that their salary can afford.

When you start to pray that God will give you something, like a trip to Egypt, you immediately begin to consider all the possibilities for how that can be accomplished. And you begin making suggestions to God for how he could make it happen, as if he cannot figure it out for himself. And if you cannot figure out an avenue through which a trip to Egypt could come, you begin to think, "Oh well, there's no way. I'll just have to forget it."

People tend to believe that God does not have the authority to get money to them in ways that are not obvious, predictable or recognized by society. It has been my experience that God can get money to you in the most peculiar, unpredictable and unbelievable ways.

Your divine originator has the authority to give you more than your salary will pay for – if you can recognize that authority and expect the fulfillment. If not, you are right: "There's no way."

"I acknowledge that you have domain over this kingdom." Do you believe that God has domain over the kingdom of cancer? Or do you believe that to heal cancer, God would have to violate natural laws of science and medicine, or that he would have to erase someone's karma, which is not really allowed according to universal law? See how our human mind can complicate this matter?

Does God have the right to do what you have asked him to do? You must consider that question carefully and make a decision. If your decision is Yes, then you can move on in the formula.

Thine is the kingdom. Examine the reality of that phrase, for you personally. Do you believe that the source that you are addressing has the authority and the right to fulfill your requests? If not, forget about praying, because your disbelief will cancel the power needed to fulfill the requests.

THINE IS THE POWER

Can God do it? Does the creative power that designed and manifested this universe and everything in it have the ability to do what you are asking? Most people believe that God can heal anything that modern medicine has found a cure for and can provide anything their salary can pay for – and nothing more. That is the limit of expectancy of most people. That is the limit of their ability to believe in God's ability to deliver.

If you do not believe that God has the ability to heal something that is rarely healed, your prayers are a waste of words. If you do not believe that God has the ability to give you something that costs more than you are able to afford, your prayers are a waste of words. In that case, there is a ceiling on your prayer effectiveness, and that ceiling is defined by your beliefs in limitation. Your prayers are limited by your capability of expectancy.

THINE IS THE GLORY

Thine is the Glory. "I'll give you the credit." Does God need the credit? Does God have an ego that needs acknowledgment and appreciation, otherwise his feelings will be hurt and he will not come through next time? If so, fire that God and get a new one.

Of the three statements of power, this one concerning acknowledgment is most important because it is the key to the other two. If you are able to believe that God has the authority and the ability to answer your prayers, it is because you have experienced it and know it to be true.

When you set a cause in motion by your prayer, recognition of the effect amplifies your belief. Your ability to recognize and identify the presence and the effects of a divine creative power in your life will empower your prayers beyond any other factor.

Imagine that there is a young man who has learned about precipitation and effective praying. He goes into his meditation room, unrolls his prayer rug, lights his candles and incense, starts his meditation music, puts on his special robe, sits down in his lotus position, lets his eyes roll back in his head, and begins to speak to God. "Now God, I have a new job, but it is really difficult to get to work without a car. So I am asking you to please give me a car. It doesn't have to be a brand new one. I just need something that's good enough to get me to work and back." About that time, there is a knock at the door. So he leaves his meditation room, answers the door, and discovers his brother-in-law standing there. His brother-in-law says, "Listen, I hope you won't be insulted by my offering this. We just bought a new car, and we still have our old one because the trade-in value was terrible, but it is still a decent car – good enough to get you to work and back. Would you like to have it?" So the young man says to his brother-in-law, "Just a minute." And he runs back to his meditation room, gets back into prayer-mode, and says, "Never mind, God. I've already got one!"

When you pray, do you notice whether what you prayed for happens? When what you prayed for happens, and you notice it, do you accept that it happened as a result of a cause that your creative self set in motion? Do you acknowledge the connection? Do you notice when the real you, the divine you, sets a cause in motion and produces an effect in your life? That recognition is the true meaning of *Thine is the Glory*.

This formula for effective prayer, given two thousand years ago, is so powerful when applied properly – when you establish a right relationship with your source, when you incorporate the Laws of the Seventh and the Tenth, and when you do not violate these three statements of power – that you can manifest anything, without fail. Your entire world will transform.

THE FINAL STEP

Amen. What does it mean? The word was used by English kings to sign legal documents and proclamations, which were displayed on posts throughout the kingdom, announcing the King's will to the peasants. It is said to mean, "So be it." It is better translated as, "I have commanded it. Let it be so."

The word *Amen* is a powerful element in this formula. It has to do with taking responsibility. You begin by shutting out everything else in the world and focusing on the source of your existence. And you speak to that source until you sense a tangible living presence and you are confident that you have made contact.

Then you say, "I want you to take over my life and make my decisions. I want you to feed me so that the spiritual side of my life becomes strong. I want you to make clear to me the lessons of life so that I learn from them. And I want you to make me strong to meet the challenges that come. I know you have the authority and the ability to do it. And every time it happens, I will acknowledge that I have set that cause in motion, and I will recognize the effect. Now I have commanded that all of this be true. Let it be so."

Can you command the powers around you in that way? Prayer does not mean commanding God. It means commanding you.

Prayer means commanding the children in you, the spoiled children of the emotions, identity, personality, ego and appetites, to form a right relationship with your source. When you start setting those commandments in motion, through the king that rules the kingdom of heaven within you, your earth will change – you will live in a different place, a new world.

PRACTICE EFFECTIVE PRAYER

When beginning an effective prayer practice, start small. Begin by praying for something that you know, beyond any shadow of a doubt, God is authorized to do in your life. Something you can expect, create and experience. Then when it happens, notice that the effect is a result of the cause. Consequently, the next time you set a cause in motion, you will have more ability to expect success.

Every time you pray, acknowledge the cause-effect relationship. And your belief will amplify. When you continue to pray in this way and see the results, your prayers will become exceptionally powerful.

Begin by praying for something that falls within the limits of your ability to expect, something you can believe in. You will need to examine your level of ability to believe and expect, in order to find out where that is. Where is the ceiling? What can you pray for, truly expecting that you will receive it tomorrow?

Make a list of things that, if you prayed for them, you believe would happen tomorrow, beyond any shadow of a doubt. Then choose one thing, pray for it, and watch the accomplishment. Afterwards, examine and acknowledge the cause and the result, knowing that you set the process in motion through your prayer. This progression will add strength to your ability to pray with expectancy.

The following day, choose something from the list that is slightly more difficult to believe in, and then pray for it. Build in increments. Pray each day for something a little greater, but still within the limits of your personal expectancy. You will only need to do this for two or three days.

Keep a record. It is important for anyone who is developing a prayer life to keep a record of causes set in motion, plus how and when the effects occur. Check them off as they occur.

If you are unable to believe in the possibility of a particular effect, do not ask for it. Do not set yourself up for failure. This is an experiment in effective praying, and you only want to experience success at this point. Do not allow yourself to fail at prayer during this practice period. Then in the future, when you have developed your skill as a pray-er, you will not fail at prayer.

Never allow yourself to fail at prayer. You know exactly what is required for a successful outcome of prayer, so to pray unsuccessfully should never happen. You know ahead of time whether your prayer is going to succeed or fail. Do not bother with a prayer that is doomed – only warm air dispersing.

If you do not know, beyond any shadow of a doubt, that God has the authority and the ability to do what you are asking – if you cannot believe unequivocally that it will happen – your prayer will fail. So do not pray. Never again pray a prayer that will fail.

Effective praying results in success every time. Every time. To do that, you must first develop a prayer life, by exercising your prayer muscles and growing stronger each time you pray, through cause-and-effect success.

Begin small. Pray for what you can expect, receive it, record it, give credit where credit is due, and do it again. Keep raising the level of expectancy until whatever you ask in prayer believing, happens. Your prayers will become powerful because you have learned their effectiveness through direct experience.

EXPECTANCY

You have a right, when you post a prayer, to believe that your request will be accomplished. Pleading or bargaining with God, and begging for the item over and over, is an indication that you do not believe your original request will be fulfilled.

If you were to place orders in the same way with a store, you would receive a dozen jackets or a dozen dishwashers! They will wonder about you at the store! So will God! Obviously you did not believe that you had already received what you requested, if you continue to ask for it over and over.

Jesus dealt with that when he instituted this formula for prayer. He said, "Do not be like the heathens who think they are going to be heard for their much speaking and their vain repetitions." (Matthew 6:7-8) Do not bother posting the same request twice.

Pray once, assuming that your prayer has power and will be fulfilled. If your request is not fulfilled, the problem lies in your execution of the formula – not in whether you begged God enough, and not in whether he felt like saying Yes or not.

PRACTICAL APPLICATION

How do you put all this into practical application? It will require going quite a way in consciousness from where you probably are.

You are here in a sensory world, and the only thing that exists for you at this level of consciousness is what you can experience through your five senses. However, if you close your eyes for a moment and begin to experience a quiet, peaceful, creative place that you can see and feel and touch and smell and hear, you will bring into play a subtler set of senses. If you can make that place so real that it becomes more real than the room where you are sitting – when more than 50% of your consciousness is in that peaceful place – that place has become more real to you than the room where you began the exercise. It is no longer an imaginary place. It is a real place.

Have you ever had the experience of coming out of a movie theater and discovering that you have a headache, that you have had it for quite a long time, but did not notice because the experience of the story had become more real than the awareness of your own existence? A similar experience occurs when you are preoccupied with a place that you create in your mind – and better when that place is of your own design, rather than one designed for you.

The moment becomes a projection of consciousness to a created place, a place that you created and traveled to in consciousness to such an extent that it became real, a place that you could experience. The reason to go there is because you want your consciousness to cause a result. The ultimate goal is to be able to attune to the consciousness of God and be effective – to go to the level of causation that will out-manifest on the level of materialization.

Prayer is only effective when a mind is trained. Prayer will not work for a lazy mind. If your mind is so lazy that you cannot discipline it to experience another reality, another place where you can go and touch what is there, and hear it and see it and smell it and taste it – if you cannot discipline your mind to that point, your mind will not be effective in causing manifestation.

There are limitless ways for you to discipline your mind. If you want to be an effective pray-er, it is a necessity. There is no substitute. You must get your mind to the point that it will do what you tell it to do.

What is prayer? It is the combined forces of your disciplined mind, your heart's intent, your level of expectancy and your unlimited beliefs. If you are saying one thing with your lips while your mind and heart are holding something else in belief and expectancy, your mind and heart will be successful, and the thing that you are holding in belief and expectancy is what will out-manifest.

Look at your life at this very moment. What you see is the result of what you are holding in belief and expectancy. If you want to change your life, you must first begin to discipline your mind. Only then can you begin to apply this formula for prayer.

The Master's Formula for Effective Prayer, used properly, can be an important tool for causing the results you desire in your life, every time, without fail. It may seem a daunting task at this moment. Going back to begging a God who doesn't hear well to do something that he doesn't want to do and that you don't deserve anyway may even look appealing right now.

It is important to remember this: You are a creative being. Every concept included here in this formula for prayer, outlined by a masterful teacher 2,000 years ago, is already fundamental in your natural state. You are the same species as your divine creator. You are a child-God growing up to be what your Father is.

Set aside what you have learned previously about religion and God and prayer, and begin by simply speaking to the power and intelligence that created you – the active, creative source of your being. Let that be the beginning of your effective prayer life, and go forward from there.

THE WISDOM OF SOLOMON

SEVEN STEPS TOWARD MEDITATION

In order to discipline your mind and develop it into a tool that works for you, you must insist that it obey you.

M ost teachers of spiritual disciplines will tell you that meditation is the act of listening in the silence, turning off all thought, emptying yourself completely, entering into a nirvana state where nothing exists, no thought, no awareness.

That is only half the truth. What you have there is essentially an inactive experience – a passive state that is actually one half of a whole. When you have reached the state of emptiness, you are only halfway through the meditation.

Effective meditation is both active and passive, and it is effective because it produces a result. The act of emptying yourself is simply stress-release.

Meditation that is designed to relax the body, through repetition of a mantra or through a guided reverie into a meadow or along a beach, is a beautiful and healing experience for the body. Stress and tension are released, and it is a positive, restful occurrence. However, by itself, it is not true meditation.

Meditation is more than that. Meditation, if used as a spiritual tool for growth, becomes a fundamental facet of life, involving what you think and believe, what you eat, how you accomplish your job, how you relate to the people around you, what colors you wear. Effective meditation does not end after the silence is broken.

In other words, meditation is a continuing experience. It does not mean taking time out of your busy day to go into a room alone and become silent for a few moments, only to come back out and continue in the same vein as before. If the experience does not have an effect on your life, if it does not become a part of the whole, then it is relegated to an isolated experience that is worth only the value of the incident itself, but is of no value to the greater experience of life.

In other words, if your experience of meditation does not change your life, it is not working as effectively as it could, and should.

Dynamic, effective meditation is a life-changing experience, because meditation is essentially soul food, in the highest sense of that term. It is spiritual food.

You have a physical, mental and spiritual body. And the body that is fed and exercised the most will, by universal law, become the dominant body. The body you consider most important is the one that you are giving the most time and attention. If that is your physical body, then you are a dominant physical being. However, a dominant spiritual being is someone who has given as much time, attention, exercise and food to his spiritual body as to his physical body, and perhaps more.

There are very few dominant spiritual beings. There are dominant religious beings, but that is another matter. Religious beings attempt to create God in their own image. But that is an act of man's will and has little to do with spirituality.

A dominant spiritual being is one who has fed and exercised his spiritual nature, the creative nature, the source of his being, until that has become the dominant factor in his life. His spiritual nature dominates his physical body. And because of that, his creativity is able to cause change within his physical body, and in the bodies of others as well.

That is the secret of the great masters throughout history. They became dominant spiritual beings. They were not dominated by the earth – instead, they dominated the earth. They followed the first commandment given to humankind, as expressed in many sacred scriptures: "Be fruitful and subdue the earth." (Genesis 1:28) Subdue the earth means take charge of matter and cause it to respond to you, instead of reacting to it.

To fulfill the first commandment, you cannot enter into victim consciousness. You cannot claim that, if you are happy, it is because someone made you happy or because the circumstances are right. You cannot believe that, if you are unhappy, it is because someone disappointed you and hurt you. That is victim consciousness.

The truth is, if you are happy, it is because you decided to be happy. And if you are unhappy, it is because you decided to be unhappy. A dominant spiritual being takes charge of how he feels at all times.

TAKE CHARGE OF YOUR DAY

As you begin your day each morning, it is a good idea to stop and remember, "This day will develop out of my attitudes. It will develop out of my beliefs and my perspective. It will develop out of my reaction to the stimuli that are offered me. What comes to me as external stimulus is simply opportunity to respond in various ways."

You are offered a world. You are offered a day. It may be sunny. It may be rainy. It may be uncomplicated. It may be full of challenge. Whatever it is, it is the raw material out of which you will make your experience.

The purpose for beginning a day with meditation is to make a dynamic, effective decision concerning what kind of day you are going to have.

Do it on purpose, consciously – because you are already doing it on purpose anyway. You already decide what kind of day you will have because your day is colored by the way you approach it from the beginning.

Then a purpose of meditation first thing in the morning is to get in contact with the creative nature that determines the day, so that you make your decision on purpose rather than unconsciously.

Subdue the earth – take charge of your experience right from the beginning. That means deciding to be a master of the day. Decide to master yourself, your feelings, your emotions and your experience. In order to create a perfect day for yourself, you must first get in touch with the creative nature within you.

CREATE A MINDSET FOR MEDITATION

There are many elements to consider in preparation for meditation. The first thing to do before meditating is to create a mindset that will result in an effective experience. If you look at your watch and say, "Well, it's time to meditate," and you meditate because it is your regularly scheduled time, and your attitude is not excited, eager, interested or curious – just blasé – your experience will be the same. The mindset with which you enter meditation will dictate the result of the meditation.

Many people today practice various meditation techniques that they have found to be effective. Unfortunately though, this is what happens: They learn how to meditate, they learn what meditation is like, and they learn what to expect each time. So when they sit to meditate, they expect to repeat the previous experience. And they do. And they call it meditation. That is not meditation – that is repetitive expectation, and possibly stagnation.

There is a difference between expectation and expectancy. Expectancy is a sense of adventure – not knowing what the new experience will turn out to be, yet anticipating the newness excitedly. Expectancy allows change and growth through unlimited possibilities.

There are two kinds of meditators. One sits quietly and relaxes, has a passive experience, feels peaceful and calm, and afterwards, may feel better than before the meditation. For that reason, it is healthy and productive.

The other anticipates the experience each day, thinking, "I wonder what it's going to be like today? How much further am I going to go? How much am I going to grow? What am I going to move into? How can I go beyond where I was yesterday? How can I grow and become what I am seeking to become?" Both meditators' mindsets will determine their individual experiences.

Consider what happens when you go to the theater and everyone is filled with expectancy. You have waited a long time to see the performance. Your favorite entertainers are present. The crowd moves to their seats quickly, excitedly, eager for the show to begin. The house lights dim, and the stage lights come up. The curtain opens, and the audience bursts into applause. The air is electric. You can feel it, and so can the performers. The atmosphere is charged with expectancy. The result: stunning performances and standing ovations!

Contrast that with a performance where the people drift to their seats in a subdued manner, wondering if the performance will be any good, not expecting much from the show or the performers. They are unmoved, and the atmosphere is dull and lifeless. The curtains open, and the performers begin the arduous task of rallying response from a "dead audience."

In either case, the play and the performers may be good, but the mindset of the audience will affect the outcome.

The same thing happens in meditation. If you enter meditation expecting your life to be changed, you create an energy, which begins to move toward that transforming experience and makes it possible. You participate in the creation of the results.

Before you ever sit to meditate, take note of your mindset. What are you feeling and thinking? What are you expecting? What is your mood and energy level? Is it what you want to take into meditation with you? If not, change it first.

If you are not smiling easily and feeling wonderful about life, take care of that first. Get excited. Do whatever you need to do. Jump up and down and clap your hands and shout if necessary. Charge the electricity of the air around you by changing the positive ions to negative ions, which are more easily absorbed and which bring energy up in consciousness. You can create free negative ions in the atmosphere by clapping your hands sharply together, by making a noise, by filling the atmosphere with the sound and the vibration.

Jump up and down, clap your hands, and shout, three times a day before you meditate. The people around you may wonder about your new technique, but never mind that. Remember that electric moment of expectancy before the curtain goes up, and recreate that feeling. Consciously produce that expectant energy within yourself. Create the mindset of joy and happiness, of electricity, before you sit to meditate.

PERSONAL MATTERS

Before meditating, you should also take into consideration the atmosphere, the order, the conditions, the lighting, the colors, etc. of the room in which you meditate. The circumstances and moods around you, the vibrations, the activities in the building where you meditate – all these factors can make a difference.

Most important to remember is that these factors are significant, not just for meditation, but also for your whole life process. If a room is properly balanced for effective living, it will work for effective meditation, because that is the process of life. It is not possible to have a scattered, disorganized, dysfunctional life, and then go into meditation and have a clear experience, and then come back out and continue with your life in the same fashion. That is not effective living, nor meditation.

So first, look in your dresser drawers, your desk drawers, your closets, all the places where you have a tendency to cram things. See what shape they are in before you meditate, because every area of your house is an externalized symbol of your mind. Whatever is in your closets and drawers is in your head.

What do the colors of your wardrobe say? Are they dark and heavy? If so, so is your consciousness – and so will your meditation be. It is not possible for you to leave this experience and enter into another one that is opposite. Your meditation will be a continuation of your daily life.

If you want to organize your thoughts, if you want to make progress spiritually, if you want to clean up your act, clean up your external act first. Clean up the appearance and orderliness of yourself, your house, your diet, your car, your bedroom, your workspace – as you order things neatly in your external world, what these things represent within will become orderly and clear in your consciousness.

If you want to take serious steps toward spiritual growth, start with the simple things around you. Meditation can only work after these things have been set right.

The best way to have a clear, productive, useful meditation is to get the rest of your life in order – especially your relationships with other people. Straighten out your relationships before you sit to meditate, because you will carry into meditation any disharmony you are experiencing with others.

That is why the Lord's Prayer says, "Forgive me as I forgive others." Forgive me exactly as I forgive others – that will do a lot to teach you how to forgive others properly. And forgiveness is indispensable to effective meditation.

Take care of all of these factors first, before you attempt to set up an active meditation life.

PERSONAL RESPONSIBILITY

In the New Age movement, it seems popular among teachers to make things easy and simple. You often hear clichés such as "Just let it flow," "Just be in the now," "Whatever happens is supposed to be," "If it happened, it was meant to be." Nonsense!

If it happened, it was not necessarily meant to be. It might mean that you did not take responsibility for it not happening. Be aware, and take charge of your life. Take personal responsibility.

If you want guidance for your life, if you want to know what God wants you to do next, obviously one of the best ways for you to find out is to go into meditation and ask. But not before you have taken all the necessary external responsibilities yourself.

In other words, take stock of your talents, your abilities, your preparedness, the opportunities available. Look at the factors in existence around you from a commonsense, deductive, logical, responsible perspective first – because God is not your errand boy.

It is foolish for you to take no responsibility for your welfare, and then go into meditation and say, "Please tell me what to do, and give me all the necessary skills, and send me there, and make the way clear." God helps those who help themselves. So what is your responsible role to play?

Spiritual growth means taking responsibility for your personal welfare on all levels. A person who has not organized his finances, who is not maintaining healthy relationships, who is not making good use of his time, who is not being productive to the world around him, should not assume that God is going to clear out a place in a spiritual community for him to touch and heal the world around him.

Be useful on your own first. Be successful in handling your own affairs. Give God a sharpened tool to use – then its perfect use will become apparent.

It does not mean that God cannot perform a change or transformation in a person. God can take a person who is completely useless on all other levels and make him something different. But I guarantee you, that that will require a dark night of the soul. That individual will have to go to the very depths before he is changed into a new being.

So you have two choices: You can make for yourself a perfectly miserable dark night of the soul, so that you can make a breakthrough. Keep in mind though that when you break through from a dark night of the soul, the chances are greater that you will break through to psychosis than to psychic. More people break through to a breakdown than to a mystical experience.

The better choice, and the better way to grow spiritually, is to take responsibility for your energy, your talents, your abilities and your opportunities, and begin to apply them. Then God will find a way and a place to use you in his service.

TURNING OFF THE SENSES

With all that in order, you are almost ready to meditate. The position, whether sitting or lying, is important so far as you are comfortable and wide awake, and that your spine is straight so that you are not hunched over and interfering with body processes.

The first step is to turn off your physical body. The challenge will be that the physical body is like a spoiled child. It has always gotten its way – the senses and appetites have always been satisfied. Now suddenly, you say to this spoiled child, "Be quiet, I want to meditate." Instead, it gets louder and louder and louder. Suddenly, you are itching in places you forgot you had. Your body is doing everything it can to get your attention.

Have you ever tried to carry on a conversation in the presence of a spoiled child? If you try to speak over him, or if you try to ignore him, what does he do? He gets louder, of course.

What is the appropriate way to deal with spoiled children? How do you get their cooperation? First of all, instead of demanding that they follow your orders, you must assure them that they are loved. Give them attention, give them love, give them care. Then they will cooperate. It is the same with the spoiled child that is your body.

Before meditating, it is important to give your body attention, by helping it to relax. The best way to do this is through simple stretching and breathing exercises.

As you go through the day thinking thoughts, you move muscles. Every time you think a thought, a muscle in your body responds.

Simultaneously, you store the feelings attached to your thoughts in those muscles, and they become embodied there and form stress.

Without deep relaxation of those muscles, the stress remains. Again, you will take that stress and the attitude attached to the original thought into meditation with you. Movement, meaning simple exercises that are not too strenuous, will get the necessary oxygen flowing to your brain. Stretching the muscles, while breathing into them, will alleviate the stress further. Effective meditation is enhanced by actively stretching and breathing, before beginning the motionless part of the experience.

TURNING OFF THE THOUGHTS

Even after you get the body quiet, the mind will undoubtedly start in, because it is the other spoiled child. Suddenly, what you left unfinished at work, what you need to pick up for dinner, and where you should spend your holiday become so important that the mind cannot stop thinking about them.

Your mind is supposed to be your servant. It is supposed to do what you tell it to do. But does it?

Most people have a relationship with the mind in which it tells them what to do. They think things that they do not want to think, and they have feelings and moods and emotions that they do not want to have. Thoughts come into their minds that they would not repeat aloud, images that they would not want to manifest. They try to control their minds. However, the mind rebels because it has become spoiled and undisciplined. When these people try to tell the mind what to do, it says, "No way! I'm in control here."

Disciplining the mind is a necessary part of, not only meditation, but also any action toward spiritual growth. It is an essential first step.

How can you clear your mind? There are two particularly effective ways: One is to use a mantra. A mantra is a word or a sound that is repeated over and over, for the purpose of producing an altered state of consciousness or a state of receptivity within. In the ancient tradition, a mantra was always a name of God.

159

Another way to clear the mind is to develop a set of subtler senses, similar to the physical senses, and then to use them to build a separate reality.

THE SUBTLER SENSES

Meditation essentially means turning from one kind of sensory input to another kind of sensory input, from one kind of thinking to another kind of thinking. It is the shift in perspective that Jesus described when speaking of using subtler senses in order to perceive an unseen force. "You are trying to use the body of flesh to accomplish things of the spirit, and it is an inappropriate body for that purpose. You are trying to use an inappropriate set of senses to receive spiritual feedback. You cannot receive spiritual information through the physical ears. You can only receive spiritual information through the ears of the spiritual body. So you must give birth to a spiritual body. To do that, you are going to have to be born again – born into a new experience, another dimension, which is a spiritual dimension. You must give birth to a spiritual nature that has a set of senses capable of hearing, seeing and sensing those things of the spirit." (John 3:1-21)

In an ideal meditation, you will find that you are capable of leaving the room where your physical body rests. You are capable of entering into another reality. And in that other reality, you have an experience of receptivity, communication and creativity. It is a very active experience, where you can receive and create. You can learn. You can even create a new life.

You communicate in that other dimension through senses that bear little relationship to your physical senses. Essentially, the way you do that is by closing your eyes and forgetting about your body.

You have always used your body for sensory input because you have been taught that that is the way to learn and experience life. If you see something, you know it is there. If you hear something, you are certain that it exists. You have been taught to rely upon your physical senses, and thus to discard your inner senses.

This is unfortunate because your inner senses are as dependable as any of your other senses – as dependable as you are honest. You can never mistake the voice of God if you are honest with yourself.

You can receive communication from your ego, you can kid yourself with your imagination – or you can receive divine inspiration. But you cannot be fooled unless you want to be fooled.

If you want to be honest about it, you can ask yourself, "Where did that come from? Is that from my ego?" If you feel uncomfortable when you ask that question, there is your answer. You must first learn discrimination and discernment in order to relearn the use of these inner senses.

A SEPARATE REALITY

A separate reality consists of a place that you design so specifically that it becomes more real than the room in which you are sitting. It becomes more than a place that you imagine. It is a place that you create by using your subtler senses. Creating a separate reality does not mean waiting for something to appear. It means deciding what you want to be present, and then seeing it and experiencing it.

The most Godlike attribute that man has is the ability to create and manifest. When you are creating, you are expressing God. So you have already begun a spiritual process as you create a separate reality to visit when meditating, as you involve your consciousness in a creative process.

In creating a separate reality, you make a place that is so real that you can see each of its individual elements. What form that place takes does not matter – only that you consider it beautiful and you enjoy being there. It can be a special room of a building, or it can be a meadow, a beach or a country road.

It only matters that you can see the blue sky and the individual blades of grass. You can feel the breeze against your skin and the cool water slipping through your fingertips as you reach into the stream. You can smell the flowers and the damp earth. You can hear the splash of rushing water and the rustling of small animals foraging in the bushes. You can taste the sweet droplets from a honeysuckle blossom and a crisp, ripe apple picked from a tree.

To be effective, this separate reality needs to become more real than the room where you sit. See the mountains in the distance, the grass waving in the wind, the myriad colors of the wildflowers. Feel the coolness of the earth under you, the heat from the sun on your skin, the slight irritation of grass blades brushing against your ankles. Smell the blossoms and the coming rain. Hear the stream as it rushes over rocks and the call of birds in the distance. Taste the bitter flavor of the straw grass you hold between your teeth.

When you can involve more than 50% of your consciousness in this separate reality, it becomes your primary reality. The room where your body rests is no longer real. At that point, you have left your body. You have projected your consciousness into a separate reality.

This is still not meditation, though. This is a preparation process. It is a preparation of your consciousness for the meditation that will follow. It is a means for stilling your mind so meditation can occur.

The purpose for using the subtler senses to create a separate reality is to move from one dimension into another dimension, to make yourself available for the process of meditation. The purpose is to empty the mind of all that exists in this physical reality, to enter a special place of relaxation, where subtler messages and lessons and realizations can come through the subtler senses.

If you have trouble visualizing the individual blades of grass and tasting the cool water on your lips, it just means that your mind is undisciplined. It will not behave itself by following your instructions. In order to discipline your mind and develop it into a tool that works for you, you must insist that it obey you. You must insist that your mind follow your instructions and that your visualization capacity develop and begin to see clearly. The result is a particular place where you can go, which is peaceful, relaxing, dependable and constant.

If you continue to visit this peaceful place, meaning you reach an extremely peaceful and relaxed state regularly, and every time you enter that very peaceful and relaxed state, you picture the same images – the blades of grass, the distant mountains, the bright blossoms – over time, the images and the very relaxed state become associated, joined. Whenever you recreate the image, you produce the relaxed state of consciousness. At that point, your separate reality becomes a trigger mechanism that causes a particular response in you. By repeating the same images and making sure that you reach a profound relaxed and peaceful state, repeatedly, you create for yourself a trigger mechanism that works as a visual mantra.

Additionally, as you involve yourself in the separate reality you have created, specifically more than 50% of your consciousness, you cannot be concerned with what you left unfinished at work or what bills you need to pay or even where the kids need to go after school, all the things that would ordinarily crowd your mind. In other words, you take your consciousness away from distractions to another place. And it causes the brainwave rhythms to shift from functioning in the left-brain hemisphere to the right.

Visualization is a valuable tool. It is one of your subtler senses. If you say, "I can't visualize," one of your senses is blind, and you are functioning as a cripple. It is important to awaken all five of your subtler senses and to use them as tools, in conjunction with your physical senses, for experiencing the rest of reality. So train your visualization and discipline your mind, until you can image what you want to image, until you can feel it, taste it, hear it and touch it.

One of the ways to train that ability is to recall a time when you walked in deep, lush green grass and you felt it under your bare feet. Remember how that feels. Remember it with such intensity that you can feel it as you sit there in your chair. Recreate the sensation of the feeling. And make that experience more real than this one.

Awaken all your subtler senses, and use them simultaneously. In that way, your special place of relaxation becomes so real that you are no longer just thinking about it. You are not imagining it – you are there. You are able to go there, to project yourself into that place.

This is an initial step toward meditation. It means taking your consciousness to a place of profound relaxation for the purpose of beginning meditation.

Ideal is to dedicate that special place for a spiritual purpose, to make going there a sacred action. Make the ability a sacred instrument that serves you. Always use it to remind you that you have a source, a friend, a teacher within, and that you must enter a subtler world to meet and commune with that being. "Except you be born of water and the Spirit, you cannot enter the kingdom of God."

You have a relationship with God, and here is a real place where you can go to experience an intimate visit whenever you want. This separate reality that you have created exists for the purpose of opening the door between you and your source. Every time you go there, do it with the expectation of meeting God. And never again will your meditation experience be limited to stress-release.

SEVEN CHANGES – THE FIRST STEP

From the place of this subtler reality, meditation can take place. However, there are still seven changes in consciousness to be met.

The first step, which defines the difference between a peaceful stress-release experience and an effective, dynamic meditation experience, is a change in consciousness into a sense of expectancy.

As already described, an individual who meditates regularly is challenged to expect more than what he experienced in his last meditation. He knows what meditation is like and what to expect, and inadvertently sets a limit on what he can receive.

It is a trap to avoid. It will help if, every time you sit to meditate, you say to yourself, "I expect this experience to change my life. I expect this moment, right now, to make a difference in my life from this point on."

If you enter every meditation experience with that sense of expectancy, you will draw that level of experience. And your life will change as a result, because you are creating a vacuum into which new experience can come.

Do not ever assume that today's meditation experience is going to be the same as what you have experienced previously. Do not settle for that. Your consciousness is what will make the difference.

You are capable of creating a new experience by being receptive to a new experience.

There is no reason in the world why, if you were a certain way yesterday, or if you had a certain problem yesterday, that you have to be that way, or have that problem, tomorrow. There is no excuse for you to continue being something unsatisfactory any longer than it takes you to recognize that it is unsatisfactory. You are a creative being. You can change your life. You can become new.

Build into every spiritual experience, especially meditation, the expectation of becoming a new person. That is the first change in consciousness, the first step toward meditation.

THE SECOND STEP

The second change is a death. Every day of your life, you should die to who you were yesterday and give birth to a new being that is appropriate for the experience of today.

Most of us go through an entire lifetime saying, "This is who I am, and this is what I am like. I know who I am and what my traits are. There's nothing I can do about it. This is who I'll be till the day I die." If this is what you believe, you poor thing. You are probably right, though, because that is your belief system and your beliefs will manifest. But it need not be so.

The beauty of reincarnation is that we grow from lifetime to lifetime, if we use the lessons that are offered. Why wait a lifetime to become new? You can be a new person tomorrow, a person that you were not today, with capabilities and attributes that you did not have today. You can become a brand new being. Who you were can die.

You probably know the criticisms that people have made of you. You know what your weaknesses are. You know the things that you would like to change about yourself. Then why should those undesired qualities live one day longer?

The second step in consciousness is a death to who you used to be. Yes, the ego dies hard. The selfish-self dies hard. It wants to live and dominate, and it will rise up again and again, demanding space, demanding opportunity. Just when you think you have killed it, it will rise from the dead! It has as many lives as you do – or perhaps, it has just one less.

Put who you were behind you. Even if yesterday's experience was good, it is still yesterday's. Why would you attempt to live in the past and miss the now? Assume that you are not going to be the same being after today's experience. Put an end to guilt, lack and limitation, by becoming a different person than the one who was responsible for the mistakes you made yesterday. Become a new person, today.

THE THIRD STEP

Out of death springs new life. In this third step in consciousness, you will give birth to a new self. "I was this, and now I am becoming new. I have died to who I was, and now I am creating the birth of a brand new being."

This third step means opening to potential and possibilities. As you give birth to this new being, you do not necessarily have to decide how the new you will look and act, what the new attributes will be. You do not need to say, "I will be this, and this, and this." All you need to say is, "I am brand new material with no preconceived ideas of what I shall become." What you will become will be decided in the fourth step.

THE FOURTH STEP

The fourth step means assuming and trusting that there is a master designer, a master teacher alive within you, the wisest part of you, who is accessible and who knows every lesson you will ever need in life. The experience of the fourth step is to acknowledge and welcome into your life the presence of a tangible energy, which can best be named living love. It is the personified essence of the divine creator and takes the expression of a real being, which acts as your mentor and mediator, a guide to reaching the next levels.

You may not be able to sense this being initially. You may not be able to see or hear it. Nevertheless, you can believe that, if it is a creator and a master, it is capable of responding to you, even if you are not capable of hearing the response.

This fourth step means speaking to the master teacher within you, which is the Christ spirit by any name: "I cannot see you. I do not know who you are or what you are like. But I think you can hear me, and so I am speaking to you. I want you to take over my life and make a difference. Start working with me, in spite of my lack and limitation. I'm sure you can do that, so I am leaving it up to you."

The necessary step at this level is a process of discharging the responsibility from your limited personality-self, which has probably already made a mess and has proven what it can and cannot do. You are taking the responsibility away from that lower self and giving the responsibility to the divine presence, the master teacher, the creative spark, the highest within you – the part of you that knows itself to be God. You are addressing that part of you and saying, "I want to know living love. I don't want to be dominated by the senses and appetites anymore. I want the divine part of me to guide my experience of life."

To make this step complete, it is necessary to love yourself, which is a result of embracing living love. You need to love yourself with all your power, all your strength, all your might, and without reservation. When your love needs are met by you, it is no longer anyone else's responsibility. Then you can turn your attention to others, and you become selfless.

Jesus said, "Love the Lord thy God with all thy strength and all thy might, and your neighbor as yourself." (Matthew 22:37-40) Love yourself, your neighbor and your Source equally, exactly – and your love needs are met. You are given power and strength. You can believe in yourself. Your posture will change. You will walk with confidence. You will exude an air of charisma. People will be drawn to you – they will want to be in your presence because they will feel better as a result. It will make you a healer to allow living love into your life. It will make you a contributor to life on this planet.

That is the power within you, which is available at this fourth level. When you have made this commitment, you can then say with absolute confidence, "All power is given unto me both in heaven and in earth, and I can do what I came to do." (Mark 28:18)

THE FIFTH STEP

The fifth step in consciousness means recognizing that you have left, and gone beyond, the experience of earth and the body. It means entering into another reality where all that exists is God. That is all there is. Nothing else matters. Nothing else claims or occupies your attention. All that exists is a living presence of God. This is the "I am" presence. I do not exist anymore. Only God exists.

This fifth step means that you enter a new and higher world where an encounter occurs between your will and "Thy will." It is the encounter between the will of the appetite-self, the personality-self, the sensory-self, which is the lower self, and the Source-self.

You have just met the master teacher within yourself, and now you say, "Listen Teacher, you know better than I what's coming up in my life. So instead of letting my rational mind, my opinions, my beliefs and my habits make my decisions, I'd like for you to make them." Essentially, you are saying, "Thy will be done."

In this new and higher world comes a responsibility to take your experience of the divine presence that exists here to other people. That does not mean preaching to others, giving readings or workshops, becoming a spiritual teacher or an evangelist.

The best way to share a spiritual experience is to live it – to be so different that other people notice and say, "What happened to you?" If no one asks about your spiritual experience, keep your mouth shut. If no one asks, your words will fall on deaf ears anyway. And if you are not demonstrating the change, it is not worth sharing.

This fifth step means continuing to live in a new and higher world, even after the meditation has ended, so that your life becomes an example.

THE SIXTH STEP

This sixth change involves taking responsibility for your meditation experience. It does not mean sharing your meditation experience with others so that they will appreciate it.

People who insist on describing sounds, lights and visions from their meditations are letting it be known that they are entertaining themselves in an altered state of consciousness. Phenomena do not necessarily define effective meditation. On the other hand, if those people are positively changed by their experience, and their lives demonstrate that change, they will not feel a need to describe the lights and visions. They will know that the change is what is important.

If you have been disappointed because other people see auras, fairies, divas and visions, consider their lives. What did the divas and lights do for them? Were those people changed for all time? Was their experience valuable to them?

If those people, through their lives, convey to you a feeling of other-worldliness, of a purer presence, and you feel as if you have been in the presence of a woodland spirit, a spirit of nature, or the spirit of the nature of God – if they have conveyed that to you by their presence – then you can trust that their meditative experience was real and valuable. Most interesting, though, is that they will have shared their experience, not by describing it to you, but by living it and thus allowing you to see in them what they saw and experienced.

That is the definition of a mystical experience. It is an experience that qualitatively changes your life, and then becomes available so that others might do the same, through proximity and observing, through noticing and becoming different themselves as a result.

Most people consider a mystical experience to be something like a magical pink flame, or elaborate visions of divine beings, or a friendly smiling Christ-figure who shows up whenever called, or a great commission from God on High about saving the world single-handedly. All of that is simply entertaining, internal pyrotechnics and bears little relationship to a mystical experience.

A mystical experience is something that produces a new being. It is a transformation that occurs as you take responsibility for what goes on within you. If you need to tell others that you are "commissioned," then something is lacking in the commission. If others can automatically see that you are commissioned because of your presence, because of your conviction and your dedication to your work, because of the nature of your work, then the change has been real, thus the mystical experience has been real.

A mystical experience always affects more than just the person who had the experience. An individual's mystical experience affects the world. A mystical experience will affect all humankind through the individual who had the experience. That evolves through accepting responsibility for what you find within yourself, and that is the sixth change. It means being willing to accept what is revealed in meditation – before it is revealed. It means commitment first.

We often ask for information out of curiosity – not necessarily because we intend to do anything with it, but because we want to satisfy our curiosity. We do it repeatedly in workshops, where we learn skills and techniques and abilities, gifts of gold that could transform the world around us. We add them to our collection and store them on shelves in our minds. To what degree do we commit to sharing what we learn, and then fulfill the promise?

Most interesting is that the particular information that is available from the higher sources of enlightenment will not come without that commitment. It cannot be had. This level of commitment is absolutely vital to the process of effective meditation, and meditation will not take place without it. You may have a relaxed moment of serene stillness. However, you will not receive the gold that awaits you in this divine storehouse.

If you are willing to take responsibility for what is revealed to you by putting it to work in your life, the storehouse will be opened, showing you the way and making clear your next step. It is the only way to reach the seventh step in consciousness.

THE SEVENTH STEP

The seventh step is at-one-ment. This state of consciousness affirms the attributes of God, which are limitless power, absolute harmony and eternal duration. They are the attributes of you when you are in this consciousness. At this level of meditation, you have limitless power when you are in absolute harmony with that which has eternal duration.

What does that mean? If you are in that state of consciousness, if you are attuned to the divine presence of God, then you want the same thing that God wants. If you and God want the same thing, you have aligned your wills, and you can produce any kind of result. And that is the perfect way to pray.

By reaching this seventh level, you have come to the proper place to pray. You are not yet at the place of meditation, because prayer precedes meditation. Prayer precedes meditation by setting the tone, by establishing the purpose, and by directing your consciousness to a specific place where you are able to empty yourself of self.

Here, in this seventh level of consciousness, is the proper place for the use of a mantra. It can be particularly effective if your mantra is a name of God. This is why. If you and I were separated by distance, and I had not seen you for a long time, but I wanted to get in touch with you, I could do that by holding an image of your face in my mind and by repeating your name over and over. By using your name as a mantra, I would attract your consciousness to me. I would form a bond between my mind and your mind. Wherever you are in the world, you would suddenly find yourself thinking of me without knowing why.

Effective meditation begins by forming a similar link between you and your source. By making your mantra a name of God, you call that presence to you, to forge a link between your consciousness and that divine consciousness.

What is a name of God? Adonai, Emmanuel, I Am, Allah, Al Rahman, Shiva, Vishnu, Avalokitesvara, Chenrezig – the list is endless. In fact, your name for God could be John or Jane – it does not matter by what name you call it.

There is a classic mistake to avoid here. For most people, God is a being – probably male, probably external – which they have placed in a small brown box with a specific label. In other words, they have told their God what he is like, and what he can be, and what he can do. As a result, their God can do no more than their religion or their beliefs say he can do. He is a packaged God, incapable of any more than he is allowed to be, which their beliefs dictate.

It is undoubtedly true that what we call God is far more than any of us has ever been capable of imagining or describing. The divine, creative being who lives within each of us is far more than religion has ever been able to describe it to be. So avoid giving that being a name, avoid giving it limitations. Do not put God in a labeled box.

Do not decide what God is – rather, let God reveal whatever it is to you, from within you. Open yourself to experiencing something that surpasses anything you have heard described thus far. That is the best way to learn of what we call God.

Say to that which dwells within you, "I don't know who or what you are. But I want you to communicate with me and allow me to experience your presence. I am going to do my part by becoming receptive. I simply want to know you better. So I will call you by this name, and wait for you to answer."

Whatever that name is, it is your name for the source of your being – not the God of a certain faith or denomination. It is your name for your source, and it speaks of an intensely personal relationship.

By using that name as a mantra, calling it over and over, you can call to yourself, and communicate with, God-consciousness, which is the purpose of dynamic, effective meditation – to lift yourself beyond the created, to the level of the creator, to become one with the creator so that you can experience a new reality, where you will live, and which you will become. You become a new being, living in a new dimension, which is heaven on earth.

The place where you call God's name and communicate with that consciousness is a place called heaven, because that is where God lives. The purpose and the effect of meditation is to take that with you, back down to earth, and to live in that consciousness throughout your daily life, so that the kingdom of heaven has come on earth for you.

SEVEN ESSENTIAL STEPS

This is essentially a description of meditation. Any effective meditation process will accomplish these seven steps. They may be described differently, but they will affect the same results in you.

You must set a sense of expectancy in order to create a vacuum into which change can come. You must let go what you have been in order to become something new. You must accept becoming new to be born into a new reality.

You must acknowledge and communicate with a higher consciousness – whether you call it a master teacher, a spirit guide, God or Goddess, a guardian angel, the higher self, universal consciousness or the superconscious mind. Whatever you call it, it is a master of your life experience. It is a teacher that knows what challenges you will meet. So it is wise to communicate with it and use it for your protection and guidance.

You must leave the earthly reality to enter a heavenly reality, where you set aside personal will. You must take responsibility for sharing what is revealed and commit to put it to work, thus creating a flow from the storehouse that is available. And finally, you must call upon and forge a link with a divine spirit, your creator.

Each of these seven steps must be taken for an effective meditative process to take place.

THE ROLE OF PRAYER IN MEDITATION

At the seventh level of consciousness, you reach the proper place to pray. Prayer precedes meditation by establishing the purpose and by directing your consciousness to a specific place where you are able to become an empty vessel. Meditation is the act of becoming empty in order to receive.

The energy of growth is expressed in the two halves of a whole that we call prayer and meditation. Prayer is the positive side, meditation is the negative, receptive, feminine side. Through coming together, they precipitate and cause a result.

The result is a form of communication. Prayer is talking, and meditation is listening. Prayer is asking, and meditation is receiving. Prayer is causing a result, and meditation is experiencing the result. Prayer is directing your consciousness in a specific direction, setting the intent. It is a positive, creative action. Meditation is experiencing the result of that action.

The positive and the negative together create a whole. Neither exists independently. There is no such thing as effective, powerful prayer without meditation, because prayer needs its negative half to provide power and reality. And meditation cannot exist without prayer, because prayer is the force that makes meditation work.

In each of the steps outlined here, both prayer and meditation are present. In each case, intent is set, and the result is received. You begin by asking to be changed by the experience, and then you wait for the change in consciousness. You create the cause, and you experience the effect. You cause it through prayer, and you receive it through meditation.

Next you want to die to the past, and then you allow the death to occur. Next you want to create a new self, and then you feel that creation begin to manifest. Next you ask to meet your source, and you wait in anticipation.

In each of these steps, you do two things: You set the idea in motion, and you experience the result. You are active, and you are receptive. In the end, you have made seven prayers, seven statements of purpose. And you have experienced seven meditations, seven moments of receptivity.

Upon reaching the seventh level of consciousness, you call the name of God, and experience the divine presence through the mantra. Calling God's name is setting a cause in motion – the prayer. Experiencing the presence is receiving – the meditation.

At each level, you request, and you receive. You cause, and you experience. You pray, and you meditate.

RECEPTIVITY IN MEDITATION

Meditation is the act of listening by awakening the receptive part of your mind. This means setting aside the active, rational, deductive, logical, figuring-out part of your mind in order to be receptive. But what are you receiving?

We tend to think, especially in today's world, that learning means taking in more information. That is not learning – that is storing information. You do not necessarily learn because you have acquired new facts or because you have been told new ideas. Learning is not information-storage. Learning is change. Unless you are affected by the experience, you have not learned.

Intellectual understanding is not always a part of that change. There are situations in life that cause you to grow – you grow from the experience, but you may not grasp it intellectually. The experience occurred, and you responded to it, but you may not have analyzed it. You may not have gained an intellectual understanding of what that lesson was in the sense that you could explain it. And that is all right.

Instead of trying to intellectually analyze and figure out what life is telling you, more important is to respond to it appropriately. It is helpful to respond to what life is putting before you, not necessarily as an intellectual analytical process, but rather as a response process, as a growth process.

Childhood is our most intense growth period, yet our growth and our changes in thinking and attitudes do not necessarily come as a result of analyzing what is happening as we mature. We grew, not because we received intellectual information or stored facts or gained conscious understanding, but because we learned to respond in new ways to various stimuli. And the change itself was the growth.

The same is true of meditation. You may come out of the experience with a more mature attitude or a wiser perception, perhaps a softening in your approach, a change in your nature, which you cannot intellectually figure out. There were no words that came into your head providing explanation. Rather, it was a transformation that occurred within your heart and your consciousness.

The receptivity you experience in meditation, the listening, does not occur in words, or even ideas or concepts. If you do not receive clear answers or intellectual concepts, the meditation has not failed. Remember that you are listening with the subtle receptivity in yourself that allows you to approach life differently, from a different place within yourself, which is beyond intellect.

Meditation is an experience of absorbing energy, life energy, which is love. It should cause you to be rejuvenated physically, mentally and spiritually. You are recharging yourself.

It is a matter of communication with the divine, not intellectual pursuit. It is a matter of being refreshed and renewed with energy, vitality, life force, love, with an ability to be secure and confident, to grow, and to respond to life in a different way. Meditation is receptivity to the vitality of life, to Life itself – which makes it a life-changing experience.

QUIETING AN ACTIVE MIND
FROM THE PAUL SOLOMON SOURCE

*T*he purpose would be to center your activities, to bring together the scattered energies of your many interests. There needs to be a period, at least three times daily, when there would be the quieting of self.

It would be helpful to fasten the attention on a physical object. The flame of a candle, or a particular object, where the attention could be focused.

It is important as well that you focus your mind at the same time, on that which is your intent, your ideal, the purpose of your soul. Fasten your mind on a particular thought, a particular growth process, a particular direction. Be aware of who "I am," that is, the true self. Be aware of the God-self within. Be aware of the Christ-

consciousness, that which you develop toward. Be intently aware of your purpose.

As you center the focus of your eyes on the object of attention, focus your mind as well on the ideal of your soul. As you focus on soul growth and your unfoldment into Christ-consciousness, subdue all that is about the body and within the body. Cause your body processes to become slower. And as there is the rest and peace within, as there is the centered focus, the eyes may fall closed, though this is not necessary or important. There needs to be a centering of all, a bringing into alignment, that you might follow a single line.

See that you study materials for spiritual growth, particularly sacred scriptures, rather than finding various disciplines of soul development and studying many different doctrines. Let your search be for the truth within.

As you direct your attention to that focal point while in meditation, as you direct your soul to that which is truth within, affirm that this is the focal point on which you would concentrate all your attention, the search for truth within.

Learning the ability to relax is important. For there is the tendency in most toward tension within, and hyperactivity. A constant need to go here or there, to find those things on which to focus the attention. The ability to relax needs be developed. The ability to turn within, to quiet the self.

The ability to relax, the ability to center, to focus the attention, the ability to turn within and realize the true self – these are the purpose. Allow that all those interests – which are presently so widely scattered, and with which the sharp mind would deal so well – lead always back to that one central focal point, which is peace within. This is what must be discovered. And through the centering of your attention into stillness, all else will be found.

WHAT IS AN ALTAR?

To acknowledge that God is really here would require behaving as if God were really here.

Imagine for a moment that there is a particular room in your house that you want to make special, reserved for a unique purpose. So you scrub that room from top to bottom. Then you paint the walls, the ceiling, the woodwork. You add a new carpet and new furnishings, only a few pieces, but selected with extreme care. You spare no expense. And the result is beautiful.

In that room, you create a comfortable place where you can reflect and meditate, an extraordinary corner with specially chosen items that move you to stillness. And that becomes the single purpose of that room – a place of quiet, centered focus. The room becomes a temple, a *church* within your house.

Every time you come to the door of that room, you enter carefully, reverently. And if, as you approach the door of that room, you examine yourself and discover that you have been angry with someone, you will not enter the room. Instead, you will first resolve what caused your anger and make peace with that person. And you will make sure that you are in a state of harmony before opening the door to that room.

Then imagine that every time you approach that room you expect to meet and communicate with a being that you love. And every time you enter, you experience a living presence there. Though the room appears empty, you know that someone is there with you. Someone is waiting for you and is ready to communicate.

Imagine that the living presence that occupies that room is divine, beyond this world – a vast consciousness with an infinite capacity for love, with intelligence and capabilities beyond your imagination, with wondrous qualities you cannot even conceive.

And imagine that that consciousness can be found in one particular spot in that room, centered on one particular item that you have specially chosen, or perhaps built with your own hands. So that item becomes an *altar*, a place of honor to that divine living presence. It has become a point of focus for that divine being's existence.

Now consider this for a moment. Imagine that a great, wise master lived in that room – the wisest, kindest, most highly revered being on the planet. And you were allowed to enter that being's room and have an audience with him or her only after you had prepared yourself. And you must enter carefully, knowing that he or she can read every thought and will know if you have prepared yourself with a special garment and with a gift to exchange for what you are about to receive.

How would you enter that room? What would be your attitude? Would you ever enter that room as if no one were there? Without acknowledging the presence of that being?

If you ever establish for yourself, either in your home or a church or a spiritual center, what an altar really is, you will never enter the room where that altar exists as if there is no one there.

A LIVING BEING

The Source has said that when a divine presence is invoked, that being will respond. And where it has been invoked, that being will remain. It will continue to live in that place.

An altar is a living thing, a living being, a point of reference for the honor paid to the venerated but unseen guest, unseen to the physical eyes. An altar is a living thing with real and vital power.

I do not often advocate that people have personal altars, because an altar is pointless until one learns about the living presence it represents and its appropriate use. Inappropriately used, a shrine or altar in someone's home can become the opposite of what it ought to be. If that altar becomes "My little bit that I do for God," or if I put my faith in the fact that I have established an altar so that it becomes a form of spiritual insurance, or if I expose that altar to the personal reactions and energies of each person who enters my house and views it, it would be a mistake. And it is a worse affront to misuse an altar than to have no altar at all.

On the other hand, it is possible to establish a meditation room that is never used for any other purpose – and an altar that is so vitally important that when you approach it, or when you visualize it in your mind, you are automatically reminded, "I live in a house that is shared by a divine presence."

If you can approach the altar you have established – whatever form that altar might take, whatever items you might place upon it, whatever religious symbols you might choose because of the response they evoke in you – with a heart of thanksgiving and devotion to whatever you believe God to be, knowing that you have set aside and dedicated the most precious place in your house to what God is, then your altar will carry the pure and powerful energy of your devotion, because objects accumulate energy and power. And they accumulate the ability to express and the ability to accomplish as you instill them with that power.

An altar should be a place or an item that brings you to a point of attunement with your divine source. It is true that a person can stack up a lot of externals and depend upon them for his attunement. There was a man who periodically came to the Fellowship to meditate. He would arrive with a rolled up prayer rug, and a special pillow, and a bottle of ginger water to ionize the air, and a meditation tape of a guru chanting, and incense and candles, and a special meditation robe, and so on and so on. By the time he got all his paraphernalia unraveled to meditate, everyone else was in stitches.

Too often, altars are established in an attitude of "Let's pretend God is here," without recognizing that God is really here. To acknowledge that God is really here would require behaving as if God were really here. And that could be challenging to sustain.

But altars are a serious business. If an altar is a true altar to what is divine, it must be treated as such. You cannot enter a room where an altar stands without recognizing the fact that an altar is there, stopping dead still and acknowledging a holy presence, speaking to that presence.

You would never enter an individual's personal room without acknowledging his or her presence in that room, without turning to that one and speaking directly. You would not walk in and turn your back and ignore him or her. Nor would you enter a place where an altar is established, where a living presence has been invoked, without communicating with that living presence.

Now in saying all of this, I am not suggesting that an altar is the place where God is. Your divine source exists within your heart, within your true self. But an altar is a place for a point of recognition of that presence. An altar is a point of reference to remind you to honor that presence. An altar reminds you that the presence that lives within you also exists outside of you and surrounds you. And your recognition of all that through an altar will evoke a response in you. You give an altar the power to do that. And the more you are affected by the presence of an altar, the more power the altar accumulates.

Everything on the altar has a purpose, has significance and should be carefully considered. Ideally, the items on an individual's altar would be made by his own hands. Technically, if a person were an occultist, he would create for himself symbols that had been made of his own hands and that had never been used for any other purpose. They would be virgin instruments, used for a unique purpose. Such an altar would never be exposed to the public, but would be a private thing, a private experience. In that case, each of the items would be a sacred instrument because each one would have a purpose, an expression, an effect on the creator's consciousness, and would serve a real and powerful purpose. Over time, the items would accumulate more and more power and have more and more effect.

When asked which is preferable, the path of an occultist or the path of a mystic, the Source has said that a mystic is a person who is depending on his master and his reverence to his master for his attainment. The occultist is a person who is taking responsibility for himself and his steps along the path as taught by his master. The Source added that the ideal is the marriage of the mystic to the occult, the formation of the Christene Occultist.

If you can look at your altar and become attuned in that same second, then your altar is working for you. In other words, if your altar has become an effective instrument in the process of your mind obeying you, it is serving its purpose. If you can step outside this physical world and bring yourself to a point of inner serenity where your body and mind and emotions begin to obey you, if you can cause yourself to be happy in a sad situation, if you can choose compassion over anger instantaneously, then your altar is working.

It is possible to baptize your altar to that purpose, by using the elements of salt and water. These are the two elements of creation that were blessed by the Master Christ. Water is a symbol of spirit and cleansing. Salt is a symbol of earth and activity, solidarity and materiality. The two elements are first blessed separately as material expressions of God. Then when joined together, they form a crystal as they dry. Whatever is invoked as the two elements are mixing is held in the crystal that is formed.

This is both literally true and symbolically true. It is symbolically true by invocation. It is literally true by the law of psychometric effect, which means that any material object carries within itself its own history. So when a crystal is formed and an invocation is made at the same time, the invocation becomes a part of the crystal. The use of these two elements together is the most effective means of protecting a home or any instrument. The occultist for example sprinkles every room of his house with salt and water with an invocation that seals the windows, the doors, the presence. This ritual of combining salt and water is used traditionally in baptisms, blessings and cleansings, usually without knowledge of the full effect or the laws in use.

Concerning what should be placed on an altar – for the average person using an altar as a point of focus for meditation – I would suggest a few symbols that represent that person's faith and beliefs, plus some living thing such as a pine sprig or a fresh flower.

What is an altar? An altar is more than a decorative thing. An altar is a physical demonstration of the importance of a person's spiritual beliefs expressing actively in his life – no longer a symbol of a person's faith, but a living expression of what that person places his faith in. The best way that a person in this physical world can express his feelings toward his God is through expressing his feelings toward a symbol for God's existence.

This may take the form of an extraordinarily beautiful table with specially chosen items, or it may be a unique stone standing alone among the flowers and grasses of a hidden garden. It only needs to be a place of centered focus that moves you to stillness so that you can commune with your true source.

It is the intention of your heart that makes an altar holy. Without your devotion and faith, an altar is just a table or a stone. God lives in an altar only because you have requested it, because you have invoked the living presence there. It is your opportunity as well as your responsibility.

A LIVING ALTAR
FROM THE PAUL SOLOMON SOURCE

*Y*our coming before an altar – your time of worship, the gifts that you offer, and even your prayers – has no meaning unless the activities that follow in your relationships, your communications, your attitude and actions, your work, your investment of time and energy, your discipline and harmony, become a living sacrifice.

The establishing of a true altar is seen in the life of one who, after a time of devotion, wastes not a word or an action, but accomplishes the fulfillment of a day – so that each day becomes an investment in being a productive cell in the body of God. So will your holiness and your righteousness be a cell in the body of God as you cause your life to reflect beauty and harmony, to express Godliness.

Not that you should eliminate coming before the altar for a time of worship. Not that you should neglect times of devotion, meditation and prayer. Simply find balance. If the room in which you live, whether kitchen, bedroom or bath, does not reflect the order and beauty of a true altar, then your symbolic altar is a lie.

Be not afraid to require of yourselves long hours of giving, on this true altar, this earth, to bring harmony, which comes from cleanliness, decency and order. For as you do, the disease will go out of this earth. You will have healed this land. And you will establish on this earth a true altar, a real temple.

A GOD SO HOLY
FROM THE PAUL SOLOMON SOURCE

*I*f there were one thing that we might express in this moment that might open you to a greater truth within you, it would be this. There is a tendency among you to understand this or that through the intellect, through discovering and using methods and techniques. There is a tendency among you to reject reverence, piety, holiness, sanctification of the body, things that you consider superstitious or ritualistic in worship.

Understand that there is a God so holy that you must transcend all that is physical to be able to stand in its presence.

So begin doing so. Begin respecting your physical body as a temple of the Holy Spirit, so sacred, so sanctified, that upon entering the chapel that you have prepared for worship, you would automatically set aside the world and enter there with reverence, such holiness that the character of the place where you worship would be altered, the nature of the vibrations would become different. You would then enter into worship naturally, without a word being spoken. It would not be a channel or a minister who would bring that holy presence. It would already exist within you.

It is not only within you, but it surrounds and permeates all that is in this universe. The universe is alive with this presence. Then open yourself to it and see how holy it is. Establish that holiest place within you, the Holy of Holies, so that he might enter, so that you might worship there.

Become aware that this holy God has been made a plaything by those who call themselves psychics, spiritual teachers, advisors, and also leaders of the church – those who would apply laws in this and that discipline and denomination, and would attempt to understand intellectually and emotionally. Let these become humble, and bow the knee, and prostrate the self before that most holy God, and remove the shoes – for they stand on holy ground.

Understand how holy is the Creator. Make it not light or simple, but give way to that holiness by dedicating yourself and all that is. Respect your bodies, respect this temple, respect the place of worship, the chapel that you set aside. And make it a holy place. So that all who enter there would feel the vibration, the holiness, and would begin naturally to worship just from entering such presences as dwell there.

So often, there have come these who are assembled at this moment on inner planes. They bless this place. They grace it with their presence. They seek to abide there always, as they have been commanded to do. And so they do. Their presence is real, and felt, and known when you recognize it. How would you recognize it but to make yourself sensitive to it? Open to such presences so that you may know, and feel, and touch, and communicate.

Give yourself often to worship in such a manner. Make it not light, make it not a simple exercise, make it not small through habit. Make it greater each time you come to worship. So that less of earth would be known, less of the physical, and more of the spiritual – so that you would transcend this plane.

Often, you could simply leave your temple behind and walk with him in the clouds. And he would take you by the hand and walk with you. For he has said, "Behold, I stand at the door and knock. If any man hear my voice, and open the door, I will come in to him, and will sup with him, and he with me." (Revelation 3:20)

WHAT MATTERS IN LIFE

Throughout our lives, one memory continues to impress itself on our consciousness: "There is a reason that I'm here on earth. There is something I came to do."

It is likely that you lived previous to this lifetime. If you do not believe in reincarnation, it is probably true nevertheless. The interesting thing about truth is that it does not require your belief in order to exist.

Assuming for the moment that you lived previously and that you died at the end of that existence, let us examine your assets at the time of your death. There were undoubtedly people involved in your life – family, friends, colleagues, people you cared for and loved. There were undoubtedly possessions as well – things you owned, things you worked hard to accumulate over a lifetime. You probably had a furnished house, a car or two, and a bank account. Because of the investment made over many years, all these things were precious. You probably had a list of accomplishments, a career, talents and skills. All this evidence of a life of commitment and effort was significant, valuable and irreplaceable.

In your last moment of that previous life, you may have remarked to yourself, "I have spent my time and energy earning these things, and they are precious to me. These relationships, this home, these possessions, this money, this career, all these people. These are what I have to show for my life. This is the evidence of a life well lived. I've given everything to acquire all this that stands before me."

Then you died. In a millisecond, all that evidence trailed behind you. All your precious possessions were in one dimension, and you were in another.

"Oh, my God!" you thought. "Everything that mattered to me is in matter – but I'm not!"

Not ready to say goodbye, you hung around at your funeral, moving in and out and through your old family and friends. You tried to get their attention.

"Hey, it's me. Here I am. Over here – or up here, I'm not sure. But I'm definitely still here. I haven't gone anywhere. Here I am! Can't you see me?"

But they were busy hovering over a discarded piece of flesh that was cold, uninhabitable and a little disgusting by now. For you, it had become uncomfortable, unmanageable, restrictive and inhibiting. So you took it off as easily as an overcoat and dropped it on the floor. Watching your friends mourn your overcoat, you realized, "I can't talk with them now that I'm not wearing the flesh anymore."

Unable to communicate, and conscious that all you gave your life for was now out of reach, you turned and looked in another direction. What you saw was a group of extraordinary beings unlike anything you had seen on earth. As these magnificent celestials looked on benevolently, you began to recall a dreamlike awareness that had originated long ago but had faded over time.

"Wait a minute. That's not what I was supposed to do while I was on earth!" you recalled as the fuzziness began to clear. "Why did I spend so much time accumulating so much stuff over there? Where's that stuff now? Why did I spend so much time and energy working hard for the big house, all the money, all the things? It's not doing me a bit of good now. It's all stuck in that dimension."

You started to feel a little foolish as you pondered the weight of the situation. "That dimension is temporary. This one is forever. I should've worked on my ability to relate to this dimension. I should've worked on my ability to communicate on this plane, because life goes on. Why did I focus on accumulating all those things that couldn't come with me? I should've focused on things of lasting value!"

The group of extraordinary beings, known as the Lords of Karma, waited silently as you came to these realizations within yourself. At last you said to them, "Please, let me make another body. Let me go again. I'll do better. I'll remember what I'm going for this time. I won't waste the experience. This time, I'll remember what I should be doing. I won't get caught up in owning things. I won't get caught up in thinking it's important to impress people, to manipulate people for my own needs, to compete to be the best and have the most. This time, I'll remember that earth is a school. I'll remember that my purpose for being there is to express as an eternal being, not limited to the earth. I'll remember that my physical body is an experiential unit, something for me to use – but not me. Please let me go back. I won't forget what I'm there for this time."

"That's what you said last time," replied the Lords of Karma.

Thinking it might be helpful to your cause, you decided to list the areas of experience that caused you the most trouble last time. The Lords of Karma helped you by suggesting three categories: sex, money and power.

"List every time that you ever used sex, money and power in a way that provided you an unfair advantage over others or in a way that did not serve you," they said. So you listed everyone you ever fought with, every time you were ever greedy, every time you ever manipulated or took advantage of someone.

After pages and pages and pages, you wondered, "Surely it wasn't that much." Feeling ashamed of the length of your list, you came back to the Lords of Karma and said, "Here it is. Here's my personal record of everything that's woven into the Great Akashic Record. Here's the record of all that I've done throughout time."

The Lords of Karma conceded, "All right. You can try it again. Now let's see that list. Here, this person whom you manipulated repeatedly and treated wretchedly, that person can be your mother. And this one whom you cheated callously, lifetime after lifetime, that person can be your father. We need a man and a woman whose union will fulfill your needs. In other words, we need a couple that will provide all the requirements on this list. In that way, you will have the opportunity to repair those situations and make things right.

"All these people on the list, where situations were left unfinished and issues unresolved, where you didn't complete the relationship, where you didn't finish working things out, where you left on an angry note, or you just left a note – we'll make sure they are all conveniently arranged within your life experience so you can finish these things, so you can resolve all these situations and relationships. We will take care of arranging everything and everyone."

So the school was set up for you. The curriculum was selected, along with the teachers you would need. You were assigned a set of parents, plus some siblings, perhaps a life partner to encapsulate all the life lessons, plus many other important people with whom you would interact throughout your life.

As your customized plan began to take form, your mother-to-be was not thinking about you. She did not want a baby. She just wanted to be in a relationship with that guy. You know, the one you cheated callously. As the two of them became intimate, there you were hovering about, communicating with her mind, trying to assert some influence on her.

"Don't you want to become receptive?" you whispered. "Don't you want to let me be part of your life?" Luckily for you, she was in conflict. Consciously, she was sure that she did not want to become pregnant, while on another level of consciousness, she was thinking, "OK, let's go for it." Soon she forgot to take some necessary form of precaution. And voila! There you were.

You spent the next eight or nine months communicating with her continuously, day and night. She was aware of your presence, and she sensed something more than just the physical body growing within her. She also sensed a personality, an expression. You established a rapport with her, and you used the opportunity to influence her choices. You did your best to get her to eat certain foods, to read helpful books, to think positively, to be calm so that her stress would not show up in your body. You maintained a sort of conversation, back and forth between the two of you, and you effectively made your wishes known to her. She responded to your wishes, so you influenced every aspect of her pregnancy.

At last the work was complete, and the great day arrived. Your vehicle came out. There it was, just as you had created it. So you put it on. It was bulky, awkward and uncomfortable. Your first response was to take it off. Instead, you hit yourself in the head. "This clumsy thing. I've forgotten how to operate one of these. Whaaa!"

Now you remembered why you took the darned thing off last time. "Why would anyone in his right mind volunteer to get in one of these things?" you thought as you wrestled to get the body to cooperate. You finally got the eyes focused, and there were all those people standing around, staring back at you.

"Are you my mom? Fantastic! You're great looking. And that guy, is he my dad? Great! Now let's talk."

There was a problem, though. All those people were busy communicating with the vehicle, the instrument, the overcoat, saying things like, "Googoo," and "Gaagaa." They had not even noticed you yet. The instrument was so uncomfortable that you finally gave up the effort to get their attention and went to sleep, meaning you slipped out of the body for a while. Now the instrument lay there uninhabited, looking peaceful. At that point, the people all said, "Isn't that cute? Isn't that sweet?"

"I'm not there! I'm here!" you shouted. Meanwhile, they just played with your instrument.

"Talk to me! Talk to me! I'm not in that thing. I'm right here!"

"What a sweet baby, so quiet," they cooed.

As you watched in disbelief, you recalled how things work in this plane of matter. If you wanted to communicate with those people, you would have to get back in that heavy, awkward instrument, get the thing to move, and make some sounds.

The first lesson a soul learns on earth is that if you are out of the matter, you do not matter. The first thing parents teach a new baby is that "You are the instrument, and when you're not expressing as the instrument, we're not aware of you. It's as if you don't exist."

So you got back in the body, and you tried to stay there as much as possible. You practiced operating it for longer and longer periods each day, leaving it less and less as time went by. You got better and better at making the parts do what you wanted them to do, when you wanted them to do it.

The body required a lot of your concentration to make it work. Over time, you began to lose consciousness of anything else. You even began to forget where you had come from, who you had been, and who you really are. And you definitely forgot the Lords of Karma and the all-important list.

The instrument required so much investment that you began to identify with it. "This instrument is who I am. I am this body."

You began to accept, as everyone around you did, that "If I want attention, I have to use this instrument to get it. If I want to communicate, I have to do it through this body. Because of their limitations, these people believe it is the only way. So to exist here, I'll have to adopt the same limitations."

FALLING TO EARTH

By adopting the same limitations, you yielded to the false beliefs of the people around you and manifested again what is called the "fall of man." The fall occurs every time man affirms himself as matter, denying his true identity as a wondrous divine creator – *in* this world, but not *of* it.

Unless the parents involved are highly aware and able to help the soul maintain an awareness of its true self, the physical, mental and emotional bodies will mature while the unconscious, spiritual aspect spends the rest of the lifetime attempting to spark a memory.

For most of us, this is the pattern that our lives take. The conscious self skips along through life with comfort and happiness as its primary goal, while the unconscious spends every moment of the day and night, year after year, decade after decade, trying to get our attention, to wake us up and remind us of the truth.

LESSONS IN THE SCHOOL OF MATTER

When you are born into this life experience, you enter a school carefully designed to match your personal needs. Your task is to use your instrument as a tool, to gather information and to put that information to work. That is all. You come to this planetary school to take charge of matter, rather than to let it take charge of you.

Your task becomes more difficult as you encounter another invalid lesson taught by those who make up the school of matter. The majority of people on earth believe that there are very specific things that matter. You are taught from an early age that it matters that you have a marriage partner, and a lot of your energy becomes focused on that quest from the time you are young. It matters that you get married and that you have children, preferably a boy and a girl, in that order. It matters that you get a good education and make good grades. It matters that you have a career, which means a good job that provides a good income because you must buy many things. It matters that you own a home and at least one car. It is important that you have status in the community, that you are respected, and that you have a good reputation. It is important that you accomplish something important. All of this is what matters according to those who live in the world of matter.

QUESTIONING THE NORM

A handful of wise people will question these predetermined standards. A few will ask, "Does it really matter that I get married and have children? Does that need to be my focus?"

A true marriage, where two people become one as their hearts and souls unite in a lasting supportive bond, is so rare on this plane that it almost never happens. A person who would marry because "it is the right thing to do" is most likely not entering a real marriage anyway, so the question of whether it matters is irrelevant. Individuals capable of real marriage provide an invaluable contribution to the world, but already live outside society's rules and do not need to be reminded of what matters.

Concerning whether having children matters, the only children important to a successful contribution to humanity are the children of your creativity. All that you create, from your thoughts to your talents, are your children and must be nourished. The responsibility of raising a child is far too consequential, for you and for the child, to be decided by *shoulds*.

Does it really matter that you have an education and that you make good grades? Studies show that there is no definitive connection between success in later life and the grades an individual makes in school. Most people who have made great contributions to the world did not necessarily receive a traditional education. What they did possess was curiosity and an ability to learn. Our educators would do better to concentrate on teaching children how to learn, nurturing their natural love of learning, than to remain adamant in telling them what to study.

Do you have to own a home, a car and lots of things? Consider this: Do you truly think that you will get to the other side of death and feel pride in the accumulated things you had to leave behind? Better ask yourself if these things will help you in fulfilling your purpose for being alive.

Certainly, we can assume that poverty consciousness does not endear us to our creator. There is no spiritual gain in being without material possessions. Nor is happiness a guarantee of ownership. Once gain, this is a question that individuals must ask themselves. Will the things you possess serve you in accomplishing what you came to do?

Is a good reputation a necessity? Consider people who have made great contributions throughout time. Are they best remembered for their good reputations, meaning they followed all the rules of society? Or are they remembered for turning the world on its ear and changing it forever? Socrates was blamed for corrupting the youth of Athens. Jesus was called a rabble-rouser. Joan of Ark was burned for wearing pants. The list is endless of people who have made contributions to humanity, and who forsook their reputations to do it.

SO WHAT REALLY MATTERS?

It matters that you relate to the challenges of life as a cause rather than as a victim, knowing that those challenges evolved in response to you, that they are a result. It matters that you learn to cause effects. It is what you came to this planetary school to learn. You came, not to be affected by your environment, but to affect your environment. It matters that you take the challenges of life and discover how to make them work effectively for you. It matters that you conquer the lessons. It matters that you respond effectively to the opportunities. It matters that you love. It matters that you are joyous. It matters that you establish and maintain a direct, experiential, two-way, profoundly intimate relationship with your source, your divine creator, your God.

During the interval of life on earth, everyone experiences a persistent memory, a feeling or a sense of something not quite identifiable. It remains with us as we adjust to this plane, as we begin to conform to what society expects, as we work on our degrees and our careers, as we work to acquire our houses and cars and things, as we try to earn good reputations and accomplish things that matter.

Throughout our lives, the memory continues to impress itself on our consciousness. "There is a reason that I'm here on earth. There is something I came to do. I feel incomplete. I'm not whole because there is some part of me that is missing. What could that part be, and how can I find it?"

It is the voice of the superconscious, trying to get our attention, trying to wake us up and remind us of the truth. It is the part of us that remains in existence after the overcoat is set aside and the incessant thoughts are finally still. It is the creator-self, the part that remains forever connected to its source. It is the part that remembers where we came from and who we are, the all-important list, and our purpose for being alive.

"There is a reason that I'm here on earth. I feel incomplete because there is some part of me that is missing. What could that part be, and how can I find it?"

The conscious self, with happiness as its primary goal, cheerily interjects, "Oh! I know what it is. I need to get married. I need to find my soulmate!"

Here is what you need to know about soulmates. It is true that you are one-half of a whole being, and you can never be complete until you join with your other half. But the other half is not walking around in a body on this plane of matter. The other half of you is your source, your creator, your origin, your God.

The emptiness that individuals try to fill by joining with another human being on this plane would better be filled by realizing that "The reason I feel like half of a whole is that I'm separated from what I really am. I'm separated from my true nature. I'm separated from my cause. I'm only the result, and any result not joined to its cause is only half of a whole. Instead of looking for the completion and fulfillment of myself through joining in a love relationship with another human being, I will marry my source. Then I will be whole."

In order to marry with your source, you must first set aside the other lovers that stand in the way. That does not mean that you have to stop dating or end your present relationship. It means that you must set aside anything that keeps you from knowing and understanding your true identity, anything that competes with the primary relationship you maintain with your source within you.

When your primary relationship is with your source, that source within you will leap for joy when you meet a particular person with whom you can create a real marriage. And that leaping-for-joy feeling will not be connected to anything hormonal or emotional. You and your new partner will feel joined in one great work together, living life together in a shared purpose. You will become one, and the child of your relationship will be new life.

The emptiness that humankind experiences as a result of a perceived separation from God cannot be filled through marriage to another person. It can only be filled by joining the real lover, the original lover.

Children born into such a marriage will be blessed. They will not learn that marriage is a series of attempts to emotionally blackmail the partner into acting a certain way.

Instead, you will teach your child harmony, love and wholeness. Your child will not hear you say, "God can provide for all your needs," while you are chewing your nails and worrying, "How are we going to pay these bills?" Your child will not see fear and dread on your face while your words say the opposite. Your child will not learn that adults are masters at lying, saying one thing and doing another. Instead, your child will mature in an atmosphere of authentic love and support.

If you want to teach children what matters in life, say to them, "Love the source that gave you life, love yourself, be kind to everyone you meet, do your best in all situations, and enjoy life."

Then realize and accept that your child may not strive for what society believes is important, nor will he always behave. Other adults will likely judge you even more than the child by whether he behaves or not. Ask yourself whether you would prefer a well-behaved child or a happy child. A perfectly behaved child may have trouble later in life, having done all the things that adults said to do, conforming and behaving as a good little adult, restricted, confined, bound in a straightjacket of proprieties. Children, who are somewhat rebellious and independent, joyous and happy freethinkers, are creatively resourceful later in life.

LOVE IS A PERSONAL DECISION

It really does not matter if you have a lot of money in this lifetime. It does not matter if you have a good reputation. It does not even matter if you succeed. It does matter that you are joyous and that you express love. When you are joyous and capable of love, you will have a valuable legacy to pass on to the children of this world.

A paradox of life is that we cannot give love. We can only express love. Other people cannot receive love from us. They can share in our love if they are already full of self-love – not self-centered, self-absorbed love, but genuine consideration and appreciation for self.

Even if your marriage is not working effectively, you can be an effective, positive influence on your children and others around you. Your partner may not be happy, and a person who is not happy is likely to be accusing, bitter and fearful. You have an option. You can join your partner in that shroud of negativity, or you can stand outside of it, choosing to be positive instead. If you have children, they can still see one person who is consistently joyous, who demonstrates that life is not threatening, who expresses joy even in the face of adversity because of a decision to do so. Your children can see someone who is joyous, regardless of money in the bank, promotions at work, peace with other family members, a good sex life, etc., etc., etc. The list of reasons to not be happy is endless.

If you are already married, you may be asking yourself, "Why didn't I know this before?" If so, join right now in a direct, experiential marriage-relationship to your source. Make your earthly marriage whole by becoming whole yourself, making sure that there is at least one whole person involved.

Be a living demonstration of a right relationship with source and the joy and the positive life experience that results. Be a symbol of the abundance of this earth by demonstrating that there is plenty, there is prosperity, that all is well even in the middle of crisis, *especially* in the middle of crisis. Be an example of faith in action, of faith in a loving creator who has made no mistakes. Pass to your child a blessing that will incubate and return ten-fold.

And who knows? By becoming whole, perhaps your partner will follow your example. Even the most obstinate partner may find irrepressible confidence and joy too much to resist, and he or she may decide, "I want what you've got!"

Even if your children are grown, what better example to present than one who has found a new joy in life and can identify the cause as internal. Be an example, even to an adult child, of what life can be.

Life can work. It can work for you. It can serve you. If you want life to serve you, become its master.

Do you have a belief that being joyful, no matter what, is difficult? Someone introduced you to that belief early in your life. Why do you choose to keep it now? Your natural heritage is to be the master of your life.

YOU ARE A CREATOR

You have created a wondrous body, which is a singularly impressive feat. You need to direct those same creative energies into building beautiful, effective, joyous experiences and relationships. Your mind is the builder, and you need to channel your life energy, through your thoughts, into masterful living.

Step into heaven. Live there. It is a matter of living where your source lives.

If you go in search of your source, and your source responds to you by saying, "What do you want?" you are really a poor, dumb creature if you say, "I want to be rich. I want to have a good reputation. I want to be well educated. I want to amount to something." If on the other hand you say, "I want to live where you live," your source is going to say, "Come and see. Come into my world with me. Step out of that place where you have been living, where you have been struggling and fighting and scraping. Step out of what feels like hell by realizing that the experience of living in hell is nothing other than walking around in heaven while looking for it. Come home with me to a place of joy and confidence, and live there."

That is what life is all about. Live where your creator lives. Live where the creator in you, the highest in you, makes the decisions. Marry the highest and best within you, and the child of that union will be effective, joyous life. By living in the name of the Father, you will live in the nature of the Father.

The choice is whether to be joyous or oppressed by life. To live joyously and fearlessly even in the face of life's relentless everyday challenges requires a shift in thinking for most of us. The place to start is in adopting the theory that choosing joy as a regular response to life is possible, reasonable and beneficial. It is important to embrace the idea completely and to consider no other possibility. Over time, theory changes to knowing through daily practice, as you reaffirm the decision minute by minute. Joy becomes a way of life.

Do you want to be an effective example to everyone around you? Then know beyond any shadow of a doubt that you are lovable and loved, acceptable and accepted.

Replace the negative diatribe of your mind with the statement, "I am loved." Say it to yourself over and over. "I'm not going to be afraid anymore. I'm not going to feel alone anymore. I'm not going to feel powerless anymore. It's my decision. And even if it isn't true, I'm going to live as if it is, because it serves me to do so. Let the rest of the world believe as it wants. Let it even try to convince me of what it will, because I have made my decision and I can't be swayed. It works for me to assume that I am a very loved child of a very loving creator, even when I misbehave, even when I make mistakes, even when I forget what really matters. It makes me happy and it makes me a better person, to believe and to know that I am the apple of God's eye." Then live as the apple of God's eye.

THE APPLE OF GOD'S EYE
FROM THE PAUL SOLOMON SOURCE

*Y*ou are the perfect creation of a Father whose needs you satisfy perfectly. Begin to think of yourself as not only a masterpiece of God's creation, but as the apple of his eye, most precious in all his universe. Begin to think of your relationship with God in that manner.

As you feel appreciated by God, you will appreciate yourself. And your relationship with God will change. You will no longer perceive him as a condemning and judgmental Father. Rather, you will feel like the object of a devoted and doting lover.

As you feel yourself appreciated, you will find the quality of your life changing. You will literally find those about you, and life itself, treating you in a different manner. It is the natural result of placing yourself in new juxtaposition to the universe and universal forces. Lessons will change and take on new scope and purpose. Relationships will mature.

Let there be a time of becoming still, a time for self-examination in relation to what God is. Let there be a time for seeking that power that has given you life. Seek that power that lives within you. That which has breathed life into your body is God, so you are the nature of God. What you are is that he loves.

Begin to see yourself as so precious to that power that it cares sufficiently to correct all conditions in your life and your body, to build strength and energy, and to provide healing in all areas. As you live in harmony with that divinity, that divine purpose that gives life and energy, there will be sufficient energy and wisdom for facing all situations.

Consider these things and set new values by developing a regular relationship with that force that is God. Visit with that closeness, in an attitude of appreciation for the life force within you, two or three times daily. Become still in a meditative mood, listening for the highest within, and visit with that which loves you. You will attract to yourself that which you seek.

Seek the highest purpose. Seek understanding. Building calm and peace and acceptance, go forth to meet the day.

How can you be sure that in this or that activity or relationship you are not entering a wrong thing? How can you be sure of making no mistakes? Better be sure that you can accept mistakes when they are made, saying this, "I know my intent for this day is to be pure and of the highest purpose. If after forming such intent and purpose, I make a mistake, so be it. I will accept that without condemnation of myself. I will learn from it and grow, but I will not feel guilty or condemn myself. I will not think myself less worthy. I will enter each relationship and situation with gusto, with energy, with joy, with life itself. And I will enjoy all these things."

New metabolism and new strength will build from this approach toward all things about you. Could the Father condemn such an approach? It is the very entering of life itself. It is the natural manner of growth. And it is in harmony with divine will.

THE WISDOM OF SOLOMON

REINCARNATION AS A SPIRITUAL TOOL

Reincarnation does not suggest that you were once someone else.
It only suggests that you have not quit being who you once were.

T he purpose here is not to hash out whether reincarnation is a fact, but rather to consider: What can we do about it if it is? How can we use it to our advantage? Reincarnation is a meaningless concept unless its process is something that we can identify and make meaningful in our present experience.

Then what does reincarnation mean to the average person? Is it possible to become familiar with the karmic effects of our past experiences? And what can be done practically with that information?

We can begin by looking at the two laws of cause and effect that govern our lives in relation to the past, the present and the future: the Law of Karma and the Law of Grace.

The popular idea of karma is that it is a form of punishment for things done to hurt other people in past lives, some kind of cosmic payment for bad deeds.

Karma would be better understood as the process of setting a cause in motion that produces an automatic effect. Karma is a natural fulfillment of the cause-effect relationship in this universe.

Forgetting about past lives for the moment, how can we deal with karma in the present? How can we identify karma in our daily lives? How can we know if something is karmic or not?

Here is a simple, effective, fail-proof test: If it happens, that means it is karmic!

No need to belabor that point. If it happened, there was a cause behind it. Everything that happens is the effect of a cause set in motion earlier. Earlier could mean a thousand years ago or an hour ago. A belief in reincarnation is not necessary in order to understand and make use of karma. Just because something is karmic does not necessarily mean that its roots are in a past life. We are constantly setting causes in motion that will produce effects in this life.

So it is not important to explore past lives in order to understand karmic situations. It is important to explore causes of karmic situations, so that we can respond to the effects more appropriately.

Remember, karma is not punishment. Karma is an indicator of a personal need to learn something in the present. Then how does that work in a single lifetime?

THREE LEVELS OF CONSCIOUSNESS

Your conscious self, which receives all its information through your five senses, is being bombarded with facts constantly, and it cannot possibly use all that information in the present moment. So your subconscious mind is storing the information that is not being used right now and making it available later if needed. Your superconscious mind pre-existed all the other aspects of you and, prior to your birth, made decisions concerning your physical attributes and talents and also carried forward some memory of your soul purpose. The nature and purpose of the superconsciousness is something like a teacher who cares what kind of result you receive from this lifetime.

You are here on earth to learn. You are here to master the laws of this plane. And lessons come at you every day of your life. If you can think of this superconscious self as a teacher and guide, then you can understand that no one comes into your life that has not been carefully chosen. Every person you met today came into your life for a specific purpose, and your teacher knows what that purpose is.

What that means is that the people who you interact with daily have special value to you. They have been specifically chosen for your personal growth. By viewing the various people flowing in and out of your daily experience in this way, you can gain new understanding of your life purpose.

The point is that life is not a series of random events without meaning. Life is a perfect blend of complementary experiences that bring us to an understanding and expression of our true identities.

THE INNER TEACHER

This concept of a higher self that acts as a teacher, screening everyone who comes into your life, may not be true. Whether it is true or not, it works. It works because it automatically causes you to care more about other people. You become curious about who they are, why they are there, what they mean to you, what purpose they are serving. You are less likely to judge people and more likely to look for the reasons behind their actions and words. At the same time that unpleasant interactions become more personally important, they become less personally offensive – more subjective, and at the same time, more objective.

You can assume that your teacher selects every situation that comes into your life, chooses it and puts it there for a reason. Every situation was screened, selected and set up.

Then when faced with those situations, which could have devastated you previously, you look at them and realize, "Hey, this is a set-up. My teacher put this person here to act the way he's acting because I needed to learn a new response to that kind of behavior. This furious person who is yelling and screaming at me – this person who I might have despised earlier for the way he is acting, and in that way returned evil for evil – I now feel differently toward him. He is acting that way for me!"

If you can understand that nothing happens to you unless you need it to happen, you will hold a very different attitude toward all people, even those who may be abusing you. Letting abuse happen is not an appropriate response, but returning evil for evil certainly is not either. These situations are happening so that you can learn what is an appropriate response.

That is the process of karma. There is a higher part of your own self, a superconsciousness that is aware of your thoughts and actions, your interactions with others, and it notes carefully how well you handle your relationships. Your higher consciousness, the highest that is within you, your own judge, the Lords of Karma, so to speak, monitor your personal growth, using relationships as the backdrop, and note how situations are handled. Before you know it, there comes someone with the same attributes as the person you just interacted with so that you can have another opportunity to handle it better.

This explanation may sound over-simplified, but that is how karma works. You will continue attracting situations in order to master them. Think about your present experience. Most situations that frustrate you occur repeatedly. Little aggravations that happen over and over and over, driving you crazy.

Is it possible that they are the same issues that were driving you crazy ten years ago? 1,000 years ago? Ten thousand years ago? We can carry these lessons on and on and on, by being too stubborn to change the way we respond to silly, aggravating, unimportant circumstances.

Karma is not punishment for refusing to make necessary changes in our responses. Karma is the inevitable result of not making those changes. There is nothing personal about it. It is an automatic, predictable process, a law of the universe. Perhaps most important to know about all of this is that another universal law provides an opportunity for release from those inevitable results: the Law of Karma always bows to the Law of Grace.

HOW KARMA WORKS

How can we describe what happens between the three levels of consciousness in the process of karma and grace? Imagine that there is a teenage boy who has just received his first car. The boy's grades were always good in school, he helped out regularly at home, and he showed maturity and responsibility in many ways, so his parents bought him a new car. Now the boy is delighted. Before long, the car becomes the most important thing in his world. He forgets about everything else. He makes sure that anyone meeting him for the first time finds him sitting in his new car. His self-worth has become intertwined with the value of the car. Soon his schoolwork suffers, and his grades go down. He neglects his chores at home. He begins to forget appointments, ignore commitments, and drive too fast. His values have changed, and nothing matters but the automobile.

What can be done? Initially, the boy's superconscious self talks to the subconscious self and says, "Listen, we're going to have to warn him about this. He's growing out of control. We're going to have to get him back on the right track. Let's give him a dream."

So the superconscious programs a dream that floats up to him from the subconscious as he sleeps that night. All night long, he dreams that his car is chasing him, trying to eat him alive. The next morning, he comes running down the stairs shouting as he passes the kitchen door, "Mom, I had the craziest dream last night." His mother, good metaphysical study group member that she is, says, "Well, let's sit down and figure out what it means." But the boy is too busy and runs out the front door, heading for the new car.

What can be done? Next his superconscious self makes a plan with another superconscious across town. "My human is not listening. He's out of control. His values are out of whack. He's let his new car take precedence over everything else. Something's got to be done about his spiritual welfare."

The other superconscious says, "My human is acting the same way. He's consumed with business. He doesn't care about other people's rights or feelings. All he thinks about is making the next deal. He's neglecting his health. And he hasn't eaten dinner with his family in weeks."

So one superconscious self says to the other superconscious self, "You have your human on the corner of 12th and Vine, headed south at precisely half-past-four today, and I'll bring mine in from the east. And we'll create a karmic experience that will take care of both humans at once."

Both cars are destroyed. Both men walk away without a scratch, except to their egos, their values, their priorities, their schedules and their perspectives. Now they are forced to deal with each of these aspects of life.

HOW GRACE WORKS

That is how the Law of Karma works. The Law of Grace on the other hand would have taken precedence at any point that the boy had realized that his values were out of perspective, that his choices were skewed – that his family, friends, grades and commitments were more important than the new car had become to him – and he had changed his consciousness as a result of these realizations. Then he would have become a different person from the one who was out of control. And that different person would not have needed a karmic lesson. Then the karmic lesson would not have occurred. That is how grace works.

There is a soul-memory of past experiences that exists in the present, creating tendencies for similar choices in the present. Having those memories and tendencies might cause fear in you around those issues if they were negative experiences, which might attract opportunities for repetition of those experiences. That is the power of fear and why fear thoughts should be dismissed. What you dwell on expands and thrives.

The paradox of reincarnation is that it only matters what you are doing in this lifetime, regardless of what you did in a past life. Become a keen observer of the karmic situations occurring to you right now. Never mind asking, "Did this come from my Incan lifetime?" or "Is this left over from when I was a rug merchant in that Arabian lifetime?" Simply notice: "This effect is happening to me right now. The fact that it is happening means that it had a cause. The cause is something inherent within me. I have attracted this lesson now. What can I do about it?"

You can view the lesson as destructive, hurtful, painful and frustrating, or you can adopt a perspective of eternity, by seeing whatever comes at you as pure gold. "I see pure gold because I know that any karmic situation coming to me is an invitation to learn a new response – that I have set a cause in motion and here comes the effect. If I respond appropriately to that effect, I will cancel the cause, and I will no longer have that karmic situation to deal with. As its master, I no longer need it in my life."

Instead of trying to discover past lives, instead of examining dreams and regressions and recall for evidence of who you were, you would do better to remember that the total of all those lives, the outcome of all your past experiences, is the person that you are, sitting right there in the present moment.

All your past lives are revealing themselves to you right now, and you do have memory of them all. You have memory that causes you to set up situations that allow you to respond to the causes you formerly set in motion. You remember exactly what you need to remember from past lives, to create the situations you need in order to learn new responses. More than that is not necessary. You only need to remember enough to complete the lessons that you previously set in motion.

HOW THE AKASHIC RECORD IS BUILT

The most shocking and relevant aspect of discovering past life memories is the similarity of the lessons of your last lifetime and the ones you are working on this time. Consider this: How different have you become in your values and in your abilities, in the development of your self, than you were ten years ago? Twenty years ago? If change and growth has been difficult in this lifetime, what causes you to think that expanded development occurred between lifetimes?

Whatever you are building into the body you have right now is what you will carry forward into your next body, unless you make some big changes between now and the time you die. In this moment, cells in your body are being born and dying, cells are constantly being replaced with new ones. New cells are born into a particular matrix. The matrix is made of the electricity produced by your brain in thought. The thought that you are thinking now becomes a part of the permanent record of your body, and it is impressed into the cells that are being created. In other words, you are building a record into your body – your body becomes the recording device of thought and action that you have built in this lifetime.

Interestingly, every new cell that is built in the body carries not only the record of the moment in which it was formed, but it also carries forward the record contained in the cell before it. So it duplicates the previous record and adds to it the current moment. As you move through the cycles of life and death, and return here to take a new body, you bring with you that record of the past, of what you have built before, and that will be the beginning of the new body. So each body is built by the soul, incorporating the strengths and weaknesses of the last physical experience.

One of the most vitally important things to learn about reincarnation, if it is indeed a fact, is that right now, through your actions and your thoughts, by the way you are using your body and your opportunities, you are building your future body, opportunities and relationships.

It has been said that you *choose* your parents and the conditions under which you will enter. Actually, the choice is most often occurring without your conscious knowledge. The people you will return with are being chosen in the present moment, right now. By the way you are treating a particular person in your life, you may be choosing your future brother, colleague or mother-in-law. If you do not finish the job that you started with your current mate, you are probably choosing that person as a mate, or a parent, in a future time. The point is: Right now you have an opportunity to change.

If you realize that the future depends on what you do now – that future lives depend on what you do with your present opportunities and that who you are now is a result of your past opportunities and experiences – the present moment becomes much more meaningful. It becomes more important to use the present valuably for change and growth – to become right now what you would like to be in a return experience, to treat your body right now in such a way that you will have a healthy instrument upon your return, to care for things that are given to you right now, to appreciate them so that you will carry that appreciation with you into a new time. Whether reincarnation is a fact or not, simply considering the possibility can change your life.

CHOOSING A PERSPECTIVE

How can you remain sharp enough in each moment to catch these karmic lessons, to recognize them as karma, and to respond to each one appropriately? The first step is to assume that the people who are presently around you are probably people you have interacted with in the past. You have attracted them to you in this time for specific purpose. Often, upon meeting someone, you can sense that there is something unfinished between the two of you – that it is going to require some balancing, some action, some loving, to overcome the residue.

The feeling that there is something to complete should be an indicator that an opportunity is at hand. That knowledge can breed one of two things. It can breed fear: "Oh no! There is definitely something unfinished between the two of us. He is going to be really bad to me, and we are going to go round and round." By setting that fear in motion, you have definitely precipitated a karmic lesson for yourself that will take some hard work to overcome.

The second choice is to instantly feel that there is something out of balance between the two of you that can definitely be corrected through your efforts. "I can feel that that person already dislikes me, and he doesn't have a clue what it's really about. He just doesn't like me, and he is going to let me know it. I know that we have interacted before. We started this some time ago. If I had finished it then, by loving him, I wouldn't be dealing with this now."

As you come face-to-face with that person, can you be strong enough to know that you are loved already, that you are secure in your own love? Being secure in your own love means that, if he does not love you, you are not threatened. Then your concern is not for whether you are loved, but whether he is. Can you give your love to him unconditionally, not requiring that he return anything? That is your challenge in this karmic situation.

If you can give love unconditionally, you will have erased your karmic debt. And the other person's choice of response will not affect you. If he handles the situation poorly, he will not work his karma out further with you, because you are finished with this particular situation. It does not involve you any longer. In order for him to finish his debt, he will find a duplicate you, someone else who needs an experience similar to his.

If you can finish a relationship by bringing it to completion, so that you have no further need of responding to that lesson, then it is an obsolete lesson, and you do not need to interact with it anymore.

The Law of Karma always bows to the Law of Grace. If you change who you are so that you become a new person – a person who would not choose that action, a person who no longer has that tendency – then you are a different person from the one who committed the act. And in that way, you are not the person who owes the debt.

Reincarnation does not suggest that you were once somebody else. It only suggests that you have not quit being who you once were.

You remain the same person until you change, and changing does not mean changing bodies. Changing means becoming different, which is a new birth experience. A new birth experience in the sense of becoming a new kind of spiritual being or a new kind of being in relationship to spirit, a new kind of being in relationship to the universe and to the lessons.

UNIVERSAL LAWS OF HEALING

These same laws apply to disease. Spiritual healers often ask themselves, "What if it is a karmic disease? How do I know that I am not taking away this person's opportunity to respond to his karma if I take his symptoms away?"

Here is a simple, effective, fail-proof test: If a person is ill, it's karmic! It is not possible to rob a person of his symptoms so that he does not have an opportunity to meet his karma. If you rob a person of his symptoms, you have only taken away his language. You have not taken his disease. You have only taken his means of telling you about his disease.

No healer should get overly concerned with symptoms. Get concerned with causes and help the patient become a new being who does not need to display such symptoms. Then you have dealt with the karma, and in that way the symptoms become obsolete.

If you want to look good as a healer, meaning effective, remember this: Obsolete diseases are easy to cure. Just help the person become new inside in his relationship to himself, to his environment, to you and to others, which means that he is in love. Make sure your patient is in love – with himself, with everyone around him, with life, with wellness, with the spirit of life. As he is developing that new love relationship to his world around him, his symptoms will become obsolete and begin to disappear.

Medical treatment should not be centered on symptoms. It should be centered on causes. Any medical treatment that focuses only on symptoms without taking into consideration the cause of those symptoms is not complete medical treatment.

Treatment of all kinds, whether it is from psychics or spiritual healers, medical doctors, psychologists or psychiatrists, chiropractors or naturopaths, ministers or counselors, should be focused on finding the source of the complaint. Healing professionals need to consider the symbolism of the symptoms – the message the patient is conveying through the symptoms – and respond to that, at the same time that they work to relieve the symptoms.

WHOSE KARMA IS IT?

When considering karmic illness, the question sometimes arises "Whose karma is it?" because one person's illness often impacts strongly on the many individuals around that person.

A few years ago, a couple from southern California requested a reading from the Source for their daughter who had been diagnosed with Cerebral Palsy. The little girl was between three and four years old when I met her, unable to walk or talk. Yet she was one of the most beautiful children I have ever seen. She had a radiant face with a smile that filled the room.

Prior to this little girl's birth, this couple had been consumed with their careers, social climbers on their way to the top. Nothing else mattered – until this little girl came into their lives. Suddenly, there was a different purpose for all their money, intelligence and attention. They investigated many medical options and made several trips to Europe to find specialists for their daughter. Before long, there was not as much money as there used to be. But interestingly, their values had changed along the way. They had become spiritual seekers.

When they received their reading, the Source had this to say: "Here is a person, a soul, who has mastered most of those lessons available on your plane. This soul has a relationship with these two people, a love relationship, and is very much concerned. She came into this lifetime as a teacher, having specific lessons to teach. She very carefully constructed a physical vehicle appropriate to teach those lessons. How dare you call it disease?"

There are many perspectives from which to view the experiences of a lifetime. Perceived appropriately, none of those situations can be considered "wrong."

SELF-DELIVERED MESSAGES

Most people go through life being treated in a similar way by almost everyone they meet. For some people, that treatment is negative – everyone criticizes them, dislikes them or is jealous of them. These people are being sent a valuable message by their superconscious self, but because the experience is continuing, it is obvious that they are ignoring the message. Instead, they are probably blaming the other people for the way they are being treated.

If everyone in your life is acting a particular way toward you, you can bet that your higher self is using those people to get a message to you. Everyone in your life will treat you exactly as you have instructed him or her to treat you, because you are sending them clear instructions. Remember that this is the *you* of you – the super you, the divine inner you, the source of your being, the you that is setting up situations designed to help you grow.

If you would get up tomorrow morning and begin the day by assuming that every single thing that happens to you will happen because your teacher, your higher self, your source, the source of your day, has selected a set of lessons for you, you would be conscious and alert for opportunities to change old responses.

"This is a karmic relationship. I am meeting this person for a reason. I want to see all that I can see in this person. What is he displaying for me? What is he telling me? What is he thinking? What is his mood? What is his personal situation at home and at work? How much can I care about this person?"

One of the side effects of becoming that interested in other people is telepathy. If you want to know what another person is thinking, you only have to care more about what that other person is thinking than what you are thinking. If you care more about another's thoughts and opinions than your own, you will give up your opinions and hear his, whether he expresses them verbally or not. It only requires caring what he is thinking, what his needs are, what his concerns are, how you can relate to him, what you can do for him.

If you begin to interact with people in that way, you will understand them at a new and deeper level. You will form new kinds of relationships, and most of all, you will be alert for that moment when something goes wrong in the relationship.

Imagine that you meet someone while you are feeling happy and cheerful, but that person lashes out and practically snarls at you. In the old life, your first response probably would have been to snarl right back. In fact, society encourages us to act that way. "Stick up for yourself. Don't take that from anyone. No one has the right to talk to you like that! You should fight back!" Which means you have the right to poison your body with toxic emotions just like he did. How absurd!

Better to notice that that person snarled at you for an unnamed reason. He has a need, and he is displaying a symptom to you. It is a symptom of a cause in him that needs to be healed. You are a healer. No wonder he came to you and displayed his symptom for you. It is not appropriate to respond by saying, "You're putting out a symptom. So I'm going to give you the same symptom right back." Zap!

When the people around you display their symptoms of discomfort, it is your opportunity to transmute the energy of that symptom, by not joining with it. You can stand there in the face of anger and remain calm and cheerful – not in a pompous, self-righteous way, but in a supportive, compassionate way, inviting that person to join with the energy you are expressing.

"I know you're really angry at someone else, and I was a safe target for your frustrations. Go ahead and do what you need to do, and I'll just keep being calm and happy. If you choose to stay in that angry place, that's all right too. But if you want to make a switch, you can join me where I am."

If we can learn a new response to angry, hurting people, even when they are expressing their worst, we can literally change the world we live in. But beware.

You may be thinking, "Yes! I'm going to do that! I want to live that way. I'm going to go out in the world, and I'm not going to be angry anymore. I'm not going to return evil for evil. I'm going to realize that everything is a lesson. I'm going to help myself and others by staying calm and cheerful all the time."

What happens next in that case is that the *you* of you will say, "Bravo! Now let's just test that new commitment. Here comes an opportunity. See what you can do with this." Zap! You walk out into the world and get knocked off your feet by a gigantic lesson in emotions management. But that is what you wanted, right?

Whether you get knocked off your feet is not as important as whether you recognize that you created for yourself an immediate opportunity to exercise and strengthen your new muscle called "giving love for evil." It was a lesson set up so you could prove that you are handling your karmic lessons in a new and different way. If you were not totally successful, you will set up another chance.

You expressed a commitment to change. The opportunity to express that commitment was inevitable. Such opportunities usually occur within twenty-four hours. You should have expected it and been prepared! Then you could have responded to karma with grace.

Responding with grace means that, instead of being worn down by karma until it finally changes you or breaks you – remember, those lessons will just keep on coming – you commit to make another response. And you do it! And you repeat it until it becomes second nature. Your divine nature!

Turning a difficult situation into grace instead of karma means looking at it as an opportunity, recognizing the lesson, ferreting out the appropriate response and committing to it. It means choosing not to become angry, or hurt, or confused.

Confusion is just another symptom. It is not acceptable. It is a cop-out. Confusion is a way of refusing to make a decision.

Choose not to become angry, hurt, confused, despondent or depressed, because these are all inappropriate responses to stimuli. And the situations will just keep showing up, until you choose an appropriate response.

Your karmic lessons are presenting themselves, one right after the other, directly in front of you. You do not need to pay a psychic to tell you what your lessons are, or who you were in a past life. You were the same person you are right now. And you were presented then with the same lessons you are experiencing today.

YOU ONLY NEED TO PAY ATTENTION
If you will respond to each present situation, however frustrating it is, as if it were a gift – as if it were an opportunity to transform instead of an opportunity to react as you have until now – then each situation becomes a gift of gold, and life becomes precious and worth living.

The past is meeting you right now. You have created it. If you are curious to know where you have been and who you have been, you only need to listen to what the people around you are telling you about yourself. They are telling you exactly what you have been busy doing in your past lives. They are acting it out and putting it before you. And they are causing you to react in a way that you have been reacting for thousands of years.

Here is a key: If you will replace their faces with yours each time they act horribly – demonstrating for you who you have been and telling you exactly how you treated them or someone else in the past, then your past lives will become crystal clear for you.

In each moment of your day, you are being shown a dramatic presentation of your past lives. The ticket for such a showing is priceless! You have the opportunity to say, "Whoa, wait a minute. I don't want to do that anymore!" At any moment, you can turn on the lights of your private theatre and stop the show – simply by changing an eons-old reaction to a more loving response. If you want to know how to respond to life in the present, simply respond as you think the other people around you should have responded.

The power of grace over karma is simply the Golden Rule. "Do unto others as you would have them do unto you." You can erase lifetimes of lessons in a single act of gold.

Life is your servant. It serves you by guiding you another step in your growth. You are not life's victim. You are the creator of all your experiences. This is the perspective of eternity.

Whatever happens in your life, even the terrible things that other people are doing to you, is something that you have created, and designed, and drawn to you. You are a creative being, you have created all these things, and you can recreate them differently.

Recreating them differently means moving into the Law of Grace. And when you begin to live in grace in all situations, the Law of Karma is cancelled. It only requires your commitment to live in a new and different way – to be a new and different person from the eons-old person you were a moment ago. Step into grace and be that new person now.

THE WISDOM OF SOLOMON

THE GREAT WHITE BROTHERHOOD:
ITS ORIGIN AND PURPOSES

There is sufficient evidence around the world proving the previous existence of highly intelligent beings for which there is no suitable explanation.

Imagine a time before the world existed, a time when the creator of this universe could be described as a great light that was a source of life. This great being – with an infinite capacity for love, with capabilities beyond our imagination, with attributes we cannot conceive – still wanted one thing. This being wanted an object for its love. This being was so filled, so vibrant, with the quality of love that it wanted an object for that love, something for the love to act upon. Because of this desire, expansion occurred. Creation began to take place. The first creative action of this great being was the birth of a son, a son of God.

This is one way to attempt to describe what is indescribable. It is not an attempt to define what literally occurred in the creation and development of the world and humanity. It is an attempt to provide a point of reference for a series of events for which we have absolutely no reference.

When trying to understand new information that is beyond personal experience, it can help to create analogies using elements that are within the realm of knowledge and experience, not so much to explain occurrences as to make relationships understandable.

Accuracy is not out of the question though. Many symbols have origin in reality. Points of reference take on validity as they result in understandings that are valid.

THE UNION OF POTENTIAL AND CREATIVITY

Imagine the beginning of time as a union of positive and negative forces, male and female. There existed a great sea of dark stillness that some call the Prime Central Stillness – peace, silence, potential. This potential, which was the female aspect of the godhead, united with the male aspect, and the result was action. Feminine potential stirred the active creativity of the male god. The union of the creative principle with potential resulted in a creation, a son. The son of God is the issue of God, or the expression of God.

A similar analogy is drawn in the Gospel of John. "In the beginning, was the word." (John 1:1) The term that John actually used in writing this verse was "logos," a Greek word that means expression. In the beginning, there was an expression of God. The male and the female aspects coming together resulted in expression. Until that point, there had existed only potential. That expression of God was the word that went forth. The word or expression of God became flesh and dwelt among us.

God expressed, and that expression went forward. It took on life. This great being that originally existed only as potential expressed itself, and the result was an expression that was now an object for its love. God created a son that was now the object of his love. The son of God was the lover of God.

Imagine God in the beginning as a large central sun, a ball of heat, warmth and light. The son that God gave birth to are the rays that go out. The son is simultaneously singular and plural, masculine and feminine. The expression that went out from God was one radiation that expressed as countless rays – each a ray of God. It might be said that God gave birth to only one son, yet there were many sparks of that one light. They all were one, and initially they knew themselves to be all one great light.

THE ORIGIN OF THE EARTH

Having given expression to himself and having created for himself a lover, there was a further step in creation. The first thing anyone wants to do for a new lover is to demonstrate that love. The next step for God was to offer the new lover a gift.

At this point, the creativity of God began to express differently. Matter began to appear. It was in this sense that stars were created. The firmament. The heavenly bodies. Even the earth.

The earth was created as the greatest gift of love that could be given to a lover, a bride. The result was beautiful, magnificent, splendorous. The Bible describes the moment of creation when "morning stars sang together and all the sons of God shouted for joy." (Job 38:7) The earth was a fascinating thing, a gift that undoubtedly attracted the attention of the lover. This lover, the son of God, was fascinated and became absolutely enthralled with the gift.

At this point, the lover, the children of God who were many, still knew themselves to be one. They knew themselves to be one with each other and one with their creator. Being sons of God, expressions of God, they were creative in their own right. As co-creators with God, they began to experience creation upon the earth. They began to affect earth by causing things to happen in matter.

During this process, consciousness affected and determined creation. Intelligent force with purpose behind it affected creation so that earth began to take on intelligent expressions – plant life. This period has been called the Lemurian Epoch. Lemuria was a place and a period in evolution when the consciousness of the son of God began to develop plant life on earth, as a co-creator with God. (Genesis 1:11-13) Plants began to reflect the consciousness of the creator. At the beginning of the Lemurian Epoch, all plants were beautiful and expressed harmony. Thorns and spines did not exist, nor fowl smelling or poisonous plants. As yet, nothing had evolved defense systems because there was no need. The existence of antagonism was impossible for it would have meant one part of a body fighting against itself. At this point, all living things still knew themselves to be one.

THE SONS OF GOD ENTER THE EARTH

During this period when vegetation developed, an interesting phenomenon began to take place. Plants could react and respond to one another and to their atmosphere. They could feel and experience existence in ways that the sons of God could not. Soon however, these expressions of God began to realize that they could have similar experiences. All they had to do to have the same experience as the plants was to identify with the plant.

Being creative, their consciousness could easily identify with the plant. So the sons of God began to become the plants, by taking on the life of the plants they had created. They experienced how it felt to be a part of physical existence and to react from that point of view. The experience was of course fascinating, but it had a secondary effect. To become a part of a specific plant required that the sons of God narrow their consciousness.

A few million years beyond Lemuria, there occurred a period called the Atlantean Epoch when animals evolved. The same phenomenon developed as these sons of God began to take on aspects of animal life. The sons of God detached from one another again, not as plants this time, but as animals, evolving into a new day. This was another day of creation – the day referred to in scripture as the day of the birth of the animals. (Genesis 1:20-23) This was the Atlantean Day and included the development of physical bodies and animals, expressions other than plant life.

Whether expressing as plant life or in a physical body, the effects on the sons of God were similar. The narrowness of consciousness required to enter and exist in a physical body caused each one to feel separate from its true identity. The true identity became increasingly difficult to remember. As long as the sons of God did not sustain identification with the bodies they had entered, as long as they withdrew periodically to realize and remember who they were, it was safe and could be a meaningful experience. Scripture describes these beings rejoicing in the beginning, frolicking among the beauties of this new creation.

Earth was created as a gift by God, and it was intended for enjoyment. Experiencing and having fun with the gift was its purpose. Imagine this great being creating for his bride the most wonderful, creative, beautiful, unique object possible. His love was so vast and generous that he wanted to fashion for his bride the greatest gift ever created – the first gift ever created.

In this account of the creation of the sons of God, we can imagine that there came a point when God's great reasoning mind said, "Now I have an object of my love. I have an issue from my being. There exists now a son of God. I have given birth to expressions of myself. But these expressions are like puppets because they have no will of their own. They have no choice but to love me because they know nothing else. They are of my nature, and they know no other nature. I will give them a gift, something that is striking and attractive, something that they could love instead of me, so they may choose. For real love is a choice."

HUMANKIND'S CHOICE

But in meeting the choice between the giver and the gift, the bride of God became more fascinated with the gift. It was as if her fascination grew until she forgot that God existed. "Oh, how wonderful and enchanting this earth is!" she said to God. "Leave me alone just now. I don't have time for you. I am fascinated with this."

The freedom of choice that God gave to his sons is what made them different from other things that he created, such as animals, plants, angels and other beings. All these evolved over time, but did not develop the ability to choose. The sons of God were different from all other creation in that they had the option of saying, "I love you, my creator. And I can experience earth and matter as a gift from you without identifying with it and losing consciousness of you."

However, that is not what occurred. The lover of God was so captivated by the gift that he became lost in it and eventually forgot the giver. The sons of God fell to earth.

The "fall of man" as described in scripture was nothing more than a loss of awareness of true identity. In terms of sin, there are no degrees. Forgetting that we are divine by nature, that we are God itself, is the only sin humankind has ever committed, and this single sin has continued over the eons – many times, many ways, in many forms.

TWO GROUPS OF SOULS

In this period of first identification with the material world, there were two groups of souls experiencing matter. The Bible calls them the sons of God and the sons of man. (Genesis 6:2)

The sons of man might be described in this way. There were beings that had created for themselves vehicles of expression.

Imagine that these sparks of God wanted to express in physical bodies on earth and knew that many other sparks of God would be expressing simultaneously. Of course, they wanted all the advantages that were available, all the options that earth had to offer.

They were aware of the oceans, and they were intrigued with flying, but they also wanted to experience life on the surface of the earth, amid the flora and fauna. They decided to be big – bigger than others who might also choose to be big. In fact, why not be huge? They wanted to go under water, so why not have webbed feet and fins and gills? They wanted to fly, so their new bodies must have wings and feathers. They wanted to reach the treetops, so they also needed long necks.

With all these things in mind, these sparks of God designed for themselves bodies in which they could experience land, air and water. Having finally created their new bodies, they entered them and immediately discovered that there were many things to do. They had to keep the organisms going. It was absolutely necessary to keep the circulation and breathing going. They had to keep cells exchanging. They had to keep organs and systems functioning.

They had to develop a consciousness of the body that would allow them to function comfortably. They had to stay so involved with these new bodies that they forgot to allow for time out of them. They began to receive all information through the senses of the flesh. Eventually, the necessary identification with the animals caused them to think that they were the animals. They began to say, "I am this animal. This is my ultimate experience. This is how I define myself."

Contact with the world of their prior existence was not immediately impossible, but was overlooked, forgotten. Soon these original sons of God became captured in the bodies of flesh and were unable to extract themselves again.

THE ORIGIN OF THE GREAT WHITE BROTHERHOOD

The second group of souls experiencing life on earth at this time still knew themselves to be cells in the one body of God. From the beginning, they had seen and understood what was happening to the others. They witnessed the fall of the sons of God into matter. They observed the other parts of themselves as they became captured in matter, as they forgot who they were, as they forgot that they were expressions of God. They watched as their partner-selves became trapped in the bodies they had created.

Those who were still in God and with God, who still knew all to be part of the body of God, attempted to reach the others in any way possible. They tried to communicate with them, to touch them, to attract their attention. They passed through the unusual bodies to stir awareness or a remembrance. But they were in one dimension now, and those in the flesh were in another.

Eventually, some made the decision to join their counterparts in the flesh, saying, "I'll create for myself a body and communicate with them through their senses, through the flesh. I'll remind them of their previous existence. I'll remind them who they really are."

These were the two kinds of beings existing on earth at that time. The first group had projected themselves into matter, either in the bodies of animals already living or in bodies they had created. Either way, they had become imprisoned by the flesh and the five senses. The second group of beings resolved to bring the captives home. Because of humankind's fall into captivity, this group of committed beings – called by many names throughout time, including the Great White Brotherhood – came into existence.

Certain members of this Great Brotherhood said, "I'll enter a body of flesh and communicate as a teacher with those captured." There is sufficient evidence around the world proving the previous existence of highly intelligent beings for which there is no suitable explanation. We have great temples and pyramids, sophisticated architecture and building methods, advanced civilizations, primitive world maps and astronomical calendars as accurate as our own today. We have stories and drawings of flying ships and other complex instruments. Legends and myths speak of ancient race-leaders.

We are left with evidence of two extremely different levels of evolution, existing on earth simultaneously – significantly skilled, highly intelligent, technically developed beings, with an awareness of science and the relationships of matter and energy, existing alongside very primitive humans and animals.

MODERN DAY APPLICATION

An important question to consider today, millions of years later, is how nearly that describes where each of us is in this moment. If we are indeed God, children of God, why do we not think with the mind of God and express all the attributes of God? Why are we not creative in the greatest sense of being God? Why are we not aware of being one with the body and mind of God? Why are we limited to the five senses of the flesh?

The Master of Masters who was the greatest initiate of this second group of souls said, "That which is born of the flesh is flesh; and that which is born of the Spirit is Spirit. Ye must be born again." (John 3:6) You must be reborn into who you were in the beginning.

Essentially, these creatures that we are describing who were imprisoned in the flesh were creatures that were being held under the mark of the beast, as mentioned in scripture. (Revelation 20:4) They were trapped within the body of the beast, slaves to the five senses of the flesh. And we might ask ourselves where we are in relation to that? To what degree are we slaves of the senses, the appetites and the flesh in this day?

THE PURPOSE OF THE GREAT WHITE BROTHERHOOD

The Great White Brotherhood set as its purpose the reawakening of the consciousness of the sons of man, those entrapped and fallen. It was not an easy task. A son of man who was born of two other creatures was even more captured, or further removed from his original identity, than the parents.

Sometimes, the fascination with the gift of love rather than the lover was even too strong for the Elders of the Brotherhood. Some of those who deliberately projected themselves into matter to teach others became captured and fell themselves. If they became fascinated and lost sight of their original purpose, they experienced a loss of contact with who they really were and a sense of separation resulted. The Elders themselves would experience the "fall of man" by failing to remember who they were and eventually disregarding their true identity.

Those members of the Elder Brethren who remained stronger than the attraction gave their entire energies and communicating abilities to the evolution of those less fortunate who were captured in the bodies of plants and animals. They formed the Brotherhood and distinguished its purpose as the lifting of humanity's consciousness. To accomplish that purpose, they set up rituals, methods and teaching facilities to remind the younger ones of their true identities. In this way, they would make the deeper mysteries available over time, as the consciousness of humanity became receptive and could understand them. They would lead those less developed, one step at a time, toward an understanding of those mysteries.

The task of the Brotherhood was multifaceted – to give to less-evolved humankind as much knowledge and information as could be understood, to further humanity's development so that more might be understood, to stimulate curiosity, and to protect and preserve the greater teachings and keep them secret until humankind became able to receive them.

The Great White Brotherhood still exists in this day, and these continue to be its purposes.

ACCOMPLISHMENT OF THE TASK

How did the Elder Brethren attempt to accomplish these purposes initially? We are considering a time on earth when the sons of God wanted to create bodies for themselves. Imagine that all the expressions of God, who were the original son of God, appeared in physical bodies simultaneously on earth. This is how it might have occurred. The son of God appeared as five expressions at once, as five races, on five continents, and all five expressions were called Adam. The number five represents the five senses of the flesh.

Yes, there was also one individual called Adam. This is a both-and situation, not either-or. There was a real Adam, one individual comprising this host of the son of God. And the one also expressed as many and populated the entire earth.

This period can be called the Adamic Epoch because it is the time of the birth of Adam, or the birth of humanity on earth symbolized by Adam. During this Adamic Epoch, the Elder Brethren stood witness as the sparks of God became captured in physical bodies – animal-like, lesser creatures, mis-shapen, hairy, perhaps with feathers and claws. Edgar Cayce gave fascinating descriptions in his psychic readings of these creatures with feathers, claws, hooves, scales, etc.

Imagine the sons of God saying, "Let us take these pitiful, lost creatures and help them. Let us perform operations to correct their bodies. We are creators and can affect matter." Knowing themselves to be God, they could perfect the disfigurements. They could affect a physical change through their creative abilities. To this end, the sons of God established healing temples for the purpose of perfecting bodies, where the sons of men were changed from animal-like bodies to human-like bodies.

THE BIRTH OF SCRIPTURE

Eons later, a storyteller within the Hebrew community wanted to describe for his people what had occurred at the beginning of time. He wanted to use terms his listeners could understand. These early events would not be easy to describe to a primitive, nomadic people. The storyteller could have said, "These sons of God who were at an evolved level took the sons of man who were at an animal level and assisted in their evolution by recreating their bodies in ancient healing facilities known as the Temple Beautiful, the Temple of Sacrifice and the Temple of Initiation, originated through the efforts of the Brotherhood to assist those beings trapped in flesh." But who would have understood?

Instead, the storyteller probably said, "God created a body, called it Adam, and blew into it the breath of life. The individual became a living soul and realized himself as such." It is possible, one of many possibilities, that the account of creation found in the Book of Genesis is an attempt to describe what happened in the healing temples of ancient Atlantis and Egypt during the evolution of humanity, guided by the Elder Brethren.

The task was not easy. To perfect the physical body, it was necessary to reawaken the mind to its true nature and to reestablish an awareness and expression of God. The older brothers began to say to the younger ones, or the sons of God began to say to the sons of man, "Look, you are a creator. You can recreate your body. You created it in the first place. You can change it to perfection. Make that arm perfect. You don't need that claw. You can have hands."

Those captured in physical bodies tried to respond with words, but found that even if they could utter words, their words had no power. The spoken word had an effect only in its original and natural expression, which might be defined as truth without ego.

EXISTING IN THE VIBRATION OF GOD

There is one vibration or expression that is the attunement of God. We cannot name it or even describe it. The vibration of God is beyond words. Even the word vibration is inadequate but will serve us for the moment.

A creative word spoken on the precise vibration of God will have immediate and intense effect. The words will invoke exactly what was described, but only if they are spoken on the exact vibration of God. If we express God in its own frequency, pitch, rate of vibration, note, harmony, expression, essence – remember that the words are inadequate to accurately express – we have spoken with the voice of God. Whatever we command with the voice of God will occur, and it will occur immediately.

A similar phenomenon occurs when spontaneous spiritual healings take place, affecting and re-perfecting the physical body. In those moments, the command for healing, which can only be the prayer of the heart, was not spoken on a personal vibration of ego or out of the senses or the intellect. Instead, the healer reached the exact pitch, the exact attunement, the exact vibration of the thought, creativity and perfection of God. It requires that everything within the individual – intelligence, ego, personality, physical senses – come into harmony with what existed in the beginning, which is divine. Meaning that which has limitless power, absolute harmony and eternal duration.

It is possible that you or I could reach that precise space of attunement, exist there for a moment, and heal someone. Yet in the very speaking of the words, the command for healing, I would simultaneously pull myself slightly off target. Just by thinking, "Hey, it worked. I did it," I call attention to myself, and that pulls me back off the vibration that I had set up. The balance between the expression of God within me and the separation, the separate state, of saying, "I did it" is that delicate. I did not do it. If I spoke on the level, the vibration, the tone, the power, the essence of the voice of God, God did it. God within me, who is me, did it.

The Elder Brethren were challenged similarly as they attempted to say to humanity, "You can heal yourself. You can bring this body back into the vibration of God. You can be God because that is what you truly are." Invariably, the response of those in lesser forms was an expression of self, even as they attempted to express God. So the Elders said, "We must take a different approach to this. They cannot understand the words, so we must create ways for them to have these experiences through which they can learn."

What are the characteristics that separate God from humankind? What are the characteristics of God that are not found in man-apart-from-God? What are the attributes that separate animals from humans as they express God? That is what the Elders had to establish. These lesser forms were little more than animals. The fully realized beings knew that to awaken these animals meant to awaken the God-self within them. Not through concepts or words, but through personal experiences.

For example, if they could awaken a lesser being's ability to appreciate a sunset, they had awakened God in it, because animals will hardly notice a sunset's creativity and color and associate that with beauty. If a lesser animal-form noticed that beauty, the spark of God within it had begun to awaken, and it had begun to evolve to a higher nature.

This gave rise to the establishment of the Temple Beautiful. "Let us herd these poor unaware animals together and expose them to beauty, music, rhythm, dance, creativity – all the things that animals do not do, the things that humans expressing God do. If we can get them to appreciate beauty, they will have begun to express God. The next step will be to help them express love – love toward another and love and appreciation for their own physical bodies, through the experience of perfecting those bodies."

THE INFLUENCE OF THE BROTHERHOOD

This was the challenge set before the members of the Great White Brotherhood. The challenge has existed throughout time. Over the eons, they have used whatever methods necessary to reunite individuals with their true identity. They have influenced the history of humanity's existence on earth to affect its evolution.

The Brotherhood teaches not only through words expressed by its members while incarnate, but also by causing specific things to happen that symbolize the teachings. A virgin who gives birth to a master soul who becomes a great teacher has often been used as a symbol for the expression of the female God, and for the beginning of time when the sea of potential stirred with activity and brought forth a son of God.

In this way, the teachings of the Brotherhood are provided simultaneously by two means: directly through a master's words, and also through the historical events that symbolize higher principles while at the same time providing a living experience of the teaching. The entire life of Jesus Christ represents a teaching that lifts humanity closer to its true self. In this way, history itself becomes a handbook for the instruction of humanity's consciousness back to God through a series of steps or initiations.

These souls who make up the Great White Brotherhood have entered from time to time in physical bodies, as with Jesus Christ. Their students, the ones awakened in the healing temples of ancient Lemuria, Atlantis and Egypt, have also lived as leaders and saviors of particular races and cultures. Each of these great race-leaders taught at-one-ment. The Law of One – that all are one with God and that there is only one God – has been the message and the teaching of this Brotherhood throughout time.

THE CONSCIOUSNESS OF CHRIST

All great leaders who taught at-one-ment and the lifting of consciousness were expressions of the One. They knew themselves to be one with God. It can be said that they were all Christ, or they were all christed beings. A Christ is one who has lost his separated, individualized identity and expresses all that God is. It would be difficult to separate the incarnations of Christ as a particular individual evolving down through historical time, specifying particular lives in different places and times. All these expressions were not necessarily the incarnations of the same entity or personality-entity. They are, however, all expressions of the son of God, which we all were initially, and still are today.

There exists only one Christ consciousness. Many expressions of that consciousness have appeared throughout time in different places. The teaching has remained the same: the birth of the Christed son of God, which was and still is the original identity of each of us though most of us no longer remember it.

THE BROTHERHOOD'S PRESENCE ON EARTH

The purpose of the Great White Brotherhood has been to illustrate the Law of One, to show humankind that we are one, that we are not separate. Its members have entered throughout history and have brought understandings as yet unreached. Some have attempted to develop the concrete, thinking mind to the point that it could absorb the concepts of higher consciousness. Others came for the development of an understanding of astrology, humankind's relationship to the universe and the stars – the relationship of God revealing himself to humanity, the macrocosm revealing itself to the microcosm – through their movements and inter-relationships. Some have initiated brotherhoods of the arts, or what has been called the Schools of the Divine. Others have affected humanity through discoveries and developments in health, science and government. Others have appeared as great spiritual leaders bringing new understandings, which have too often become buried in dogma. Others have appeared as great philosophers, even political leaders.

Imagine that there are those walking among us today who at some point said, "I realize myself to be one with God. I have reached a point in my evolution where I know my true identity. It is as if I am walking on a beam of light, moving toward a shining city where I will be one with my Father. I have completed all that I need to do on this plane. As I look below the beam of light, down to the lower levels, I see what I was and where I have been. The creatures there are mis-shapen, with claws and fangs. They scrape and fight for survival among themselves. They tear at one another and destroy one another. They are oblivious to anything else. I look back at my beam of light, and I think, 'They should be here with me. They should be one with me.' So I tell my comrades who are walking with me toward the shining city, 'I can't go on without them. I'm going down to help them.' My comrades respond, 'Don't do it. Don't go down there. They will destroy you. The only way you can live among them and teach them is to take on their form and descend into their level.' I explain, 'But I must. I must descend there.' And the brothers say, 'They will destroy you. They have always destroyed anyone who descended to their plane. They have pulled them apart with their claws and fangs. Look at what they have done to the pure and good throughout time. They will do the same to you.' And I say, 'I must go. I cannot go on without bringing these others, because they are the same as I am. We are one.' So my comrades on the path say, 'Then we will protect you. We will overshadow you. At any point that you decide to withdraw, we will protect you and bring you back.'" A pact is made.

The Brotherhood overshadows the one who descends. That one descends into a grotesque, ugly world because it is the creation of that that separated itself from God. Earth became a point of reference and a symbol for that separation. It became the opposite of God, to give a point of reference for what God is. It was the gift created by God so that the son of God might know and choose his true identity, which is the nature of God. Earth is simply a line of demarcation so that we may discover what God is. That is its purpose.

That one descends and walks among men while still maintaining contact and communication with the Elder Brethren. In that way, he serves as a channel for the teachings of the Brotherhood. Upon entering earth, he may not know that he is a channel nor have any memory of the Brotherhood. He may simply be one who brings messages, as Edgar Cayce did. Or he may be one who introduces a concept or enables a discovery, without even knowing that it came from a spiritual force. He expresses what he is and the creativity that is within. Thus the world receives the gift of that he has brought from the level of the Great White Brotherhood. If he does not know himself to be of the Brotherhood while providing these teachings on this plane, that realization will come to him as he re-ascends – unless his treasure has been found here on earth and again the gift has become more fascinating than the giver. That possibility always exists.

We begin to understand that the Brotherhood is far greater than a fraternity formed on this earth. The movements of the stars in their paths are affected by its influence. Yet the importance of its scope should not take away from its personal nature. As this consciousness generates influences that affect humanity as a whole, simultaneously it affects the individual mind of each person on earth.

Chapters of the Brotherhood exist on earth today and are available for study and for relationships. The Brotherhood is not a visible body, labeled as such. Groups that claim to be the Great White Brotherhood are not necessarily the result of that work. Essentially, you can recognize that a group is being influenced by the Brotherhood when the focus and central purpose of its work is the lifting of humanity's consciousness back to at-one-ment with God. In such a group, the members will not teach or advocate separation, differentiation, hierarchies, etc. Teaching at-one-ment with God is an explicit stamp of the Great White Brotherhood. In addition, all who teach that concept, whether as individuals or within groups, are being influenced by the Brotherhood even if they do not know it.

In considering the work of the Brotherhood on earth today, it is helpful to look at a book written in the first half of the 20th century by Dion Fortune, called *The Esoteric Orders and Their Work*. In an introductory essay called, "The Work of the Inner Plane Adepti," Gareth Knight explains, "A Fraternity is founded by one of the Inner Plane Adepti, or Masters, as they are often called. It is a very difficult process, for the Master is on the inner planes and has to make contact with someone on the physical plane in order to found a physical group. Thus this person on the physical plane needs a fair degree of developed psychism in order to contact the Master readily, plus a strong personality able to overcome all the practical difficulties of starting a society, and also must be a comparatively advanced person esoterically. There are a few people who have all three of these qualifications. There are many dominant personalities about, quite a large number of psychics, and a fair sprinkling of spiritually advanced people; but the combination in any one person is rare because psychism goes almost invariably hand in hand with a sensitive temperament which cannot cope readily with all the administration and finance involved in starting a group from scratch." The scarcity of such leaders is why more chapters of the Brotherhood do not exist.

Knight further says, "In this way a group or society is established which trains students to become contacted individuals of the inner Fraternity. The Order behind the Fraternity was there all along in the Master who started the group initially. There are various inner plane Orders but it would be of little point to give their names as the little that can be said would only lead to fruitless speculation – and all Orders anyway are aspects of the One Order, that of the Hierarchy of Master or the Great White Lodge."

THE CHALLENGE IN TODAY'S WORLD

Throughout time, the message has always been available and accessible. It will remain so for anyone who is willing to turn within to discover a relationship with his true source, to recognize himself as a spark of God, to know that he has become encased in flesh while remembering that it is not his true nature. That person will be drawn to the true teachings of God in a form that God will provide.

On the other hand, it is typical of the nature of humankind to seek drama. We want phenomena. We want visions of God as we close our eyes. We want lights and colors and voices. And we want a direct link without an earthly intermediary.

God chooses and sets among us channels, psychics, prophets, ministers, teachers and leaders as the contact point for that Great Cloud of Witnesses. But we tend to dismiss the messenger and thus the message, choosing instead our own avenues of listening. It is true that every individual can find that link within himself to talk with God and hear God speaking directly to his heart. But the individual who has truly found God within himself will also recognize God in others.

When one has been chosen as the leader of a group for the establishment of a society of the Brotherhood, individuals who are of like faith and vision and are of the same nature and following the same path will be drawn to that leader and to that group. They will recognize a spark of God in that group. That recognition will grow into a compelling desire, even an obligation, to serve the group and its particular work. This feeling arises because God has established his work in that way since the beginning of time, setting a leader among people who is a magnetic focal point. This method is effective because it is certain to bring the people together as one, and lessons are learned through the experience of participating in a group – the group dynamic of working together, the humility of serving another, and the assimilation of the Law of One by becoming one with others in common purpose and common cause.

When an individual steps onto the path, he chooses an area of spiritual work or study in which he can invest his time, energy, dedication and money. If that work is not connected to a group or to the support of someone, it should be suspect because it demonstrates separation and individualism that oppose the Law of One.

We are not discussing good or bad here. We are acknowledging the expression of Oneness as opposed to its opposite. The individual who steps onto the spiritual path will quickly be faced with a fork in the road. The Path of Oneness is not one of isolation and individualism but of many, and it will be connected with the support of others through associations with groups.

TWO POWERS EXIST

There are two powers in this world. Whether we like it or not, there is a dichotomy of power. We often deny the dichotomy by asserting that there is really only good in the world, as if we can focus on good and all else will fall away as a result. But the dichotomy definitely exists.

To recognize good, most individuals need evil as a point of reference. A fully realized being is one who can recognize good without the presence of evil. As long as individuals still believe in their own separation from their source, they will continue to experience evil in order to recognize good. Thus there is the opposite power acting as an adversary to work against us as we step onto the spiritual path.

But what form does that opposite power take? Where is the evil that would work against us? It could be the family members and friends who say, "I don't believe in psychics. I don't believe in past lives. I don't believe in communication with dead people. You're crazy to believe in that stuff." Or perhaps it is the people who make fun of us or even persecute us. No, that line of demarcation is so obvious that those people are no threat at all. Then where is the threat?

The threat comes from within. Typically, an individual is drawn to a teacher. The teacher says, "There is available to you a point within you where you can hear the words of God if you become quiet and still enough to listen." The eager student begins immediately to ferret out that still place. Nothing is more important to him. He trains himself to shut off the outside world and listen within. Eventually, he hears a voice. He is so excited that he neglects to investigate the source of the voice. He forgets to try the spirits by examining the way they work and the way they lead. Invariably, the first voice says to the neophyte, "Your teacher has an ego problem. You don't need to follow him. You don't need to work in his group. He is building a group centered on himself. What you need is to be a free agent. You don't need to associate with any group. You just need to work back and forth between groups without serving anybody in particular, just God." It is the message of individualism, which is the message of separation.

The true voice of spirit will bring us into association with other people, in groups that can effectively carry on the work. Being a supportive member of one group does not require avoiding other groups. There are many systems within the body of God that serve different purposes. There are many groups that serve the purpose of God on earth. These groups are set apart for the work that they are to do, and they have identity and personality as the systems, the organs, the mechanisms in the body of God.

If individuals are of the same master and share the same purpose, they will likely mesh and mingle and work side-by-side in harmony. Or they may be totally separate, never crossing paths.

The work of the heart is totally separate from the work of the lungs, yet the cleansing power of the lungs is necessary to keep the heart functioning properly. And both the lungs and the heart are necessary for the purification of the blood to support the brain and its activities. No system can work independently of another.

Beware if you discover a voice within that guides you to say, "I don't need your messages. I don't need your teachers. I don't need your systems. I don't need your group because I have found my own source. I don't need to listen to you as a source any longer." It is a dangerous message for the beginning student. We all go through it. Eventually, we outgrow it, saving ourselves lifetimes.

If you discovered a group that caused something to awaken within you, it is that group that got you started on the spiritual path. If you quickly outgrew it and no longer needed the group, or its people, or its leader, and now you hope that someday they can catch up with your progress, beware.

The truth is that you owe that group a great deal. If that group helped get you started on the path, it is time for you to go back and take a second look at the group's present needs. If you have not helped to meet those needs, you have created an imbalance. You may argue that the group served to awaken you and that was all it was supposed to do. You outgrew them quickly, and your meditations have been your real teacher. Consider this: If they forged the link that opened you to the God that dwells within you, you owe them a debt of gratitude for life because they gave you life.

When such a link is forged, what does the Brotherhood do? What is their work in this day? What is the work of the Great White Lodge?

THE MECHANICS OF THE BROTHERHOOD

Remember that any attempt to describe these beings or how they originated is a metaphor. It is an attempt to describe what cannot be described, or even comprehended.

Consider that there were worlds before this world. There were cycles of evolution before our root race began. There were beings that lived and evolved on this earth and in a sense preceded this earth, as we know it now. Those who evolved beyond this earth were like realized-gods. As our root race began, they were among us as those whom the Bible speaks of as men without beginning or ending of days, without father and mother. (Hebrews 7:3) They manifested among us because they had mastered the laws of the plane. They implanted teachings in the early race, in its silent stone monuments, and then disappeared. Occasionally throughout history, one has returned to lift the race a little closer to the Godhead. But the body of these has remained on inner planes.

Now this great body has no location or place. It is beyond time and space. However, smaller groups or concentrations called Star Lodges do exist on this plane. The Star Lodges exist in various places where a channel has developed and focused the work.

This Brotherhood of Lodges is second down from the Great White Brotherhood itself. Star Lodges are guided by beings that have passed on from this earth and are servants on the other side, but they are not masters. These are servants on the other side who attempt to correlate the work here. They are drawn close as we develop inwardly.

When individuals develop the kind of sensitivity that would allow them to channel, they produce a light that is like a glow seen from inner planes. That light bears a mark that is the mark of the individual's master. That individual has given up free will and said, "I accept this master as lord and ruler, decision-maker in my life." Many traditional, exoteric churches have called this valid experience "salvation," being "born again," the "conversion experience."

At that moment of transformation and dedication when a person says, "I don't want to be ruled by my conscious, programmed self, my lesser self, anymore. I accept the teachings of my Master. He is lord and ruler of my life," an allegiance to that master is formed. The resulting glow, produced by the student and visible from inner planes, is the glow or color of that master.

When a Star Lodge is established, a communicant from the Brotherhood of Lodges is attracted to the channel. As often as the channel opens up to that communicant in meditation, prayer, a trance reading or any form of altered state, the words that come are the words of that mystic Brotherhood. If a channel or a psychic has once channeled a message from the Great White Brotherhood, it does not conclude that every message in the future will be from the Brotherhood. As the channel becomes sensitive and prepares to open up, the intent and centering must be directed toward God. If so, the individual may totally lose consciousness of self and become a pure channel for the work of the Christ, which is the original son of God that we all comprised in the beginning. Whether the words come from the Great White Brotherhood is immaterial. If the channel opens to God, the message will be of God. If the message comes through the Great Brotherhood, it will be because its members are the servants of the Master of Masters, the Christ, the Father, God.

If the message identifies itself as from the Brotherhood, consider it suspect. When someone says, "This is the Great White Brotherhood channeling through me," he is attempting to give importance to the message to serve his own ego. Remember that if the message is valid, it will stand on its own merit and will not need recognizable or exotic-sounding names attached for credibility. The Great White Brotherhood will not attract attention to itself. It is only a service body for the consciousness of Christ and does not need to identify itself.

The practicality of the application is in realizing that there are those who have grown beyond this life experience and that we can attune ourselves to their message, remembering that it is a service arm of the Christ and not to be worshiped. It is important to serve God without becoming distracted by an awareness of the Brotherhood. Knowledge of their work serves to make our experiences understandable so that our personal journey is more easily understood and accomplished.

PERSONAL RESPONSIBILITY

It is important that we individually open ourselves to a work of service by finding what we can do for and with others who are doing the same. Find others who are doing a building work, a service work of the Christ, and be of service to them. Do whatever you can to build that work and reach the people who need that message.

The channel or leader of that group has been presented with a difficult task. That person has accepted the job of building an organization. Others may be critical, saying, "I would work with you because I want to serve God, but I'm not going to because your ego gets in the way of everything. Someone needs to keep your ego in check." See how the task of the leader becomes doubly difficult? The purpose of the members of the group is to share in the work. God's task is to worry about his channels' egos.

The expression, "Two heads are better than one," was never truer than in the service of God. There is no other way to be of service to God. Remember what Jesus said: "In as much as ye have done it unto one of the least of these my brethren, ye have done it unto me." (Matthew 25:40) You cannot serve God directly, but you can serve indirectly by working side-by-side with those people who are serving God's work on this earth.

God's work is about teamwork, togetherness, family. And it is accomplished in groups and through organizations.

The best way to assess a group is through its work, by what it accomplishes and what it awakens in people. No one should give blind devotion to any group or organization. Instead, devote yourself to the higher ideal that the group serves. There are many groups whose members receive mystical influences and reveal them, but your service should always be to the purpose and the ideal of the group rather than to its members.

God's work is always conducted by someone incarnate on this plane, not a master. The masters are never incarnate on this plane. They are on inner planes. Anyone who claims to be a master, whether on this plane or inner planes, is not.

The channels, the servants, the workers that channel the masters, are on this plane. Not because of what they know, but because they have become a receptive vehicle. They are motivated, energetic people. They can get the work done, organizationally, or as a psychic channel, or as a teacher. They have some talent that the inner planes have found useful, and therefore an organization has built up around them. It is the work of a group guided by a master. It is not the work of one person.

Moving from one group to another as an individual, without being loyal to anyone, is a waste of energy. Remember that you cannot honor God without honoring the channels sent. There are people whom God has selected and set apart, and their ability has been revealed and proven. If you have seen them at work and can identify the work as that of God, the fact that you are aware of it indicates that it is your direction. It is a calling of God to you to work with them. So find the task that you can do best and be of service.

Make sure there is a balance. Do not take what you can draw from that channel or that group without giving in return. Certainly do not take from that group saying, "You've got something good. I'll take it and make my own thing out of it. Then I'll go here and there and teach it my way." Always remember the allegiance you have established and give back more than you have received.

The Great White Brotherhood works on inner planes, and it can take you there and teach you as you sleep. However, if you decide that you do not need the groups that the Brotherhood has established on the outer plane, you will stop its work in your life, and whatever you are doing on your own will fall flat on its face. Test it and see.

Try the spirits. "Believe not every spirit, but try the spirits whether they are of God, because many false prophets are gone out into the world." (I John 4:1) Discover the Brotherhood's secret presence in your personal world. Know who they are and where they are applying influence in the world by the work that they do. When you find them at work, get behind them and do all you can to share in that effort.

It is every individual's certain destiny to grow in the knowledge of his true nature and to rediscover his source and origin. The Great White Brotherhood was born of a purpose linked closely with that destiny. And in time, the Brotherhood and all humankind will succeed as One.

WITHIN ONE STEP OF ENLIGHTENMENT
FROM THE PAUL SOLOMON SOURCE

*T*here are few, in any given generation of humankind, who are prepared for perfect enlightenment. This is not meant to suggest that perfect enlightenment is difficult or impossible. *We rather comment that the self of self, what you would call the soul, is in fact perfectly enlightened. The one who is the Christ is alive within you. We refer not to a historical man of 2,000 years ago – rather that the child born of God is alive, is here, and is within you.*

The veil of separation between the perfect soul of your enlightenment is only a cloud of unknowing. The separation from perfect enlightenment is a veil so thin, so fragile, that in moments of perfect asking – without wanting, without wishing, in moments of willingness to be as enlightened as you truly are, by nature – that contact with knowing can come.

The perfectly enlightened one is one who knows love without fear, one who is Christ-conscious, one who is God-conscious. One who lives with the consciousness of God is simply one who has attained the ability to recognize good without evil as a point of reference. This is one who can experience and express perfect love that casts out fear. A Christed or enlightened being is one who experiences absolutely no fear, who can live without the expression of fear in the heart, the mind, the life.

Perfect love without fear is the way of life of one who is joined with God and has no concern for whether he was enlightened one moment ago or whether he will be enlightened one moment from now. In this present moment, he knows, "I Am God. I am no one else. And any voice from within me that expresses separation from God is a creative voice of imagination, a false voice. It is a voice of fear. It is a voice of doubt. It is the voice of the veil."

There has never been a time when you were not. You have existed as a soul from the dawn of the consciousness of God, when God breathed the first breath and from that breath came the universes. In that first breath of God, you breathed as well.

There are souls who yearn for at-one-ment with the Father. There are also souls who yearn to experience and express themselves as independent individuals, separate from God. Those souls who are prepared for the experience of enlightenment are those souls who no longer fear loss of individual identity. If one is afraid that losing identity of self, that merging with God, will cause him to lose consciousness of self, this fear will keep him separate from God. It was expressed by the Master Jesus in this manner, for he said, "He that findeth his life shall lose it, and he that loseth his life for my sake, shall find it." He who sets life aside for the sake of being one with God will gain his life.

If you are willing to be perfectly God, without being self-separate-from-God, you can be enlightened. That is the experience of enlightenment – to know self to be only God, and not man, nor self, nor separate. Who you are is God projecting himself into this world through a body. You are not the body. You have a body for the expression of God in the world. You are not your personality. You have a personality as an instrument to express God in the world. But if you are afraid of the loss of that body or that personality, if you are afraid of not being you, that fear will maintain the veil of separation between who you are as God and who you have believed yourself to be as separate from God.

You already know these things. We have said little in these moments that you do not already know. Yet we have said them for a purpose. Giving voice again to these words, these ideas, these thoughts, these teachings, sets a vibration in motion again which creates a vehicle for the consciousness to realize that which the soul knows. We create a sound, as a vehicle, for the soul to express what it knows. The simple repetition of these words, heard again and again, can become a vibration and vehicle for self-realization. Just as a chant can become a vehicle and vibration through which the voice of God, the essence of God, can be given vibratory life in this space, so every word becomes a mantra for touching the consciousness of God.

Many among you long for particular places and times because in your soul memory you remember particular times of closeness when you had the opportunity to be near those who walked with God. Some among you had personal contact with the souls who manifested as Jesus and as the Buddha, at a particular moment, in a land you now refer to as Egypt. You would recognize the names differently, for he who became the Buddha was known in that time as Enoch. He who became Jesus the Christ was known in that time as Hermes. These were, in this early day, teachers from an older world. They were called the Manu – those who brought light from a previous world into this age, old souls who came again in this particular time of history. They have appeared here and there among you over time.

It could be said of them that they are not human. These are souls who project themselves into a body to remind those evolving beings who are human of the fact that they can be released from humanity – that they are God projecting himself into matter, rather than man attempting to be God.

The greatest disservice done to these great souls who were teachers is that men have chosen to worship them rather than emulate them. Repeatedly, humankind has had the opportunity to see a pure, realized soul, and with a sense of reverence, he has said, "I will honor that soul. But I know I could never reach to such height. It would be presumptuous of me to think I could be such a realized soul." In your humility, you attempt to elevate the enlightened ones, while denying that same light that exists within yourself. This does not honor the enlightened being.

If the holy presence of an enlightened being causes you to feel unworthy or causes you to think, "I am human. I am not, and cannot be, divine," the divine one has affirmed your belief in lack. The wish of the enlightened one is to provide a light, an example, a hope. By affirming your belief in lack, he has done the opposite, reinforcing the negative, which is the separation. His true message is that you can step beyond the separation and be the Buddha, the Christ, the enlightened expression of God in the world.

You have come to a time when many see the essence of truth that is found in the mysteries of Buddhism and in the teachings of Christ, without experiencing the walls of separation that say, "This is Yoga, this is Christianity, this is Buddhism, this is Tantra, and these things are separate and different." Jesus the Master did not teach that Christianity is something other than Buddhism. Enlightenment is enlightenment. Truth is truth. There is not one truth for Christians, and another for Buddhists, and another for Muslims.

It is to your credit that you can point out the pearl of each great religion without communicating that it is separate, different, in disagreement with, or somehow better than, the truth spoken in other forms. Because you recognize truth without walls, you are just a single step from perfectly realizing and perfectly remembering who you are.

So many who were present in that ancient day are meeting again in these last days of this era. You stand right now at a precipice. You stand at a moment in history when this planet, this mother upon which you live, has been so scarred and abused that it is as if the soul of this great mother has been made sick and must erupt to shake off the abuse, so that it may be made new.

This precipice, this critical moment in time, may be experienced as a great cataclysm. It has happened before in history, or prehistory. This earth was in essence destroyed in that time. There was an age during which man, as you know humankind, no longer lived on this planet. And so, she was renewed, and a garden grew in Eden. That was the dawn of this age. That was the time when these great teachers came and attempted to teach responsibility for this earth.

Now you are at the brink of a new age. As you attain enlightenment, you express a desire to give to the world a gift as great as that given by the Buddha and by the Christ. The gift that must be given is the message that says, "Live in natural, perfect harmony with the laws of this earth, or you will destroy this earth and yourselves with it." Not with a voice that will bring fear to the people of the earth, but precisely the opposite. It is the learning of the Law of Love without fear that brings salvation.

One who lives in perfect love without a moment of fear does not believe that the environment must be manipulated to force it to provide what is needed for life. The technology of modern science asserts that man must de-nature and destroy the plants and the resources of earth in order to force it to provide energy for life. Such practice disavows that everything that is needed to sustain life on this earth is quite naturally present in the environment around you and is provided by God. One who knows God knows the abundance of life and knows that it is not necessary to force nature to be de-natured, that it is not necessary to create unnatural conditions to force the earth to provide for humankind. All such technology is fear-based, meaning that it is born of a fear that God will not provide.

There is a handful of people coming together to re-establish the understanding of the Law of One. So there is created in this time a unique opportunity for those who have brought themselves within one step of enlightenment to step across that line. A handful of enlightened beings on this earth can save this earth from destruction. It will take a miracle, but miracles are available.

THE PARABLE OF THE DIVINE LOVER

When all your other lovers have lost their power over you, you will no longer be captured in the divine lover's gift.

Before there was matter, before the actuality of time and space, there existed only the expression of a great love. There was no world, no universe, no being, no experience, no intention or urge. There was nothing beyond the silent, motionless expression of great love.

This expression was without beginning or end, measure or limitation. It was the divine creator. It could express anything, create anything, possess anything, but was without need, will or endeavor. No want or wish – only the peace of infinite stillness.

Yet there came a point when this great love roused from its eternal haven and resolved to know one thing. It stirred to experience a recipient for its love. This great love was infinite and permeated all, however no object received and returned its love. There was no sanction of its love.

So this divine creator caused for itself a bride with whom it could share love. It reached inside its bosom, and from beneath a rib, took the bottom of its own heart, the tenderest and most sacred part, and it fashioned a partner.

The divine creator gazed upon his creation and knew her to be a perfect expression. He embraced her, he encompassed her, he shared with her his essence, and then awaited her response. She inhaled his spirit and made it her own, being in the nature of him. Compelled, she returned his love.

Were there time or measurement, eons might have passed until, observing his bride, the divine creator reflected, "I have chosen her. I have fashioned her as I pleased. Yet because she had no choice, she has not chosen me in return. She returns my love because she *is* love, and can do nothing else. She loves me because there is no alternative. Would she love me if there were something else to love?

"For her love to be actual, it must be the effect of choice. She must choose me in preference to something that appears equally appealing. Only then will her love be authentic and complete."

For the divine lover's bride to love him by choice, there had to be an alternative. The alternative had to be attractive. The choice must be real, unfeigned. There must be an exciting alternative lover, someone she might truly consider. The choice must be between a great, deep love on one hand, and attractive appeal on the other.

So the divine lover fashioned a universe. He spangled the night with the moon and the stars. He lit the sun and set it blazing in the heavens. He fashioned a world that was beautiful and fascinating.

He created the earth as a gift for his bride, and the morning stars sang together in celebration. Certain that his gift was perfect, the divine lover presented it to his bride. She now had an alternative.

The earth was attractive, appealing, fascinating. The bride gazed upon it and became intrigued. "How wonderful," she exclaimed. She was dazzled by its beauty. She was thrilled by its excitement. Fame and fortune, appetite and pleasure had been fashioned especially for her to enjoy. She was enraptured, captivated. The divine lover gazed upon her delight and remained motionless, emotionless.

The bride wanted to hold her new gift and reached out to touch it. She could taste its delicious flavors and hear its wondrous sounds. Eventually, she entered it, wandering among its marvels. The divine lover observed as she savored his creation, his serenity still immovable. She continued to explore, fascinated and excited, relishing each new discovery.

"Are you pleased?" he asked, at last.

There was no answer. His bride was not listening – she could not hear him. She was engaged with the gift. She became intoxicated as she felt it, tasted it and experienced it. She saw that it was good and ate insatiably from it. And her eyes were opened.

Over time, she became lost in the earth, and she no longer remembered the divine lover. She perceived only the tangible, palpable conditions and circumstances that surrounded her.

A bond was formed, and her new identity became her encounter. She forgot who she had been. She knew only the gift. Once only captivated, she had become a captive.

Fame and fortune, success and power, appetite and pleasure were the creations of the divine lover, his labor to create an alternative choice. They now came to life as handsome suitors for the new bride.

They took shape and kissed her hand. She was amused. They made proposals and promises. She was enthralled.

She chose popularity as her first suitor. His allure was provocative, and she was seduced by his assurances of satisfaction and fulfillment. But popularity was a callous and fickle flame. They made love, and she bore his children – jealousy, possessiveness, depression and helplessness. The more she served popularity, the more demanding he became, and the more dependent she grew. She became a slave to his vile deceit.

Desperate, she chased after money. She worked hard to win his heart. He teased her and beguiled her. She worked for him, and he allowed her existence. She owed him her life, and he imprisoned her. She was a bond slave.

She courted power and ego, and found neither satisfaction nor fulfillment. She chased after sex and pleasure, sensuality and passion. Moving from one cheapened affair to another, she lost self-respect. She felt undeserving and worthless.

Eons passed, and she grew old and tired. Honor was gone, integrity lost. She was an adulteress and a mistress to many. The handsome suitors had only pretended love. They were thugs who betrayed her and pirated her sanctity.

Where once she had been a likeness of her creator, an expression of great love with capacity to enliven all – now she could love none, not even herself.

Far back in the hollow of her remembrance was the shrouded vision of a great and noble ruler, a wise and selfless lover. But she believed it only an apparition, because such purity could not possibly exist alongside the pain and desolation of this world.

Exhausted and full of sorrow, she lay down and cried. She called out for an end to it all. As she hovered near deep sleep, she dreamed.

She dreamed of a prince who was powerful and loving. He owned the cattle on a thousand hills. The fowls of the mountains, the wild beasts of the field, and every beast of the forest were his. The world was his and everything in it. He had once proposed marriage to her, and she was to be his bride.

"I am the rose of Sharon, and the lily of the valleys... I sat down under his shadow with great delight, and his fruit was sweet to my taste. He brought me to the banqueting house, and his banner over me was love." (Song of Solomon 2:1-6)

With his right hand he had embraced her, as his left hand held her aloft. Yet she had declined his devotions and gone in search of other lovers, abandoning the sanctuary of his divine love.

Was it only a dream, or was it reality? Had it happened in another place, in another time? Could she possibly find him again? Would he take her back?

By night upon her bed, she sought him whom her soul loved. Unable to find him there, she wandered the darkened streets in search of him, looking for a face she could almost remember. She asked the watchmen that went about the city, "Have you seen him whom my soul loveth?" She described him in detail. He was fair as the moon, clear as the sun, altogether lovely. She sought him, but could not find him. She called him, but he gave no answer.

Pain and yearning marked time upon time – until at last the divine lover appeared before her. She gazed upon his face and cried out to the heavens, "It is he! He is the one whom my soul loves and for whom my heart yearns."

In that instant, she remembered all. She recalled a time before life – when she existed as the most sacred portion of his heart.

But now she felt dirty and used, hopeless and unworthy. How could he still love her?

She fell to the ground before him. Her tears fell on his feet, and she wiped them with her hair and kissed them. She used her last precious earthly possession, an alabaster jar of ointment, to soothe and cool his skin.

At last she dared to speak, "Once I was fair and young. Men sought after me, but I made the wrong choices, took the wrong lovers. Over time, I forgot your face. Now I'm old and used, and you could not want me, not as a lover nor a companion. Won't you take me sir to work in your household? Is there nothing I could do to make it easier for you? I want only to serve you, to serve who you are. I'll give you my life. I'm not expecting to be your bride, only hoping to serve. Will you have me? I'm not afraid anymore. I'll do all I can for you. Is there nothing I could do to make it easier for you?"

In that moment, squandered eons fell away, as if never lived. Spent lovers ceased to exist. Fame and fortune, success and power, appetite and pleasure vanished like vapors in a mist. She was emptied of adulterous affairs – a chaste vacuum, receptive.

"Rise up, my love, my fair one, and come away," spoke the divine lover. "For lo, the winter is past, the rain is over and gone."

She rose from the dust where she had lain at his feet. Bliss purged her as he took her in his arms. Again, she inhaled his spirit, being in the nature of him.

In time, she yielded to sleep and rested, silent and motionless. When she woke in the darkness, an angel stood before her. She felt young and pure, virtuous and virginal. The harlot was a far-off dream.

"Fear not," said the angel. "I am the illuminator. I have come to kindle in consciousness your true identity, to remind you of who you are. You are the bride of God who loves you and would have a child with you. And the child will be new life – the perfect expression through you of your original divine creator."

Throughout time, there has been only one story. It is told in many different forms, in many languages and cultures, using many names and likenesses.

It is the story of the soul's journey through physical incarnation, back to its creator. The incarnation process of the God-force, realizing itself through matter.

It is a story of personal relevancy. Wherever told, in whatever form or language, it is a story about *you*.

Whether you are a man or a woman, your soul expresses a female quality in relation to its source. You are yin to your creator's yang. You are receptive potential, while your creator is active force.

This story is about you because you are God's lover and you have fallen into an adulterous affair with the material world in which you live. You have chased after fame and fortune, power and success, pleasure and sensuality. You have born the children of sadness and disappointment, and they haunt you. You were seduced by alternate lovers, and you became captured in the gift. You are, at this very moment, engaged in an adulterous love affair, and you are its captive.

In the Book of Genesis, the soul is first described as Eve, the one who rebelliously falls to temptation in spite of the warnings provided. She is later described as a harlot and a sinful woman, Mary Magdalene. She is caught up in adulterous love affairs and loses self-respect. When confronted by the sight of the divine lover, she feels unworthy. She falls to her knees and begs to be the servant. Elsewhere, she is described as the virginal Mary and receives new life, which is the expression through her of her original lover. Lastly, she evolves into the queen of heaven, clothed with the sun, with the moon under her feet and a crown of twelve stars.

That is the complete story of your own spiritual journey. It is recorded to help you recognize your true identity. You represent potential. You have a womb, a receptive place inside you that can be impregnated by a divine presence. It can be filled with new life.

The Bible was not meant as a simple historical tale. Its metaphors form a carefully constructed roadmap for your spiritual growth. It should be considered personally, as if you had dreamed the story and its events portray personal meaning for you specifically. Look at the events and characters and discern what they symbolize for you.

In the dream, you appear as Mary, an innocent young girl. Then an angel emerges. What does that mean? Imagine that you have been struggling against life, and life appears to be winning because you are beaten, helpless and hopeless. Nothing is working anymore. One day, you drop the struggle and say, "I just don't know how to make it all work, where to go from here." In that moment, you become empty, like a vulnerable young girl. In that state, any new possibility, any new idea that appears, can impregnate you. You are vulnerable, receptive and open to anything different.

Mary comes from the word, Mara, meaning bitter waters. "Out of my dark night of bitterness, hurt and pain, I come to a point of being vulnerable. I am empty of ideas and solutions. I realize that I don't have the answers. I'm open to another type of answer, something from outside myself."

Suddenly, a light appears – it might be an angel, a messenger, an idea, an answer, a solution, a spark of truth. In the story, it is called Gabriel. Gabriel says to you, "Don't be afraid. I've come to tell you that something fantastic is about to happen. I've come to tell you that you are fortunate and blessed!"

Life has not worked out well. You are empty and used up, out of answers. A messenger appears and says, "Here's a new idea. God is going to plant a new life in your being, and you are to call that new life, Emmanuel, which means *God is right here inside me* – no longer living in some far-away place, unreachable and unknowable. You will give birth to new life, and it will conquer the enemies that surround you. New life will be crowned king. This king will establish a kingdom in your life. It will be called heaven, and you will live in that place. This king will gather around him the twelve powers of life, the twelve abilities, the twelve lessons, the twelve challenges, the twelve principles. And he will teach them. They will become his servants. Your talents and abilities, your mind, your personality, your physical expression, will become his servants. He will guide and transform them from students and disciples into Apostles – emulators of the things that he can be, expressions of the things that he can do. They will become active in your life. They will become cause-factors in your life. Your life will be transformed."

As the servants are mastered, the soul becomes the queen of heaven. She wears a crown of twelve stars, one for each of the schools of life. She has overcome the lessons of earth and is crowned by the challenges that she has mastered. She is wrapped in a robe of light, and the earth has become her footstool. Her robe is a wedding dress of light as she embarks to meet her groom.

In this moment, as you are reading this, I am Gabriel, and you are Mary. Whether you are a man or a woman, your soul represents the female qualities of receptivity and potential. I am here to tell you that the divine lover made you and is deeply, joyously, crazy in love with you.

You have chased after alternate lovers and born their children. But the great love out of which everything was created is still in love with you, still cares about everything that happens to you, still resides within you, still waits.

When all your other lovers have lost their power over you, you will no longer be captured in the divine lover's gift. You will be free to choose to live according to your true nature. You will find yourself empty and pure – a virgin. The divine lover will impregnate you with himself. Your heart is the womb where his expression will be incubated, your soul is the cradle to nurture supreme love. And you will give birth to a son called new life – an active expression of great love on earth.

Hail, Mary! Know who you are.

PREPARATION FOR EARTH CHANGES

*Any law that we can see reflected in the material is just that:
a reflection of a spiritual law.*

Concerning what has been commonly termed *earth changes*, the Source has repeatedly said, "You do not need prophets to predict and foresee the future. You only need to study history, which is your most precise prophet, because your history has repeated itself again, and again, and again."

Throughout history, as there have been periods of extreme prosperity, they have consequently been followed by periods of extreme famine. As the pendulum swung to one extreme, it eventually swung correspondingly to the opposite extreme. As humankind experiences one extreme, it can expect with assurance that the other extreme will follow.

In our lifetime, in the western world, we have experienced one of the greatest extremes of prosperity that the world has ever known. The opposite must come as well. Even those who do not believe in prophets and psychics can recognize the inevitability through the demonstration of the fact that we live in a world of opposites and opposing forces. This polarity determines that we must experience the opposite of those things we have experienced.

The greatest prophecy is to be seen in what is going on around us this very moment. Intelligent individuals, observing what is happening in today's world, should be making preparations for the inevitable movement of the pendulum in the opposite direction.

Polarities in our time have created a separation between science and spirit. We have lost sight of the reflection of polarity, or the other side of the Hermetic law, which says that where there are two ends, the same thing exists between them. We cannot simply relate to the

253

extreme ends of something. We must also know the synthesis that joins them as one.

There must be a marriage of science and spirit. We must realize that we cannot put spiritual life on one side and material life on another side and create a separation between the two. Spiritual life is only spiritual when it is married to the material.

It is not simply a matter of choosing between the scientists who are looking at the laws of this physical plane and the psychics who are looking at the laws of spirit, in order to understand earth changes. It is a matter of listening to those who bring a marriage of the two. It is a matter of understanding that any law that we can see reflected in the material is just that: a reflection of a spiritual law. And it is absolutely impossible that they could disagree. That which the scientist finds through his proper recognition of material law must be a reflection of a spiritual law.

THE VOICE OF INNER NATURE

What practical action can you take from this? Anything that seems foreign to your inner nature, if you are opening honestly to your inner nature and looking for truth, is not appropriate action for you. That means that some people will react to talk of earth changes by moving to the mountains. Others will remain in the thick of urban life. Some people will become a part of a community by separating themselves from the world. Others will be guided to a different choice.

Long before the birth of Jesus, there were individuals known as the Essenes living in Jerusalem, Nazareth and Galilee. As they grew less in accord with the world of their time, they said, "I cannot practice all that I need to practice for total attunement in this environment. I need to withdraw from this busy community. What is happening in the marketplace in Jerusalem no longer matters to me. I want to get away to a place where my time, energy, thoughts, conversations and activities can be devoted to understanding the spiritual plane and my relationship to it. I want to be a part of a spiritual community."

And so in the mountains around Carmel, there developed a group of people who said, "I must give all day, every day, all of my life, all of my thought, and being, and purpose to my spiritual development." These were people who felt compelled to create a different way of life.

They felt that way, not because someone told them, "This is what you should do." They felt that way because they understood their inner nature, and thus their appropriate action. They withdrew themselves from the city and gathered at Carmel, and they began to establish a community.

If that community had been established because a prophet said to do it, it would have lived as long as the prophet and then it would have collapsed. But this particular community of the Essenes was established because the people felt guided from within to withdraw.

The same thing is true in this time. There are communities of people drawing together all around the world because the individuals know, "This is what I want to be a part of. This is what I know is right for me. This is where I can best serve and grow."

Even when the Essenes gathered around Carmel and built their hospital, their School of the Prophets and their community, there were other people as well in that time who were attuned to an expectation of the Messiah. These were people who were growing ready for his arrival, yet were not part of the community of the Essenes. They were expectant, like the Essenes. They were preparing themselves, like the Essenes. Yet they were preparing in a different way, according to the calling that existed within them.

PERSONAL CALLING

This is most important to understand. When we have asked the Source, "Should we store food? Should we get to the mountains? Should we build places to store necessary items?" the Source has answered, "Look at the periods of history that preceded this. What happened?"

One of those periods of history tells of Joseph's experiences in Egypt. While there, he received a prophecy similar to those that we are hearing today. The seers and prophets are saying today that there is a period of famine coming. There will be a period of extreme shortage of many things that we need – food, clean water, shelter, fuel, money. That a loaf of bread will be of far greater value than a fistful of dollars. And that the ability to produce food personally will be most valuable of all.

Joseph said to the Pharaoh in that time, "The interpretation of your dream is that you have had seven years of plenty. Now you are going to have seven years of famine. Therefore you must build storage bins and save food."

Joseph did not spread the message to the world. He only alerted the people of Egypt. The people of Egypt stored food wisely for the future. Important to learn is that, in the end, the stored food became a storehouse for the rest of the world.

Should these disasters come upon us in this time, anyone who chooses to hoard food for himself or chooses to hoard material things of any kind for himself – without thinking of those who are less fortunate, less informed, less wise, less prepared – will lose all. And his efforts will have been in vain.

On the other hand, those who prepare with the specific purpose of being servants to all humankind including those who do not recognize truth, making preparations for themselves and for others as well, will be ready for whatever happens. Those who see that by recognizing truth they are given responsibility for the care of those who do not become stewards of the creator's goods, like Joseph.

Those of us who recognize that there is a time of shortage coming should be preparing to be of assistance to others, knowing that this earth still has plenty, and will yield plenty, even through the worst times, if we become responsible for caring for and distributing that plenty properly. That is the purpose for preparing ourselves. That is the personal calling of every individual on this planet.

PERSONAL RESPONSE

How does all this become practical? We must learn in this time to turn inside ourselves and know that when we receive answers, we are responsible to act on them. It would be easy to let others take charge, to hold the prophets responsible. Many of us would like for someone else to spell it all out for us – to let a channel say, "Here, this is the plan of action."

Though many prophets will intuit and receive effective plans of action, if it were done just that way, each of us would be robbed of the most important asset that we must have during any time of change – our own ability to respond properly to what we find within.

Our ability to listen within for our appropriate action will always be our most important asset. If instead, we are given the rules and instructions for doing this and that in preparation, we will cease listening within and that muscle will atrophy.

We have already been told what the need is. Do we then need further to be told how to meet it? If we do, then we are not prepared within ourselves to respond appropriately. We have not made the necessary first preparation.

The time is now for us to take what we have been told and respond to it. What we have been told is this: The time of plenty has come to an end. It is finished. Not next year. Not five years from now. It is *already* finished. We have already entered the decline of economics, of food, of all the assets and resources of this earth.

It is no longer appropriate to say, "There will be an energy shortage in twenty years. There will be a shortage of land, water, food and fuel in twenty years." We should now be saying, "We have already overused the resources of this earth."

Now is the time to respond as if the shortages have begun. Right now we should begin using the earth in a better way – not waiting for the last crash, because by then, it will be too late. We should begin right now to place our values on things of value, and live now as we will live when shortages are evident and painful. We need to begin to tilt the balance the other way now. The period of plenty has already come to an end.

THE BIRTH OF A NEW AGE

Through this period of the pendulum's extreme swing in the other direction, we will experience greater polarity – a greater recognition of good and evil, right and wrong. In other words, we will experience the dark side now. We will experience some loss and deprivation. And every moment of that experience should be viewed as the exercising of a muscle, as if it were developing and making stronger something within us. It should be seen not as a punishment, but as a tool.

"These experiences are preparing me for something that is just beyond. This is a period of darkest night, and it is going to break into morning soon. Unless I receive all that I can from this period of night, I won't be prepared for the morning."

The Source has described this period of deprivation that we are entering as the pains of labor, because earth is giving birth to a new age. During this period of labor, we should feel like expectant parents giving birth to a new child – not filled with dread but with expectancy and even delight concerning the new life that we know is coming. We are the pregnant ones giving birth to a new age. Each change in life as we know it marks the coming of a new heaven and a new earth.

EARTH CHANGES
FROM THE PAUL SOLOMON SOURCE

*T*here remains a great deal to be done before that you refer to as earth changes upsets the lifestyle and the thinking of those about you. Realize that what remains to be done remains to be done in spite of the earth changes, not because of them. That which needs to be done should be done for its need in the present – not as a matter of preparation for extreme change – for it is the imbalance that is causing the change. Correct the imbalance, and the changes will not matter so much.

Begin first with the realization that the essence of man, that which has eternal value, is not flesh and is not subject to the laws of the flesh or the experiences of the flesh within the material world. That which man should identify with has little concern for the changes in the earth's surface – except that he is responsible for such changes.

Then your best service is to demonstrate a change in values, by putting your value in things that are of true value, things that cannot be destroyed or even changed by the events that occur. One can hardly demonstrate a new set of values while showing concern for those things that will be destroyed. The most important single thing that can be done in this time is to restructure the values.

The best way to heal any disease is to discover what that disease can cause you to realize and become. That is the purpose of the disease. By realizing the purpose of the disease, and by understanding what can be gained from it, the gain can take place and the disease will have no further purpose.

So it is with the changes coming in the earth, which are merely symptoms of misplaced value.

If man would lift his values to those things that are of true value, then those things of lesser value would not need to be taken away – for all those things that are presently considered of value will be wrested from the hands and the life during the period of change. And the greater the attachment, the greater the suffering when those things are lost.

Those who pray to avoid these changes, saying, "Let us pray, and then we might avoid the earth changes," would do better to pray for a new set of values. Better to restructure the thinking and cause others to see the possibility of living within a set of true values.

As to survival itself during these times, even survival will depend upon values, for those who value love and one another will survive. Those who put spiritual relationships before self will survive. Those who scrap for pieces of food, placing survival first, will perish.

Banding together in communities specifically designed for spiritual growth and improvement – not communities designed in paranoid reaction or fear of loss – those spiritual communities will survive by lifting their people to a higher consciousness, even during the time when those unaware, and those who choose not to be aware, still refuse to speak of earth changes.

Your message should not be a message of fear for what comes, saying "This will happen, and that will happen." Your message should be of confidence in a new day saying, "Things of true value cannot be taken away, cannot be lost under any circumstances. If those things are valued more than things that can be taken away, we will live a new kind of life, an effective life."

Hold dear what is of true value. Begin now, before you lose those things of false value in order to learn to recognize the greater value. Begin at home, in your own life. And know that there will come opportunities to assist others by teaching them to adjust to the changes, to adapt to new lifestyles, to feel thankful for the knowledge.

Systems you have depended upon are coming to an end, and a new order will be established. There are among you those few who are beginning to commit themselves to transformation in a new way, with a new level of commitment. You have about you a growing concern for integrity. Not so many can maintain that integrity to which they aspire. But the thought, the aspiration, is becoming a motivational force, building in increments, so that the building becomes a living movement.

In these months and years that are upon you, you will find a continuation of war, pain, disease, death, changes in the earth, in the weather, in the economy, and such. When you discover that love is a power stronger than fear and life is stronger than death, and as these thoughts reach a critical mass for change, you shall see suddenly the dawning of a new day.

Become then the new Essenes, and with your expectation create that power that will produce a critical mass for the transition. And as there is transformation among you, so will there be transformation on the earth. And that transformation will be a reversal of polarity, but we speak not of destruction. We speak rather of a heightening of power. The lifting of the earth into a new expression that is not one of polarity, so that you will no longer encounter good and evil, life and death – but rather, new life shall reign for that time, for that season.

THE KARMIC DESTINY OF AMERICA

*If there were one, or two, or twelve in this nation who would
follow his or her karmic destiny perfectly, fulfilling his or her life
purpose exactly, the whole world would be changed.*

It is interesting to understand the different forces at work at the
time of the founding of the United States of America. There were
three men in particular called together, assigned the task of
establishing the founding principles of a new nation and creating a
constitutional charter. The three men were freemasons and
astrologers, and they shared their understandings of ancient
disciplines as they considered the monumental task and responsibility
before them.

One was particularly concerned with esoteric principles. Another
was Christ-oriented. Another was schooled in the ancient traditions
of Egypt and their symbolism. Eventually there evolved a marriage
of the various systems.

The men were aware that two great forces would influence the
new nation. One force would be its establishment as a spiritual
institution. They would invoke that force through their knowledge of
astrology, occultism, ancient rites and Christine principles. And they
would weave it into the very fabric of the new nation's existence, as
protection and as a guide.

The second force would be the nation's karmic destiny, which is
the balance of good and evil. This second force would be just as
strongly influential as the first, and it would also be invoked
consciously and deliberately, because in a return cycle, one
automatically carries with him what he has built. America had
inevitably carried forth in her fabric, already woven, both the
accomplishments and the mistakes of earlier times and experiences.

Through the efforts of the Founding Fathers, the newly born nation of America was consecrated to serving a higher power. However, that could not override the fact that the nation was bound to the repetition of patterns set in motion in previous times.

As there is a repetition of patterns, there is as well a repetition of souls. To fulfill karmic destiny, the souls that participated in the earlier times reappeared. And there exists now in America a deep-rooted soul memory and a tendency to repeat the same patterns, unless particular effort is made to attune to a higher power. In other words, there is equal possibility and opportunity to succeed as there is to fail.

THE PORTENT FOR TODAY

We have arrived at a moment of particular karmic destiny, and it is demonstrated in the current happenings within and surrounding this nation. What is the karmic tendency? To rely solely on humankind's own understandings, ego and devices. In other words, to worship personal power.

There are signs that this karmic destiny is manifesting, as we abuse and attempt to control the forces of nature, and as we aspire to gain and maintain power over others. We have reached a time when it is vital that this nation stop and re-examine the principles on which she was born.

To what purpose is America dedicated and what does she serve? God or power? The highest principle or the lowest?

We have done a number of things right. Even those leaders who are obviously serving the lower principles, in times of national disaster, call the nation to prayer. Somewhere in their political minds, they realize that, at the heart of America, there is a great faith in prayer and in a divine power.

This is a time for listening within because the answers are there waiting. This is a time when we can turn from trying to overcome nature and beat her at her own game, and instead listen to nature and discover that, inherent within her, are the answers that her creator placed there. It is time to turn within, to discover a new order.

People throughout the world, of all ages and backgrounds, are saying, "The old answers aren't working anymore. Traditional religion isn't working anymore. I want to study something – whether it is yoga, or the Qabalah, or Buddhism, or mind control – anything that will show me a new means of thinking, a purer set of values, and a new identity for myself."

It is not a time to resist the signs and indicators that have come to us. It is not a time to ignore the conditions – intense weather patterns, draught, famine, natural catastrophes. However, worry and concern are not an answer. Our best approach would be to utilize the opportunity, by sharing what we have with those who need it and by preparing to care for more in the future.

If you feel removed from the karmic destiny of America, not being a lawmaker or a decision maker, understand that the karmic responsibility for the time at hand is intensely individual. One single person meeting perfectly his place in karmic destiny could lift all others a bit closer to God. If there were one, or two, or twelve in this nation who would follow his or her karmic destiny perfectly, fulfilling his or her life purpose exactly, the whole world would be changed.

You stand right now at a moment of choice in your life. You can place your value on things of higher value, or on things of temporal value. If you are scraping in order to own a bigger house and a better car than the guy down the street – living above your means in order to maintain a certain status quo – if that is your system of values, you will experience what happens to those things at that level. Those things will be burned and consumed, and the consciousness that is fastened to them will know a similar experience.

However, the person who has released those things and has set his value on higher ideals will not be affected by their destruction or their disappearance. If he does not have them, he will not suffer. If he sets his value on higher ideals, they cannot be lost – and the lesser things will be provided as well.

Seek first the kingdom of God, and everything else will take care of itself. (Matthew 6:33) Put all your energy, concentration and faith into the pursuit of higher values, and everything else will come to you in higher measure.

It is a time for prayer, a time for listening, a time for a new manner of thinking. Listen within and consider higher values. Then share your values with others, and expect great changes.

LOVE, FEAR AND ARMAGEDDON

If you are tired of living in a world where pain, starvation and war are considered normal and expected, there is an alternative. If you are willing to take responsibility for creating that alternative, it is possible to produce a new world.

Everything in existence on this planet is performing perfectly and naturally, exactly according to its nature. And it is the nature of all things existing on earth to participate in recycling.

Humans, animals, plants and minerals all grow as a result of the death of other things. Death is not the end of life. It is the recycling of life energies through new forms.

Humans may be repulsed by the mental image of a dead carcass that is beginning to bloat and stink. However, to a vulture or a maggot, dead meat looks like a banquet because it is their nature to gorge on decaying flesh. There is absolute perfection in the creation of the maggot, the housefly and the buzzard. Earth was perfectly designed to renew itself continuously by cleaning up its waste. Thus the lowly earthworm is one of the most useful beings on the planet. It may even be one of God's favorites for that reason.

As part of this grand recycling system, it is the nature of some animals to be predators. Built into our human nature as well is the predator instinct of killing and eating, causing death and recycling life. It is our natural way of participating in the life and death cycle of earth.

It is also the nature of all things existing on earth to participate in reproduction. It is instinctive for everything on this planet to want to express sexually and to reproduce. Nothing could be more natural.

Everything about the nature of earth and its inhabitants is natural and is an expression of its creator. It is absurd to suggest that earth's creator did a poor job.

HUMAN NATURE

Humans are naturally capable of more thoughts, moods, emotions, feelings and appetites for good and bad than any other living being on this planet. Included in who you are is the ability to express a range of so-called negative emotions including anxiety, resentment, anger, jealousy, hurt and hate. All these expressions are perfectly natural.

It is natural for you to feel, think and do all the things that you feel, think and do. It is natural for you to feel angry and vengeful, even to fantasize about killing someone. It is even natural for you to kill, given certain circumstances. It is natural for you to have sexual urges and fantasies because all these expressions are natural and are all right to experience. You cannot express incorrectly. You can only express what is in your nature.

It is important to know, though, that you did not make that nature. That nature is an aspect of this planet earth. It is an aspect of a living beast that occupies this planet and lives within its inhabitants. It is natural for you to express that beast within you, which includes the complete range of emotions and feelings that God ever created and put on this planet.

Here is an important key for understanding this point: Outside this planet, you would not experience the nature of this earthly beast. It is a consequence of living on this planet.

As a result of living on earth, you express the beast nature that rules this planet. The king or ruler of the beast nature of this planet is called by many names, including Satan. Satan's kingdom is the kingdom of earth. And all of that is all right. It is natural for the beast to act like a beast, which means to participate in the life and death cycle of this planet.

Consider the lesson of the frog and the scorpion. The scorpion wanted to get to the other side of the river, so he asked the frog to carry him across. The frog answered, "You'll sting me if I let you ride on my back." The scorpion responded, "Surely I wouldn't sting you because then we would both drown." The frog, trusting in this logic, allowed the scorpion onto his back and began the journey across the river. Halfway across, the scorpion stung the frog. As both began to sink below the surface, the frog cried out, "Why did you sting me? Now we will both die." The scorpion stated matter-of-factly, "I couldn't help myself. It's my nature."

It is important, even crucial, to understand that your personal beastly expressions are natural and that they are all right. A scorpion can be nothing but a scorpion. Individuals who resist that part of self will wrestle needlessly and unsuccessfully, so it is important to accept all aspects of the beast nature within you.

Confusion arises when you try to put all of this into a religious context, believing that you are supposed to behave in a "morally good" way. It is impossible to force the beast to act in a way that is not like a beast.

THE OTHER NATURE

The only way you can stop the beast from doing what it is created to do is to take it off, like any other piece of clothing. How do you do that? First, you need to know that there is another nature, which is not the beast.

The other nature is not a participant in the life and death cycle of this planet. The other nature is the creator of that cycle. The other nature is a continuous, sustaining, creative consciousness. It does not grow through the death of other things. It has no natural instinct to kill and eat, to cause death and recycle life. It has no appetite for reproduction. That which does not die does not need to reproduce. The other nature can only create. It only grows. It is an archetypal, everlasting nature – and it is yours. It is your intrinsic divine nature.

THE PROPER ROLES OF MAN AND BEAST

When the beast that inhabits earth was created in the beginning, God suggested that humankind participate in this divine occurrence called life. God suggested that we rule over the beasts in the garden, that we give them names and train them to behave as we wished. From the beginning of time, we have done that. All the beasts in the garden do what we command them to do, providing we take charge of them. When we do not take charge, the beasts run amok. Then the beast in man rules man, to the point that man forgets he is the creator and believes he is the beast.

Obviously, the question that arises on a personal level is, "Who's in charge?" Who is making the decisions in your life? Is it your beast or your divine nature?

There is a battle raging within you at any given time between these two natures. That is where the real battles of life are being fought. The bumps and nicks and scars occurring on the surface are outward manifestations that reflect your struggle to regain control of a beast that has grown seemingly insurmountable, lifetime over lifetime.

That is where the madness is. That is where heaven and hell lie. That is where God and the devil meet. You may have been convinced that God lives in a peaceful paradise above the clouds and that Satan rules a fiery pit down below. You can continue to believe that they exist out there, outside yourself. Maybe they do, but those externals are not the ones who are influencing every thought, feeling, mood, interaction and circumstance of your practical daily life.

The God that lives within you causes you to feel uplifted as you respond to a divine presence. That God is alive, and there is no need to question it. Serious theological debates concerning the existence of God and Satan are not necessary. You only have to ask yourself if there is a force at work within you that makes you feel good about yourself and about life, that makes you respond with hope and healing when you see particular images, when you hear particular music, when you encounter particular people, when you experience particular events, or when you just pay attention and appreciate life as it is.

In those moments, you have experienced a force coming from within you that inspires you to know that you are all right. When you commune with that force, when you talk with it, you feel good. That force causes you to feel alive, without regret for the past and without fear of the future. You are alive to the present. That creative, life-giving force is God within you.

There is another force living within you as well. You cannot deny it, and it would be ridiculous to try. There is a force within you that sometimes dreads, fears, worries, judges, condemns, hates and becomes melancholy and depressed. That force causes you to feel bad, discouraged, not all right. You can call that force, Satan, the devil, the lower self, the beast nature, or any other name you prefer. The truth is that it exists. When you talk with that force, you feel worse. And that is the definition of evil.

LIVE vs. EVIL

It is both poetic and ironic that the English language provides us two words that are mirror opposites: live and evil. Evil is live spelled backwards and could not be more appropriate.

Whatever makes you dead is evil – whatever makes you hurt, whatever makes you feel guilty, whatever makes you fearful. Whatever makes you less alive is evil. All the studied categorizations of morality and sin provided by traditional religion – this is good but that is bad, this is acceptable but that is not – are unnecessary. The definition of evil is very simple. Anything that makes you feel worse is evil. It is the opposite of life. It does not enliven you. It un-livens you.

Whatever takes your life away makes you more dead, and that is the nature of evil. Anything that gives you liveliness, that makes you more alive, more lively and life-filled, is Life and God. Scripture tells us that when asked to identify himself to Moses, God said, "I am that I am." (Exodus 3:14) "I am that which lives. I am life. I am the living one. I am what makes life live." Let that be your definition of God.

WHO DECIDES YOUR ALRIGHTNESS?

You have the right to be totally alive on all the levels of your being – physically, emotionally, mentally and spiritually alive. This right to be alive on all levels can be called your alrightness. The very fact that you are not dead should confirm to you that you are all right, perfect as you are. Being alive means being all right.

On the other hand, you can also choose to experience life according to the dictates of others, letting others determine how you should feel, think and act. If you do, you also give them the right to hurt you, the right to make you angry or sad, even the right to make you happy.

If you choose to surround yourself with people who decide whether you are all right, it means those people are important to you. It is a system that serves all of you because those people want to be important to you, particularly because they have probably given you the responsibility for their alrightness as well. If those people are important to you, they can assume that you will give them what they want, especially assurance that they are all right. As long as you remain important to them, you can expect them to give you what you want as well. An unspoken agreement is formed. You agree to pretend responsibility for each other's alrightness.

THE GREAT CONSPIRACY

A great conspiracy is taking place on this planet, and most of the world population is involved. The conspiracy consists of an agreement to pretend that you determine my alrightness and that I determine yours. It is not a conspiracy to believe that this is so. It is a conspiracy to pretend that this is so. No one really believes that their alrightness is dependent on what other people think of them, but almost everyone pretends that it is so.

The truth is that your alrightness depends on absolutely nothing but your decision to know that you are all right. You are inherently all right and cannot be otherwise. It is your choice to recognize it. You can choose to know that you are all right, or you can leave the decision to someone else and join the conspiracy.

Individuals learn to be conspirators at an early age. A group of young boys will refuse to let a girl play with them. She is the only girl, which means there is something different about her. The boys exclude her, not because they do not like her, but because they need to form a clique. To form a clique, there has to be someone who can be rejected. Since the girl is different, they can use that difference as a way of setting up their in-club, with her out. What they have actually formed is a conspiracy.

The girl buys into the conspiracy as well. She protests, until she believes her own words, "Poor me. They're mistreating me." Of course, she is not obligated to agree to the conspiracy. There are other options. For instance, she could become intrigued with her own activities, and in the end the boys might even want to play with her. Participation in the conspiracy is always a choice.

The adults around the girl buy into the conspiracy as well by saying, "Poor little thing." They could communicate another message such as, "Others don't decide whether you're all right or not. Those boys have agreed to pretend that something is wrong with you, but that doesn't make them right. There is absolutely nothing wrong with you. You can have fun wherever and whenever you want, even by yourself, especially by yourself."

More likely, the adults will try to flex their importance by imposing rules. "You can't play the way you want to play, because it's not nice. What I say is the rule because I'm an adult, which makes me more important." It is all part of the conspiracy – having more power, being richer, being smarter, being more beautiful, being taller, being thinner. It is the survival of the fittest, or the best at manipulating.

We teach children to sell out to the conspiracy through our examples, through the values we set, through the messages of our media, through the means to our goals. We teach children far more by who we are and what we do than by what we say. We teach them to conspire for alrightness.

We teach each other in the same way we teach children. Sometimes, we try to convince others that "I'm not important, but you are." Other times, we try the opposite, "You're not important. I am. And what I say goes."

The biggest contribution we make to the conspiracy is that we remain victims ourselves. Each time we allow ourselves to be hurt by someone, we buy into the conspiracy and we model the conspiracy for our families and our friends.

As you grew into your adolescent and teen years, you probably began to experience tremendous guilt. It was difficult to determine what caused the feelings. Most adolescents think that the feelings come from disappointing people, from being bad or just not good enough. "If I'm a bad person, people will get mad at me." You probably longed to find someone who thought you were all right just as you were.

The guilt of adolescence results from trading your integrity for the beliefs of others. Adolescents and teens literally writhe in discomfort over the decision they must make. "Do I conform to society? Do I act like I'm not all right unless someone tells me that I am? Or do I find my individuality in breaking the rules to prove that I'm different and not like them? Or do I break out of the conspiracy?" Hardly anyone considers the last question.

By adolescence, most people are so strongly committed to conspire that they cannot see what they are doing. Breaking out is barely an option. They have already agreed to pretend that being popular, wearing the right clothes, making good grades and trying their best, always saying the right things, being seen with the right people, never acting like a fool, and always being cool are what matters. Or perhaps they have decided to pretend the opposite – that being seen with the wrong people, wearing the wrong clothes, and not trying at all are what makes them all right. Either way, they have decided to do whatever it takes to fit into the group that promises to support their alrightness.

They handle the guilt of selling out by suppressing it. They stuff it down in the subconscious to avoid examining its validity. Then they set about creating an existence that maintains the lie. They work hard to forget, to remain unconscious and to anesthetize their feelings about having given control of their emotions and alrightness to others.

The conspiracy is an agreement to pretend that you determine my alrightness and I determine yours. The amount of power that I agree to give you is the amount of importance that I give you in my life. Then we call that loving each other.

What it means is that I will give you the power to control my life and I will make you prove your love for me by testing how far I can push you. I may need to prove my importance to you by saying, "How important am I to you? Am I important enough for you to put up with this?" Zap! Lovers do it regularly.

If the beast in me is fearful, and I make you responsible for the way I feel without taking care of my own love needs, because I am too busy participating in the conspiracy with you, then I can call you wrong, bad and evil. I can blame you for the quality of my life. Then we can have a family feud.

I can even call you an agent of Satan, and we can have a "holy war." Have you ever wondered how two such contradictory words can stand side-by-side in a rational sentence, in a rational world?

I can go to war with you. Satan does not care on what scale the wars are managed. Small, seemingly insignificant family feuds feed on fear and hurt, on suppressed, unconscious resentments, and they keep the planet in a state of disharmony. Strife is expected and reasonable. Hate and conflict are so seemingly innocuous that they continue without resistance and become habitual and commonplace, a way of life. In other words, the beast reigns in his kingdom.

There is no crime in participating in the conspiracy. It does not mean that you or your co-conspirators are wrong or bad. You certainly do not lose your alrightness as a result. It is important, however, to do it consciously if you are going to do it. If you prefer sadomasochism, hurt the hell out of each other. Just know that you are doing it by agreement, because you want to. The relationship is sadomasochistic in nature by mutual agreement. If, however, you want to step out of the conspiracy, you can quit any time.

STEPPING OUT OF THE CONSPIRACY

The more you practice your right to be alive, or alrightness, through the decisions of others, the more you forget how to make the decision for yourself. Then how do you stop the game?

All you have to do to step out of the conspiracy is to become conscious. Being conscious of what you are doing is called enlightenment. Just admit what you are doing and name your action. Call it what it is.

Here is the good news. Admitting what you are doing will cause what you are doing to change. You cannot change your actions through trying. If you try to stop an action, you will make it more important, and it will grow larger and more dominant through your attention. You will become more entrenched, and it will hurt you more.

Recognizing that it is a game that you and your cohorts have been playing will steal its power. Like a deflating balloon, it will look silly. The action will become futile and foolish as you acknowledge that it does not serve you anymore. And you will no longer give it energy and importance. The very act of performing the action will remind you of its senselessness.

Buying out of the conspiracy means being conscious. Enlightenment does not require learning great truths. It only requires that you turn on the lights, become conscious, own what you are doing, and be honest with yourself. Enlightenment is simply shining a spotlight on the truth of your actions.

By acknowledging the conspiracy, you will begin to notice what others are doing as well – not the feigned interpretations that the conspirators have agreed to, but how things truly exist. When you observe the conspiracy that others are playing, resist the temptation to suddenly blow the whistle on everyone's game. Just see it for what it is, make note of it, even laugh at it. It, not them. Remember, you were just there.

Individuals may say to you, "That means you don't love me anymore." That is not true. It means, "I don't need for you to tell me that I am all right anymore. I don't need to give you the power to hurt me in order to feel important and loved anymore."

Stepping out of the conspiracy may seem lonely because there are so few doing it and because you no longer get to depend on others for your alrightness. Beware. The feeling of loneliness is part of the conspiracy, because loneliness is a feeling-reaction based on the belief that others are responsible for your alrightness.

Removing yourself from the conspiracy results in independence, which does not equate with loneliness. Not having needs that others must fill is not a problem. It is an advantage. Only then can you love because you want to and because you choose to, not because you have to in order to get your needs filled. That is real freedom.

A journalist once said to Fidel Castro, "You are totally dependent on Russia, even for your survival. You are the most dependent nation in the world." Castro responded, "With all that you have said I will agree, except one thing. We are totally dependent on Russia for our survival. But we are also the most independent nation in the world because we are not dependent on the United States, our big neighbor. Everyone else is. We have chosen to be dependent on somebody else, and that gives us our freedom."

He was completely accurate. They were still bond slaves, but they had chosen their master. In choosing your master, you are not mastered. You are free. It is not whether you serve that makes you free, but what you consciously choose to serve.

There are only two choices, love or fear. If you serve love, you serve life. If you serve fear, you serve death. By serving fear and death, you remain a slave no matter how free you think you are.

You do not become free by breaking the rules. You become free by choosing to respect the rules, the universal principles on which life on this planet is based. You do this because you want to, because you recognize that they are authentic and work effectively for everyone simultaneously. No one is free to live in abeyance of these principles, except to the extent that we choose our master.

Who is the master of your life: Love or fear? Life or death?

PERSONAL RESPONSIBILITY FOR A NEW WORLD

The sacred texts of many civilizations predict a time on this planet when there will be no fear, no pain, no hunger, no disease, no crime, no war, no death, no longer any reason for tears. A utopian world of peace and plenty will manifest.

People generally consider the concept of a peaceful, plentiful world to be a fantasy, a metaphor, a myth, a joke, not real-life, religious folly, something that may occur in some elusive place called heaven. Almost no one takes personal responsibility to see that it absolutely occurs within our generation.

Sacred texts also predict that this new earth will come because of specific conditions. There will be a group of people present on this planet who have already begun to live in the consciousness of that new world. At some point, those people will catch the rest of the population up with them. They will cause other people to join them in that consciousness, and the new world will manifest.

According to these texts, at any given moment, we are presented with two options. We can choose to live in a world with so much pain, anger, fear, disease, sadness, cruelty, crime and war that it has become the norm – a world where people believe it is impossible to make a difference, and that self-interest and self-protection are the only answer.

The alternative is to choose not to live there. Should you choose this other option, you will be glad to know that what may look difficult to accomplish turns out to be less troublesome than what you are already experiencing.

There are two ways to go. We can continue on our present path perpetuating actions that have become habitual since birth, destroying the earth and ourselves in the process. Or right now within our lifetime, we can make a commitment to become the parents of a new world where the children yet to be born will not know sickness. They will wonder what it means when people speak of something that used to exist on earth called death. They will be unable to understand such concepts as war, competition, limitations or hurting one another. That option is available to us.

Perhaps that sounds far-fetched. It is more far-fetched that humankind is considered the most evolved of the living beings and yet purposefully hurts and kills members of its own species for no useful reason and is systematically destroying its home planet. Which world sounds more far-fetched, and which sounds more feasible?

If you are tired of living in a world where pain, starvation and war are considered normal and expected, there is an alternative. If you are willing to take responsibility for creating that alternative, it is possible to produce a new world.

The knowledge necessary for accomplishing a new world has always been present. The wisdom to do it must be achieved.

Why was death introduced into the world? Why does death exist? The answer is simple. But we have complicated our lives, particularly through what we tell ourselves about what goes on around us. It has become the job of wise sages in our time to make truth sufficiently complicated to be appealing to people.

TWO POWERS EXIST

Only two powers exist on earth. Everything derives from those two. We can call them the expansive force and the contracting force, or life and death.

Life includes anything that grows, supports growth, expands, increases and builds. The energy of life includes joy, healing and health, happiness, effectiveness, expansion, abundance, prosperity, productivity, growth, encouragement, support and power.

Death is an energy that contracts, decreases, interferes with or destroys growth. It includes hurt, pain, limitation, competition, disease, illness, worry, negative emotions and negative perspectives.

These two powers that enliven the universe are in constant war, battling against one another. Each attempts to recruit you to its camp, meaning your vitality is invested on one side or the other of these two expressions of power. You believe in one or the other. You accept and depend on one or the other as your source of security, vitality and life. You have confidence that it will support and sustain you. Whichever of the two powers you have confidence in will motivate you and empower your life.

These two forces can also be called love and fear. The term love means everything within you that is expansive, everything that makes you feel better, more alive. Love nurtures and sustains.

HOW DID FEAR ORIGINATE?

How did we become separated from what sustains, feeds and causes us to grow? How did the power of destruction gain control? How did fear gain the power to take life away from us?

To have the experience of existence on this planet, you created a piece of equipment. That piece of equipment has sensors, abilities, personality and identity. All these things were your creation for the purpose of a sustained experience, long enough to gather the information that you wanted to gather, to feel and to experience earth.

Imagine a time before time when you had no physical body. You were a creative intelligence. You were so vast that being contained in one of those minuscule physical-units of earth was unimaginable. However, as you watched the occurrences on that magnificent planet, you were fascinated and entertained. When you observed the savory experiences available to material beings through their senses, you became curious and said, "Why don't I just go ahead and make myself one of those things?"

You made yourself a unit equipped with senses, a mind, emotions, feelings and abilities. The life span of the unit was meant originally to be temporary. After all, it was just something to put on for a while for research purposes, and then to take off when the experience was completed. It certainly was not you, any more than planet earth was your home. What a ridiculous notion!

You gave to the unit an awareness that its usefulness was limited and temporary. But over time, you developed an interest in extending the duration of the experience. Life on earth was fascinating! So fascinating that you began to forget life outside the unit. In response, the unit began to view its temporary quality as a frightful limitation and developed survival anxiety, or the fear of death. By allowing an original belief of limitation of time available in this earth, and then by allowing that belief to lead to a feeling of anxiety, you introduced fear into your existence.

The interesting thing about fear is that it requires fantasy to exist. It has no reality of its own. By definition, fear is a fantasy of something that has not yet occurred, creating an unreal image in your mind of what could happen. You can only fear something by fantasizing it and imagining that it may happen. You can even fantasize fear to the extent that you can affect your ability to experience what is occurring in the present. That is fear's only relationship to the present moment.

WHERE THE PLAN GOES AMISS

For most infants, the first encounters with the world bring love, nourishment, attention, warmth, security, admiration, praise, even worship. Further on, that experience changes – even though the needs of the individual do not. People continue to need love, attention, admiration, even worship, throughout life. The biggest challenge comes as those who are providing love and praise to the infant begin to express disapproval. To regain their approval, children must begin to act differently. Children must begin to act according to the expectations of those who are disapproving.

For the first time, an artificial element is introduced into the child's life, something unnatural. As love and approval are withheld, a fantasy called fear is introduced, a fear that something needed will be withheld. If children decide to supplant their own desires, aspirations, even intuitions, with the desires of others in order to get the love and approval they need, they join the conspiracy to act as if others determine their alrightness.

The fantasy of losing what is needed for survival can develop into an energy of fear that becomes a focus of life. The constant conversation occurring in the minds of all individuals known as selftalk can become dominated by this fantasy.

As children grow into adulthood, their selftalk will express as fear thoughts. "I'm afraid of being rejected. I'm afraid they won't like me. I'm not worthy. I feel so guilty. I don't deserve to make good grades. I don't deserve to get that great job. I don't deserve to marry someone nice. I don't deserve to have a good life."

Thoughts born out of fear of lack or limitation have two things in common. First, they are lies. They do not tell the truth about you or about others. Second, they either devalue something that has value or they limit something that is limitless.

Negative selftalk will devalue you by depreciating your inborn value as a human being. It will also devalue the possibilities of your future. Negative selftalk is false, yet it has the power to impose effect on reality because you accept the false limitations as real. The result is decrease and death. If the source of your selftalk is fear and its content is limiting or critical, it will make you less. All thoughts coming from limitation produce death.

THE NATURE OF SELFTALK

All thoughts coming from love, life and prosperity produce life and growth. If the content of your selftalk is approving, if it accepts and supports reality just as it is, without wishing it were different due to fear of what might be, it will cause growth and increase strength. Resistance to life just as it is will decrease strength and growth.

A perfect example is how tiresome and depleting worrying is. Wishing life were different or fearing what might or might not happen will drain energy from your mind and body. Consider those relentless conversations that run inside your head where you rehash what you should have said yesterday or last week, or you go back and forth about how you should respond if someone does this or that in the future. These fantasy-based thoughts have the power to zap you physically and mentally.

You are a creative being. So creative that you can successfully make a body and arrive at destination planet earth. If you dwell on thoughts about limitation and turn those fantasies into something called fear, that fear can divert your attention from the present. You can miss what is, by fantasizing about what is not.

In that way, you lose consciousness of what is. Losing consciousness of what is means being dead to the present. Attending to those inner conversations will cause you to miss what is happening right in front of you.

The less conscious you are, the more dead you are. Everything that involves fear, to any extent, is another degree toward death. Total lack of consciousness is a step deeper in your fantasy of annihilation and non-existence, but it is not real either. Total lack of consciousness can deprive you of your unit, but it is not real, and it does not equate with death.

The *you* of you does not have limited existence. It does not have survival needs because survival is not an issue. You will survive no matter what, even if you take off the unit. Survival anxiety has no basis in reality.

OUR FASCINATION WITH DEATH

There is only one thing in the universe that a human being cannot do and that is to cease being. You cannot even imagine not being. If you try to image yourself as dead, you will picture a body in a casket, a funeral, lots of flowers, solemn words and mourners dressed in black. But you are still there. You are simply observing from another vantage point.

In the beginning, God said, "I will let you do anything and everything except this: You cannot die. I have placed a flaming sword in front of the Tree of Life so you cannot eat from it. You cannot die." (Genesis 3:24) And since that day, humans have been fascinated with death and danger.

We thrill at being "scared to death," entertaining ourselves through dangerous death-defying feats, creating faster and faster ways to propel ourselves from one place to another, creating and allowing access to more and more methods for killing ourselves and each other. We attempt to corral death with costly coffins of impenetrable metals. And as a final insult to death, we toy with cryogenics and cloning.

Still, the most popular and widely used method for exploring death remains the choice not to be alive in the present. The mind can easily put itself somewhere else, choosing to live outside present-time. You live in the past and blame it for being inadequate in the present, or you live in the future and dread what might or might not be. Thus your fantasies allow you to escape living in the now. You are as good as dead to the present.

Of course, you are not really dead, only pretend-dead, but there is little difference. Both allow you to escape what is around you in the present moment. How often does your mind wander from this experience and go to tomorrow, or next week, or last week? And this moment is lost. You will not remember what was said. You will have to check someone's notes. Then you will lose that moment as you try to recapture this one. All because you were busy living in another time instead of the present one. You killed the present.

"But there is so much past to relive and to regret," you say. Existing in a world of regret and guilt means that you are dragging who you used to be along with you through the present.

"I really regret that thing I did last week." Instead of being alive right now, you try to relive last week, at a moment when you were at your worst. How smart is that? Last week, you acted like an idiot. To regret being an idiot, you have to remember that you were an idiot. This means reliving the experience and pretending in your mind to be an idiot again right now, just because you were one last week. Why do it again on purpose?

You will never accomplish the possible-human you could be if you have that big garbage can filled with past events strapped to your back. Yes, the one you swear is not there!

There you are, after all these years, still feeling guilty for that incident that occurred eons ago. Long after the event, you are still begging, "God, please forgive me. I'm so sorry." Till God cannot take it anymore and finally says, "Hey! Get over it! Just forget it! I did! I don't want to hear about it anymore. Forgive yourself, and be forgiven, and get over it. Be who you are right now!"

Many people allow experiences from the past to control who they are today. "My potty-training was traumatic, so now I'm neurotic." "I lived through the depression, so I can't think differently about money." "I suffered a business failure. If it weren't for that, I wouldn't be like this." "I was raped when I was younger, so I will never feel right again." "I was betrayed big-time once, so I will never trust again." "I had a nervous breakdown, so I'll never be able to handle this." "I was abused as a child, so I can't succeed at anything."

Yes, tragedy happens. Not a single person gets through life without experiencing some kind of tragedy. Allowing past tragedies to determine the present doubles the tragedy. It is also called being dead in the present by trying to be alive in the past. Are you having a nervous breakdown right now? Are you being abused today? Are you addicted to drugs right now? Are you failing this very moment? If you are, get some help, immediately. If not, move on. Stop letting the past control your present.

If you are waiting to live until you make your fortune, until you get your degree, until you get married, until you become a parent, until you get out of debt, until you get thin, until you get sober, until you get your act together, you are trying to be alive in the future.

Those of you who are dead, please just lie down so the rest of us will know how to relate to you. Have the courtesy to go ahead and fall over on the floor if you are going to be dead in this moment.

NEGATIVE MEDITATION

"But I need to worry about what might happen," you say. Worry is the most practiced form of meditation in the world. It is practiced far more regularly than positive meditation where the mind is focused on good, body systems are strengthened and stress is reduced.

Worry is a universal religion, subscribed to by millions of people, mainly out of a feeling of obligation. "If I don't worry, it means I don't care. If I don't worry, I won't be ready when it happens. If I don't worry, who will?"

Worry is faith in evil, believing in darkness, expecting the worst. It is the one god that almost everyone on the planet worships, regularly, at least once a day.

The effect is predictable. The rewards reaped are tensed, stressed bodies and contracted, diminished lives.

FEAR vs. PRUDENCE

There is a positive counterpart to fear and worry called prudence. Prudence means being wise enough to act with common sense in threatening situations, to deal with an adverse power sensibly. Prudence produces confidence and is the opposite of worry. Fear is a lack of confidence and appreciation. The best way to overcome fear is to appreciate, respect and care for the thing that you fear.

Many people are frightened by snakes, including the harmless ones that are beneficial to us. People who fear snakes usually have little knowledge of them. The best way to overcome a fear of snakes would be to study them, because it is difficult to fear something that you understand. A person who understands snakes will be prudent. People who milk dangerous snakes have the necessary confidence because they are informed. Their knowledge allows them to act wisely. Because they are informed and because they act prudently, they no longer experience fear. If they did experience fear of the snakes while milking them, they would put themselves in a dangerous situation, which counters the popular argument that fear is wise in some situations. It is not. Fear is dangerous in all situations, and there are no exceptions.

Prudence means acting sensibly in a situation, not because you feel overwhelmed by the situation, not because you feel victimized by it, but because wisdom calls for it. Fear is a victim response. Prudence is taking responsibility and causing a positive result.

If you fear a disease, you will give it energy and power. If on the other hand you love yourself and inform yourself to understand the disease, then you will approach the symptoms, and their healing, with prudence, which means that you will take the actions that are appropriate to cancel the effects of the disease. At the same time, you will not be victimized or overwhelmed by the fear of illness.

CHOOSE TO BE ALIVE

Let go of worry. Let go the habit of dreading the future. Let go the habit of regretting the past. Let the dead bury the dead and choose to be alive right now in this moment. Even in a moment of excruciating embarrassment, and we all have them, choose to find worth in that moment. Look for something valuable.

You are a divine alchemist. That means that you can find something of value in the worst experience. If you do, you redeem the moment. To turn chaos and destruction into gold, you need to find value in the world, value in the experience of life, and most of all, value in yourself.

Choose to actively create in your mind and in your surroundings joy, excitement, adventure, prosperity and expansiveness. Believe that you can make a difference, that you can contribute to the world, that the purpose of life is to live!

Stop trying to live in the future or the past. Just be alive now. Accept the past, and the future, and most of all the present, just as they are, without wishing they were different. Stop resisting. Be all right with who you are, and the people around you will learn to love and support you just as you are. Or else they will go away, which might not be a loss.

Believe confidently in life. Live with divine selfishness. Divine selfishness means believing that what is ultimately good for you, what is in your best interest, must be in the best interest of everyone else.

What is good for you will be simultaneously good for all who share this planet. It could not be any other way under the divine order under which this universe operates. There is a good reason for believing this way. From our knowledge of the universe, we can assume that if this planet had not produced in abundance everything needed for humankind's survival, we would not have appeared and developed on this planet as a species.

Turn your consciousness and your attention toward the source of life, as the source of energy and power that supplies all your needs and sustains you to exist, grow and function. In that way, you can stop fearing things and people, and thus stop creating death and everything related to death. You can eliminate fantasy from your life and experience the real thing instead.

Becoming conscious has been glamorized through terms like "enlightenment," "God-consciousness," "cosmic-consciousness." All enlightenment means is to wake up out of fantasy into reality. That is all you have to do.

You already are – always have been and will be – God-conscious, cosmic-conscious and enlightened. Who you are is all those things and more. You do not have to work at enlightenment. All you have to do is stop the fantasy of something else and experience reality.

If you can make a switch in identity and wake up to who you really are, you will change your relationship with your body. Instead of it being you, it becomes yours. You will change your relationship with your mind. Instead of it being you, it becomes yours. You will change your relationship with your emotions and feelings. Instead of them being you, they become yours. All those things become tools that belong to you, rather than who you are.

By stepping into identity with the creator-you, you can observe your personality, your thoughts and your feelings just as you would observe another person. You can notice what is occurring, and more importantly you can notice what is not working effectively or supportively. You can see how you are acting, how you are thinking, how problems develop.

It is easy to see weaknesses in another person, but difficult to see your own missteps when you identify with the created. When you remember that you are the creator, you can step back to observe the created-self and what it is doing and the results of its actions. You observe from the perspective of a creator, a teacher, a friend, a parent and a source. From that perspective, you can determine the best choice of action. You become a co-creator with God.

Self-integration is a popular term. Being integrated means being one with the real self, the source. Being one with your source means that you have integrated what your source has built with what your source is. It is a natural, normal experience for you, and anything else is unnatural. If you want to wake up to naturalness and be who you really are, you need to stop creating fantasy and living in that as if it were real.

LOVE AS A KEY TO METAMORPHOSIS

Recognize that you are a source of love. When you give love, under any circumstances, you give the power of life. It is demonstrable. Say something or do something that is appreciated by another person, and that person is likely to smile, hug you, give you a compliment, express appreciation in some manner. When that happens, allow yourself to be sensitive to what it does to you physically, mentally and emotionally.

Physically, you will find that you suddenly have more energy. You were given energy by that exchange, by receiving appreciation, love, any positive expression of attention from another person. Emotionally, you will feel good about yourself. Mentally, you will feel revitalized, as if your battery received a charge.

That is what love is. Not the emotion, but the energy. The energy of love is the energy of life. It will heal you. It will enlighten you. It will give you life. It can perform miracles. It is the source of transformation. It can allow you to experience a metamorphosis.

Metamorphosis occurs when fantasy and fear die, and love lives. You become the cause of your body and what it experiences, instead of being the result of the functions of your body and its mind and emotions. You use the created to experience being the creator.

There are some keys to producing metamorphosis. First, you must give love to all that you have created, including your body, your mind, your ego, your personality, your thoughts, your emotions and feelings, your habits, your abilities, your weaknesses, your name. Everything that you have identified as you needs to be given love.

That sounds like it will keep those old parts of self alive. After all, love is the source of life and nourishment. But the death-birth experience of metamorphosis does not mean that the body crumbles and dies. It does not mean that the mind dies in the sense of annihilation or the end of existence. Metamorphosis means a death to the old self's existence as your identity. You die to the old self, and you are born again to a new relationship with it.

There are six things needed to survive. Five are commonly recognized: air, sunlight, shelter, water and food. There is a sixth one, and that one is love. Love is a source of life, and it is more important than the other five survival needs. It is vital, and humankind will do anything to have it.

It is common among individuals to try to get another's supply of love, which means, "I need to get you to give me your love. So I'm going to strike bargains with you. I promise that if you give me your love, I will give you my love. Of course, I don't really mean that, because I'm only willing to give you my love as long as you are serving my needs, being productive in my life and causing me to feel loved. As soon as I suspect that you are being unappreciative and not feeding my need, I'll withdraw from you."

Then we can go through something called falling out of love, and we can get divorced. We made an agreement that we did not know how to keep: "I will give you my love if you will give me yours," which really means "I am trying to get you to satisfy my love-needs by giving me your life." Life and love are the same thing.

There is something that you need to know about love. You cannot love anything or anyone that you need. You can only use that thing or that person to satisfy your needs. Real love is a choice. It is a choice to give life and to support life in another person.

When we came to this planet, we knew that we had to have love to survive. Knowing that support is necessary for life to exist, we probably agreed to support life. Any time that we do not support life, in even the slightest way, we introduce death. We introduce pain and hurt, and we are guilty of murder.

All I have to do to fail to support your life is to attempt to make you less alive in my mind or in the minds of others. Making you less alive means making you less important. I deny your existence in as much as I am willing to criticize you, to make you little or to make you not matter. To cross you off as unimportant is to say, "You don't exist. You're not alive." To do that, I only have to deny you love.

When an individual feels threatened by another, a common reaction is character assassination. Another word for it is gossip. Most individuals are too civilized to actually obtain a weapon and kill those who seem to present a danger, so they attempt to make them less alive by killing them with words, spoken to others. They want to make them less important to others, so they criticize or make fun of them when they are not around. They take away life and produce the energy of death. All individuals are constantly either giving life to others, or taking it away.

When people approach you and say, "How are you?" you can go on to tell them all your problems and tragedies and illnesses, and you can watch them deflate and lose liveliness while they listen respectfully. Try it and see. If you think your problems are killing you, just pay attention to what they are doing to others. Better to see if, in your response, you can keep the life going in those unwitting individuals. Practice making yourself and others more alive through your exchanges. In that way, you become a healer of individuals.

THE SOURCE OF YOUR SELFTALK

Remember that there are only two powers. There is love, and there is fear. If the conversation in your mind is coming from heaven or love, then you are supported. You are supporting yourself and your whole life, including your health, your prosperity, your feeling of security and confidence. You feel supported, and you can handle life no matter what comes along.

If the conversation in your mind is coming from fear, you will fear life. You will feel inadequate because that is what fear does. It tells you that your future is limited, that you will never accomplish your goals, that you will always be poor, that the wonderful people will elude you, that life is not yours for the asking and taking. Talking with fear is talking to hell. It means living in hell while on earth.

Talking to love makes you feel better, simply because you talked to it. It makes you feel good about yourself and life. Love never limits you. That is how simple it is. There is no mysterious technique.

If the conversation in your mind makes you feel better, it is coming from love, and it is supporting you. If it makes you feel worse or makes you feel afraid, it is coming from hell, and you need to get hell out of your head. Let it exist as a fiery pit down below for others if they want, but eliminate it from your life.

THE WORLD DEPENDS ON YOU

Whatever you do for yourself, you can also do for others and for the planet. Anything that you can do to make yourself or another person more alive and more joyous is practicing God. You are giving life, and you are being God-alive.

If you are willing to deny love and life to anything on the planet, you introduce death. You become responsible for the fact that death exists on earth. If you do anything at all, in thought, word or deed, that introduces death, pain, hurt or fear to the planet, you become personally, wholly responsible for the fact that death exists on earth. You are supporting it because you are putting it here.

That is the difference between life and death, between responsibility and irresponsibility, between creating a new heaven and a new earth and sustaining the pain and the imbalance that is here now. The pain and the imbalance will cease to exist when we cease to create it.

If we want to create a new heaven and a new earth, we must not introduce limitation, hurt, pain and death. We must be willing to support the life and worth of others at all times. If you become unwilling to introduce fear into this world, this world will automatically experience metamorphosis and become a new heaven and a new earth. If you are not introducing limitation, limitation will not exist. If you are not introducing fear, fear will not exist.

That is what life is about – being as alive as we can possibly be in every moment and supporting life in everyone and everything around us. That is what it is to be spiritual. That is what it is to be God. That is what it is to practice life, to experience it, to give it, to share it. That is the purpose of life.

What matters is whether you live while you are alive. Be alive now. Do not make yourself dead through worry or regret or any other thing that causes you to escape reality in this moment. You are alive now for a purpose.

There is no reason for not being alive and full of joy in this moment. If this moment changes so that you find the world crashing down around your head – your money runs out, your health deteriorates, your career falls apart, your home is gone, your friends betray you, you are left alone – there will still be no reason for not being alive and full of joy in that moment.

Choose whether you will suffer, or whether you will look for value in all experiences. You have every reason to be fully alive and happy, regardless of circumstances. Be a person who needs no excuse for experiencing and expressing pure joy.

If tragedy arises, and it always does, you may be knocked down. You may think, "I can't handle this." You may need to grieve, or feel shame, or retreat from chaos. But know that those responses are temporary and that you will handle whatever comes.

What makes a difference is how you handle it. You can continue to suffer long after the experience has ended, or you can grab what is valuable. You can grab the life in that experience! You can hold onto the life within it, which is the healing power that will get you through it. It is what will make that experience, not a dead event in your past, but a living experience that contributed to and empowered who you are in this moment.

TALK TO YOURSELF ON PURPOSE

Tell yourself the truth, and the truth will make you free. When that conversation of selftalk occurs in your mind, just ask one question, "Is this the truth?"

If it takes away from your value, it is not the truth. If it takes away from your future, it is not the truth. If it takes away the value of other people, it is not the truth. The truth is always supportive. The truth is always a vitality that will get you through the challenges of the next moment.

As you tell yourself the truth, an interesting thing happens. There is a horizontal line of chatter going back and forth in your mind at a furious rate. This horizontal line of thought makes up your rational, logical thought process. It depends on experience, the knowledge stored from learning and living, and whatever you tell yourself about yourself. When fear is a factor, your negative thoughts will form a furious, churning vortex, at the level of that horizontal line, that keeps you worried, afraid, sick, incapable, all the products of fear. Vertical thought, which includes intuition and insight, cannot get through that churning mess of negativity.

Meditation is a process of getting the horizontal conversation to stop, enabling the truth to come to you vertically. When the mind finally rests, when the incessant verbiage finally stops, guidance can advise you what to do in any moment. God can talk to you, and does. Living love will talk when you let yourself be quiet enough to listen.

Whenever that conversation in your mind is racing, just stop and ask yourself, "Is this the voice of love?" If not, change channels. Listen to your true divine nature for the answer.

THE BEAST NATURE IN YOU

When we enter this material universe, we must use a body to experience the laws of this planet and to learn the lessons that this planet presents. Our spirits are housed in these bodies for a time, yet these bodies have a nature of their own that is not the nature of God. It is a beast nature. It is an aspect of the living beast that occupies earth and lives within its inhabitants. As long as you inhabit the body, that beast nature will be a factor in your experience.

Rejection of any kind of animal causes problems. Without understanding and acceptance of its ordered nature, the animal will rebel. In gaining control over a wild animal, there are a couple of options. The spirit of the animal can be broken, pitting will against will. Or the animal can be tamed through a gentle, tolerant process of winning trust and cooperation.

Most often, when a horse is broken, control is gained through brute strength and illusion. Horses are physically stronger than humans, but they are made to believe the opposite through methods that can be cruel. Similarly, the beast in you is naturally stronger than any fabricated or forced desire within you to change your nature to something you consider to be good. Trying to break the will of your beast will not work.

The goal is not to change wild tigers into docile pussycats. It would be an insult to the creator of those beings if we did. When we try to discipline our minds and our bodies into a forced obedience of rules and codes of behavior that are contrary to our natural desires, yearnings and appetites, we get restrained, inhibited, explosive, unnatural human beings. Religions produce them. Society produces them. Families produce them.

When we try to control our natural yearnings and instincts by force of will by saying, "I want to make myself behave so that I can fit into society and meet the criteria of religions and laws," we fight against our natural will. When we fight against something, it perceives that it is unacceptable, condemned, feared and hated. Any animal sensing those feelings in an owner will become stubborn, or will become wilder and lash out in rebellion.

Your body and its nature will do the same thing. It is the nature of the beast to do so.

As you exist in this physical body, it is not wrong for you to experience your nature in all its aspects, including your emotions, your feelings, your instincts and your expressions. However, it is inappropriate for you to believe that the nature of your body, your animal, your beast, is your only or true nature.

YOUR TRUE DIVINE NATURE

There is a divine nature in man, which is the uniqueness of humankind. All other beasts, as far as we know, have a nature that is born of earth, and they follow that nature accordingly. Unless humankind intervenes, animals act according to nature, the way they are supposed to act. And that is perfect.

The divine nature that lives within you wants it to matter that you were alive. There is something in you that wants to make a difference that you were here on earth, beyond the fact that you attended to the creature comforts of your body. There is something in you that wants to make a magnificent contribution to the world.

That divine part of you cannot be killed, but it can be overruled. You can overrule your real self so that it stays entombed. You can lock your divine nature away in a tomb, and the stone rolled in front of the door is called "behaving according to expectation."

The stone that hides the magnificence that you are is your conformity, your submission, your refusal to do anything that is outside the bounds of acceptable behavior. You cannot let the divine spirit in you rule without being extraordinary, because the divine nature in you is not an animal nature. It is not even a nature of this planet. It is the nature of the creator of this planet.

If you try to tame the beast in you by breaking its natural spirit, you may succeed in breaking your own spirit. Then what will you amount to? You will simply become complacent, strictly disciplined, perhaps a very religiously and morally good person. You will not have to be paid for being good – you will be good for nothing.

On the other hand, you can discover the divine nature within you, which is the natural desire to love and be loved. The creator is proud of his creation, including your appetites, your emotions, your yearnings, your hates and your fears. All those things are a part of the animal nature and are natural. It is all right for them to exist.

WHAT ABOUT THE BEAST?

There are two ways to effectively relate to the beast in you. Become completely happy with being the beast and experiencing and expressing the beast. Revel in your emotional outbursts and your lascivious and gluttonous lifestyle. Do it and have a ball!

Or let the beast be loved and accepted by the God in you, by the highest part of yourself, by that in you that loves naturally. Let the beast in you be accepted, loved, appreciated, and approached gently with confidence and reassurance. At the same time, let the warm, beautiful, loving parts of your nature that you want to encourage be nourished, robustly and regularly.

Christ taught, "Resist not evil." (Matthew 5:39) Do not give the beast nature in you more power by trying to force it to behave differently than it does. Your nature, in all its oddities, is acceptable to its maker. The beasts and the animal natures exist as part of a beautiful and harmonious plan, a divine plan. While that is the nature of the animal, the body, the planet and the universe we live in, know that it is not inherently your highest aspect.

There is within you a creative being. It is the part of you that wants to love. It is the part that wants to participate in creation. If you will allow that part to come forward, as you love and accept all the various parts of yourself, you will know who is in charge. The spirit of love, which is the source of life, will hold dominion over all the beasts.

Who is in charge? Man was put into the garden and was told, "Have dominion over the fish of the sea, and over the fowl of the air, and over every living thing that moveth upon the earth." (Genesis 1:28) Adam was instructed to name the beasts, identify them, become familiar with them, tame them and guide them. He was told to be responsible for them, to care for them, to love them. In the presence of living love, without fear, even the lion will lie down with the lamb.

OUR RELATIONSHIP TO ARMAGEDDON

In northern Israel, there is a hill that overlooks the plains of Jezreel. On that hill are the ruins of an ancient royal city. It is called Megiddo, which means *place of troops*. The name has become synonymous with terrible conflict and grief due to the vast number of battles that have taken place there over time. Megiddo was important in the ancient world because it was a crossroads. Many countries including Israel and Egypt depended on caravans that came from the East and passed through the plains of Jezreel. Whoever controlled those plains controlled the commerce of the world in that time.

Scripture foretells that the plains of Jezreel, the valley of Armageddon, will be the sight of the last great war of this planet. "For they are the spirits of devils, working miracles, which go forth unto the kings of the earth and of the whole world, to gather them to the battle of that great day of God Almighty.... And he gathered them together into a place called in the Hebrew tongue, Armageddon." (Revelation 16:14-16) The result of that final battle will be the end of the earth as we know it and the beginning of a new kind of life, a new relationship with earth.

Scripture is clear as to the adversaries in this great final battle called Armageddon. One takes the form of a dragon, ugly and menacing, and causes the inhabitants of earth to worship the beast. He has great powers and performs miracles, winning the people over. "And he causeth all, both small and great, rich and poor, free and bond, to receive a mark in their right hand, or in their foreheads.... Let him that hath understanding count the number of the beast: for it is the number of a man; and his number is six hundred threescore and six." (Revelation 13:16-18) Without that mark, no one can buy or sell, and those without it should be killed.

The other participant in this great battle takes the form of a lamb. "A lamb stood on the mount Sion, and with him an hundred forty and four thousand, having his Father's name written in their foreheads." (Revelation 14:1) With the voice of heaven, those who stand alongside the Lamb of God sing a song whose words only they know.

Those wearing the mark of the beast do not know the words to the song, because they do not sing with the voice of heaven as long as they speak with the voice of the beast.

JOHN'S MESSAGE

Many of today's prophets predict that a world dictator will take power soon and that the inhabitants of earth will be forced to wear tattooed numbers, necessary for buying and selling goods. By interpreting the message of John's Revelation of Christ to mean that there is a ruler who is going to threaten the whole world, we can effectively externalize the message and make someone else responsible for it. We can look at nations with suspicion and fear, and justifiably add millions to our military defense funds. We can watch dictators and rulers who rise to power around the world, wondering if he or she is the one. We can watch for the number 666, thinking that will confirm our identification of the beast. Yes, then we will know who the beast is.

Searching the horizon for the beastly dictator is part of the great conspiracy, because it keeps our attention outward, and it sustains the battle between love and fear that rages within us.

Two mistakes are commonly made in interpreting the warning of John's Revelation. One is to externalize responsibility. The other is to cast it in the future.

The beast is here now! His power is already revealing itself. He is already dictating to people whether they may live or die, whether they may feel good or bad, whether they may feel loved or rejected, whether they may feel alive or not. The beast is the animal nature within you, and it uses the senses and the appetites of that nature to rule over you.

When the appetites of the beast dictate whether you can feel good, or whether you can be happy, joyous and alive, or whether you can express your true self, you are already tattooed with the mark of the beast. The beast is alive, ruling your thoughts and your actions. The vile dictator has claimed power over the world, your world.

Standing on the mountaintop is the part of you that is marked with your true identity. The name of your Father is written on your forehead. Standing on the mountaintop is the *you* of you that sings with the voice of heaven.

Know who you are. Know your true relationship to your creator. Recognize your opportunity and your responsibility, no matter what you have done in life, no matter how you have lived your life thus far, no matter how enamored you have been with the gift causing you to forget the giver.

OUR RESPONSIBILITY TO PLANET EARTH

The great creator of this planet earth gave us the responsibility for her care. She is a living, breathing, conscious being, at the mercy of our actions.

Interestingly, in this century we have manipulated the environment so that the climate and the temperature of the planet have been altered. We fill the atmosphere with pollutants, putting filters between the earth and the sun – our planet and her Father, so to speak. We have altered delicate balances between carbon dioxide and oxygen, acid and alkaline. We are the dubious inventors of acid rain. As we destroy trees without replacing them, we alter the delicate balance that sustains this planet, and we leave her surface, which is her skin, to become hard, brittle and cracked.

The order of this Eden was so specifically designed and set in motion that, left alone, a perfect balance would be maintained to produce and sustain life. But humankind continually attempts to improve what is perfect by manipulating it. We create acres and acres of one kind of plant, providing a banquet for certain insects and inviting imbalance in the delicate symbiosis between plants that naturally grow side-by-side to nourish and protect each other. Then we use chemicals to destroy those insects, and we poison our children and ourselves simultaneously.

The patterns of destruction go on and on. We are destroying our own life support system – the planet for which we were given responsibility – and ourselves simultaneously.

Yet it is almost certain that the planet will outlive our generation, and our children's, and their children's. It takes a very long time to kill a planet, though we seem to be up to the challenge.

More relevant to each of us personally – even more relevant than the ecological issues – is another factor. Anything that destroys the life of our planet is the expression of the beast. Anything that we can use as an opportunity to escape responsibility for the maintenance of this planet, its health and its joy, is the very nature of the beast, the enemy in the battle of Armageddon.

It is observable that almost everyone on this planet is already living under the mark of the beast. People are living so that the beast, which is also named fear, is dictating to them whether they are happy, whether they are contented with life, whether they are afraid of life. People are living as victims.

It can be tested. Just walk up to anyone on the street and say something unkind or insulting. With just a few words of attack, you can alter the body chemistry of another person and elicit a negative, even harmful counterattack. For that reason, the test is not recommended, which proves further that the beast is ruling most people.

We are children of fear, living in darkness. It is a serious matter. Billions of people on earth, 99.9% of us, are living under the mark of the beast. Armageddon is already here.

Do not give into the conspiracy that warns against some future event, a rising dictator, a world economic system that employs tattooed numbers. That would be too obvious. Satan is clever and deceitful, and knows how to appear as a prince of light. The personification of evil, darkness and fear can disguise itself to look like anything other than what it is.

We are destroying our planet by the methods we use to manipulate her ability to grow and provide for us. We assume that ecological matters are for someone else to solve and that it has nothing to do with Armageddon. Better rethink that one!

It is time to realize that whatever gives you a reason to express anything other than total love to yourself, to other living beings, to mother earth and to your source of life is a part of the great conspiracy that creates hell on earth. If we are supporting the enemy in our relationships with each other, we are engaged in the battle. And we are on the wrong side.

You can no longer say, "Some day I will learn to manage my emotions, but right now it hurts my feelings when you say that. Eventually, I'll get around to learning how to communicate better, but for now, what you are doing is making me mad! I'm trying to become a better person, but right now I don't feel like being nice to anyone."

If anyone's words and actions can still create negative feelings in you and cause you to express without love, who rules your life? Is it the beast?

THE TRANSFORMATION

In the new heaven and the new earth described in sacred scriptures, there will be no fear, no pain, no hunger, no disease, no crime, no war, no death, no longer any reason for tears. It will be a utopian world of peace and plenty.

It may seem that this earth would have to be utterly transformed in its very nature to produce such a place. It would. And it might seem that the magic required to produce such a transformation would be complex and mysterious, something we could not comprehend even it were revealed.

That is another part of the conspiracy. The magic required to transform this planet does not require a dazzling nor catastrophic bolt of cosmic energy that God will use to recreate the planet. The recreation of the planet will be accomplished by God within us.

God in us will transform our relationships with each other so that we are ruled by love, support for one another, kindness and peace. By building a consciousness of family that reaches every individual in every city and village on earth, the kingdom of heaven will arrive. The earth will be changed as if by magic. Eden will be reborn, and we will live in a new heaven and a new earth.

It will also be the "Second Coming of Christ" described in scripture. The spirit of Christ will rule this planet, alive and well in all, universally known and recognized in one another. The consciousness of the Christ-force will appear in all places at once and will rule the earth, not as a leader sitting on a throne in a particular country, but sitting on the throne of consciousness within you, the source of life and enlightenment.

ALLIES IN THE BATTLE

If you are overwhelmed by the fact that there are millions of children of darkness on the planet and only a relative handful of children of light living without fear, there is something that might make you feel better about the odds.

When God created this planet, his children were set there and were assigned specific tasks for maintaining the health of the planet. Most of those children play their roles perfectly to this day, from the lowest to the highest – except one, humankind, who is capable of manipulating and making decisions against its best interest. All the other children are still doing their best to serve their mother earth.

Perhaps the least significant of God's children is the lowly earthworm. Interesting creature, the earthworm. It crawls under the surface of the earth, aerating her skin. What a dirty job, you say? His assigned task is to help mother earth's skin breathe. As he goes through the soil, his castings make the earth richer than what he took in. He spends his entire life feeding the life of his mother, doing his best to keep her healthy, returning more than he takes from her. That is his nature. Wonderful beast, the earthworm.

There are billions of humans on earth. Thank God, there are billions more earthworms, and they are all working in earth's best interest. They are all children of light.

Every plant, every tree, every animal, has a spirit of life. And those spirits are our allies in this battle called Armageddon. Additionally, there are spirits all around us, called angels, who work through us. There are a few billion of those as well, and they are allies with the children of light.

Additionally, as we discover more about our universe, we find that in our galaxy there are more billions of stars than we can count. There are any number of galaxies, which fill any number of universes that stretch from here beyond our ability to detect them. Billions upon billions of stars.

Deborah, a prophetess of ancient Israel, writes in her song that "They fought from heaven; the stars in their courses fought," by the waters of Megiddo. (Judges 5:19-20) Even the stars changed their courses to involve themselves in the battle, on the side of the children of light.

So on the side of love, we have the forces of light that include the stars, the angels, the earthworms and the other creatures, the spirits of nature, and the spirits of balance and harmony. The odds seem better already, don't they?

100 CHRISTS

What happens when a few children of light choose to express love and nothing else? We do not know because it has never happened in recorded history.

We do know what happens when a single individual expresses only love. The expression of God who was Christ, living and walking among us 2,000 years ago, totally changed the course of history.

What would happen if there were 100 Christs alive today, 100 individuals expressing God as Christ? It would likely produce a new heaven and a new earth.

Does it seem impossible that 100 expressions of the Christ could live on earth today? How about one then? How about you?

The consciousness of Christ lives within you, and you are a decider. It is your decision whether you act like Christ, whether you let the Christ within you determine your actions. It is a decision you face in every moment.

Even if no one else does it, you could. If you are as effective in expressing the consciousness of Christ as the man called Jesus was when he did it, you could change the course of history again.

"He that believeth on me, the works that I do shall he do also; and greater works than these shall he do; because I go unto my Father." (John 14:12) Convention tells you not to take those words literally. It is heretic to think that you could do more than Christ did. But think it anyway. Consider the possibility that he was telling the truth, that you are potentially all that he is, and more.

A utopian world of peace and plenty is not a fantasy, a metaphor, religious folly, or something that may occur in a far-off heaven. Living in a new heaven and a new earth may be as simple as choosing against pain, suffering, hurt and fear, and for joy, love and life. It is a personal choice and a vital responsibility of each individual to see that it occurs in this lifetime.

The rewards are great. From a sensible point of view, the choice seems obvious. Still, we have the option. The choice is put before you this day whom you would serve: Love or fear? Life or death?

Make your choice. The battle has begun. The allies stand ready. The earthworms and angels are cheering you on!

YOUR PROPHETS HAVE SPOKEN
FROM THE PAUL SOLOMON SOURCE

*Y*our prophets have spoken of a time when this planet may be consumed by fire, utterly annihilated, destroyed. Your scientists have already begun to discover these prophecies revealing themselves in a manner of ways. For example, has it not been seen by those who measure such things that the hole in the protective layer of the earth, the ozone, this increasing rupture in the protective envelope of your atmosphere, exposes the earth to the possibility of destruction by fire?*

Your prophets have spoken of the change in the natural balance of rain, which throughout history has been alkaline for the renewal of the earth, and is now changed in PH balance to become acid. It becomes increasingly acid with each day that you live in the manner that you live, with the burning of fossil fuels and the use of unnatural substances, changing the nature of the environment about you, even the production of oxygen which is obviously necessary for breathing on your planet. There is already a measurable change in the oxygen/carbon dioxide ratio about the earth in your day.

We do not speak of the future when we speak of these things. We speak of what is occurring now. These things continue to change at an alarming rate. The spin of the earth upon its axis becomes slower with each passing decade. These imbalances are upon you now.

Your prophets have spoken of critical periods concerning these changes in the earth. Their words have been only partially understood. Understand that certain of the prophecies have occurred. They have occurred in this manner. Already the economy has gone past the point of balance. Though you cannot see the literal fall or the crash of the world economy, it is observable that you have entered into a false economy in which measure for measure, equal barter value, exchange for exchange, does not occur in this time. The stability of the financial environment is already lost.

You have looked for an earthquake, particularly in the year 1984. Understand the words of the prophets. The conditions that could produce an earthquake were available in that year. That was correct. What occurred in that year was a change in the environment that is irreversible. The year 1984 was used as a marker for passing a line of irreversible damage to the environment. Much of the environment, the systems upon which you depend in this time, has already been damaged irreversibly.

At the same time, there is much that can be done to redeem the earth and to renew her resources. In practical measure, if you were to start today, what are the things that you would set in motion to prevent the complete destruction of the earth, the alteration of the landscape of the earth and the destruction of many people?

If there were a single practical step that could be taken virtually overnight, it would be this: Throughout the earth, there should be planted a tree by the hands of every living being on the earth. If every person planted at least one tree, you might reverse a trend. The trend being that, throughout the earth, every nation is destroying more trees than are being replaced by planting gardens and forests.

We mention this as a critical point for this reason. Your climate has changed on earth. The climatic conditions, the zones of weather, of rain, of desert, have been altered dramatically. The relationship of carbon dioxide to oxygen has been altered dramatically. These are the effects of the destruction of your forests, of the alteration of your rivers and streams, of the balance of nature. The oxygen on which you depend for your very breath is provided by your forests, your trees. Your ability to breathe is being lost with every tree that is cut. It is suicide to maintain this rate of destruction of the natural surface of the earth.

That which holds together the skin of this holy planet on which you live – the living, breathing being on whose surface you live – is being destroyed, is being made sick systematically, by your relationship with your earth.

You must walk upon her as if she were a holy altar, as alive as you are, knowing that her surface is a skin as alive and vital as the skin about your body. Imagine doing to your skin what is done to the skin of this earth on which you live. The deep gouging, the destruction of the plant layer that is the surface life that maintains the health of the body, the destruction of this organism that has a circulatory system, which has a breathing system, which has chakras as you have chakras, which has magnetic poles as you have magnetic poles in your head and your feet.

This planet has all the features that you have, even consciousness. And this living being has tolerated your presence almost as if you were parasites on the skin. But how long can the presence be tolerated when it is destructive, as if it were a cancer upon the surface of this planet? You come to a time when the illness of the planet will cause a convulsion that will shake the earth to its very core, will shake about it those who live on the surface, and will change the landscape.

Consider the trees to be holy, for you breathe in oxygen and you exhale carbon dioxide. The trees inhale carbon dioxide and breathe out oxygen. Knowing that, would you destroy a tree?

Take that which stands beside you as your brother and maintain the possibility that you have your very breath. Let there be established on earth a new philosophy of the relationship between humankind and the environment.

Now you have one coming into your midst, in your time. One who is called John. He has been spoken of by your prophets as one who will establish a new order of things. What is meant by a new order of things? Let us attempt to describe it.

All that you know of science and technology in your day is a science and technology rooted in fear. The relationships between you as individuals are established on a basis of competitiveness, as if two of you had reached for a single grape at the same moment and had realized that "If he takes that grape, then I will not have it for myself." In that precise moment of belief that "your interests compete with mine," there was established on this earth a fear-based relationship between individuals. This fear-based relationship was established thousands of years ago when man began to defend himself against man, when neighbor defended himself against neighbor, believing that personal interests compete. In that day in history, there was born the law of duality, of separateness, of selfishness, the law of fear. And there was what you call the "fall of man."

In that day, man began to fear man instead of realizing that "What is in my best interest is also in your best interest. Our best interests do not compete. There is no reason to live in fear of you."

Fear is ruling your relationships with one another – fear and concern that "You may not accept me, you may not love me, you may not act in my best interest." Even in the moment when one meets another to shake hands, there is in the solar plexus and in the heart the little tinge of worry and fear. "What will this one think of me?" So pervasive is this energy of fear in the relationships between you that it has penetrated your institutions – your churches, your schools, your businesses, your governments, your technologies and your economies.

Fear has become the basis for your science and technology. Your technology is based on the principle of destroying matter to release its energy in order to support life. Consider that philosophy carefully. Your science is based on a belief that that which lives must die in order to release living energy to support life. It does not even sound reasonable, does it? It is a technology of death and destruction.

The energy sources that you use for fuel are produced by the breakdown of matter – taking life away in order to attempt to support life, producing death to support life. We speak of a very basic violation of natural law, built solidly into the infrastructure of your science and technology, your lifestyle, the way you live on a daily basis.

When we say that one will come who will bring the new order, we speak of this. There is one to come among you who will introduce a very simple, vital formula for a new technology, a technology of a new age. This is in reality a re-instituting of an ancient technology, for there was a time on this planet when it was possible to move about this planet in ships – ships that flew by a principle that allows stone to float in the air.

What you call the Great Pyramid of Giza was created by floating stones in the air. Now that sounded strange when it was spoken from these records many years ago, yet recently it has been discovered that ceramic material, being a superconductor when lowered in temperature, causes a piece of stone, slate, ceramic to float by the magnetic field produced within it. This is observable in your laboratories in this day. The qualities of superconductive ceramics begin to demonstrate the principles of stones floating in the air.

Discovering these materials, these new relationships between materials, will allow your technology to discover that ships may fly, not only through the air, but through the earth and water as well. You are beginning to realize in your technology that your body is not as solid as it had seemed, that the space between the molecules and the atoms could easily accommodate the spaces between the molecules of the earth.

As your understanding of physics is altered, to see the earth as it is, to see the relationships between the bodies as they are, so your new technology will allow for the communication of lines of force, not around the earth in satellites and such, in such a ridiculous system as circling the earth to allow communication with the opposite side. By using the superconductivity of the earth's core, communication can be passed from this side of the earth to the other without time lapse. The energies that are now passed in the atmosphere around the earth from one side to another can be passed through it. Travel can be accomplished similarly, moving through the earth.

The establishment of the new order depends upon a simple formula – the introduction of the principle of accessing energy at its point of entry, rather than accessing energy by the breakdown of matter, which forces it to release the energy that gave it life.

This simple formula for the revolution of science will make energy available in a way that makes current science obsolete overnight. All the current means of production of energy become obsolete in the moment that it is discovered that energy is available about you on the surface of the earth and can be accessed without the destruction of natural resources. The atmosphere of the earth can be made to supply electricity freely without the breakdown of matter, and without the enormous cost, and with the availability to each person, the freedom of energy about him.

Such instruments will be invented as a great ion generator that could gather from the city about you the destructive materials that you call smog, to be collected and recycled to the earth. Such instruments will be invented as anti-gravity devices, instruments for moving into what has been termed hyperspace.

All these instruments that sound like advanced technology will come through the simple understanding of the blending of the interests of life with life, living naturally upon the planet.

These formulas for a new science are the establishment of a new order of things. Live simply and in harmony with the earth, and that which is needed as a basis of life will be provided.

You have heard that there was a civilization called Atlantis, that it was an advanced civilization with an advanced technology. Yet you have not found evidence of that civilization, hybridized materials, metal alloys. You have not found evidence of a technology that suggests a science out of harmony with nature. Why? Is it because there were no flying ships? It is not. It is because those flying ships were harmonious with nature. What you find of the remnants of that civilization will appear very much as natural substances on the earth. A technology that is in harmony with the earth should not leave debris that will not breakdown and harmonize with the surface of the earth.

We are not allowed to pass to you this simple formula of which we speak. We are not allowed because we are not allowed from these planes to interfere in the laws and the lives of humankind. We are allowed to inspire you. We are allowed to electrify your imagination. We are allowed to say to you, "Pray." We are allowed to say to you, "Stimulate your scientists to change their thinking from destruction to the promotion of life on your planet." We are allowed to say to you, "Publish this idea that challenges science to access energy at the point of entry rather than bringing destruction for the release of energy." We are allowed to say to you, "Challenge your scientists and those who are in control of your lifestyle to make a difference, to save the planet before it is too late." We cannot drop in your laps this formula. We can say, "Tell your physicists, tell your scientists, tell your researchers, 'Search for this formula which is so simple, which is basically accessing energy as it enters earth and as it is available in the atmosphere. Revolutionize your thinking about the manner in which energy is accessed.'"

This is your salvation. Without the understanding of this simple law that will establish a new order, you cannot save your planet.

How will John access this understanding of a new science and technology? The instruments we speak of – instruments for renewing the earth, for repairing the ozone layer, for building ships that make stones float, for creating machines that can almost vacuum the destructive elements from your environment – these instruments exist and are set aside in a tomb near that monument you call the Pyramid of Giza. If he – John – has prepared himself, this Initiate of the Law of One may enter the Hall of Records, and these instruments might there be found, along with the living formula for a new basis of technology and science.

Understand that the one that we call John is not necessarily a single man upon whom is placed the burden for bringing a new order of life to earth, although such a man does exist. But we make this point, which is vital that you understand. There are among you some who have been, in an earlier time, initiated into the Law of One. If you can bring yourselves to the point of remembrance, you may begin to teach and to bring initiates into the understanding of the Law of One. As you begin to make this change in consciousness, if you can make it complete, you provide an environment into which John can come and reveal himself, and establish this new order.

You must not wait for John to come and make a difference in this earth. It is upon you that the burden is placed, individually and personally. How will you do it?

Begin in this simple manner. Create harmony within yourself. Replace with harmony the argument that occurs in your own mind. Replace with harmony the insecurity that speaks in a conversation between the poles of your mind, the conversation that produces fear and hesitation, the conversation that makes your mind bipolar, that keeps you separated from the source of your own thought, that maintains the veil between the hemispheres of the brain, that maintains the law of duality and prevents the Law of One, prevents the integration of the mind with its source. Begin with yourself, your wholeness. Create wholeness in the relationship between yourself and your source, so you access the Law of One within yourself.

What will the evidence of this be? How will you know when you have harmonized with self, initiating the Law of One?

When you have become comfortable with yourself and with your relationships with the environment and with your neighbors. When you begin to notice that you no longer tense in the presence of another person, feeling afraid that this one will disapprove or that one will not serve your interests. When you have so overcome fear with love that you are filled with confidence.

Disease does not occur in the body of a human being who knows no fear. That which you know as physical death does not occur to a body that has never known fear – unless the occupant of that body gives up that life for another, as did Jesus the Christ. The power of life and death over disease and destruction, over war and peace, is given to those who know love as the power of life and who do not entertain thoughts of fear.

If you can give up your belief in fear and believe instead in the Law of Love, you can become enlightened beings. You can live as enlightened ones, as whole beings, as Initiates of the Law of One. And so you will have a voice to teach and to say, "The science based on the law of fear is obsolete. Governments and institutions based on the law of fear are obsolete."

Your nations around the world criticize one another. One nation criticizes another for building barriers to hold its citizens within the country, to prevent them from leaving. The country making the criticisms builds barriers around its country to keep others out. One nation keeps its citizens in. The other builds barriers to keep others out. And they criticize one another. This is the life of disharmony.

Open the barriers between nations. Tear down the walls between religions. Remove the threat of fear between you. So you will begin to understand the Law of Love, the Law of One.

The Law of One is knowing that "My interests are not competitive with yours."

Your world does not need a new religion, but you do need a synthesis of religion. For that you call religion exists here, and there, and there, and there about the planet – a pearl of great price and great truth surrounded by dogma, as if surrounding a pearl of great price with beliefs and rules enhances the value of the pearl.

Take away the dogma and string together the pearls. Then you will find that, at the core of man's need to communicate with his source, at the heart of every valid religion, is the Law of Love, the Law of One. Collect and examine that which is holy, that which is valid, that which is truth within every religion. Then show man how he may come together across religious barriers to worship together in international, interfaith fellowship.

This is a small step toward breaking down the walls and barriers that maintain the destructive technology and lifestyle that exist on the face of your earth in this time. This is a contribution that each individual can make. This is a way to create a difference.

THE BEST EVIDENCE THAT GOD LIVES
FROM THE PAUL SOLOMON SOURCE

*W*e speak in words, and words by their nature are symbols. Symbols are reflections and can only reflect the image of truth. Those who have known truth have been reduced to attempting to express it through words that are dead.

However, truth lives! Is living! Truth must be approached, not as a concept, but as a living being who reveals the living self to you. Knowing truth is knowing a friend.

When there is a feeling of peace within you, living truth is speaking. When you see beauty and are inspired, living truth is speaking. When appreciation wells up within you and causes you to know with absolute certainty that God lives, truth is speaking. When you know that life itself is evidence that God lives, truth has revealed itself to you.

That which lives is truth, for life is greater than death, and light is more powerful than darkness. That which lives cannot be overcome or destroyed by that which is dead.

If you want to know the truth, walk with that which lives, that which assures and reassures life. Walk with that which speaks of harmony, of peace, of confidence. Worry and concern are manifestations of fear. One who worries believes in the power of darkness, of confusion, of destruction. He believes that darkness can somehow upset truth or life.

Understand that the great war of Armageddon is already being waged. The battle has begun. This battle – call it World War III if you will – is being waged on earth at this very moment. It is being fought between the forces of light and darkness, between life and death. This ultimate war manifests on your planet as the destruction of the evidence of life on earth.

Understand though that all you need to know of this great war is that all things that live are evidence that God lives, for they express through life. And all that expresses life tells the truth that God lives!

If, however, there is belief in the power of evil or darkness to overcome life, and that belief is stronger than the belief in the superior power of life, the evidence of the stronger belief will manifest in the destruction of bodies, plants, nature and earth itself.

However, understand this principle that we will call the Law of Twelve. If there are twelve men, or twelve women, just twelve people on earth who know absolutely that the power of life is greater than the power of death, and out of their assuredness they walk with absolute confidence in God – confidence in truth, confidence in love and life, without a worry in their heart, but with a peace, knowing that life is, because God is – there can be no destruction.

Life is the best evidence that God lives. And you can no more destroy life than you can destroy God. God is the source of all that manifests. And that which has been manifested cannot be greater than its source. It cannot be more powerful. It is not capable of the destruction of its source.

You cannot destroy God. You cannot destroy your planet. God is. Life, which is God, ultimately overcomes death. Love overcomes fear. Death is only a point of reference for recognizing life. Death itself bears witness to the fact that life lives.

As long as God lives, there is life.

Do not worry that so many people live in darkness. It is true that, because of their allegiance to fear and worry, because their belief in the power of fear is greater than their belief in love, they will pay allegiance to this power through suffering.

Those of you who have reached a stage of compassion care. You care for the whole world. You care for each other, for nature, for the planet. Out of your compassion, you want to see harmony throughout the world. You would love to recreate harmony in order to save your planet. Yet worry will not save your planet.

The best that you can do is to walk in complete peace, within nature and among people, with an absolute confidence in your heart – confidence in the power of nature as a manifestation of God. Walk within nature, among humankind, in the midst of life, and say to nature and humankind and life, "You will overcome these difficulties, and I know that. Therefore, I will not fear. I do not worry."

Though the evidence seems to abound that man is determined to destroy himself and to destroy life on this planet, you must have complete and absolute confidence in this one thing. Man simply does not have the power to destroy life, nor is it given to him. It cannot be given to him.

There is no power great enough to destroy God, who is life. Life lives! It can do nothing else.

Life will continue to live in the face of all destruction. Life will return, and return – for God is, God lives, truth lives.

When you know truth, you will know its voice within you. It is not a principle. It is not a religion. It is a living friend. Communication with God is not a communication of words, though you would do well to use your words to talk with God. Communication with your words will lead to real communication. And real communication with God is an absolute knowing of the heart. It is the peace and stillness within you that knows God and reveals God.

In every moment when the mind is troubled, when the heart is troubled, when there is worry, that is not the voice of God speaking to you. It is not the voice of truth, for worry is not truth! Fear is not truth!

Truth speaks its name with confidence. Truth is confident of its invincibility. Darkness cannot overcome light. Fear and death cannot overcome life and love.

See this tiny planet in the perspective of the vastness of the universe, in spite of the destructive power of humankind on earth. See

311

what a tiny speck earth is in the magnificence of the universe. See how tiny is man's ability to be destructive.

All the universe is a manifestation of God. And all the universe is your home. If one small ball of matter, which is not in itself a light yet, were completely destroyed, it would be nothing more than the passing of a cell in the body of God. The spirits of the living would continue to inhabit the vastness that is still the manifestation of the beauty and the light of the living God.

There is no tragedy that can befall you. You descend into matter for a time, and you develop concerns about matter and its limitations. And after a time, you are released. Eventually, you enter matter again. This time, with the intention of making a contribution to harmony and peace, to communicate the truth that it is possible, to live in the world with complete confidence in the power of life to overcome death. But again, matter concerns itself with matter, and logic concerns itself with evidence. Thus confusion reigns, and worry and fear manifest.

Return to confidence. Let not your heart be troubled. You believe in God, that which lives, the source of all life. Believe also in life! Know that life lives, that God lives, that God is completely in control. Know that man, with all his destructive power, is limited to changing the way matter manifests. He cannot destroy matter. He cannot destroy life, for life is greater than death. The evidence of that is seen all around you in life renewing itself and constantly overcoming death. Life is great enough to overcome all the forces that humankind and the power of darkness can manifest against it.

Therefore, be not afraid or worried for your planet or for life. Do not be afraid that man can crucify his God – for has he not tried again and again? Yet God lives! Life lives! Beauty lives! And so do peace and harmony.

Believe in that which lives, and partake of these things. Feed yourself on the beauty that manifests in nature. Wherever the forces of manipulation of darkness have not intruded, walk amid the beauty that is natural and drink of it. When thoughts of concern or worry come, have nothing to do with them. Simply dismiss them and return to a belief in love and life, in joy and happiness, in harmony and peace. Let it fill you and renew you, so that life wells up within you.

Know the truth. Know life. Know that you have a supportive friend living within you and that friend is called confidence, peace. That friend manifests as your own ability to experience life, love, peace, harmony, beauty and joy. Spend your time with that. Focus your thoughts on that.

Feed upon it so that you might become one of the twelve. Just twelve are required to alter the coming changes, including war. The requirement upon each of those twelve is that he be one who lives with complete and absolute confidence in God. He must believe in God more than the power of destruction.

When one is afraid of the power of destruction, one's knees are bent before the altar of destruction. Worry is the act of worshiping destruction because it is the manifestation of believing in the power of darkness and fear.

Confidence is the fruit of worshiping love and life. You are empowered by who you believe in. This is the truth that will set you free. Know the truth that life is greater than death and overcomes it, that love is greater than fear and overcomes it, that light is greater than darkness and overcomes it. Believe in that so thoroughly that you know with confidence that it is true.

That is the truth that will make you free, free of worry and free of fear. So free that, where your footsteps walk, the earth feels confident for here is one who knows God, knows truth, knows that life is greater than death and overcomes it. Nature, where you walk, will spring to life and be encouraged, for it is written: "How beautiful upon the mountains are the feet of him that bringeth good tidings!" (Isaiah 52:7)

The very footsteps of those who know God bless nature and bless life. Earth herself is encouraged by the feet of one who walks as a manifestation of complete confidence that God is alive and well, that life lives and cannot be stamped out, that all the forces of hell and darkness, of destruction, of evil and fear, have no power to stand before the Living One!

You know the truth when you know the Law of One. There is but one God, one truth, one life, one power of love and creativity. And it is greater than all the forces that appear to work against it.

313

Let absolute confidence reign within you. Believe in truth, believe in God, and share that knowledge. This is the truth given by all religions in their original intent, and this is the salvation of yourself and the earth.

If the challenge of enlightening all humankind seems too overwhelming, then consider the challenge of producing just twelve — twelve people who simultaneously express complete confidence in life, in God, in harmony and in truth. And so, you can change even the manifestation of destruction on earth.

Twelve individuals can stop an earthquake. Twelve individuals can stop a war, a World War. Twelve righteous people can bring Armageddon to a close without another shot fired.

Twelve people among you represent the consciousness of the earth, and that percentage of consciousness is sufficient to affect the consciousness of all others on the globe and to enlighten humankind. If it seems that great campaigns are needed to reach the politicians, the governments and the masses of people, all these things are not done in vain. Yet the greatest you can do is to establish complete confidence within yourself.

One! Become one of the twelve, knowing that you walk beside two or more others who also have such confidence that all is right, that life is in control and is not worried about destructive forces, but will continue to live and thrive and grow and manifest in spite of the powers of darkness. Complete confidence is required to know God.

It is also written, "Greater is he that is in you, than he that is in the world." (I John 4:4) You might take that to mean that he that is within you, he that is life, is greater than the evidence that you see around you of destruction. Greater is the life that is in you than all the powers of the world.

Healing at its ultimate comes from this absolute confidence in life, in love, in harmony, in peace. When absolute peace is in your body, there is no war between factors in your body that can manifest as disease. Health itself is a manifestation of harmony within the being. Certainly it is healthy to eat in balance, to live in harmony with the rhythms of nature around you and to avoid altering the substances that nature offers you. It is well that the body be cared for because it is an instrument for expression. However, one should not worry for the health of the body or for its physical manifestations. What you should focus on is complete peace and confidence.

When there is conflict within you, when you are worried about the planet, when you are worried about what man is doing, the worry is internalized. Conflict is set up within you, and the result is fatigue and disease. But when one comes to peace, peace manifests in the muscles of the body and in the nerves and the tissue. While it will not necessarily regenerate the physical body, it can release power in a person and renew strength.

There is no greater secret of health than peace within your spirit. Harmony with truth within you renews, invigorates, rejuvenates and heals the body. One who comes to perfect peace prepares a body that might well pass from this physical plane in peace, releasing the soul to greater life. In such a passing, there is no tragedy. Nor in such a life of harmony is there ill health. One who walks in such confidence blesses the earth upon which he walks. And those who pass by him are influenced by his nature. They are touched by a force of peace.

Then be about the settling of issues within you that cause concern and worry. Let peace, harmony and truth rest upon you, in complete confidence that life overcomes all. From a point of confidence, harmony and peace, you can speak with a voice of inspiration and reassurance. Not so much a voice of warning, although man must be warned of his destructive action for it is simply kind to do so. Humankind might be made aware that there is a better way, a more harmonious way, a more peaceful way, a way that serves his interests better.

The prophets sent by God will continue to speak so, but not out of fear, not out of worry, not out of concern. They will speak with a voice of reassurance. They will give assurance that all is well, that God is not so small that he can be threatened by the actions of humankind or by the forces of destruction or darkness.

Then be not afraid! If God is not concerned, neither should we be. The very nature of God is harmony, the Law of Life, the Law of One, the Law of Love. If you would know God, then you must know him as he is. You must know him in peace, in harmony, in love and in confidence. Then you will know him as the supreme force. Then of what can you be afraid? What can be the concern?

Let your voice become a voice of confidence. Let your heart become a heart of peace. Know God and know truth. Walk with him. Feed upon him. Let that be your source of strength to renew the mind, the body and the spirit, to give direction and guidance, to make the walking of your feet a blessing to the earth and to all that you touch. May it be so.

THE X-FACTOR IN HEALING

You are intricate, delicate, complex, highly responsive and fascinating.

I spent the first thirty-three years of my life being orthodox, conforming to the rules of others including those of the church. That lifestyle worked for me until I became fed up with a popularly worshiped God who rules through fear, punishment and havoc. At that point, I decided to get even. I spent the next five years showing him who was the boss. I lost the battle, but you might say I won the war, because at the end of that period an extraordinary thing occurred.

I discovered a new world that had not existed for me previously. To this point, I had lived as a classic victim. My experience was not unusual since everyone around me lived life the same way. I was dissatisfied most of the time, meaning I usually wished that things were different. When I was happy, I often felt guilty about it. After all, I was living in a terrible world that was getting worse all the time. This was confirmed by the media, the daily news, the preachers, my neighbors, my colleagues, even my family. Additionally, almost everything that was enjoyable was illegal, immoral, fattening or all three. Apparently, the purpose of life was not to enjoy it.

The purpose of life seemed to be to grow to maturity – concerned, rational and seriously responsible. Things were certainly important. I was supposed to apply myself diligently to making money, so I could buy things, so I could be successful, so I could be a responsible adult. Of course, I had all the attendant diseases. I got sick every winter as soon as the advertisers announced that "The cold season has arrived." I got headaches and backaches due to stress. I developed high blood pressure due to my lifestyle. I was right on track with the rest of the collective race.

Then one day, unexpectedly, I made an extraordinary discovery. I realized that there is more to my mind than I had ever suspected, or had ever used. I had been taught that my mind comprises the five external senses of my body, collecting and storing information, calculating and computing responses. We make an observation, we make a comparison, and we draw a conclusion – rational, logical, deductive, conclusive reasoning. Most of us have been taught, or have assumed, that this is all our mind can do.

There came a time for me when the answers I needed would not come through this function of the mind. I had problems for which I could not find solutions. Eventually, I became desperate – so desperate that another function of the mind revealed itself to me. I discovered that if I would shut up and listen, if I could stop the incessant babble of my mind and thoughts, I could get answers another way. I call it intuitive reasoning instead of conclusive reasoning. Instead of logically figuring things out, I simply listened and received answers.

THE REST OF THE MIND

I discovered an ability to communicate with the rest of my mind, the source of my mind. I like to call this greater mind the *cause mind* or the *source mind*. The reasoning is this: The mind that I have ordinarily identified with, the mind that I have believed was the limit of my mind, is a result of brain activity. But the originator or creator of the mind, which is the source mind, must be the cause of the brain activity, the cause of the result.

So there is a result mind, and there is a cause mind. If these two enter into a conversation with one another, extraordinary things can happen to the individual. That is what meditation is all about – teaching the result mind to be still long enough to listen to the cause mind, which is its source.

If we refer to that source in religious terms, we can call it God. If we prefer to avoid religious terms, God will not be offended since she has no ego.

As I began to talk with this source mind, I could get answers that were previously unavailable to me. I received answers that were meaningful and applicable to my life.

One area that I explored was healing. I believed that there were people who could heal others. I wondered if this ability was something that an individual was born with, a gift that some people have and others do not. I wondered why there was the differentiation. Perhaps God liked some people better than others. Or was it something that could be learned and developed? If it could be developed, then how? I asked these questions of my source mind.

EXPERIMENTAL HEALERS

Four friends joined me in asking my source mind this question concerning healing. We waited for the answer.

"If you want to be healers, let each of you go out and buy two young tomato plants," instructed my source mind. "Love one, and hate the other. The one that you love will grow, thrive and produce fruit. The one that you hate will begin to wither and die. And when it starts to wither and die, then learn to love it as well. If you can cause the dying tomato plant to revive and produce fruit, you can heal a human being in the same way."

Excitedly, we all rushed out and bought ten tomato plants, two for each of us. We brought them home, set them out on the back porch, watered them, fed them and gave them plenty of sunlight. And as instructed, each of us loved one of our plants and hated the other – until they all died.

Undaunted, we assumed that we had over-watered them. Back to the store we went. We bought ten more tomato plants. This time, we asked the man at the plant store for specific instructions. Back home, we gave the plants nitrogen. We carefully controlled the water. We gave them just the right amount of sunlight. Each of us loved one of our plants and hated the other. And they all died again! By now, we had killed twenty tomato plants!

At this point, three of the participants decided they did not want to be healers after all and dropped out of the experiment. The other two of us went back to the store, bought four more tomato plants, and brought them home. This time, I decided to love both my plants, thinking that perhaps the hate was rubbing off onto the second one. In fact, I decided to love my friend's plants as well, just in case.

It did not reassure my confidence that my father raised tomato plants successfully every summer – hundreds of them. He did not love them. He did not hate them. He just set them out, and they grew like crazy. And he went on vacation every year with the money they produced.

I wondered what was wrong with me. Was God warning me not to try healing a human? Would I experience the same lack of success as with my tomato plants? Feeling apprehensive, we set the four plants out, and we watched them lovingly. This time, they actually grew a little taller before they died.

That was enough! The experiment was over! I decided to ask my cause mind different kinds of questions. From that point on, I would ask questions about meditation and spiritual growth. At least I could not kill anything that way.

Important issues have a way of resurfacing in our daily lives. One day, I was in a plant store with another friend of mine. He and his wife had an apartment full of plants, thriving and beautiful. Their home resembled a garden and was a wonderful place to visit. I wished that I could nurture plants to grow in that way, but I knew it was impossible. I was certain I would kill them. So my house was without a single plant. On this day, here we were at the plant store. My friend was picking out plants to purchase. I looked around, wishing that one of these beautiful plants would be safe with me.

Then I spied a display of cactuses, and I thought, "Who could kill a cactus?" Well, if anyone could, I probably could. I decided to buy two, just in case. Then I thought, "If they both die, I'll never forgive myself!" So I bought two dozen. They could not possibly all die.

I took them home and created a miniature desert in a beautiful dish with many fascinating variations of cactuses. It was wonderful. "To be safe," I decided, "I'm not going to love them, and I'm not going to hate them. I'm not even going to come near them because I don't want to kill them. I'll just leave them alone."

I attempted to stay away from my cactuses, but I was continuously drawn back to enjoy their beauty. After a few days, I realized that I could not possibly avoid them. I cared about them, and I wanted to look after them. I wanted to look at them and enjoy them. I also realized that I was drawn to some more than others. As I cared for them, I realized that certain ones meant more to me and that I would not be terribly upset if certain ones died. There was one that was my favorite.

Eventually, a bell went off in my head. I realized that I had never really loved or hated any of the tomato plants. I was doing an experiment, and love is not an experimental thing. You cannot turn love on and off, for experimental purposes. I believed that I felt real love for some of my cactus plants, but I never loved any of the tomato plants. I never hated any either. I was simply indifferent to the tomato plants. They had probably died from over-watering!

The principle of loving, which my cause mind had discussed, was seemingly more complex than I had realized. What did I really know about loving something or someone in such a way?

As I watched healers at work over the next few weeks and months, in conferences and workshops, it seemed that sometimes they were most interested in being known as healers. At times, their focus seemed to be more on themselves than on the patient. I wondered who was giving whom energy. Was the healer taking the attention of all the observers and participants by drawing attention to his skills? Was he taking valuable energy from the patient – energy that the patient needed to get well? By claiming "I am a healer," was he not focusing attention on himself, perhaps at the expense of others? Every human being needs love, attention, and positive energy, including the healer. But in these instances where the healer was receiving acclaim and attention, what was the patient gaining?

THE X-FACTOR

As I considered all these things, I understood that the caring and the concern of the healer for the patient must be genuine. My caring must be real. And it must be greater than my concern for my success as a healer. I can never lose sight of the primary goal, which is the well-being of the one I am caring for, the patient. As I genuinely love someone, so effectively that my caring moves as a tangible energy from me to that person, it carries a force that is a healing mechanism.

Right now cells are dying in your body. Simultaneously, new cells are being born. There is a factor present in you that is creating new life out of death. That factor is the intelligence that created you, and it has been with you and within you since your beginning.

This factor that is the source of all life, which makes new cells out of dying cells, is the healing source. It is the power that produces all healing, of any nature.

If you should scratch your finger, you would probably feel pain, and the pain would attract your attention to your finger. Because you care, and because the pain focuses your caring, your caring is likely to go to the point that needs that energy. That source energy is carried to that point and is focused and concentrated there, and it causes healing to begin.

It is an observable fact that if you do not care about life, that healing process will be considerably slower. If you are tired of living, if you are disgusted with life, if you are depressed, if you are life-weary, that healing process will be considerably slowed and less effective. Caring – for yourself and for life – is a primary factor in self-healing.

When love for yourself, your body and life is present, healing is accelerated. Thus love, which means caring for the life-force in all things, is the X-factor or the carrier that delivers life energy to a focal point to cause healing.

What if I can care more for you than for me? Then that same energy that would repair the cells of my finger can leave me and go to you and participate in the process of healing in your body.

Caring for someone else more than ourselves is a valid process of communicating a healing response. Can you move your caring from yourself to another? Can you move the process that builds your body and lend that to someone else to increase their ability to respond?

Of course, there are those who will say that the process is simply psychological, that the patient knows that the nurse cares, thus stimulating a healing response. If I can communicate to you that I love you, perhaps that does cause the healing process. And perhaps there is not a mysterious energy that moves from my body to yours. It does not matter.

If genuine caring has the power to accelerate the healing process, then that is what we must develop as healers. I believe that anyone who can learn to love on that level can learn to heal.

The most important factor in learning to love on that level is security with self, or self-appreciation. Unless I am secure in my own love, it will be difficult for me to forget about myself, to love you more than I love myself. If I am afraid that I am unacceptable, I will be busy trying to prove something to you, and I will draw energy from you. That will oppose the healing process. If I want to share healing, with myself or with another, I must begin by accepting who and what I am.

THE SOURCE OF DISEASE

It is likely that disease exists prior to manifesting in the physical body. For example, if you have a problem in your marriage or any other relationship, you already have a dis-ease. This is the point at which disease needs to be diagnosed and treated. If not, you will embody it. You will find a way to put the stress of that difficult relationship into your body. You may put it into the muscular system first, which may affect the skeletal system, which may affect the circulatory system and the nervous system. You do not know how it will eventually reveal itself. Perhaps in the kidney. Then you have a symptom that is observable. The next step is to take your body to a body mechanic and tell him, "Fix it."

What will he do? He will look at your kidney. He will not ask you, "Are you having a problem with a relationship?" He will fix your kidney if he can. Then he will give you back your body, so that you can go back to your argument with your partner – and develop another symptom in another part of your body.

This is how we keep the body mechanics employed. It is not healing. It is not the correction of illness. It is the treatment of the result of illness.

Each of us has been given a wonderful instrument – intricate, delicate, complex and highly responsive. It is responsive to our thought process and to our communication process. It is especially responsive to the food we put in it and to stress. It is most responsive to caring.

You were given an instrument and told, "Love it." Your body needs love, attention and caring. Chemical changes take place within your body when it receives attention. Depending on the quality of that attention, the result in the body may be of a healing nature, or it may be destructive. If it is destructive attention, such as hurt, hate or fear, the chemical response will be destructive in the physical body.

Imagine a world where the practice of healing is elevated to a level where we heal our communications and relationships with self and with each other before disease ever shows up in the physical body. I believe that such a world is not only possible, but that it is also our natural state.

We can begin right now by communicating with one another in such a way that we do not put the stress of our relationships into our jaws or our lower backs. Do you know that you can exert forty pounds of pressure with your jaws when you are tense? And do you know that such pressure can send stress all the way down your spine and into the rest of your body?

Of course, then you will take your body to a body mechanic, and he will work on your back. He may even successfully ease some of the tension. But does he ask, "Where did that tension come from? Why were you clamping your teeth? Why were you holding your shoulders so rigidly? What made you so anxious that you did this to your body?" Why do our body mechanics not treat disease at its level of origin?

You have a body that is amazingly capable of successfully responding and adapting to what attacks it. There are enough carcinogens in a room to kill us all. But we are not getting cancer, are we? There are enough disease-producing organisms in the mouth of any one of us to kill us.

If it is germs and bacteria and microbes that cause disease, why are we not all sick right now? Perhaps because we are not under the right condition at the moment to take on that kind of problem. Perhaps we have not produced the weakness necessary for disease through our relationships, communications and lifestyles.

Disease starts in the way we live and the way we think. Nutrition plays a role. Sanitation plays a role, the control of bacteria, germs.

But even the best nutrition may not be enough when faced with the stress factors that we are capable of creating.

THE ROLE OF LOVE SUBSTITUTES

We need to begin by giving our body exactly what it needs. It needs love. It needs love as much as it needs food, water and air. And it will insist on getting it.

If it does not receive love, it will seek attention in some other form. We all have ways to make people pay attention to us. If your relationships with your partner, children, parents, colleagues and neighbors are not loving, it is certain that you have found a love substitute – something to take the place of the love you really want. You have found a way to gain attention, even though it may be destroying your relationships.

Do you know that we, as average humans, will accept disapproval, anger and even hate as a love substitute? We will not be fulfilled, but our craving for attention will be temporarily satisfied. Meanwhile, we will embody the anxiety created in those situations. The result will be symptoms of illness, which we will attempt to correct without treating what created them.

YOUR BODY IS ABSOLUTELY FASCINATING

To correct the cause of the symptoms, you must begin with your most personal and intimate relationship, your relationship with yourself. You have a body that needs love. Do you know that you should love it, in spite of the fact that you have been taught it is not all right? Do you ever look at your body and say, "Wow! Perfect!"? Do you tell your body, "You're a miracle! You're beautiful!" especially if society or your partner says you are not?

What has true beauty got to do with an exclusive standard of aesthetics? The human body comes in assorted sizes, shapes, contours and colors, with all sorts of unique accessories. And every single one of the six billion is fascinating.

If I stood before you naked, and I may have the most distorted body of all, would you not be fascinated? Of course, some of you would not admit to being interested. But the fact is that the body is definitely absolutely fascinating.

Your own body is so fascinating to you that you have probably spent hours studying every inch of it in mirrors. Your body is intricate, delicate, complex, highly responsive, wonderful and fascinating. And you should admit it.

You should accept the truth and begin to live accordingly. Begin to feel good about the miracle you are walking around in. Accept your body, own it, make it yours, and stop comparing it to some other, saying, "I wish I looked like that," while disapproving of yours.

Guess who is listening. Do you realize that your cells have consciousness? Do you know that they can be hurt? Do you think that is not possible? Do you think that is something a child would believe? Well, wake up! You had better believe that it is possible. It is absolutely true that you can cause chemical changes in your body by disapproving of yourself.

This does not mean that we should just accept what we are without concern for improvement or continued growth. Improvement works best when joined with self-acceptance. Accept your body exactly as it is and give it your attention, love and affection.

Why in the world would you choose to deprive your body of what it needs most? Talk to it sweetly, endearingly, lovingly. Let it know you care. End the disapproval that will stop you from being effective. If you want to lose weight, be where you are now first. Know that you are beautiful as you are now, and start there. Drop the disapproval, hate and hurt, which are love substitutes like every other addictive substance.

WHEN FACING DISEASE

If you have a health problem, get to know your body and its processes intimately. Get to know what part of your body is affected and how that part functions. What does it look like and how does it relate to other parts of your body? What is it supposed to do in a state of wellness? How should it look and feel?

Your doctor does not have time to get to know your body intimately because of the economics of medicine. Your body differs from every other body slightly. So does your personal history – what you eat, your level of exercise, your environment and circumstances, your relationships, your communications, your relationship to money, and your sexual experiences.

Ultimately, you are responsible for your body. Do not leave your healthcare in the hands of a doctor, thinking, "He will take care of everything. I don't have to worry about it." Medical doctors, chiropractors, naturopaths, osteopaths, dietitians, healers, whoever you choose, can only supplement your personal relationship with your body. If your relationship is not right with your body, no matter how good your healer is, you will counter his or her efforts. Your body will continue to express what is out of balance in your life.

If you do not have a right relationship with your life, your source, your family, your body, your work, your food, your existence on this planet, you will embody those imbalances. And you will build disease.

You have an instrument that is responsive to your thoughts and actions. It cannot be otherwise. Even if the response of disease is corrected, your body will find another way to express the problem that exists in your relationships.

Ultimate healing is a correct relationship with yourself, with your source and with others. A right relationship with life will be reflected in your physical body and in your joy of living.

BEING JOYFUL IS ALL RIGHT

It is all right to enjoy being on this planet. Most of us have been taught that as adults it is appropriate to look concerned and serious and to go around with a furrowed brow. If you walk down the street laughing and smiling to yourself, or talking and giggling to yourself, thoroughly enjoying your own company, society will worry about you. According to society, if you do not appear pensive, you are not serious enough about life. You are not a responsible, mature adult.

Consider this: If God had not meant for us to enjoy ourselves on this planet, surely he would not have expressed his sense of humor in the comical way that most of us turned out.

Perhaps the place to begin is to stop holding God responsible for our dis-ease. We take everything personally and seriously, we become worried and concerned, and as a result, we embody the distress. Then we expect our doctors to search our inner recesses, looking for a cause, when the only thing they can possibly find is a result of what is happening on the outside.

Why not externalize the process? Why not develop a group of doctors who treat the way we interact with each other and the way we interact with life, saving us from disease before it develops inside us – before they have to cut us open to find it?

Why not begin with a healthy relationship with self? Your body may not be in its optimum condition right now. It may not be where you want it to be. However, it is absolutely true that your body is functioning perfectly, even if it is diseased.

WHAT IS PERFECT HEALTH?

Perfect health is the ability of the soul to experience exactly the symptoms that it most needs at any given moment, to respond to those symptoms, release them, and move on to new experiences.

You do not have to be symptom-free to have perfect health. You only have to respond appropriately to the message of the symptoms.

Your body uses symptoms to send you a message. It is up to you to learn the language and decode the messages.

Let me give you a hint. Look for clues to decoding the messages in your relationships, your communications, your sexuality, your prosperity, your daily emotional responses, and your ability to feel gratitude for life.

Appreciation and gratitude are the keys to being symptom-free. Begin by appreciating what you are and what you have right now. Look at your body, accept it as it is, whatever its condition, and be grateful. However terrible your experience of the conditions and symptoms, it is still responsive, still fascinating, still exceptionally wonderful. Begin to believe in that, knowing that your body is listening. Your body will begin to respond to your new beliefs about it. You will witness a difference.

Of course, there are always other options. I spent 33 years living a soap opera – a very sad tale about a terrible world, getting worse all the time. Viewed through a conservative, dogmatic Southern Baptist lens, the world appeared evil – until I finally decided to change the script. I made a simple decision to begin enjoying myself and life. I began to look at the world in a different way. As a result, my world, which had been evil, fearful, destructive and doomed, changed to a world that was exciting, adventurous, full of new information and getting better all the time.

That change in perspective had physical effects as well. I literally began to feel differently. I experienced life differently. I developed a new responsibility for my body. I used to take it to body mechanics to get it fixed when things went wrong. Now I love it, and I take responsibility for the way it works.

THE POWER OF A SINGLE DECISION

It is possible to make a decision, in this moment, that will alter the course of the rest of your life. When every moment that follows is a confirmation of that decision, life changes dramatically.

Accept your life in this moment, and build a healthy attitude toward your circumstances and the people around you.

The people in your life need love – your family, your boss, your coworkers, especially those people who pretend that they do not. People who lash out with hurt and hate and gossip are hurting. People who are unloving are displaying symptoms of dis-ease. And you can be a healer.

How valid is it for a healer to look at a patient and say, "I don't want to be around you. You've got symptoms that I just can't stand."? That is what we tend to do with the people who are expressing the most common symptoms in today's world – the ones who are afraid, impatient, irritable, and who lash out in anger, but who are really saying, "I need love desperately."

You are a source of love, a generous source with ample supply for a whole world. Begin by loving yourself, and go from there.

PERSONAL RESPONSIBILITY

Because the healing process is a process of love, it is important that you fall in love with yourself. Forget what you have been taught about conceit and self-centeredness. We are talking about self-appreciation. To appreciate and love yourself, it is probably helpful to love every organ of your body. That requires that you get to know all your organs intimately.

Know what they look like and how they function. Know their functions so thoroughly that you can close your eyes and actually see a portion of your body and know precisely what is occurring there. You may visualize it incorrectly. Perhaps you will not know exactly what every cell is like. What is important is that you care what every cell is like. Form an image of how you think the organs, the glands and the cells appear as they go about their individual functions. Get in there. Visit your heart. If you have a heart problem, get to know your heart and try to see how that problem looks, in intimate detail.

You have a consciousness that is involved in cell building. The process is unconscious, but the consciousness that fulfills that process lives within you. That unconscious process is influenced by the stresses of life, and it uses them in building cells. That is how disease occurs.

If you can change what is occurring in your life, you can change what is used to build your new cells. This may be the most effective technique of healing in existence – the patient's conscious participation in the function of the organs and glands and the building of cells, in his or her body.

That is ultimate responsibility – participation in the renewing of your own body. It is common to take care of your nutrition, to manage your activities responsibly and to monitor your exercise. Take the next obvious step by restructuring the way you think.

Spend time each day with your body's processes, instructing your consciousness in how to build healthy cells, glands, organs, tissue and systems. Visualize this taking place and know that you are consciously participating in building and repairing the functions of your body. Finding the time may not be the biggest obstacle. Loving yourself may be. Visualizing a perfect body will require that you care for yourself, that you love who you are, just as you are.

It is perfectly all right for you to sit for a few minutes each day and tell yourself, "I love me. I love being me." If you have not yet loved being you, try it. See what it feels like to just enjoy being you instead of wishing you were like somebody else. Whatever state you are in, whatever your attractiveness, or talent, or personality, you are still your own best friend. Make a decision to love being you. Say, "I love being me!" And say it often enough to convince yourself.

Do not pretend to love being you. Really love being you! You have every right, and every reason, to love being you, to enjoy being who you are, to have fun with you, and to appreciate how fascinating you are.

You have to have love in order to live. And since people around you are preoccupied with getting the love that they need, it makes sense that you be responsible for loving you.

We all work for approval. We work to succeed so that other people will tell us that we are all right. We look to others to give us the approval that tells us we have earned the right to be alive. But there is a problem inherent in that plan. I am trying to get all these people to tell me that I am all right, while all these people are preoccupied with getting me to tell them that they are all right. And somehow, it never quite happens for any of us. Hardly anyone is told that he is perfectly all right and acceptable just as he is.

You struggle to get people to tell you that you are all right, but you try not to be too obvious about it. Often, if you want someone to notice you, you become silent, somber and serious. The other person thinks, "Uh-oh, wonder what's wrong with him?" Of course, you really want her to say something wonderful. But instead, she is thinking, "Mmmmmm, better not say anything." So she becomes silent. You respond by becoming even more somber. Until finally she says, "What's wrong?" And you say, "Nothing!" "Want to talk about it?" "No!"

We find it difficult to communicate our need for acceptance, approval and love because we have been taught that it is not all right to say to somebody, "I need for you to tell me that you care about me. I need your attention, your love and your acceptance. And I need it now." We are taught that it is inappropriate to say those things, especially for men. What man ever says to someone, "I need to be loved. Please tell me that you love me"? If a man ever has the courage to come up to you and say those words, please validate his effort by telling him you love him!

The truth is that no one can establish my alrightness but me. I have to give myself that alrightness. I have to say to myself, "I'm all right. I've decided it. I'm the authority on my alrightness, and I've decided I'm all right."

If I let you decide for me and you decide that I am all right, I will not believe you anyway, because I know that I am the only one who can establish my alrightness. How do I do that? By accomplishing something? No, that will not work. That will only establish the alrightness of the accomplishment. But I still will not feel all right.

Establishing alrightness is actually simpler than that. It only requires a decision: "I'm all right with me. And I don't need any better reason for deciding that than the fact that I think I need it. I'm worth that decision."

If I have decided that I am all right and I am not dependent on your establishing that for me, I can stop living my life for your approval. I can get on with the more important reasons for being alive. I can even spend time sharing with you that you are all right.

If we handle our security issues first, we rid ourselves of a lot of anxiety. We are no longer vulnerable to the many insecure and paranoid people that we encounter every day. We do not react to insults, gossip or accusations, because we know better. We know that we are all right. If someone thinks otherwise of me, it is because he does not know me well enough yet.

If I am all right with me, I can function successfully in a world of people who have not established their alrightness. When they strike out with harsh words, when they try to hurt other people, when they gossip, I know that I am not the target. Their actions and words have nothing to do with me. I am only witnessing symptoms in people who are in pain, and I do not need to be vulnerable to their symptoms. I do not need to take those things into myself. Their disease is not contagious. I can instead be a source of love, life, caring and reassurance. I can give wholeness in return.

People who are all right with themselves have established a source of love to give to others, and they give it freely. They give unselfishly because they do not have to prove that they are better than someone else. They are not on ego trips. They are secure.

THE LEVEL OF LOVE THAT PRODUCES HEALING

People who give themselves the time and attention that they need, while giving caring, concern, love and healing to others, discover a new level of preventive healing. This level requires new kinds of relationships with individuals, with self and with life, where stress is not embodied.

At this level of healing, I notice difficulties in my relationships and my communications as they arise. I work to repair those difficulties while they still exist at that level, before they become embodied in my physical body and appear as symptoms. If these difficulties do become embodied, rather than try to mechanically correct the physical symptom, I take the first step of feeling loved. How do I feel loved? Simple. I make a decision.

You are a generous source of love with ample supply for a whole world. You have love to give. You can give it to yourself, and you can give it to others. Do that; do it freely because you want to.

At the same time, decide to enjoy your life because you want to enjoy it. Realize that if you experience life as a miserable situation, you will make insurmountable problems for any healers attempting to work with you. It is very difficult to heal someone who is determined to be miserable.

On the other hand, it is all right to be miserable. You can keep your disease if you want. If you insist on being miserable because it serves you to feel that way, your healer should simply let you have it. Good healers do. No good healer should take away your disease until you are finished with it.

If you have decided that you are ready to drop that and get onto something else, get onto some other form of entertainment, then begin to look at the exciting aspects of this planet. It is a very interesting place. Get your mind on something else. Give yourself some other things to do. Avoid becoming morbidly preoccupied with your symptoms, including treatments, medications and doctor visits.

Focus on your body and how it functions effectively, rather than your symptoms and how they work. Get to know the correct function of your body, not the incorrect function. Visualize and encourage the right function. Build it through creative visualization. And cause your body to respond by functioning in that way.

Spend only the time necessary for that, and then focus your interest on other things. Use your time, your life, your energy, your interests constructively. Get interested in life. Enjoy living. If you can become a joyous person who is excited about life, in spite of your present life situation, you present to your healer an interesting, excited, joyous, loving person who is easy to love and easy to work with. Then your disease won't have a chance!

Disease and pain find it uncomfortable to live in a joyous body that is loved and full of life. Disease tries to escape such a body because it is out of place, it is out of harmony with that environment.

That is the beginning of the healing process – a formula for self-healing. Decide to enjoy life and look for opportunities to express that joy. Decide to love yourself and tell yourself at every turn that you love and appreciate yourself. Appreciate the beauty of your life experience and dwell on that.

If you are going to play back memories, then reminisce about beautiful experiences. Avoid worrying and brooding on negative experiences. While you concentrate on negative experiences, your body is involved in building cells. And guess what it will use to build those cells. Reliving a negative experience, which you have already used to build your symptoms, is not the way to heal. Fill your consciousness with thoughts of beauty, harmony, love, joy and healing. Dwell on those things.

There was a wise healer who said it simply and precisely. "As a man thinketh in his heart, so is he." This does not mean that disease is all in your mind. It is not that simple. People who are ill are understandably dismayed by the situation. However, it is true that the way you think will strongly influence your choice of lifestyle, including diet and activities. When you love yourself and life, making wise choices that assist the healing process will be considerably easier. You will be better able to cooperate with the healer when you believe and accept that you deserve to be well.

CHANGE YOUR IMAGE OF GOD

The process of self-love is a process of self-forgiving. If you have not forgiven yourself for the mistakes you believe you have made, feelings of blame and guilt will continue to reinforce your negative symptoms, even when a healer begins to help you clear them up. You will grab those symptoms back if you feel you deserve them.

Forgive yourself. Know that it is all right to make mistakes. Let your alrightness include everything you have ever done or not done.

Most important is that you develop a healthy relationship with your source. We all make mistakes. We do things that preachers like to call "sin." We even enjoy it initially. Then guilt sets in, and we embody the negative emotions.

When a child does something naughty, he is able to enjoy what he is doing until he becomes afraid that the parent has noticed. Then he becomes convinced that the parent disapproves of what he did and so does not love him anymore. We have a tendency to think that God operates the same way.

When a child has been naughty, does the parent stop loving him? Is it likely that when we make mistakes, God stops loving us?

In forming an attitude of forgiveness, it is important to separate ourselves from our actions, just as a parent must separate a child from his actions. We must avoid embodying age-old concepts of a punishing, fearful God because that will build symptoms in our body as well.

Forget about God's disapproval. Concentrate rather on how your source adores you. Your source is absolutely nuts about you! You are the apple of your creator's eye!

THE ROLE OF VISUALIZATION

The abilities of concentration and visualization are important because they are the focus of the power of your creative consciousness. Your mind should be your servant, not your master. If it wanders from one thing to another without direction, and you cannot focus on a particular point, your mind is not much use to you. You need to tame your mind by making it obedient. This will require that you spend time each day focusing on mental imagery. Learn to visualize by learning to see a particular thing clearly and distinctly.

Choose a beautiful setting. A quiet meadow, or a grassy spot beside a bubbling stream. Create whatever scene you can enjoy. Build the ability to see it in detail, until your mind obeys.

In that act, you can develop both concentration and visualization. Having developed the ability to see with your mind's eye – if you can see that special setting so well that you can discern a blade of grass casting a shadow on another blade of grass – you can turn that same visualization process toward healing your body.

Visualize your body's processes and travel through its systems. Where there are processes not working appropriately, focus on what they should look like. Spend time every day creating in your mind the correct image. In that way, you will correct the physical process.

BEGIN WITH YOURSELF

The process of healing yourself and others begins with yourself. Begin first with self-love, self-acceptance, right relationship with self, right relationship with your source and with life.

Begin with appreciation for the magnificent instrument that you are. Admit the truth of it and be grateful. Allow yourself to feel loved and approved of by your creator. Remember that if you have an imbalanced relationship with yourself, your relationship with your source can be no better.

If you find yourself beautiful, acceptable and all right, you will build a relationship with a God that finds you beautiful, acceptable and all right. Your communication with that being will reflect the personal knowledge that you are loved.

Starting from feeling loved and all right, begin to believe that you actually deserve to be whole and healthy. If you have a disease right now, drop any questions you have about whether you deserve to be healthy. Make the assumption that you do deserve to be whole, healthy and beautifully all right.

Then love, and expect to be loved. Expect to be cared for. Accept the caring that comes from others without resistance. Let caring – from yourself, your source and others – be applied to the systems of your body. Accept it and enjoy it.

Then allow yourself to give your caring and love to others who need it. As you heal yourself, you can give that healing to others. As you give your caring to others, you heal yourself. One supports the other. Your love is your greatest asset, and there is no greater power of service.

MAINTAINING A PROTECTIVE AURA
FROM THE PAUL SOLOMON SOURCE

*F*ear not. Never again allow the energy known as fear, which is synonymous with evil, to enter your mind or spill from your lips. Be an instrument of peace. Allow yourself to be filled with calm, absolute contentment and self-confidence.

Forget, and put far in the past, the times when you have appeared to be a victim. All these experiences are only seeds of wisdom, to know and understand the depths of hate and hurt of which one is capable when one is in pain.

Humankind is born to love. Humankind is made of love. It is natural and normal for all humans to be loving in every word and deed throughout their lives.

To act otherwise is abnormal, and subnormal. When any being who is human, the expression of God on earth, feels loved and alright with self, such a being will never act in an unkind manner.

No human will act unkindly unless dis-eased. That person is without ease, meaning alrightness, security and love within. Being in pain, that person strikes out.

An individual in pain will even attack the person he believes can help him out of his pain, just as a wild animal will attack the one trying to rescue it. Such an attack is a plea: "Help me overcome my pain."

The fact that people have lashed out at you and hurt you is a statement in itself that you can help release them from their pain. They do not understand it, even as it occurs, because it comes from a deep, primordial sense within them. Yet it is, in an odd sort of way, a complement that these people attacked you.

You are not the target. Their pain is the target. You are seen as the key to unlock their pain. In that way, you are also seen as the keeper and the manager of their pain. And so they turn to you, as the one who can release them – at the same time they blame you, as if you are responsible for imprisoning them. The confusion they experience is the darkness of one who has not yet known the light, one who has not yet embraced love and understood it.

Give enlightenment to them. Always give mercy and love, without condemnation. Hate no one. Direct fear toward no one. Be

337

without blame toward any person. For to resent one who has lashed out at you is the same act as a healer blaming a patient for being sick. How can such a healer heal a patient? Never blame a sick individual for having symptoms.

That is the nature of the cleft between darkness and light, which man himself has created. It is not a creation of God.

You are a healer. You were born in love. You are made of love. Drop sympathy and self-pity right now, and forget all that you have experienced and endured.

Engage the angel of the power of evil, and say to that angel, "I will not let you go until you bless me." Having done so, having insisted, and then having the power of the angel ruling over the matters of your life, that angel – once you refuse to resent or hold a grudge or blame – becomes in your employ, a servant to you, and will overshadow you and overpower any resentment that such sick ones can direct toward you.

First, you must know that you are not the target. You must know that their extreme pain is the target. Pity not yourself, but rather that one who strikes out toward you, who is always in much more pain than you will ever know.

You are love personified. Be nothing else. Know only that. Simply love people. And you will have accomplished the will of God.

Be aware of the nature of the auric field about you, as best it can be explained. Visualize this sheath about your body as maintaining a distance of some eighteen inches or so from your body's surface, and following more or less the contours of your body. The outer surface or protective layer, the portals of the auric field, are composed of layers of what might be called light – an electromagnetic, biomagnetic field made of layers, similar to the scales of a fish, one overlapping the other – that will seal the aura.

When the seal is open, in order to sense the vibration of another, the scales separate themselves, the upper from the one below it, like shingles opened. For visualization purposes, think of it so, as if the wind were blowing against these scales, and they open and allow energies to flow in and through.

You have a tendency each day, when you go forth from your home, to open these scales, in order to feel the environment and the atmosphere of the day. And at that moment, you are extremely vulnerable and can allow attack from without, into the auric field. And it can be experienced as discomfort in the area of the solar plexus and the forehead.

You must learn to literally use, not only the mind itself through your intent, but even a motion of your hand, smoothing as it were, closing down layers which rest one atop the other, about your body.

Notice what occurs when these protective layers begin to part and open, and grow more sensitive to the effect. You become open to all forms of both darkness and light. Begin to smooth these, as you would smooth your hair, and even use an oil of lanolin or sandalwood in smoothing the skin surface itself, to reinforce and symbolize the closing and the sealing of the aura.

In the opening verses of the oldest writing contained in the Bible, the Book of Job, there is a comment characterized as Satan, or the power of evil, addressing God with relation to his servant, Job. And Satan challenges Job's devotion saying, "He is faithful to you as a servant because you have put a hedge around him and his house and all that he has." (Job 1:10)

Now use this as an active image combined with affirmations. This sealed aura is the fence or hedge around the servant. Build that hedge by using your hands in a motion that describes a vertical ellipse and a horizontal circle about your body, defining limits that extend as far as your fingertips can reach – and within that limit, invoke the living Presence of the Christ, inside your auric field with you. In that way, you live with the resilience of the Christ-force, which fills you and surrounds you.

One could no more pierce that veil than he could pierce the protective sheath of the Living Master himself. And it is well known, by those who understand the closing of this field of what is called the chi or ki, the life force, the kundalini, that neither arrow nor bullet can pierce this armor when it is closed.

It is time for you to live in an envelope, a sheath of pure peace, pure harmony, no fear whatsoever. Within this sheath, you must listen to the voice of the Living Master every day saying to you, "Be not afraid. Be still and know, I am God. You are safe in my arms, and there is nothing that can touch you."

Know this without a shadow of a doubt. You are embraced by his holiness and none can touch you. You are not available for persecution, for victimization, for being humiliated, hurt, none of this. For the armor that you have created is so great that what is cast at you returns immediately, without time lapse whatsoever, to the sender, causing him to be seen for what he is in the eyes of all who behold wicked attempts.

Beautify yourself by every means including your body, your manner, your carriage and all that you wear. And with a great deal of pride, go forth to face those who have dared to lift a finger or even the volume of their voice against you. Defy them to take any thought or remark against a servant of the Christ.

You are as holy as the one you serve. And no one can touch you any more than he can wound the flesh of God himself. Simply know it, and live in peace from this day forward.

WHAT LOVE IS AND ISN'T

There is no greater talent than the ability to give others a feeling of hope.

Most people think they know what love is and spend their lives in search of it. The truth is that most people know very little about real love. They do not know how to recognize it, how to cultivate it, how to use it, or how to give and receive it.

What is often thought to be love between individuals is a set of pretenses used to mimic love, to substitute for love, when love does not really exist. These are communication practices that do not constructively serve anyone in the relationship. They are not loving communications. They are disguises for love practiced unconsciously by individuals who are ignorant of, or who are not choosing, real love. Real love is conscious, purposeful, supportive participation.

It is helpful in understanding what love is to first understand the disguises for which love is most often mistaken. By defining love substitutes, it is easier to discard them and choose real love instead. Here is a look at what love definitely is not.

DISHONESTY DISGUISED AS LOVE

A common disguise for love when real love does not exist is dishonesty. Dishonesty occurs when an individual refuses to hold a friend accountable for destructive actions. Instead, the individual pretends that nothing harmful is happening. He withholds the truth out of fear and calls it being nice. Real love means holding another person responsible for his self-destructive acts.

It is usually easy to recognize self-destructive acts in another person. But pointing them out may seem harsh or hurtful, thus demanding on the relationship. "I don't want to make him mad. I want him to love me. And I want to be loving to him." We imply that the behavior is all right, while we only share with others our true thoughts about the individual.

Dishonesty disguised as love occurs in all types of relationships, including relationships between parents and children. Dishonesty produces permissive parents. "I'll never punish you. I'll never say you're wrong. I'll never call you on your destructive habits. That way, you'll always like me."

However, dishonesty between individuals prohibits one really liking another. Respect will not be possible either. Both individuals will settle for dishonesty, without knowing love. The silent individual prefers to remain nice to be around. However, he is actually just easy to ignore.

How often, in the name of love, are we dishonest instead? How often are we afraid to communicate the truth, which would bring the relationship to a point of truth, because we would rather not create problems, rather not rock the boat, rather not take the risk?

Every individual on this plane is a tool of your divine plan, including you. Our purpose here is to grow, and we are constantly used to teach one another, to point things out to one another. We often miss divinely inspired opportunities to deliver honest observations that could change another person's life for the better. Instead, we act dishonestly, pretending not to notice and avoiding the matter completely.

Your inner teacher is working constantly through the people around you, even as you are acting as a teacher for others in the external world. However, if you are more concerned that others find you smiling, placid, warm and friendly – so you avoid being honest, never caring enough to point out those things that do not serve another's growth, and thus avoid working with others – you will miss the opportunity to be a teacher, the outer representative of an individual's inner teacher.

Being honest is a double-edged sword though. In attempting to be honest, you can be cruel. You can be so determined to make others aware of what they are doing, and thus teach them a lesson, that you forget to be kind. You may even use honesty in your relationships as an opportunity to unload personal hostility, blaming rather than helping.

Being honest means being absolutely honest, with the other person and with yourself. "I will not pretend that what you are doing is effective when I believe that it is not. Nor will I force you to fit into my beliefs of right and wrong by using guilt to manipulate you."

When an individual makes an agreement of responsibility, and then avoids that responsibility for whatever reason, people who love that person will point out to him what he is doing. People who do not love him will be quick to support his lack of responsibility, which helps him justify his actions. Through their dishonesty, they are participating in that individual's destruction.

Other people who also do not love him may go over to him and say, "You jerk, look what you're doing. Look at the trouble you're causing us." Blaming is also not helpful or effective.

Naming reality accurately is helpful. It can be as simple as saying, "I notice what you're doing, and it's all right. I'll support you as long as you continue to do that. But I do notice, and I want you to know that I notice." That is all you need to say.

Just a look can say, "I notice." You may not have to say a word. "I'm not going to accuse you and make you wrong. I don't want to make you feel guilty. You'll do that all by yourself, if that's what you want. All I have to do is notice. I don't even have to be in your presence. I can be across town, and you'll still know. You'll always know that I'm not going to lie to you. The fact that you know that I know what you're doing, and that I won't lie to you about it, is enough." That is real love.

Reality, just as it exists, is honesty. Denial and avoidance support what is not, because they are dishonest. Supporting what is does not mean making others wrong or speaking up every time they do something you judge to be wrong.

Loving and supporting someone means being an example for recognizing what is real. At the same time, it means being willing to live with another person's action and supporting that person, especially while he is not supporting himself. But supporting that person does not mean pretending he is not doing what he is doing.

You can know your love is working effectively if a person avoids you when he is doing something that you both know is counter-productive. That person expects you to challenge him to right action, and so he avoids you. His avoidance does not mean he does not know you love him. It means he is not ready to change the destructive behavior.

It is typical group dynamics that someone who is out of sorts with a group of people who are happy and being supportive of one another will go off in a corner to be alone. If that person notices that someone else is also unhappy, he will single that person out. Together, they will support each other's unhappiness. But they will avoid the group. They will talk about the group and make the group wrong. When one returns to the group, the other will have to return to being alone or at last confront the group. Those are the choices.

People do not usually go to other people who they expect to tell them that what they are doing is ineffective or destructive. People who do not want to face what they are doing do not go to the people who will point it out to them. They already know what the problem is, and they do not want to be told.

What they need is someone who is honest and loving enough to be honest and loving. That individual's unwillingness to support their negativity will be instrumental in helping them face their negativity at some point. Such individual's are rare, just as true love is rare.

LEECHING DISGUISED AS LOVE

Another commonly used disguise for love when real love does not exist is leeching. People leech the life force from others when they require them to be aware of their presence or when they require them to feed and acknowledge the fact that they are alive. If a person cannot tolerate not receiving attention, he will leech that attention in whatever way possible.

If you are the person being leeched and you resist, your attention and energy will be drained. However, if you give that person attention because you want to, you cannot be drained, even though the other individual will still be leeching.

Leechers try to make themselves so important in your presence that you cannot possibly ignore them. This can take place through various forms, including complaining and showing off, and entertaining and lecturing. Whether a person is leeching depends solely on his motivation and attitude – whether he requires that you be consistently, actively attentive to his presence.

Western culture has produced a population of people who as children were not absolutely certain they were loved. As adults, they enter relationships believing themselves to be in love, when they are actually searching for someone to prove that they are lovable. Individuals who do not love themselves have a great, unfulfilled need to be loved, which will drain the life force from any relationship. The individual who does not love himself and who is not sure he is loved will constantly do things to cause another to prove that it is so.

Leeching occurs in all types of relationships including marriage relationships, parent-child relationships, workplace relationships, friendships, and student-teacher relationships. The leecher wants someone else to provide what he has not provided himself: knowledge of his personal worth. Of course, that is impossible. And rather than a sense of love and worth being gained, life force is lost.

GIVING DISGUISED AS LOVE

Standing opposite the leecher is the constant giver, which is also a common disguise for love. In this relationship, the giver is the one with the need to have his worth proven. The giver gives attention, energy, support, money and gifts to others constantly, so they will want him around. His giving springs from his great need to be needed.

Leechers and givers often end up together in relationships. The constant giver supports the ego and the attention-needs of the person to whom he gives. The leecher buys into the pretense and validates the person who needs to be needed, forming a symbiotic relationship. The constant givers give and give and give, while the leechers take and take and take. One denies himself in support of others, while the other denies others to his own advantage. And it is all done in the name of love.

Parents do it to children. Colleagues do it to each other. Teens do it to their peers in order to fit in. Teachers do it to students. Partners do it for the duration of the marriage.

"I'm a leecher. I need for you to give me attention constantly so I'll know I'm worthy. But if someone more appealing begins to give me attention, then I might drop you."

"I'm a giver. I need to give you my attention so that you'll need me, because if you need me, I'll feel loved. But if you don't need me anymore, then I might hate you."

The truth? We do not need people to need us in order to be loved. We do not even need people to love us. We can give ourselves the love we need. And then, we can choose whom and when we want to love.

If you are challenged by the concept of a world in which nobody needs you, you are misunderstanding love. You have confused love with need. The truth is that it is impossible for individuals to truly love anything or anyone that they need and cannot live without. People can choose to love whomever they want to love because they want to, which has nothing to do with need.

PASSION DISGUISED AS LOVE

One of the most common disguises for love in our western culture is passion. We are taught through countless avenues, from birth till death, that love is based on a feeling of excitement, a chemistry that happens spontaneously between two people. "Oh, you'll know when it's real love. You'll get that funny feeling in the pit of your stomach."

A woman looks at a man and thinks, "He's mysterious. He's strong. He's different from the rest." She finds those qualities exciting and stimulating. Her passion is aroused. Endorphins are released. She falls in love. She forms a relationship and enjoys the feeling for as long as it lasts. Over time, she discovers that he is just like other men, probably quite different from the one she first encountered. Eventually, she says, "There's no more romance in our marriage. Where's the excitement gone? He's changed. He's become so boring. Maybe we should break up. He just doesn't turn me on anymore."

The truth is that he never did. The passion was built on the image she created of him, which was never him in the first place. She was turned on by what she believed him to be and felt stimulated and excited by that image.

People feel passionate toward others because of fantasies built in the mind. Relationships built on passion are based on personal need. They remain the self-satisfaction of one person rather than an experience of real love between two people.

If a man looks at a woman and thinks she is beautiful, he may become sexually aroused. To translate that into "I love you" is far from the mark. It is rather a potential opportunity for passionate, physical involvement with another person, which can be very enjoyable, but should be called exactly what it is – passionate, physical participation with another person. If passion occurs with a person we love, it adds a dimension of expression to the love. But passion itself is not love. And it should not replace love or be considered its equal.

Aroused passion mistaken for love can lead a person to say, "I love you. I have to have you. I need you. I can't stand to be deprived of something I want. I'll risk everything to have you. You have to be with me. I can't help myself. I know I should, but I can't. I have to have you. I love you." That is better named blind passion. It has nothing to do with love.

If you "can't help" yourself, realize that you had better help yourself! Release your passion when and with whomever you want to because you have decided to do that. Otherwise, you deny yourself a range of choices and the fullness of what life is.

When passion is aroused and released without your control, there is a potential for denying your creativity, your ability to make decisions, your purpose and participation. In spite of what society has told you, can it really be desirable for your body to just go around releasing itself without your decided participation, like a can of soda that sat too long in the sun? There goes your body again, doing its own thing, without your guidance or consent!

Take responsibility for the fact that you can make decisions and that you must live with the consequences. Never say to yourself, "I don't have a choice. I can't help it." The day you have no choices and options is the day you are dead. Without the ability to choose and create, you have denied your reality. You have denied your divinity.

The divine spark within you is a creator, a chooser, a decider. To deny that is to deny your relationship to your source and your true identity as the child of that source.

Passion is the energy that you put into a physical act or an expression of love or emotion. It is the release of your total energy, your investment of self. Love can be, and often is, best expressed passionately, because love is something worthy of the investment of yourself. Love passionately. Release your total energy. And do it with conscious, deliberate participation.

OVER-PROTECTIVENESS DISGUISED AS LOVE

Over-protectiveness is another disguise for love when real love does not exist. A protective parent is usually thought of as a loving parent, but the two are not the same thing. Protectiveness means that an individual tries to protect another from himself and specific things within his environment. What keeps protectiveness from necessarily being love is the motivation behind it. When protectiveness exists for the purpose of proving an individual's importance and indispensability, it has crossed over the line where love does not exist.

Protectiveness most often occurs between parents and their children, but it is also practiced in other relationships, including men who want to protect "the little woman," and women who want to "mother" their husbands. The intent is to protect individuals from harm, from making mistakes, from being hurt, from negative emotions and painful feelings.

Keeping individuals from making mistakes, especially children, robs them of their right to flex and strengthen their decision-making muscles. These skills atrophy under the watchful eye of a protector. Children, spouses and students who are protected into inertia grow to be bland, dissatisfied people. At some point, all the pent up expressions and feelings will explode as resentment makes its way to the surface.

Protectiveness prohibits the other person from expressing who he really is. An image that the protector believes is better becomes the goal. "You have to act this way in order to please me. I know best how you should act and what you should do in this situation. And I want to make sure that you don't make any mistakes. Do as I say. If you don't, I will blame you and make you wrong and cut off my energy to you until you do it my way. I know what is best." And they call it love.

The truth is that love is expansive and is not capable of creating limitations in a person's experience of life. Protectiveness is helpful when it becomes a device for teaching a person how to protect himself. This is discernment combined with wise response. Done successfully, protectiveness leads to independence. Done without the presence of love, its purpose is to allow the protector to feel important. "You need me. I will protect you."

Security is an illusion. No matter how good you are as a parent, you cannot ensure that your children will survive into adulthood. Parents cannot control everything. And children will do what they are going to do, often in spite of you rather than because of you.

Protectiveness has a place as long as it does not destroy other people's options and as long as they are allowed to grow to a point of independence. For this to occur, the protector must relinquish all need to be needed. Only then can love be present.

POSSESSIVENESS DISGUISED AS LOVE

If a person is protective, he is probably possessive as well. A possessive individual will want to possess another's attention. And he will want his partner's joy to be centered on him. If his partner is having a wonderful time, he will want that enjoyment to result from something he did, something he suggested, something he gave to the partner as a present, or just his presence in general.

"I don't want you to have fun unless I'm the cause of it. If you love me, you won't have fun if I'm not around." A possessor will need to be the cause of his partner's happiness. And if he is not involved, he may even want the partner to be unhappy. The possessor forms a container that prohibits the other person from expressing naturally, all the while believing that he is demonstrating love. "I love you too much to let you go."

What is an alternative to possessiveness? What works is when individuals enjoy one another because they want to, and love one another because they choose to do so. "I want you to stay with me as long as you enjoy being with me. I want to be with you because I enjoy being with you. I want it to be a choice every second."

If a marriage license has come to mean, "You're obligated to love me," there will be no room for love in the relationship. Then it is only a fraud supported and perpetuated by the government and the church. It is not love.

Parents own children, husbands own wives, wives own husbands, teachers own students, ministers own congregations, bosses own employees. In this society, official certificates of ownership are provided to parents and couples, in the name of love. And the rights of the individuals, the "shoulds" of the relationship, are the restrictions and demands of ownership. "You should do this, and you should not do that."

You do not own your children. You do not own your partner. No one can own another.

With that understanding, individuals can make some agreements. If they willingly keep those agreements, they can enjoy love together. If those agreements are kept because one of the individuals owns the other and has created a sense of obligation, because the license says so, one of the individuals has become, not a lover, but a slave. Anyone who remains in a relationship with a possessor sells his soul by agreeing to be possessed in order to feel loved.

Over-protectors and possessors must resort to manipulation. "Well, if you love me, you won't do that. If you really cared for me, you wouldn't spend your time in those places, or do those things, or spend time with those people. If you really cared about me, you would be interested in the things I like. If you love me, you won't see that person anymore. If you love me, you'll do this for me." The truth is that, if an individual really cares for another, these statements will never come up in the connection.

The result of possessiveness and ownership is jealousy. In fact, "If you're not jealous, you must not love me." Individuals unable to live without another will require that one's attention, will try to own that person, and will use fear to maintain the relationship.

Jealousy is the result of a relationship based on fear. "I'm afraid of losing you." A jealous person will always experience the fear of not having the other person, and will never be able to experience the joy of being in the relationship. The fear of loss will override the enjoyment of the experience and will become the working factor in the relationship. The individual who fears exists in a relationship with fear, not a relationship with the other person.

Real love will require you to be precisely and honestly conscious of your true motivations. "I want to make you happy every moment that I'm with you to the extent that I can. And I want you to enjoy the moments that you're not with me. If I'm enjoyable enough, you'll come back. And we'll enjoy being together because we want to do that, not because we're obligated."

FLATTERY DISGUISED AS LOVE

Another commonly used disguise for love is flattery. Flattery usually exists as the flipside of criticism. "If I never criticize her and always praise her, then she'll want me around."

Flattery is dishonest praise. It is another form of dishonesty disguised as love. People want flatterers around. They want the flattery, accepting it as praise, but they do not care for the individual.

People who are honest in relationships become tools for recognition of reality. They require other people to be real and honest. If you temper praise with truth by calling things what they truly are, realistic points for improvement combined with support and encouragement, people will respect you because you support reality and honesty. Only in that atmosphere can real love exist.

Individuals in search of real love will change and adapt in order to support love and growth. Other individuals, who want to maintain status quo and who are not interested in the honesty of reality, may hate you. No one will take you for granted because you will not be easy to ignore. People will love you or hate you. Whichever they choose, you can expect them do it with passion, if you are real.

PROVIDING DISGUISED AS LOVE

Providing for others is another disguise for love. The provider is a person who wants to be responsible for the fact that you are surviving. The provider gives in order to experience being needed. And you had better love and appreciate that because the provider will never let you forget your indebtedness.

The truth is that you can appreciate what the provider gives, but you cannot love it. Love and appreciation are not the same thing. You cannot love others because they provide for you, but you can love them because they are who they are. If they stop providing for you, you can still love them. But appreciation may last only as long as the meal ticket lasts. That is natural. A good cause-effect relationship means feeling gratitude for the things that people do for you. But do not call it love.

You cannot love a provider, until you are meeting your own needs and until that individual is no longer providing for you. Then that person can give to you, but not to get your love and not because you need what he has to give. He can give to you because he enjoys doing it, because you receive pleasure from accepting it, and because he enjoys your pleasure. When you establish your independence of that person, then you can feel real love for that person.

Love does not occur because you are supposed to love, because you owe it. Love does not grow out of a sense of obligation. You cannot love who or what you need to survive. If you want to love someone that you need, you must stop needing him or her first. Eliminate the need, and then make a choice.

Your choice might surprise you. It might surprise the other person too. That person may not like your choice, but that will not matter because you will no longer need him or feel the need to please him. He is not your provider anymore.

He is not the provider of your alrightness or your love. If you need a provider to fill those needs, then you have not found a source sufficient within yourself. And if you cannot love yourself sufficiently, you cannot love another.

If you find yourself in such a situation, demonstrate to yourself that you can live without the external source of support. Then choose to love, not because of need, but because of choice. You can only do that after you prove to yourself that you can live without the other person. Proving that does not require that you do anything. You do not have to chase another person away to prove to yourself that you can live independent of that person. You only have to become conscious, examine your need, and know that you have the ability to handle that need yourself. And the relationship will immediately reflect that new healthy balance.

You can perform in many ways that look like love but are not love. You can be someone's white knight and appear unselfish by making sacrifices for that person. You can open a soup kitchen or a drug rehabilitation center and measure your worth by whether you save society. You can receive rewards for your unselfish work, including gratitude and recognition, praise and appreciation, awards and trophies. But if you are performing these wonderful deeds for you, to fulfill your own need to be responsible for someone's survival, you cannot receive love as a result. Your actions must be motivated by your desire to perform the actions, not a desire for particular results.

If it is love you want, realize that people will never love you because they need you or because you are meeting their needs. People will not automatically love you because you are supporting them. People will truly love you only if they choose to love you, and they can only make that choice if they are independent of you.

LIVING VICARIOUSLY DISGUISED AS LOVE

Living vicariously through others is another disguise for love. Individuals sometimes postpone, or cancel completely, their own experience of life in order to live through others – causing those people to feel obligated to live a certain way, creating for them a burden that they cannot possibly manage – in order to prove the worth of themselves.

Vicarious living can appear loving, generous and unselfish. Someone attempting to live vicariously through another will do wonderful things for that one because one of the goals is to have a vicarious experience of the other person's joy. But because dependence is caused in the other person, resentment inevitably forms, and neither person finds enjoyment.

Parents may live vicariously through their children. Divorced couples sometimes continue their unresolved relationships vicariously, communicating anger, jealousy and hate through their children. The children become vicarious instruments of negative communication and cannot possibly handle it.

Vicarious living does not really occur. It is not possible to use others as a vehicle to experience the world. We can only utilize another person as a point of reference for how well we are experiencing the world, as our relationships indicate how well we are handling our lessons of life.

THE IMPORTANCE OF TRUST

Of course, all these loveless functions of relationships are practiced unconsciously. Why choose one of them over real love? Love disguises arise from an inability to trust life.

The divine plan for this earth made of it a great school of the mysteries, designed in such a way that every lesson needed by an evolving person will be designed and presented in an appropriate and timely fashion throughout that individual's lifetime. There is no room for mistakes in the natural divine order of this planet. Teachers and lessons are present at every turn. And within each of us is a personal, loving, caring inner teacher who is not protective or possessive. That teacher will let you experience all that is needed for your growth, knowing that what is eternal within you cannot possibly be harmed.

Most parents, on the other hand, decide that they know better than God how to run this school, and they attempt to safeguard their children from the experiences of the school. They interrupt the classes, stop the lessons, and thus thwart the child's potential for learning and growth.

It is a wise individual within any relationship who listens within for guidance in how to relate, what action to take and what words to say. By letting individuals taste of life, rather than protecting them from it, both children and partners will discover for themselves what choices are ineffective, what does not work in life, and what does not serve. Yes, they will suffer some tough consequences – some they could have been protected from by one already experienced in the same area. But only through their own experience will they learn how to make wise decisions next time.

That knowledge comes through lessons provided by the inner teacher. Otherwise, the relationship with the inner teacher is never developed. Instead, a relationship of dependence on another person develops, the possessive protector. And the school of life cannot work effectively to fulfill its purpose.

YOU TEACH PEOPLE HOW TO TREAT YOU

People will only treat you as you have taught them to treat you. Hear that again: People in your life at this very moment are treating you exactly as you have taught them to treat you.

You teach them how to treat you by consistently responding in a certain way. If you teach them that a certain word or a certain look will get a particular reaction from you, you have taught them to use that word or that look whenever they want that reaction from you.

Some people want flattery, and they have taught you that that is the way they want you to relate to them. Some people are susceptible to manipulation, and they have taught you to manipulate them. Some people are responsive to possessiveness. All the people with whom you relate have taught you specifically how to treat them. And you have done the same with them.

Teaching others how to treat us is often taken to rash extremes. Some people teach others that the only way to get their attention is to brutalize them. They become martyrs, blaming their attackers, which never stops the attacks.

If an individual wants to teach another that something is not acceptable in their relationship, it will not be accomplished by protesting the treatment. It will not work for that person to rant and rave. "I won't put up with this! You can't treat me like this!"

What will work is to leave. Refuse to be present when a person is doing something that is unacceptable in your relationship. Do not rant and rave about it. Do not waste words. Just do not be there. If you leave every time a person starts to do something that is unacceptable, that person will get the message and stop doing it, if he does not want you to leave. He will learn how you want and expect to be treated.

If punishment is the only form of concentrated attention a child can get, he will seek punishment. He will do anything to get attention, so punishment will become a reward for his efforts. Do not give children punishment that has become a reward. That does not necessarily mean to ignore them. That means be conscious enough to notice that it is attention that they want and are trying to get. If you do not want a child's action linked to the response of punishment, do not give it to him. Whatever children want, do not give it in a moment when their behavior is unacceptable, or you will teach them to repeat that behavior every time they want it. Fill the need for attention at other times in positive ways.

Refusing to be present when a person is doing something that is unacceptable in your relationship does not necessarily mean that you have to go away, removing your body. It means not providing the response that the other person is seeking. If a person is trying to make you angry, do not teach them how to do it. Do not give people that power over you. Do not show them where the appropriate buttons are, uncovered and labeled as if waiting to be pushed.

If you are triggered by something that an individual does, disable that automatic reaction. Do not be triggered anymore. That means the individual's action does not work on you anymore. It has no power over you. He will then stop doing it because people do not do what does not work.

If you cannot stop being triggered, then you have a problem. Recognize that the problem is with you, not the other person. Do whatever it takes to stop reacting. If you feel uncomfortable that you are only suppressing yourself, then change your reaction. Give an unexpected reaction. Respond differently. Respond in a way that the other person does not expect.

A new response in you will train new action in the other person. A predictable response only teaches people to treat you in a predictable manner. They will treat you precisely as you have taught them to treat you thus far in the relationship.

In this world, consistency can only exist within us. Limited, predictable responses are only a tiny piece of the spectrum of all that you can be. In that case, you are predictable to others, and you are never your total self. If you are consistent in being the whole you, what you are will be unpredictable. You will operate from points over the whole spectrum.

Where you are on the spectrum of all that you can be at any given moment is your personal choice, and no one else can determine what that will be. No one can make you mad. No one can make you angry. No one can hurt you.

If you allow your life to be predicted by others, you end up with a roller coaster ride of experiences and emotions, a lot of ups and downs. In that case, you will not experience consistent joy of life.

Being consistently joyous is the result of one thing: being willing to take responsibility for being consistently joyous. When you allow others to determine your experience, you get the opportunity to blame everyone else for everything wrong in your life.

Blaming others is not right or wrong. Life is not about right or wrong, good or bad. There are no universal shoulds and shouldn'ts.

Life is about cause and effect. Are you willing to live consciously with what you have set in motion? Are you willing to be honestly aware of the consequences you have caused? Are you willing to deliberately set the life that you want to experience in motion?

CHOICES OF ACTION

In examining love disguises or love substitutes, it is important to ask, "What do I do in the name of love that is not love at all?" without judging your behavior as bad or wrong. All these things that we have mentioned can indeed serve as functions of love.

There is nothing wrong with vicariously experiencing another person's joy. There is nothing wrong with filling another's needs, or even seeking another to fill your needs. It can be supportive, and it can be fun. However, these expressions do not necessarily indicate the presence of true love. So if you are experiencing these expressions in your relationships and you are calling them love, assuming that they guarantee love in yourself or in another person, you are mistaken.

All these expressions are choices of action. When used in a particular way, they can be motivated by love. But they are not love. When the motivation is for self, they are what love is not. Yet these same actions can all be supportive forms of expression as you learn what love is and choose to express it consciously and appropriately through any of these functions.

Then the question becomes: "How do I experience what love really is? How do I build relationships that are based on real love rather than one of these disguises?"

The first step in building a strong, positive, loving relationship is to become familiar with who you are. You are a powerful creator. You occupy a body that you made. There is an aspect of you, a consciousness, an intelligence, an awareness, that designed that body. You also created a design for your life experience. You are the creator of every occurrence in your daily life. And you are able to creatively affect the people around you. You can even affect their body chemistry. When you feel really good and are beaming with confidence and enthusiasm, the people around you are affected. They are lifted and encouraged.

If you simply went to someone who you really care about and said, "You are really beautiful. You mean a lot to me. I feel fortunate to know you," do you know what would occur in the blood chemistry of that person? Do you know how much you can affect people around you if you just express the truth? How many people have you been fortunate to know? How many of those people have you told lately? How often do you validate the presence of the people in your life? When did you last say to someone, "I'm so glad you're in my life."?

We have a tendency to think that the lovely, wonderful, important people in our lives already know that they are lovely, wonderful and important. The truth is that most of them do not. Most people would be surprised if you told them how much they have meant to you. And it would make a considerable difference in their lives to know that.

PEOPLE NEED YOUR LOVE

You are a powerful, intelligent, creative being. And you are absolutely, perfectly beautiful. There are no exceptions. Do not hear that statement as a member of a mass audience. It is true for you individually and personally. You are beautiful, just as you are, without changing a thing.

And so is everyone else in your life. And you are a person who can affect others with your beauty. Your love is something precious, and it is worth having. People who receive your love are fortunate. Love is your greatest asset because whatever you love is affected.

When was the last time you told yourself that you are beautiful and others are fortunate to know you and to have your love? You need to know that as the truth. Not just a clichéd self-help statement. Not just as my opinion of you, or your parents' opinion of you. It must be your opinion of you, your truth of you.

Recognize your own value as an individual. Look at the body you have made and say, "Yes, as a matter of fact, it is complicated. It is delicate and precise. It is an absolute masterpiece. It functions well to provide me with every lesson that I need. Even when there is weakness, even when there is disease, I can recognize that as a message from my body. It is a communication device, and it is trying to tell me something. Even then, it is operating beautifully and perfectly. Even when I call it sick or weak."

The first step in forming a true love relationship is being whole and complete and loved, even if no one else loves you. Before you can love anyone else, or be loved by anyone else, you must first come to the point of loving who you are. That means loving your body because it serves you well, loving your ability to create and respond to life, loving your ability to be a cause, to affect life and the people around you, loving the divine spark that is within you – and then, feeling loved by all of that.

You must feel good about yourself, good about life, and good about your relationship with the source of your existence. Even if no one else expresses love for you, you must feel secure that you are loved. When you feel all of that, you are ready to form a relationship with another person.

SELF-SABOTAGING RELATIONSHIPS

If you are not already confident that you are loved when you form a relationship with someone else, you will require that person to constantly assure you that it is true. You may be so convinced that you are not lovely or lovable that you sabotage the relationship. When that person says, "I love you," you may think, "Oh yeah? We'll see about that!" Then you will do something obnoxious to challenge the validity of that person's love for you. Testing the validity of the love will become more important to you than receiving the love.

Why do individuals sabotage the success of their relationships? Often they enter relationships thinking, "If she ever finds out what I really am, I wonder if she will still love me. When she really gets to know me, she won't want to be with me." They enter relationships as a paranoid individual, feeling unlovable and undeserving of love. They make the partners jump through hoops, to prove to themselves their partner's love cannot really be true love because "How could anyone love me? I'm not lovable. I don't even love myself."

People who love themselves, who recognize their value and worth, who know themselves to be loved no matter what happens in the external world, can enter a love relationship saying, "I love you." That means, "I care for you exactly as you are, and I recognize your right to be exactly who you are. I don't require you to change or meet any of my expectations. I love you exactly as you are. And even if you don't love me in return, I'll still love you."

Only people who are already secure in their love for themselves can say those words and mean them. Only people who feel loved can enter relationships saying, "I love you without requiring that you love me in return. If you aren't capable of loving me in return, I will know that that has nothing to do with me anyway. It only has to do with your own insecurity and your difficulty in loving yourself. I love you enough to want to see you grow into security in your own love."

WHEN PEOPLE CANNOT LOVE YOU

People who take personally another individual's inability to love them in return simply do not understand what is occurring. Anyone who does not love you is only experiencing a problem with himself. It has nothing to do with you. It only has to do with something that he thought that he saw in you, which probably was not there in the first place. It was probably the reflection of something that he did not like in himself, that was demonstrated to him through you by some phrase you said or some gesture you made or some action you took. It has to do with his relationship with himself. So how can you be offended? How can you feel hurt if a person fails to recognize who you really are or if a person fails to love you?

People who lack love, who are love-starved, make it obvious to others that they are seeking to be loved. But they also make it obvious that they do not feel loved. They put out a double message. "I want you to love me, but I bet you won't. I want you to love me, but I'm going to make sure you notice how awful I am."

People who feel un-loved often appear to be less than beautiful. But an interesting thing occurs as they grow into being loved. They become satisfied, secure and comfortable in that love. And their appearance begins to change accordingly. They develop a glow that is attractive to others. As people who want to be loved begin to generate that love within themselves, for themselves, they become showered by the external love they were originally seeking. It is amazing to watch, and to experience.

As a young person, I felt unloved and unlovable. I used to think that I was ugly and hopeless. I thought that not even my family loved me. As a result, I entered relationships fully expecting to be rejected. And I was. I was rejected in love relationships, in family relationships, in job relationships. In the army, I never expected to get promoted, and I was not. In my professional jobs, I never expected to succeed, and I did not.

I believed that, if anyone did feel love for me, it was because they did not know me. If they really got to know me, they would stop loving me immediately. I hated myself. I was ashamed of who I was. I was certain that I had failed God, my family, my marriage, myself. I had failed everything. And I was perfectly prepared to be a failure in whatever I tried next. I knew I could be successful for a short while, but that was only because people had not yet figured out the truth, that I was a failure.

When I was "in love" with someone, I could really pour on the effort. I would become successful for a while. I would perform well on the job and make money, and I would start feeling better. I would become successful for that other person. When I was not in love with someone, success did not matter, and I would begin to fail again.

It never occurred to me to be successful for me. I never considered that it was all right to do things for me, to buy things for me, to be successful for me, to love me. I lived for whomever I loved. When I saw nice things, I said to myself, "Wouldn't my sister like that?" or "Wouldn't my brother like that?" or "My mother would really love to have that." It never occurred to me that it was all right to say, "What about me? Why don't I buy something for me?"

It never occurred to me that I did not truly love any of those other people. I did not love in marriage. I did not love within my family. I did not love in the relationships where I was blaming people for not loving me. I thought, "I'm so loving because I do so much for them. I'm always buying them nice things. So why don't they love me? What's wrong with them?"

Today, it is not surprising or uncommon for someone to approach me at the end of a lecture and ask a question, obviously expecting to be rejected, brushed off. That person might as well be wearing a nametag that says, "I expect you to reject me. Go ahead and do it. I know you are going to reject me. Everyone does. But you might as well know that I am going to resent it when you do it. And just in case you don't do it, I'll imagine that you did it. I'll project it on to you." People who do not love themselves will make certain that they are not loved in their lives.

How did I break the pattern in my own life? It occurred in the initial months when the Source began communicating through me. The Source said to me directly, "It's all right to be successful for you. Why don't you do it for yourself?" It was a completely new idea for me. In fact, the idea that it was all right to do anything for me – to be successful for me, to buy things for me, to earn money for me, to be successful in my relationships for me – was shocking.

At that point, as my relationship with my Source began to develop, I discovered that it was all right to love me. In fact, if I did not do it, no one else ever would.

YOU MUST LOVE YOU

You must love what God has given you, as if it were a child, a baby, born to you, given into your care to raise. I am speaking of the preciousness of your heart, your self, the true essence of what you are. You need to fall in love with that as if it were a newborn baby.

As soon as you begin to express that to other people, your family relationships, your love relationships and your work relationships will begin to change, regardless of how they were initially formed, regardless of how dysfunctional they seem at the moment. As you quit requiring those relationships to feed you, and you instead become whole within yourself, loved totally, those relationships will change.

The change that comes may be the ending of those relationships. With or without those relationships, know that you are loved. With or without the excitement, the drama, the satisfaction of being right about not being loved, with or without whatever reward you are receiving from those relationships, know that you are loved, secure, whole and all right.

What you can give to a relationship is beautiful, good and worthwhile. Then give it, knowing that it is precious, but without requiring that anyone else notice how precious it is. That other person may not be mature enough to recognize the value of what you have to give, and that is all right. That does not decrease its value. The people who need your love most are not capable of returning it. They are caught in a negative pattern of giving like for like. When they receive anger, they return anger. When they receive hate, they return hate. You must give love, always, freely, without requiring that others notice. Make that enough.

Form your love relationship with your true soulmate. Then your relationship with a partner on this plane will take care of itself.

What is your soulmate? It is that part of you that never descended into matter. It is that part of you that is divine, always has been – has remained in the bosom, in the heart, of God for all time. Form a relationship with the other half of you. Stop requiring your life mate on this plane to return love to you. Stop making such demands on the relationship. Instead, nourish yourself, and thus the relationship.

What about divorce? What about separation? What about getting out of the relationship if it is not working?

That is fine if you want to come back and try again at a later time. Divorce does not end anything. If you do not resolve that relationship effectively, you will definitely receive another chance. That is how the universe works. That is the universal law of cause and effect. We cannot repeal the law.

The relationship is not finished because you have a divorce decree tucked away in your personal files. It only means that you do not have to deal with it right now. It only means that you received a temporary reprieve. And that may be helpful in growing into a person who is better able to handle the relationship next time. Just know that you must, at some point, deal with everything in that relationship that was a challenge to you, everything that you did not handle well. And the reprieve may be shorter than you expected. You may be resolving those same lessons and challenges with other people in your life at this very moment. The challenges of that troublesome relationship do not have to be resolved with that particular person. You may have met the same lessons you attempted to escape through divorce in the next person you met after coming out of the courthouse doors.

YOUR KARMA IS WITH YOU

All karma is within you. All karma is with yourself and the source of your being, not with any other person. You do not have karma with your ex. Other people only provide the backdrop for you to work out the karma you have with yourself. Everything that did not work out must be, and will be, worked out eventually. So why not stick it out with the relationship, at least until the challenges are resolved? Work it out within yourself and become a different kind of person than the one who could not handle the relationship. Become the kind of person who could handle the challenges of that relationship, and you will not need to have the relationship, or end the relationship, to prove it. You may still choose divorce as the next step, but the relationship will be finished because the challenges have been resolved.

Resolution of karmic challenges is possible as you grow inside yourself, as you fall in love with the source of your being and with its handiwork. Love not only God, but love what God has manifested through you. Forget false humility that says, "Me? I'm not much. I don't have any talent. I can't accomplish anything. Everyone can do it better than I can. I can't do anything." The creative source of your being designed a delicate, beautiful, complicated instrument. For you to say, "That's not much," is an insult.

Self-love includes a simple appreciation for the tools that God gave you to manifest in this time. What defines a brilliant talent? Is it being able to perform on a concert stage? Is it being able to give readings or to speak before great crowds of people? Is it being able to write words into an important book? What is really valuable? What is the most important contribution? What does this world need right now more than anything else? More books? More performances? More technology? More progress?

Right now, more than any other time in history, this world needs people who can look at one another and say, "You are absolutely beautiful. This world is nicer because you are here. I'm glad that I know you."

This world needs people who can help lift others out of darkness, who can encourage them, who can make them feel better about themselves and about life. There is no greater talent than the ability to give others a feeling of hope. You have that ability.

By using that ability, you become as beautiful as any being who ever walked on earth. You can be to someone the most beautiful person they have seen today, by giving to them your beauty, by giving to them an expression of your love.

But that is difficult to do unless you are absolutely secure in your love. It is difficult to approach someone and say, "You are beautiful. I really care about you," because we do not want to appear crazy. You will be afraid to say that to someone if you are not in love with you. If you fear being rejected, you will fear being bold enough to love.

That is the paradox. If you are not love, you cannot love. If you do not love yourself, you cannot give love to others. Loving causes you to feel loved. Feeling loved causes you to be loving.

I LOVE YOU ENOUGH TO MAKE YOU MORE BEAUTIFUL

Where do you start? Begin one day at a time and make it a project. Begin to notice how much affect you can have on other people. Make it a project to make other people feel better. Do it for a week. See how many people you can make feel better.

When you walk into a restaurant and speak to a waitress, be the person who made her day. When you walk into a grocery store and interact with the clerk, be the person who made his day more beautiful. When you pass countless people on the sidewalk who are serious, preoccupied, worried and fearful, be bold. Smile. Be the one who, if only for a moment, causes them to think of something else, something that lifts their spirits.

How much difference do you want to make? I believe that a handful of people could change the world. The Source says it would only take twelve people. Just a handful of people could change the consciousness of this earth – if they begin to love who and what they are, if they begin to love the source of their being, and if they begin to give that love freely to other people. Love is contagious. It is infectious, and it will spread beyond anything you could imagine.

Fall in love with yourself. Fall in love with what you are, with the manifestation of God within you. Begin to give this love to other people in your daily life. Begin to heal your love relationship with your husband or wife, with your children, with your parents, with other people around you. You may receive negative responses in return. But that does not matter because that negative response does not determine your worth, does not deprive you of being loved, and does not stop you from being a loving person no matter what.

Do not be a victim in your relationships. Do not let other people determine how you will feel. Be loved and secure, and continue giving love to those who find it difficult to receive. If someone snaps back at you, if someone returns hate and anger for your love, then consider that you are a healer who has just discovered his patient and his patient's symptoms. That is all.

People who cannot give love in return are hurting. And the appropriate thing for you to do in that situation is to give more love. Give love as a cause, and at some point, they may begin to experience and feel it, and even welcome it.

The challenge and the lesson in relationships is to become a cause rather than a victim. If you can become love and its expression, you can change the world in which you live.

WHAT LOVE IS

Love is what makes communication possible between people. It makes healing possible. It makes relationships work. Love is the X-factor in healing, in communication, in relationships, in everything that is creative, positive, supportive and expansive. Love is the vital energy out of which the world was made. It causes life-supportive results. It is the energy that gives vitality to your body and propels you through life.

Living love dwells in a sacred place within you. You can visit that place and encounter all that is good and alive and vital. In that place, there is a wisdom available that can communicate with you, that always serves your best interest, that always makes you feel better for having been in its presence and never makes you feel guilty or unworthy. It always makes your life more important, always makes your future more important, and is always supportive of your abilities and your worth.

Living love consists of three qualities, which are each two-fold. So there are six aspects of love when it is expressed as an action. This is very important to remember: Without all six, love is not complete.

KINDNESS AND CARING

Kindness and caring form the first two-fold aspect of love in action. Kindness and caring are not the same thing. They express two different qualities of an aspect of love.

Kindness is unmerited and is expressed without reason. It is simply human nature to be kind. In fact, this one bit of knowledge, taken and used constructively by all individuals, could produce ultimate productivity and harmony on this planet. When people feel loved, when they feel good about themselves and the condition of their lives – when they are not experiencing fear for themselves or for those they love – they are naturally and automatically kind.

Caring, on the other hand, is not a natural state. Kindness is a noun, while caring is a verb. Caring is an action you take, something you do on purpose. Caring requires an object upon which to express. You can express kindness to a stranger on the street, but you will not truly care about that person unless you make a connection with him. Caring often results as a response to another person's need. It is necessary, in some way, to know the other person's experience, in order to care.

Caring communicates that the other person matters and has value to you. When caring is combined with kindness, it forms the beginning of real love. Kindness opens the heart of the other person, which makes it easier for you to care. Then caring opens your heart to the other person.

Expressing kindness and caring means acting on a desire to be supportive. It means committing to being a person who gives life, support and love. It means being a person who decides to make a positive difference in a situation and in another person's life.

UNDERSTANDING AND ACCEPTANCE

Understanding and acceptance form the second two-fold aspect of love in action. Understanding may be the most sought after aspect of love. The desire to be understood is often the driving force in our interactions with others, even to the point of preventing us from hearing what the other person is communicating. The challenge is that understanding is not an intellectual function. It does not occur as a result of logical thinking, and so cannot be attained through explanation or justification.

Understanding occurs by means of empathy. It occurs when you care so much about the other person that you actually forget about yourself for the moment. Understanding means discovering not only what the other person is thinking and feeling, but how he is thinking and why he thinks the way he does. You come to know his experience, and as a result you are filled with compassion for him.

As a parent, your child may come to you with a seemingly impossible situation. Someone broke his toy. You cannot rebuild the toy. The other child cannot replace the original toy. "See, it's hopeless," is your child's message. There is nothing that can be done. If you say, "Oh well, that's not important. We'll buy another toy," your child will likely cry, "No! I don't want another toy!"

Masked in that kidcode is the child's true message. He is right that he does not want the toy. He wants understanding. Understanding is what everyone wants and seeks. If the child receives your understanding, his next response will likely be, "Oh, it's all right. I didn't like that toy anyway," It is ineffective for parents to attempt to simplify and make unimportant the problems of children when children are seeking to be understood.

We should not assume that anyone in this world fully grows up. People never outgrow the basic needs they had as children for love, attention, affection and understanding. The basic needs of humans remain the same throughout their lifetimes. The child is still present in the adult and needs to be related to as a child. Every adult still needs kindness and caring, plus understanding and acceptance.

Understanding involves a willingness to hear what a person is saying. For instance, we say that a man could never fully understand what a woman goes through in labor. In an intellectual sense, that is true. A man cannot have the physical experience of giving birth to a child. However, he can experience understanding. Understanding occurs through listening, caring about, and supporting what the other person is experiencing.

Understanding occurs through interest. It is a result of curiosity born of caring and wanting to know. A man gives understanding in the birthing relationship by wanting desperately to know what it is like and by communicating, "I care what it's like, and I'm hanging onto every word, every indication that you can give me of what it's like, so that I can perceive it as thoroughly as possible." That is the nature of understanding: caring enough to want to know.

Understanding is not complete until the person who needs understanding feels understood. And there is no point in going any further to try to resolve or heal a situation or a relationship until such complete understanding is communicated.

Acceptance, on the other hand, has to do with unconditionality. Love makes no reservations. To love another is to accept another person exactly as he is.

Love says, "Even if you never change, even if you don't do it my way, even if you don't want my help, even if you don't love me in return, I still accept and love you exactly as you are in this moment. I may disapprove of your actions. I may even abhor them, but you are still sacred to me. And I will never withdraw my support from you."

For example, a parent knows that his child needs to change her behavior because her rudeness is sabotaging her ability to have good, functioning relationships. He can see that her behavior is not working in her best interest, so he makes a thorough and efficient list of the things she is doing. And he tells her, "If you will stop doing this and if you will do this instead, I believe that things will go better for you. I'm telling you this for your own good. I'm trying to help you in your relationships with other people."

The child will hear his words. She undoubtedly already knows she is sabotaging her best interest and even feels guilty about it. She will hear the instructions for how to correct it. She will know what to do and how to do it. No big mystery there. Most importantly though, she will also hear the message behind the words. What will she do? She will go right on expressing the rude, brash, ill-mannered behavior. Why? The kidcode behind that behavior is, "I understand that I need to change. I can change. I'm even willing to change. But I will not change, come hell or high water, until you accept me exactly as I am without changing."

The child does not need instructions for how to behave appropriately. The child does not misunderstand the problem, or even the solution. The necessary instructions on good manners have been effectively communicated over the years. The child is even surprisingly willing to follow the rules when she is ready. Children will bend over backwards to please those they love, as long as they feel unconditionally accepted.

When unconditional acceptance is communicated – and there is no such thing as conditional acceptance – children can change quickly and automatically. You may be amazed by how brilliantly they can suddenly acquire and effectively use all those tools you have been trying to instill in them over the years. All it takes is a clear and honest message of, "You're acceptable to me just as you are without changing a thing. You are absolutely perfect."

So how do we communicate unconditional acceptance of other people? We communicate acceptance by supporting a person exactly as he is and by telling him directly, "You don't have to change anything in order to get my love, my caring, my understanding, my acceptance. I'll support you just as you are."

The question that arises for parents is, "If I do that, how will my child grow and also learn not to make mistakes?" The child will never learn to change, or even to avoid mistakes, until acceptance is part of the formula.

What is true of a child is also true of the child that still exists within you and the child within every other individual in your life. When we feel accepted without condition by someone, we will actually approach that person and ask for advice. Change is easier through the objective support of someone who is not hanging onto a vested interest in the outcome. When a person is not willing to accept us as we are, we are likely to refuse their suggestions for change, no matter how kindly given.

Acceptance and understanding are two sides of the same aspect of love. And without both sides, that aspect is not complete. You can say, "I accept you, but I just don't understand you," but it is impossible. You can say, "Well, I understand that, but I don't accept it." Also not possible. Remember, to understand someone does not mean to have figured someone out.

I once knew a person who had a fascination with inflicting pain and having pain inflicted upon him. Initially, I found his behavior repulsive, unacceptable and stupid. But I wanted to understand why he did what he did. He described an abusive childhood where the only concentrated attention he received from his parents was through punishment and pain. His child's mind had learned to associate pain with fulfilling his need for love.

His explanation made his behavior more clear, but I was still reluctant to accept it. However, in order to understand and accept him, which was my goal, I had to release my preconceptions of how he should be, and just let him be who he was. I still refused to accept the behavior. But in the end, I had to accept him doing the behavior. I had to stop requiring that he change his behavior so that I could understand him.

The point is that if you put limits on your acceptance and understanding, you allow yourself to be self-righteous. You allow yourself to reject the people that you disapprove of and the people whom you fear.

You have the ability to make people bigger or smaller, more or less. By rejecting people, you make them less, less important in your life. By loving people, you make them more important in your life.

By loving them, you give them more ability to affect your life. You support them. You stand under them. You accept them as they are, and you make an effort to understand them. You make yourself vulnerable to them through acceptance and understanding.

Sometimes, the vulnerability that results from accepting another person unconditionally can lead to a different kind of challenge. Others may place expectations on you to prove your total acceptance.

How can you accept a person who has expectations that you do not want to fulfill? First, you must discern the difference between accepting the person and meeting his conditions for whether he will believe that he is accepted. Some people will never acknowledge your acceptance of them, no matter what you do, because they have a basic belief that they are unacceptable. There is nothing you can do to change such a belief and attempting to convince them of your acceptance will be fruitless.

People commonly put out the message, "I'll believe that you love me if you do this for me." Then you are supposed to jump through their hoops to prove something that they are not capable of believing at the present time anyway. What you must do instead is say, "I do love you, and I'm not willing to do this in order to prove it. I accept you just as you are. And I'll express my love to you in the most effective way that I know how. But I won't accept your conditions, just as I won't put conditions on my acceptance of you."

Conditions created in order to get people to prove their love are not fair, logical or even possible to meet. When a person places expectations and conditions on you, you must find a different way to express your love and acceptance that does not relate to those expectations. Your choice of action needs to say, "I hear that you want to know that I love you. I'll give you that as effectively as I can," without accepting or challenging the individual's conditions.

Do not get caught in the trap of "How do I get my love across? How do I convince him that I accept him?" There is no how. Acts do not prove love. There is nothing you can do. Simply know within yourself that "I do accept you as you are." When that is completely real for you, your message will be clear to the other person. If he is capable of hearing and accepting it, he will.

Concerning understanding, adults, just like children, are rarely looking for solutions to their problems. People are looking for understanding that they have a problem.

A colleague comes to you complaining that the boss gave another person permission to go to a convention out of town where there will be many new developments to discover plus a good time in the off-hours. "He got to go last time. Why can't I ever go to these things? Why do I always have to be the one who stays back and does the work?"

Of course, you are quick to respond, "Well, he didn't actually go last time either. And it is information that his department needs. And your team is working on that project that has to be done next week. You'll get to go one of these days."

"But you know, it's just not fair. I could use that...."

You are trying to provide a solution. But your colleague does not want a solution from you. Your colleague wants understanding from you. Just like a child – because his child is still very much alive within him – he will argue any solutions you provide, continuing to whine and complain about the unfairness of life.

The colleague already knew the answer to his complaints. He knew the solution. He probably even knew that you care about him. He just wanted to hear you express it through understanding that he has a problem. He was trying to tell you, "I want love, understanding and approval right now." Forget trying to fix the problem. Forget trying to explain, trying to justify, trying to resolve the issue. His communication is not about an issue. His communication is about a need he is feeling, a need for your approval, understanding, interest, caring and assurance. That was his real inquiry. Answer that question, and he will take care of the rest.

There is one question behind all the questions you will ever hear throughout your life. That question is, "Can you show me love? Can you show me where love lives, what it's like, how it feels, where I can find it?"

If your answer is, "Oh, your problem is not so serious. Here's the solution," you have missed the real question. If you respond with, "I care, and I will stick by you while you are dealing with this," a miracle will happen, a miracle of communication that is beyond

373

intellectual function. He will figure out his own solution, but more importantly, a communication between two hearts will have taken place.

Understanding and acceptance cause trust to evolve between individuals. If your partner, or children, or friends believe that you will only accept them if they change in some way or if they behave in a certain way, they will carry a fear of not meeting your expectations. That fear will become the foundation of your relationship, and it will always be present in your interactions. That is not love. That is not a love relationship. You will never understand them as intricate and unique beings. You will never understand the special ingredients that make up their distinctive choices of lifestyle, actions, beliefs and thoughts. Consider the wonders of variety that you will be missing.

Perhaps you will never approve of the other person's choices, but could rightness ever be worth more than your relationship with someone you love? Let the people in your life know that you accept them completely, without conditions. Allow them to feel safe, secure and trusting of your support. Open the door of your heart for understanding and acceptance to take place.

SERVICE AND CHALLENGE

Service and challenge form the final two-fold aspect of love in action. They express two qualities of the third aspect of love. Supportive challenge is the greatest service, while challenge without service is a violation.

If you can cause someone to become aware of a destructive pattern of behavior that he is expressing yet unaware of, you can help that person free himself from limitations and self-sabotaging actions. You can create a potential for that person to establish a new pattern, even a new life. And in doing that, you cannot give him a greater gift.

You serve a friend or loved one when you make it possible for the best in that person to express, when you make it easier for him to convey his personal gift to the world – whatever that gift may be. Sometimes, that means telling that person what is not working in his life. But that can only be accomplished in an atmosphere of real love.

Supportive challenge needs an atmosphere of kindness and caring, and it cannot take place without them. Supportive challenge is not hostile confrontation. It is not telling another what is right and wrong or what he should do. Supportive challenge means helping another to see the results of his actions and to determine whether those results are working in his life. It means helping him take responsibility for the consequences he has caused. But none of that is possible unless that person feels supported, not threatened. Supportive challenge provides strength and energy for him to move forward in an effective way, to take his own next step.

Supportive challenge requires courage and clarity of thought to perform. If you feel hesitant about challenging someone by naming for him what he is doing, you are probably afraid of his rejection. Remaining quiet may appear more loving. You have to ask yourself, "Does my feeling of alrightness depend on whether he likes me? Can't I find a supportive way to say it, with kindness and caring, a way that he can hear?"

Supportive challenge is the most difficult aspect of love to apply. It is often mistakenly viewed as mean, imposing and unnecessary. But consider this: Are you loving enough to tell a friend that he has bad breath, or that he talks too much and chases people away, or that he yells at his children too much? Are you loving enough to tell a friend why her life is not working effectively?

Are you loving enough to listen when another person tells you these things? Do you love yourself that much? Or have you conveyed the typical unspoken message to your friends that if they butt in, they will no longer be your friends? Most people are afraid to speak the truth to others because of the likely negative repercussions.

Can you imagine a love that is so great that it will risk being cut off forever in order to serve you? Do you have friends who love you that much, who are willing to risk losing your friendship in order to help you?

What measure of friendship does it take to be willing to serve in that way, to say what the other person does not want to hear, knowing that the relationship may end as a result? We would all be fortunate to have such a rare friend.

How can you challenge others without risking rejection? It is necessary to choose the words carefully, of course. But there is something even more important, which is a formula for supportive challenge. When you compliment the other person twice, he is better able to tolerate the criticism. Consider it a sandwich, two pieces of compliment with a piece of criticism in the middle.

The order of your statements is important. If you put the criticism first, the individual will not be listening by the time you get to the compliment. If you give a compliment and a criticism and stop at that, the individual will only remember the criticism. If you give a compliment, a criticism and a compliment, the criticism will lie in the center, hugged by the compliments that will take precedence in the moment. But the supportive criticism will eventually float to the surface of consciousness later.

If your ego becomes involved so that you have a vested interest in being around when the criticism reaches the surface – if you need to witness the person's reaction to your criticism – your compliments will not be delivered in sincerity. And the individual will hear none of it. If you are able to let the person enjoy the two compliments and let the criticism lie there quietly until it becomes active and floats to the surface, the person will consider it when he is ready.

This ability to remain objective requires the second two-fold aspect of love, understanding and acceptance. To deliver challenge supportively requires first accepting the individual just as he is. Whether he changes is not an issue for you. "You don't need to change a thing for me. And here's this sandwich, if you're interested."

When delivering supportive challenge, it is important to remember that you are not delivering criticism. You are providing a service. People want whatever will make them feel better, look better, sound better, love better, be more effective in life. Therefore, what you are giving that person is not mean or destructive, or even negative. And he will not hate the discovery. The challenge then is in giving the gift in a way that the other person can receive it without feeling threatened by the delivery.

Supportive challenge can only be given in an atmosphere of kindness and caring, when understanding and acceptance have been established. Simultaneously, if kindness, caring, understanding and acceptance are present without the service of challenge, they can only remain impotent.

Here is the formula for love in relationships: "I'm willing to do anything in the world to help you change, if you want to change. And I'm willing to do anything in the world to prevent you from being forced to change, if you don't want to change, because I accept you exactly as you are."

Love in relationships allows for invitation to challenge, because trust is established. That challenge carries with it a responsibility for service. Challenge means putting before that person an ideal for change to which you both make a commitment. Service means supporting that person's efforts toward that change, in an atmosphere of kindness, caring, understanding and acceptance. When all six of these qualities are present, love is complete, and it is unconditional.

THE FIRST STEP

Love in relationships – with partners, friends, colleagues, parents, siblings and children – is not possible until you have given unconditional love to yourself. You will treat others the same way you treat yourself. If you require yourself to be perfect in order to get your own love, you will require other people to be perfect in order to get your love. And they will come no closer to earning your complete love than you do.

The first step in applying these six qualities of love is with yourself. If you are ready to give love to yourself, you are kind to yourself and you care for yourself. You accept who you are, without excuses or apologies, to God or anyone. When you are willing to accept yourself with all of your particular judgments, beliefs, habits and weaknesses – when you are willing to accept all that you are and take responsibility for it – then you will begin to understand you. You will begin to understand why you do things that are against your own best interest. But you will not understand until your acceptance is complete, meaning unconditional.

When kindness, caring, understanding and acceptance are in place, you will be able to serve yourself by challenging yourself. That does not mean being perfect all the time, suddenly having all the right answers and insights, taking only brilliant and correct actions. It means challenging what you have been doing so far, discovering whether those actions are serving your best interests, and making decisions for right action based on cause and effect.

Patterns develop because familiarity is easier than being conscious. It is easier to do things automatically than to do things deliberately and consciously. When you begin to notice what is not working in your life without feeling guilty, without explanations, without justifications, without excuses, without apologies, without denial – you cannot stop doing what you do not know or will not admit that you are doing – without getting caught in whether it is right or wrong, something interesting takes place. It is called transcendence. You rise above the tendency. The pattern loses power when you name it.

We rarely have the opportunity to see ourselves as others see us. If we did, we would probably immediately set about changing our perspectives and reconstructing our habits and our ways of expressing. The only way we can receive the gift of another's perspective of ourselves is to give other people permission to give us that gift. We tend to give that permission to very few people in our lives. We sometimes give it to therapists, psychologists or psychics, sometimes to teachers, but rarely to close friends, and almost never to family.

But guess who is most qualified to give you that gift? Your family! Your lover, your husband, your wife, your father, your mother, your children, especially your children. They are astute observers, unfettered by beliefs, politics or vested interest. If you have the courage to ask your family members "What do you see me doing that is not serving me?" you will likely receive gold in the form of wisdom and concrete material and incentive for change. In that case, do not explain, do not justify, do not apologize. Simply listen. They may not be right. But they will undoubtedly open doors for consideration.

By observing what you are doing, unsupportive actions will change. You will not change them. They will change.

You are in a process of growth. You could scarcely stop it if you tried. You grow by observing the cause-effect relationship of your actions. You cannot outgrow things that you are unwilling to notice. But if you are willing to accept yourself as you are, if you are willing to understand yourself by noticing that what you set in motion causes an effect, if you are willing to be responsible for the effect without trying to blame someone else or explain why you did it, then you have served yourself by challenging yourself to continue to grow. And when you serve yourself, you have served everyone around you. It is not possible to serve yourself without serving others.

If kindness, caring, acceptance and understanding are alive in a relationship, the challenge aspect of love may be exercised without fear. These six qualities of love, when present, form a whole. Love exists, and it is golden beyond measure.

LOVE IS YOUR GREATEST CONTRIBUTION

There is no greater service than our active, conscious participation in life, which in its highest form is to notice another's happiness and to experience joy as a result – to notice another's joy, to congratulate it, to support it, to have no part in trying to make that person feel guilty for having more, to want nothing for self.

To allow another to have everything that you have, and then to have delight in his having it, is to express as a parent. A parent, by definition, is one who looks into the eyes of a child and hopes that that child has more intelligence, more compassion, more talent, more beauty, more of everything than he or she ever had and is perfectly willing to rejoice in that fact.

That is real love, to experience delight in another's happiness.

Love is participation in the lives of others, without a need to have more, be the best, have the most or be the greatest. If you can be joyous at the sparkle in another's eye, you will be filled with love. And you will be more alive as a result.

Participating on this level means expressing the part of you that is love incarnate. Love alive. Living love. The part of you that speaks encouragingly to you, that makes you feel better about who you are, that makes you feel better about your life and your future, that makes you feel better about others – the part of you that is naturally joyous and causes others around you to feel joyous. And joyous people make the planet a better place.

Love is a simple contribution. It is your greatest contribution to the world around you.

THE POSSIBILITY OF COMMUNICATION

If you feel all right about yourself, your right to communicate and your right to think as you do, you will communicate with integrity, and all your signals will say the same thing at the same time.

Y ou are naturally clairvoyant and naturally clairsentient. You can see, hear, feel, smell and taste with a set of subtler senses, beyond the external physical senses.

These subtler senses have been with you since the beginning, and the five physical senses are the result of these original ones. However, because of belief structures and habits built into our western culture, you probably neglect these five primal senses and instead use the five grosser senses to communicate. The problem with that is that the grosser senses rarely communicate truthfully.

We learn early that we can communicate anything we want through the five external senses, even if it is not true. At the same time, we know inherently that that is not possible with the subtler senses. In fact, you can never tell a lie with the external senses without telling the truth, at the same time, with the subtler senses. We will send a double message when necessary, to compensate for a verbal communication that is false.

And verbal communication is seldom true. We rarely say precisely what we mean. Instead, we say what we think we are supposed to say under the circumstances, while our nonverbal signals communicate what we really think and feel.

One person meets another on the street. He does not really want to visit with that person but wants to be polite. A big smile spreads across his face as he says, "Hello, how are you? Delighted to see you," while crossing his arms over his chest as if to protect himself. A practiced eye can learn to interpret nonverbal signals consciously because the messages being transferred are coming through loud and clear.

HOW TELEPATHY WORKS

Communication is occurring non-stop between individuals, in one way or another. At a particular subtler level, communication that does not require the physical body or the voice is taking place. It can be called psychic communication, although psychic is a misused and misunderstood word.

What we really should say is this: Your mind has field properties, which means that a source of energy can affect something else, a receiver, at a distance without an obvious means of connection between the two.

Your mind is capable of emitting energy that can be received over long distances by anyone who makes himself or herself receptive – on the same wavelength, for lack of a better term.

In other words, if you should care about another person, what that person is thinking and how that person is feeling, more than you care about yourself, you will experience that person's thoughts and feelings. That is telepathy.

If you want to know what someone else is thinking, all you have to do is care more about what he is thinking than what you are thinking. That level of caring will cause you to give up your own thoughts, ideas and opinions. As a result, you will be able to perceive that other person's thoughts. Most individuals are too lazy or indifferent to do this on purpose, but it occurs accidentally quite often.

It often occurs when people fall in love. An individual falls in love, and suddenly all the issues that were previously important do not matter. And for a period of time, that individual seems mindless, because his mind is always on that other person, often caring more about that person's thoughts and feelings than his own. The result can be a series of psychic experiences, such as when the phone rings and he knows ahead of time that it is the other person on the other end, or when both individuals say or think the same thing simultaneously.

If you learn to care what another person is thinking, you will make yourself receptive. It is not simple to do deliberately, because when you start doing it deliberately, your mind wants to consider whether you are experiencing success, which means your mind is on yourself again. In other words, the caring must be genuine. Genuine caring will cause you to be magnetically receptive, and by being receptive, you will receive thoughts from the people around you.

Caring is not the only way to become receptive. Not experiencing your own thoughts deliberately can also cause you to feel and experience the thoughts of others. It is less healthy than doing it on purpose, but it occurs all the time.

There are two kinds of thinkers, or two ways of thinking. One is a deliberate act of thinking, which produces a positive polarity. The other is receptive, negative, feminine thinking, which is the act of being empty in your consciousness, such as when you daydream. When you are empty in your consciousness, you become vulnerable to the thoughts and feelings of the people around you.

To avoid unconscious thinking, you need to take responsibility for your communication on several levels. There are two halves to every experience of communication: what you are giving and what you are receiving. Two halves make a whole, and every whole has a positive and negative polarity.

The positive is what you are trying to give. And the negative is what you believe you are receiving in response, which directly affects the next communication that you give. Communication is a rhythmic movement, flowing back and forth, between individuals. Whatever you communicate with another is built on what that person communicated to you. Your task is to be sensitive to what others are saying, what others are asking, and what others are telling you concerning what you are saying.

That means taking responsibility for being both receptive and active in communication. The key to doing that is to realize that verbal communication is probably the least important of all possibilities. When we speak words, people consider our expression, our other body language, the myriad conditions under which we speak, and the way we word our sentences. What we say is better understood when considered in the context of what we do not say.

INTEGRITY IN COMMUNICATION

The secret to whole, responsible communication is integrity. The word integrity is a variation of the word integral, meaning one – not separated into two parts, not split from itself, not doing or saying two different things simultaneously, not saying one thing and meaning something else.

Integrity in communication means identifying what you mean and admitting it to yourself. People who lie in communication usually lie first to themselves. They do not want to believe they are being dishonest, so they will excuse themselves by finding some justification for saying what they are saying. Society provides ample justifications, by saying that it is important to be polite, to be non-confrontational, to be discreet, to not make trouble – more important than being honest.

Integrity comes from examining who you are and what you want to say, and forming a right relationship with that. If you believe that what you are communicating is not acceptable, you are split from yourself. You will feel dishonest, and you will indicate that on some level. We are not capable of lying on all levels. So we will use our body to indicate our discomfort with whatever we just said. That is communication without integrity.

Integrity comes from self-acceptance. You can communicate with integrity anything that you believe, if you believe that it is all right to believe it, and you are all right with you, and you have given yourself permission to think what you think, and you have given yourself permission to communicate that. If you feel all right about yourself, your right to communicate, and your right to think as you do, you will communicate with integrity. And all your signals will say the same thing at the same time.

When all your signals say the same thing at the same time, even people who do not know how to read multilevel signals will notice something unusual about you. They will think that you communicate with confidence. Confidence is a result of integrity in thinking.

We are not using the word integrity here in the moral sense. Integrity in communication is not dependent on whether your thinking reflects moral codes. We are not referring to what you should believe or say. In fact, that has little to do with integrity!

Integrity means harmonizing with yourself on all levels, being one. Being one means being able to think a thought, even one that would be considered immoral, and being able to express that, and being all right with it. Your belief about it is that it is all right, because you have found it acceptable to you. Everything is in agreement.

Your thought and expression, and your belief that both are all right, may violate codes set by other people based on their beliefs. But if you have formed a right relationship with you, if you have accepted you as an individual, if you have decided to take responsibility for what you communicate and the consequences, then you can communicate what you truly think – instead of communicating what you think you are supposed to say under certain conditions, while simultaneously thinking, "I wish I didn't have to say that." That is a double message, a multilevel message.

We create in ourselves, and in our children at an early age, the tendency to communicate one thing while believing another. And we simultaneously tell our children "You are supposed to be honest." We tell children that it is important to tell the truth, while we teach them to lie through our double messages. It is difficult to fool children. They definitely know when we are not saying what we mean. And they can usually detect what we really mean instead.

Double messages get caught in the physical body. It is not possible to communicate a lack of integrity without tightening muscles. The place where you tighten the muscles usually relates to the subject. If you are talking about sex and moral considerations, you will likely tighten muscles in the thighs and lower abdomen. If it concerns your job, such as working overtime because you feel guilty about not getting enough done, you will likely tighten your lips and shoulders. You are shouldering a burden.

The majority of your communication is accomplished through your emotions and your physical body, not your words. People around you discover what you are trying to say, by the way you use your physical body and your emotions to manipulate them to get what you need. You tell them that you are feeling good or bad, or that you need this or that, by expressing emotion.

To actually begin to communicate with integrity, to give ourselves and others permission to say what we really mean through our words and signals simultaneously, would be like getting out of prison. The change would be so major that it would affect our physical bodies: our facial muscles, the muscles of our jaws in particular, the vertebrae of the back of our necks, the muscles across our shoulders, the muscles up and down our backs. And that would in turn affect our hearts, lungs, kidneys, endocrine glands, and on and on. Being completely honest, with yourself and others, would heal your body and transform your relationships and lifestyle.

How do you begin to get honest with yourself and communicate with integrity? By getting in touch with yourself, how you feel about you and about what you have been saying to the people around you.

COMMUNICATION IS ALWAYS SEXUAL

Communication is a multilevel sexual relationship. It is sexual in the sense that it is an interaction of a positive with a negative. When a positive and a negative interact, one impregnates the other, and the interaction becomes sexual. If something new is born, birth takes place. The interaction may occur on several levels. It may be positive on one level and negative on another at the same time. You are a multilevel being, capable of interacting on many levels simultaneously.

For instance, you may express anger at a person for something he has done. He in turn may express regret and contriteness. You may receive and experience satisfaction from his response, at the same time that you continue to express anger.

Your expression of anger is an active, masculine, positive communication. That expression causes an effect in the other person. You receive satisfaction because the person is communicating back to you what you want. Receiving is an accepting, feminine, negative communication. It causes a result in you, which is a new feeling. The feminine in you conceived and gave birth to a new feeling.

So three things have occurred: You put out a masculine, you received a feminine, then you incubated that and gave birth to a new emotion as a result. That is a multilevel sexual relationship.

THE POSSIBILITY OF COMMUNICATION

MALE OR FEMALE?

Your soul, the *you* of you, is not male or female. Your soul is androgynous. Physically, you are expressing as male or female in this lifetime because it best suits your needs right now. That body that you are wearing is most appropriate for what you came to do. But it is not who or what you are.

What you are is an androgynous being with masculine and feminine qualities, capable of conceiving, incubating and giving birth to ideas, emotions, expressions, creativity, all sorts of things on many different levels. In communication, you can be male on one level and female on another, or female on all levels, or male on all levels.

We are constantly having interactions that produce results. These interactions are essentially sexual or reproductive in nature.

Communication is the act of having productive relationships on both subtle and observable levels. It is the act of becoming masculine in order to impregnate a feminine receptor, which may be in a masculine body, to produce a result. The result may be a thought, an idea, or an image. In any case, it is the offspring of the impregnation.

The goal of every communication is to give birth. But in every case, abortion may occur instead. It often does.

Two masculine expressions will always result in an aborted communication. When one person is expressing actively and the other person interrupts, also expressing actively, no one is expressing femininely, and abortion is the result. When one person expresses actively and the other takes a feminine mode, the active one is drawn out by the receptivity of the feminine, and the two incubate a result.

Every communication, every conversation, should result in a birth of a child. That child is the understanding that occurs between the two individuals as a result of their communication. If the child is not born, if the conversation is aborted, communication did not take place.

LOVE IS THE KEY TO COMMUNICATION

Love means the feeding of one another with available energy that allows us to have mutual intercourse, not necessarily on the physical level. Every human being has an intrinsic need to be loved.

And if a being does not feel loved, that being will go to drastic lengths to get a love substitute.

There are many substitutes for love including sympathy, hate, rejection and disapproval. The thing that human beings can tolerate least is being ignored. Keep in mind that hate is not the opposite of love. Indifference is the opposite of love. We will accept either love or hate, but we cannot accept indifference.

Hate is love expressed with disapproval. You cannot hate someone you do not care about. And that caring is what love is all about. People have a need to be cared about, no matter what form that takes. We have a need for someone else to care that we exist. Because of that, we often enter into unhealthy relationships.

All your relationships and communications center on acceptance and love – not necessarily the expression of love, but your need for love. Your need to be loved is a critical need that you cannot deny. Your relationship to being loved will affect all your communications. Every time you communicate, even if only to ask for a glass of water or to say hello, you will make a statement about your current love relationship – your need for love and your current status concerning the satisfaction of that need.

If a stranger says hello to me, I can tell you almost immediately about his relationship to love – whether he feels loved, whether he believes he is loved, how deep is his need for love, whether he is receiving it, how he feels about receiving it, whether he feels worthy of it. In every relationship, in every interaction, all of this is the basis for communication.

Your greatest need as a being is to love and be loved. And the physical body is only an instrument for the expression of that. It is an instrument created for experiencing communication and relationships, in order to love and be loved.

Communication does not occur through words, sounds, facial expressions, body language or any other physical means. It occurs in a subtler dimension, if at all. Words can only facilitate our recognition that communication has taken place.

The key to communication is love. Without it, communication does not, and cannot, occur. You cannot communicate with a person you do not love, a person with whom you do not have a love relationship. You will have an exchange of words, but you will not have a communication.

ORIENTAL THOUGHT ON COMMUNICATION

The ancient system of divination called the I Ching originates through oriental traditions and legends of a time when a wise woodcutter lived alone in the forest. Over time and through focused observation of the nature surrounding him, the woodcutter became aware of patterns in nature, as demonstrated through the constant interactions – the animals interacting with each other, and with the seasons, the environment, the sun and the earth. Through keen observations and reflection, he discovered patterns – the relationship between the sun and the earth, how the sun's energy is absorbed by the earth and restored to life in the plants, and all the cycles that evolve out of that phenomenon.

The woodcutter began to record the patterns. In doing so, he realized certain principles represented in the patterns. There were two basic fundamental building properties that he applied, called yin and yang. Yin is receptive, passive, negative, feminine, and is a womb for incubation. Yang is assertive, active, positive, masculine, and is an impregnating force. In considering the interaction of those two properties, he developed eight basic principles that eventually became known as *trigrams*.

Within those trigrams, each time he saw the active yang principle at work, he expressed it with a straight, solid line. When he saw the receptive yin principle at work, he expressed it with a broken line.

He realized the relationship of humankind to heaven and to earth, and the function of humankind learning to harmonize the active and receptive energies, in the world around him as well as within. He recorded the principle of heaven, which is our creative source within us. And he recorded the principle of earth, which is the vehicle that we build, the body and the mind, the result – the temple that we build to house the creative force and where our consciousness is designed to harmonize the two energies, active and receptive.

In between heaven and earth is humankind, and various interactions are occurring among the three at any time. There are times when heaven is being active, earth is being receptive, and in between those two, man is being receptive. Sometimes, heaven is being receptive, earth is being receptive, and man is being active.

The woodcutter noticed that all three of these, heaven, earth and humankind, interact with the basic yin and yang principles in eight different modes. Those modes became the eight trigrams of the I Ching, which eventually became a system for divining the wisdom of the universe. The woodcutter described these universal principles within the context of nature because that was his life. His writings concerning these principles became the sacred scripture of that time, also known as The Book of Changes.

In our western culture, the word *change* generally means something changing into something else. It is true that the body changes. Parts of the body are always dying and being reborn into new forms. And the mind changes. Our perceptions, beliefs and thoughts are always changing. The body and the mind are results, and it is true that results are always changing. However, the cause is consistent. The cause consistently expresses into the result, and the result changes, while the cause remains the same.

Western culture is result-oriented, and we have come to mistakenly identify ourselves as a body and personality, a collection of beliefs, emotions and thinking patterns. "I am this result that I have created." Now we must re-learn to identify with the cause, the creative source that made this vehicle.

Oriental thought, on the other hand, has not forgotten to identify with the cause. In oriental cultures, change means growth. The people experience change from a perception of consistency, rather than a perception of becoming something different. They do not have to become something other than what they are. They recognize change as a learning, growing process, as an opportunity for expansion of awareness, rather than a painful, death process.

Centuries after the woodcutter recorded his observations, there was another wise man named King Wen. King Wen was imprisoned for a time, and during those years of solitude, he studied the I Ching and began to record his thoughts. He contemplated the principles and relationships of nature that the woodcutter had detailed – how water related to wind, how wind and wood related to the earth and sun –

and he applied them to the realms of social behavior, the political system, and economics. He considered how the principles operated universally as man interacts with his inner and outer worlds. His commentaries became known as Judgments.

Today's study of the I Ching includes books based on King Wen's interpretations of these universal principles from nature and their operation and influence in the lives of man. Later, King Wen's son went on to write the Commentaries on the Judgments. The most famous commentaries on the I Ching and the Oriental mysteries were written by Confucius, including the Ten Wings.

Oriental legend tells of a student of the I Ching who lived in the Shaolin Monastery, in the Henan province of China. One day, the student was sitting in meditation when he heard a scuffle in the courtyard. He went to investigate and discovered a crane and a snake fighting. He sat for a long time watching them, and as he observed the efforts of these two creatures, he noted the interplay of the principles he was studying.

The crane would strike out, and the snake would adjust its position, to avoid the strike. The crane would strike again, and the snake would yield and readjust. The battle continued in that same manner for hours, the two creatures moving rhythmically back and forth. All the while, the student observed the principles operating.

In the end, the snake was victorious, but not by being actively aggressive, not by striking over and over, as the crane did. Instead, the snake derived strength by yielding, by absorbing the crane's attack, by adjusting himself to whatever the crane did. He remained yin to the crane's yang. And the crane simply wore himself out.

THE TAO OF COMMUNICATION

The Tao is an ancient Chinese word, very roughly translated as the "right way." Taoism signifies the peace that occurs when positive and negative forces are in perfect balance. It refers to mastery over universal elements – mastery through integration, not defeat.

The principles detailed in the I Ching are represented in the Tao as yin and yang. In every effective communication, there exists an interplay of perfect balance between the yin and yang forces – thus, the Tao of communication.

Communication cannot occur if there are two yangs, or two yins. Communication is a rhythmic movement back and forth, to and fro, from yin to yang and from yang to yin. If communication occurs, it is because one person remains yin while the other is yang.

Compare that with an argument, where yang meets yang. When two yangs talk, they both attempt to get their points across, and they both listen with their mouths open, rather than their ears, waiting for the other to stop talking so they can give their point of view again. They begin to raise their voices, as force meets force. Both parties express assertively, and no one hears anything said.

On the other hand, when yin meets yin, no one expresses actively, and there is indecisiveness: "What do you want to do?" "I don't know. What do you want to do?" Both parties remain receptive, and nothing is decided.

Communication requires moving from yin to yang and back again, as necessary. One person will always be yin when the other is yang. When that person switches to yin, the other must become yang, for communication to occur.

Being yang is common in society. We are taught that it is important to be assertive, to get our point across. We believe that in order to be worthwhile, we must have something to say – and that something needs to be appreciated. If it is not, that equates with insult or rejection.

We give others the ability to manipulate our feelings by listening to us or not. Anyone desiring power over us knows exactly how to achieve it – by not listening to us. They do it passively by putting their consciousness somewhere else, even as they look us straight in the eyes and politely reply, "Yes... un-huh... yes...." They do not listen, to prove that they do not have to listen, even while they appear to be listening attentively. That is not communication.

The inclination is to think that the yin side of a conversation is weaker. The martial art of T'ai Chi proves that incorrect. It is based on developing the strength of yin, the receptive, and allowing the yang energy of the attacker to defeat itself.

Its originator said, "Nothing is harder than stone, and nothing is more yielding than a river. Yet over time, a river will wear away stone." For centuries, T'ai Chi has existed to teach individuals to become receptive, to be receptive to God, by developing their yin aspects. In the process, also developed is the art of the yin listener in conversation.

THE EFFECTIVE YIN

For the effective yin listener, it is unnecessary to make a point of disagreement with another person. The effective yin knows that it is more important to not establish a point. Why? When a person is insisting on his point, he is being yang. And an important key to communication is to know that no one can hear when he is being yang. It is impossible.

A person cannot hear you when he is yang, so there is no point in raising your voice or repeating your point. As long as the other person is being yang, you will waste your energy by speaking.

However, by remaining yin, you have the power to win the argument. It is called the Socratic method and consists of drawing the other person out by asking questions. You cause him to explain his point further and further, so thoroughly that he eventually comes around to your point on the issue, by looking at all the angles and examining all the views including yours, as a result of your questions. The two of you will end up saying the same thing.

Even if the other person does not end up agreeing with you, you will find yourself in a new position. By asking questions, because you really want to explore and learn, because you are not threatened by his point of view, you will learn everything that he knows. As a result, you will know everything that you already knew plus everything that he knows, while he still only knows what he already knew. Who is in a better position?

The yin listener knows that when one person remains consistently yang while the other remains yin, the yin person will end up knowing everything that he already knew, plus he will gain an understanding of what the other person knows, feels and thinks. The yang person, on the other hand, ends up receiving nothing new. That is not whole communication. The yin person has received and is richer for it, but the yang person has not moved forward simultaneously.

A consistently yin person will not lose what he already knows and believes, if there is value in it. Yet he will gain what the other person has. A consistently yang person will only remain where he is, in his beliefs and his knowings.

Being an effective yin listener means drawing people out until you know all that they have to say. Do not give them your side unless they ask for it. Eventually, they will. If you really want people to hear you, do not insist on being heard. Draw them out until they finally say, "Well, don't you have a point of view?" Answer the exact question, "Yes, I do have a point of view." "Well, tell me what it is!"

At this point, the other person has become curious. He is finally yin and can hear you, at least your first sentence. If his mouth flies open again, stop speaking. He wants to present his side again, which you have already heard, and he can no longer hear what you are saying. Resist the temptation to become yang again. Remain yin.

An effective yin listener knows to immediately become yin when the other person's mouth flies open, even figuratively. It may be only a raised eyebrow, or a flash of the eyes. His body language will give away his uncontrollable need to make his point again. Listen to what he has to say. Become curious. It means more than just sitting quietly while he talks. It requires sincere curiosity. You must want to know and understand.

The secret of being effectively yin is wanting to understand another person's point of view – caring more about the other person's thoughts and feelings, and giving up yours in order to absorb and understand his. An effective yin listener wants the other person's knowledge, no matter what, even if that person has cut himself off from the possibility of receiving anything in return.

The superior communicator is the student of life – the person who does not miss a chance to learn. He wants to know what others are thinking, and it is always more important than getting his point across. When asked, the yin listener shares. If not asked, he simply takes what is offered.

It is impossible to argue with an effective yin person. He is too busy listening and learning to argue. It is not true that other people start arguments with you. It cannot be done without your participation. It takes two people to have an argument. And it only takes one person to stop one. A yin person who wants to know the position of the other person will stop an argument. And he will become stronger and will learn more than the one who cannot stop being yang. People who recognize that skill as a greater, not lesser, strength can be tremendously effective communicators.

THE EFFECTIVE YANG

It is also important to develop as an effective yang person. What makes an effective yang? Two things.

Number one: You must recognize that your point of view has value just because it is your point of view. Whatever you think has value, and it is important to share. If you are not afraid of being judged on the basis of what you think, then you can communicate what you think without fear.

This brings us back to integrity in communication. If you believe that what you are communicating is not acceptable, you will feel dishonest, and you will indicate that feeling on some level.

Integrity comes from self-acceptance. You can communicate anything that you believe, if you believe that it is all right for you to believe it. When you have self-love, self-worth and alrightness, you can communicate yang effectively.

Number two: To be an effective yang, you must have the ability to become an effective yin in a split-second – as soon as you see the other person becoming yang.

These two abilities make an effective yang. One: self love, alrightness and confidence that your point of view has merit. Two: the ability to notice when a person is not listening and to immediately become yin, to draw the person out.

THE EFFECTIVE YIN PARENT

It is customary to believe that children should remain feminine and receptive to the wisdom of their parents, while the parents should always be yang and wise. That works well until the children grow to about twelve years old. At that age, a natural milestone in their growth and evolution occurs, and it becomes essential that they develop more independence and their own ability to make decisions.

So at that point, they start expressing differently. They become more masculine, more yang. Even if they do not have a lot of knowledge or all the answers, they want to communicate their expression and their ideas.

What is most important for parents to know at that point? It is best for you to become feminine in the relationship. Begin to ask questions effectively. Instead of telling them to do something, ask for their feelings about what they want to do. Ask questions without manipulation, only drawing them out. Your challenge is to remain yin, feminine and receptive. Your role is to listen.

You must allow them to express in a new way, as a cause, in a new cause relationship with their world. This new expression begins for all children during the adolescent years.

If you find that they absolutely refuse you, especially later as adults themselves, it is not because they object to what you are saying. It is because they object to your continuing to act as a cause for them in their personal lives.

They may very well agree with you. They may have the same idea. If they are allowed to give birth to the idea, to be the instigator of the idea – so that you become the incubator and allow them to become the cause – you can end the impasse. You must make the transition, from being a cause factor in their lives, to being the incubator. You must allow your child to be the source of the suggestion, the communicator of the idea, while you absorb it, take it into you, be curious, discover, listen and understand.

As they grow into their masculine, cause expression, whether they are girls or boys, communication cannot take place if you are also expressing as masculine, as yang. You will only end up butting heads together. Your child will think you mean one thing when you mean something completely different. And vice versa. Communication and understanding will be impossible.

As your children grow and change, your relationship to them must change. You must become the feminine, receptive one – the effective yin listener.

IMPREGNATION BY ALTERNATE LOVERS

Your caring will allow communication to occur, by making a womb available within you. Whatever your physical gender, you have within you a female aspect that is capable of being a mother. That female in you is capable of bearing a child. Your womb will incubate whatever you allow to inseminate the receptive part of you. If that is ambition, you will bear ambition's child. If it is power, you will bear power's child.

Whatever you believe will bring you satisfaction is the lover that you will allow to inseminate you, and you will bear its child. If that lover is not love itself, which is the source of your life, the child that you bear will be an alternate lover, a love substitute: money, ambition, success, opinion, popularity. And the children of these lovers will dominate you but never fulfill you, because they are not satisfying. There is always a feeling of "If I can get just a little more, I'll be satisfied." A little more fame, money, popularity, power, substances, material possessions, whatever is addictive.

If you want to communicate with the source of life – if you want to bear the child of God in your life – the only thing you must allow to impregnate you is living love. If you are impregnated by love, you will be able to hear, when another person is angry, that that person is really hurting. You will hear the pain over the anger, because you care, because love lives. You will listen to what is behind the anger, knowing that anger is an ineffective technique for communication. Anger does not communicate any better than words do.

What does communicate is your heart. And the only way you can hear someone communicating is to have a link with that person's heart. The only link that occurs between hearts is love. That means, no matter how angry, or unkind, or bitter, or undeserving someone is, you will have to care – you will have to care why – if you want to communicate. Most of the world gives hate for hate, anger for anger, hurt for hurt. But if you truly want to communicate, you will have to give caring instead.

GOING BEYOND THE FACADE

We are expressions of God on this earth. And it is not normal for any of us to be angry, bitter, unkind or undeserving. If you allow yourself to abort communication by judging another and by believing that the facade you see is who that person is, you will never know what you missed. What you will miss is the divinity of that person, the real self, the divine self, the Christ-self.

We were given eyes that only look outward. Therefore, if you want to see the consciousness of Christ, you must see it in another.

"Have I been so long with you and yet you do not know who I am." (John 14:9-11) It was a technique used effectively by Jesus when he told his apostles how to know who he really is. "Find that which is alive in me."

To do that, you must go beyond the facade. The facade is the mask. A person's mask may be anger, a sense of inadequacy, anxiety, gluttony, greed, lust for power, weakness. What is the you that you put out there in front?

We are tempted to point to the facade and say, "Look at that person. That's what he's like." Because of that, we continue to believe in the facade and miss the truth. The facade is true in your perception, which does not mean that the person is not being and acting that way. Your perception is probably accurate. In fact, that person is probably doing worse than what you have noticed so far.

Here is what you need to remember: That is not who that person is. So do not stop at that initial barrier. You must go further to find what is inside. Go past the facade, and you will discover who that person really is – a child that needs desperately to be loved, and who wants to love everyone, but puts up barriers that say, "You can go only this far, because if you go any further, I will feel threatened."

We carefully and deliberately create our facades. And every facade is a lie. There are no exceptions. It is your front. It is what you tell me about you because that is how you want me to relate to you. Your facade may say, "I'm vulnerable. I'm helpless. Will you help me find my way across the road?"

Society tells women that helplessness is a good facade for them to wear. If you say, "That's who she is, she's just like that, so I have to relate to her that way," you are reinforcing her facade.

We may relate with each other daily, for hours at a time, with our facades intact. And we may assume that we are communicating. We are not. We are only gathering information concerning each other's protective mechanisms. We claim to communicate, meaning we talk, but communication does not occur. Instead, the conversation has been an investment in reinforcing each other's facades.

People even wear facades within families. Spouses want to impress each other, and if one is not impressed, the other is hurt. Children want to impress their parents, and if their parents are not impressed, they are hurt.

How do we impress anyone? There is only one way, and that is to pretend, which is another word for lying.

The alternative is to tell the truth. What must you do to tell the truth? Drop all the stuff and care why – why another person does what he does, says what he says, thinks what he thinks, feels what he feels? What people do and say does not matter. Why they do what they do matters.

What is it that we are all hiding from one another? What is in each of us that is so precious that we are compelled to keep it secret and protect it?

It is our Holy Grail – that which contains the blood of the Christ, the divine spirit, the life-force. We have been hiding it within ourselves for centuries, for so long that we have forgotten that it even exists. Knights and pilgrims have come seeking it, but we have hidden it behind fortresses, behind great structures with thick walls – behind our facades.

The key to the fortress, the key to getting beyond the facade is to know that it exists. When you know that it exists, you can consistently refuse to believe the lies created to support it.

You refuse to believe in an angry, bitter, inadequate, sensitive, unworthy person. That is not who others are, and that is not who you are. The more that you suggest that it is, the more you challenge others to discover the real you.

Loving means caring with a deep curiosity, caring to know the uniqueness of another person, caring to see the uniqueness of the divinity in that person. Instead of using words to communicate, you must get beyond the words. Each part of that person that you get to know is only one facet of a fabulous multifaceted diamond. Only when you know and accept each facet, can you know the complete person.

THE REAL YOU

There is within each of us a precious child. There are no exceptions. We all have a child within us who needs love to survive. There is nothing abnormal about that. Your inner child must have love to live.

If you will give love, acceptance, caring, alrightness, confidence, encouragement, empowerment to that little child in you, he or she will grow stronger, bigger, healthier. And the people around you will probably say, "I've seen something very loving in you that's growing."

Congratulations, you just allowed people to see the real you. Perhaps it was just a glimpse. Perhaps it will take time for you to love yourself so completely that you feel confident to be all that you are and to let others see that. That is all right because there is time enough. That is why we are here.

Communication occurs only through love. If love is missing, what occurs is a substitute – processing words and symbols to rearrange pre-held beliefs, opinions and prejudices.

As you communicate with love, something else occurs that has to do with your life purpose, your purpose for being on this earth. Ordinarily, in deciding a life work or career, you would use words to examine various factors, possibilities and opportunities, weighing one against another. You would attempt to become clear and directed. You would research different avenues, assessing your talents and background, your experience, and your opportunities. All these things would be relevant for the cognitive decisions you want to make.

Or, you can communicate with living love in you. By communicating with the love that lives within you, you become an expression of love through something that you do. That something becomes the form through which you express love. And it does not matter what that form is, because you can express love effectively in any form. It may be as a garbage collector, a teacher, a writer, a secretary, a bookkeeper, a musician, an artist, a politician or a priest.

The interesting thing about that list is that it elicits judgments. Garbage collector sounds bad, while artist and priest sound good. The truth is that neither is good or bad. And the sooner you drop those judgments, the sooner you will experience harmony. We are simply talking about different methods for the expression of love, and no one form is better than another. The superior form is the one that gets the message across – and the message is love.

Do not assume that the plan for your life purpose is to accomplish a successful career – not even that of a spiritual teacher. That will never be your life purpose. You can decide to be a doctor, a priest, a garbage collector, a teacher, a factory worker, a chiropractor, whatever you want, because it does not matter. Pick one, any one.

It is relatively unimportant which one you choose. It is only a bottle to pour the juice into – the juice is what is important. What's the juice? The expression of living love, your life force.

Whatever the form that you pour the juice into, do it extremely well. But do not let that cause you to think that it is anything other than a container.

If you are a chiropractor, and you do a wonderful adjustment on a spine, but you do not have love, the stress will remain there and the joint will go out again within hours, days at the most. You will have done little good for your patient. On the other hand, if you cannot quite figure out how to do the adjustment, but the touch of your hand communicates your deep caring for what is going on in that life, while you are working, that person will begin to speak. It is like oral diarrhea. They will tell you all their troubles and not even know why.

You will probably say, "I know why you're telling me this. Sure, you need to get all these thoughts out. Yet what you need more is to feel loved."

How long has it been since you told someone I love you? How long since you said that to someone who is not your spouse, child or parent? Do you think it is corny, or risky? What is your belief about it? Fortunately, you can say it without words. You can say it with your eyes, with a touch, with an action.

WHY ARE WE HERE?

Your life purpose is not to accomplish something great. Your life purpose is to find out who you are, and in the process, to find out who the people around you are – and to love all of us, with all your heart, your soul, your mind and your strength.

Find a way to communicate the fact that you love. You can do that by making things, by selling things, by writing things, by teaching things, by cleaning things, by healing things. But that is only packaging, no matter what it is. That is the container for your love, which is your real purpose. Do not worry about what your career should be. Know that it is just a container and fill it with the love that is you. And use it to cause people to feel loved and to know that they deserve that.

If you can teach people that you love them, that is a first step – a small one, not even halfway. If you can teach them that they are loveable, that is the ultimate goal and the purpose of life.

Teaching them that you love them pumps up your ego. Teaching them that they deserve to be loved is a gift of pure gold, and much more difficult. Teaching them that they deserve to be loved will make a difference in their expectations and their experience of life. You will have given them the keys to transformation.

And of course, you must love yourself first. What is loveable about you is that little child inside. All the rest is packaging – bravado, pretense, facade. Sometimes, it is nice – brightly colored papers, ribbons of satin and velvet, beautiful sparkle and glitter. Packaging to be appreciated and complimented – but only packaging.

What is loveable about you is that you are an absolutely perfect, yet vulnerable, expression of God in this world. If we can always remember that about each other, then we can always live in the consciousness of Christ. The moment that we accept another's facade as the truth, we fail to see the face of Christ, and even blame it on that person. And we step out of the consciousness of Christ.

THE FOUR ELEMENTS OF COMMUNICATION

In communicating effectively, it is important to understand ourselves and in the process, to understand the people around us, and to communicate love. It will help to be able to identify and understand behavioral qualities that we all express through our personalities and our communications. We can do that by associating those qualities with the four elements of our material experience: earth, air, fire and water.

For most people, one of these elements will be dominant in most of their communications. That does not mean that a person is always "earth," or always "air." It means that a person most often behaves in a certain way, which is representative of a specific element. It is possible to switch back and forth, from earth to air, or from fire to water, depending on a person's choice of action in a given situation – or to put it more accurately, a person's non-choice, meaning that most people react without forethought.

Within each of these elements, there are positive and negative forces. There is positive earth and negative earth, positive air and negative air, positive fire and negative fire, and positive water and negative water. We all, at one time or another, express the positive and negative forces of each element.

Communication involves several factors. While examining the expression of these four material elements, it is helpful to consider four factors in particular: the situation, the feelings that arise, the other person(s) involved, and self. When we express the negative force of any of these elements, we usually emphasize one of these factors, while ignoring or omitting the others. And an imbalance occurs. For instance, when a person expresses negative air qualities, he tends to emphasize the situation to the exclusion of feelings, others and self. It is possible to recognize which element a person is expressing by noticing which of these factors is being emphasized and which are being ignored. This will become clearer as we look at each element and its positive and negative expressions.

POSITIVE AND NEGATIVE EARTH

Positive earth can be described as clear, direct, concise, accurate, realistic, assertive, purposeful, sensible, practical, reasonable, grounded, logical, organized, disciplined, structured, honest, fair and responsible. Positive earth communicators state the facts without exaggeration, dramatization, emotion, extravagant language or illustrations. They stand solidly and use only a few gestures that support what they have to say. Nothing superfluous. Their expression is one of conviction and firmness. When positive earth communicators make an effort to add feeling and emotion to the facts, their communication becomes genuine and supportive.

Negative earth can be described as emotionless, dispassionate, factual, cold, lifeless, boring, argumentative, thinking they are always right, like stainless steel, a know-it-all, calculated and manipulative. Negative earth communicators are computer-like, without feeling or concern for others.

In the case of negative earth, the essential factor denied or omitted is feelings. All feelings are overlooked, and only the situation is important. The people, self and others, are acknowledged to some degree. However, most notable is negative earth's open declaration that he does not care how you feel, period.

Negative earth parents are earnest, serious, straightforward, straight-talking, honest, truthful, while also being computer-like and lacking warmth and emotion. Just the facts. "This is the way it is. I'm not impassioned about it. I'm not going to punish you. You're wrong. I'm right. Don't try to argue with me. I'm the head of this house, and I make the rules. That's the way it will always be." Always right, cannot be reasoned with, no emotion, no drama, no apologies, no feelings, no warmth. Negative earth can be devastating to anyone.

POSITIVE AND NEGATIVE AIR

Positive air can be described as easy, unfettered, light-hearted, cheerful, bubbly, optimistic, charming, generous, loving, disarming and idealistic. Positive air communicators do not take anything too seriously or consider it too important. They are masters at finding humor under any circumstances. They make light of heavy situations, do not indulge in crisis or drama, and do not make matters terribly important. Positive air people are the angels who can fly because they take themselves lightly.

Positive air is a good mode for parents because anything can happen within a family and a home and it is important to maintain a sense of humor about it all.

Negative air can be described as fickle, evasive, avoiding, illogical, unreasonable, inappropriately emotional, irrelevant, insecure, over-sensitive and over-reactive. When the situation is crucial, and people count, and feelings are important, the negative air communicator dismisses all of these essential factors. Everyone else is working to resolve the situation, while becoming more and more frustrated because the airy-fairy, negative air person is everywhere and nowhere.

Negative air communicators make irrelevant comments, such as, "Just let it flow." "Whatever will be, will be." "It's all in divine order." "Let go, and let God." "Whatever is supposed to happen will happen." These are all beautiful statements, but only useful when combined with practical, earthy application and fiery determination. Negative air communications rarely have anything to do with the situation and are of little use in finding resolutions.

Negative air parents may know that the child is stealing, or smoking cigarettes, or worse, but will never bring it up. They do not know what to do about it anyway. "Whatever happens, happens. What is, is." They are not in touch with what is going on in the family and are surprised when crisis arises, because they are involved in so many things outside the family – whatever allows them to avoid dealing with the home. Children have a very difficult time getting a negative air parent's balloon back down to earth.

POSITIVE AND NEGATIVE FIRE
Positive fire can be described as energetic, spirited, full of life, active, fiery, questing, ardent, dramatic, emotional, warm, supportive, comforting, loving, passionate, caring, giving, enthused, inspiring, encouraging and motivating. Positive fire communicators are take-charge, make-it-happen kind of people – leading the pack, out there on the edge, making decisions and carrying them out successfully.

Negative fire can be described as intense, fierce, consuming, demanding, scorching, over-emotional, dangerous, manipulative, temperamental, self-righteous, turbulent, forceful, blaming, explosive and violent. Negative air communicators emphasize feelings, so they dismiss the situation, other people and even themselves. They use their over-emotional states in an attempt to make others feel guilty and to manipulate them.

A negative fire parent can be a child's worst nightmare. Explosive anger, quick outbursts, screaming and yelling, physical punishment. All part of negative air's destructiveness. Only feelings matter, not people or facts, so out-of-control behavior is justified.

POSITIVE AND NEGATIVE WATER

Positive water can be described as yielding, flowing, caring, giving, helpful, sharing, generous, altruistic, receptive, incubative, sensitive, compassionate and understanding. Positive water equates with servant consciousness.

Negative water can be described as wishy-washy, self-effacing, passive, servile, placating, weak, overwhelmed and incapable. Negative water communicators can be doormats, victims, and martyrs. They emphasize others and negate themselves. They are often derogatory and belittling toward themselves, and put themselves down in a way that seems phony and sticky to others.

Positive water is giving. Negative water gives in.

A negative water parent will stand by while a negative fire parent abuses the children, rather than become a positive earth parent who would not allow it. Negative water communicators always take a back seat to whatever is happening, giving others authority. They vacillate and are unreliable. They do not make decisions or enforce rules. There is no consistency, because there is no intrinsic understanding of right or wrong, or the need for rules.

The child of a negative water parent exists in confusion, never knowing what the rules are or when he has broken one. Meanwhile, the parent says, "I'm so sorry. I'm always wrong. I make so many mistakes. I know I'm not a good parent." The child ends up with no role model. There is no indication of a responsible, loving adult who loves self.

GETTING THE ELEMENTS TO WORK FOR YOU

All four of these elements – earth, air, fire and water – exist as facets of your personality and your communications. And you express the positive and negative aspects of each, in response to the different situations that arise in your daily life.

What is most important to know is that you can call upon these elements, at any time, according to what fits a given situation. That is why it is important to be able to know how they inter-relate and impact on your world, how you can move from one to another at will, and how to use them constructively.

Obviously, the negative aspects of these four elements can be disturbing and will not serve you. They are computing, irrelevant, blaming and placating. Do you recognize those qualities in yourself? Do you tend to emphasize the facts above everything else, always maintaining order, in spite of others' feelings and needs? Do you tend to de-emphasize everything and everyone, not wanting to "get bogged down in intellectual stuff," practicing denial and avoidance? Do you lose control and scream at others, over-dramatize everything, "guilt" others into getting your own way, use a carefully chosen voice and facial expression in order to get attention? Do you placate and whine? Are you a martyr, claiming to not matter, to avoid responsibility? If so, don't feel bad. Almost everyone else is doing the same thing!

Most important is to be able to recognize when you are doing it and to monitor any destructive effects. Keep a journal of how you see yourself expressing. Name the names of what you are doing. And then ask someone who knows you well if he or she agrees with your assessments. It is amazing, when we do this in workshops, how often people who know each other well do not agree. So keep researching. Get clear.

Then it is important to take control of your mode. When your self-image is positive, healthy and confident, you tend to move easily through the positive aspects of all four elements. And you can call on them whenever you choose.

The positive aspects of these elements will help you become an effective communicator. You can be direct, solid, down-to-earth and attentive to the situation when it is appropriate. You can be humorous and light-hearted, and lighten the situation when necessary, dismissing heaviness and causing a note of cheer that others will welcome. You can move others with your dramatic energy, encouraging and motivating them, and helping them to express and feel their personal emotions and enjoy doing it. And you can be receptive, caring, accepting, understanding and loving, which is healing to yourself and others.

The point is: Know the mode that you are expressing at any given moment and be responsible for it. As you go through the day, think about how you are acting, what element you are expressing, and whether you are expressing its positive or negative aspect.

Ask yourself, "Am I deliberately creating the experience that I want? Am I relating to others, and to myself, in the best way that I know I am capable?" Simply be responsible for your experience and for your communications.

CREATING AN EXCHANGE

In order to deliberately make your style of communication more meaningful and effective, what would you do? Would you decide what you plan to say ahead of time? Would you determine before hand what result you want from the conversation? Would you be clearer in your statements? Would you try harder to give the right response?

None of these have anything to do with communication. They have to do with how to be heard. They have nothing to do with how to hear. They are about getting a point across, but not about listening, or even communicating.

Communication does not occur through words, or vocal sounds, or facial expressions, or body language. The key to communication is love. Communication does not, and cannot, occur between two people where a love relationship does not exist.

Communication is an experience of harmony between two individuals. If harmony is not present, communication cannot occur. They may believe that they understand each other, but if they have not harmonized with each other's reason for saying something, they cannot understand what is said. No matter how well they intellectually process verbal symbols, verbal symbols will remain inadequate to communicate what the other person thinks and feels, his motivations, and who that person is. Words simply cannot contain that.

All verbal symbols will do is cause us to reorganize our own verbal symbols. They will help us sort out our past experience, and allow us to draw conclusions, as a result of the other person's stimulation of our process.

Some of the most effective communication you have ever experienced has occurred when you were not talking. For example, there may have been a time when you were with a friend, walking through the woods. On the way, and even as you entered the woods, the two of you chatted on about various things. But at some point, you both became quiet. The stillness and the peace of the surroundings affected you, and you walked for miles without saying a word. And an unspoken feeling of understanding came over each of you.

Communication occurs when two people experience harmony together. When they allow themselves to experience approximately the same thing, and through the experience, are able to understand one another. Then at some point, they make an exchange, which may occur only with the eyes, or with the hands, or simply with the heart. Perhaps the exchange occurs over a distance. There is no limitation. Communication requires nothing physical, not even proximity.

Communication requires that individuals take turns moving into yin, then into yang, then back into yin, as if swaying in unison, as if in a dance.

When love is present, caring allows communication to occur.

THE WISDOM OF SOLOMON

THE MARATHON
COMMUNICATION EXPERIENCE

The Marathon Communication Experience was designed as a means to build a heart-bond between two people, beyond what generally occurs through normal interaction. A level of understanding and caring occurs through the process of a Marathon that is not often experienced otherwise. For that reason, it is recommended to people who are preparing to join, or who are already joined, in any type of relationship or partnership.

• The Marathon is designed to take place in a neutral setting, away from your normal environments. You need to set yourselves apart from all distractions, including people, pets, jobs, televisions, telephones, computers, newspapers, chores such as cleaning or food preparation, and all responsibilities and commitments.

• The Marathon is designed to last forty-eight hours. Each person in the partnership will take a turn talking for twenty-four hours and listening for twenty-four hours. Naps are possible, when necessary. Meals should not become a distraction from the process. Walks are possible, if you are not likely to encounter other people, distractions or interruptions. The emphasis is on constant communication between the two of you for two full days.

• The talking partner is expected to talk about himself or herself for the full twenty-four hours. What to talk about? Your life story. Your earliest memories. Your hopes, dreams, fantasies, desires and aspirations. Your disappointments, hurts, conflicts, concerns, anxieties and fears. Your philosophies, beliefs and values. Important events and people, and why they were influential. Why you feel the way you do. Why you made particular choices. Anything is appropriate, as long as you talk about you. This is your opportunity to share who you are in a unique way, which you have not previously experienced.

• The listening partner is expected to listen without reaction, comment, facial expression, gestures, judgment, approval or disapproval – without response of any kind, for the full twenty-four hours. You may ask simple questions, but only for the purpose of keeping your partner talking, not for the purpose of leading your partner in a direction you desire. How did that make you feel? What did you do then? This is your opportunity to witness and understand who your partner truly is in a unique way, which you have not previously experienced.

The Marathon Communication Experience is designed to create a safe place where communication from the heart can take place – as protective facades dissolve, and judgments and interpretations fall away. You will come to know your partner better, even if you have been living together for years. You will experience greater trust, understanding, and acceptance – for yourself and your partner. You may experience forgiveness that was not possible before. You will gain clarity about yourself that can provide answers and direction.

The lasting gold of the Marathon Communication Experience is a new way of looking at your partner – through the eyes of the heart.

MONEY IS GOD IN ACTION

Begin to think of your body, your mind, your personality, your talents, your determination and resourcefulness, and your stubbornness as spiritual tools – no less spiritual than your soul, or whatever you call the container that carries God within you.

Money, sex and power will influence most of the challenges you will face in your lifetime. For many people, money will be the most difficult. Money will likely be the toughest and most conniving dragon on the path to mastery. Many people will spend their entire lifetime as money's victim, rather than as a cause of money.

Mastering the money dragon involves more than filling your wallet. It also includes comprehending true value, establishing a prosperous consciousness of alrightness, working in harmony with universal laws, expressing acceptance and appreciation, finding happiness in another's prosperity, sending your money out to perform a contribution to the world, and more than anything else, it includes loving and being loved.

Prosperity is not a matter of how much money you have. It is not a matter of how successful you are. It is not a matter of how many possessions you own. Money and the success that produces it have little to do with prosperity.

Many people have ample money and possessions and have done well in their careers, yet prosperity eludes them. At the same time, others do not succeed in prestigious careers and never accumulate money or possessions, yet they are prosperous. Money and success can be the results of prosperity, but they do not determine it.

If money does not determine prosperity, then what does?

Prosperity depends on whether money and possessions are obeying you as servants, or whether they are ruling your life as masters. If the money that you have is working for you, doing what you want it to do in your life, accomplishing things that are important to you, you are prosperous.

THE RELATIONSHIP OF PROSPERITY

You may believe that prosperity means a right relationship with money, with goods and with the bounty of earth, but go one step further. A right relationship with money, goods and the bounty of earth is contingent on your relationship with yourself. The panacea to set your life in effective working order is a right relationship with yourself, not with your bank account, so hopefully that is not where your security has been based.

To understand prosperity, we must look at humankind's search for alrightness, which is the personal knowledge of one's innate perfection. It includes recognition, attention and security, which add up to love, the sixth survival need.

As a substitute for love, some people drive themselves to accumulate money, but it cannot provide satisfaction. When money has become a love substitute, people find that the more money accumulated, the more difficult it becomes to be prosperous. Money begets power, and power is another love substitute. The more money they have, the more power money has over their lives. They must accumulate more and more, but more is never enough.

Truly prosperous people are individuals who experience their needs being met. You are not busy worrying about how to meet your needs. Instead, you are accomplishing purpose and reaching goals that are important to you. Money alone will never meet those needs. Neither will property, power or approval.

This is a serious issue because your need for alrightness and your ability to satisfy that need will determine whether you are prosperous in every area of your life. You cannot possibly be prosperous in one area while experiencing lack in another. You are either prosperous, or you are not. And that will be determined by your relationship to your own concept and acceptance of alrightness.

When your relationship with yourself is all right, your relationship with money, possessions, career, success and other people will be all right. A person who meditates and prays regularly, perhaps even heals people, but who worries about how to pay the mortgage and meet the bills, and how to ever get out of a paralyzing financial rut, is not prosperous, nor spiritual.

IT IS NOT SPIRITUAL TO NOT BE PROSPEROUS

There is nothing sacred about being poor. A person with constant financial problems has a spiritual problem.

If you are applying God's universal laws properly, it is impossible to have financial problems. If you do not have the money needed to function well and contribute to life, there is an imbalance in your spiritual relationship with the universe. Spirituality means working in harmony with this universe and its laws at all levels.

You cannot be spiritually prosperous while lacking in other areas. Each area affects and reflects another. Your condition in the physical, including your physical body, your finances and your household, reflects your spiritual nature and your mental nature. It is impossible for you to have an uncluttered and effectively working mind if your house is not clean. It is impossible for you to have a prosperous spirit if your habits are undisciplined. You can look at your desktop and your refrigerator shelves to assess your thought processes and how well you use your mind in experiencing universal laws.

Everything in God's universe operates according to God's laws, including God. If you are setting the laws in motion correctly on one level, it will be reflected on other levels.

MONEY IS ONLY A SYMBOL OF VALUE

When you use money, you exchange symbols. And there is nothing more spiritual than taking charge of the symbols in your life and exchanging them in a system of barter with others. You make a statement of value whenever you move money.

Money is a symbol of how effectively you are using your energy. If you are using your energy well, the symbol for the flow of your energy will be moving well, in and out of your life. That does not necessarily mean you will have a lot of money. It does mean that you will have *enough* money and that you will use it effectively.

You will not be victimized by money. You will be able to cause the results you want with it, because those results are important to you. They are contributions that you want to make in the world. And they will be the measure of your prosperity, the measure of your spirituality, and the measure of your awareness of your innate alrightness.

MONEY CANNOT LIE

Money is a communication device, and it cannot lie. Money will tell the truth, even when nothing else in your life is doing so, because it is a sacred instrument.

We are masters at fooling ourselves, better than we fool anyone else, because we fear reality. We sometimes manipulate facts to fit our interpretations. We pretend things are different from what they really are. We assign false value to things. We lie to ourselves and to others with our words and our actions. But there is one aspect of our life that can never lie – money.

Money can only tell the truth. It may be the most honest energy you will ever encounter. If you want to know the depth of your commitment and the value of things in your life, your meditation could provide that answer. Or you could pay for a psychic reading. But for the most accurate answer, ask your money.

LET'S ASK YOUR MONEY

You have three bodies, and each wants to be fed and nourished. Your body and mind are strong and relatively healthy from the nourishment they receive daily.

But what about your spiritual body? How often is it fed? When was the last time you exercised it? Was it when you had some extra time on your hands and decided to meditate? Was there a crisis in your family, so you quickly decided to pray? When a friend was sick, did you try to heal him? How often do you seek inspiration to feed your spiritual body? Once a day? Once a week? Once a month? Can you remember the last time you fed your spiritual body? Have you checked if it is starving, or even still alive?

When your gigantic, richly-fed, well-attended physical body becomes sick with the sniffles, you tell that poor, hungry, weak, emaciated spiritual body, which has not been fed in months, to "Heal him! Yeah, the big one!" And then you wonder why it does not work.

If I ask, "Which is more important to you, your mental, physical or spiritual body?" most of you will answer, "My spiritual body, of course!" Then I will say to you, "Do you mind if I ask your money?" Your money cannot give a false answer.

If we compare the amount of money you spend on your spiritual body with what you spend on your mental body, the amount spent on your mental body will be generally five times greater. If we compare the amount you spend on your spiritual body with what you spend on your physical body, the amount you spend on your physical body will be generally twenty times greater.

Which body is more important to you? Where does your money go? What are your investments? What is it you most value? Physical comforts, entertainment, mental activities?

MONEY TALKS

Money is nothing more and nothing less than a written statement of what you value. You will spend your lifetime passing out small, colored paper statements of what you value. If, at the end of your life experience on earth, we want to assess the progress you made, we only need to tally your expenditures and say, "To what did this person give written statements of value?" Your money will tell us the truth.

If you want to be honest with yourself, begin watching your money. You cannot make it say something about your values that is not true. Money is a sacred instrument, so it is extremely important, but not because it has inherent value of its own. Whatever the state of the economy, whether money is devalued or inflated, it will symbolize your values accurately and consistently, throughout your lifetime.

You may say, "I want to make a difference in the world. I want to cause global peace." I will respond, "Would you like to give some written statements demonstrating the relative importance of that in your life? How important is world peace to you?" You may say, "Oh,

I'll do anything to bring peace in the world, but I don't have any money." My response is, "Did you eat today? Was that meal more important than peace in the world? Was it more important than teaching people to love? Was it more important than being love?"

These questions are not to intimidate or produce guilt. They are to facilitate honesty. If you are honest and back it up with right action, your spirituality has a foundation on which to stand. If you have intensity, inspiration, conviction and powerful words, but lack honesty, your statements will be like a puff of wind. And people will know you to be ineffective.

THE GLOBAL EFFECT

You may ask, "What can be done about the starving people in the world?" That is definitely a problem in this earth experience. Many people are starving for lack of food and money. Why? Because some people in other parts of the world have a wrong relationship with money. They have money, but they are not prosperous because they are greedy. They are greedy because they lack security, which means they lack love. They are trying to substitute for the lack of love, joy, contentment and fulfillment in their lives by hoarding money, which cannot make them secure or prosperous. Because their money is ruling them, they cannot rule their money.

It is not necessary to hoard money and gather more needless possessions in order to prove success or to assure security. The planet is prepared to supply the needs of all humankind. When all individuals have established a right relationship with money, which means a right relationship with self, everyone will prosper and all people will be adequately fed.

CAN MONEY PROVIDE SECURITY?

Many items in our homes are there to make a statement. We want our families, friends and neighbors to know we can afford them. Why? Because we need recognition from others. We want other people to admit that we are successful.

We try to impress each other to prove that we are all right. We choose our words for that purpose. We dress and decorate our homes for that purpose. We drive a particular car for that purpose. Merchandisers recognize this and give us a wide gamut of choices.

We are expressing an emptiness inside that says, "I want to earn my right to be on this planet. I want to have assurance that I am all right." If we do not feel all right with ourselves, we will do whatever it takes to establish our alrightness through the feedback of others. We will work for money, strive for important jobs, accumulate expensive cars and homes and clothes and whatever leisure toy is current. "If I can get you to be impressed with me, then you will admit that I am all right. Won't you?"

It is a societal trap because you will never admit that I am all right. Instead, you will keep me guessing while you are busy trying to get me to admit that you are all right. It is true, and it is pandemic, and it is dangerous to humankind's existence. If we were more concerned with feeding the world than with proving that we are all right, there would be ample supply for everyone.

WHY ARE WE HERE?

Many people spend their lifetimes making a living as if someday that is going to support the opportunity to make a life. Then when they finish making a living, they are dead. And unfortunately, there was no time left to make a life.

The truth is that we did not come here to make a living. We came here to make a life. What is your greater life purpose? That is the first question for you to ask in understanding your personal prosperity.

If you could accomplish something meaningful on this planet, if you could cause a result that you think is worthwhile and makes a difference, what would it be? Seriously ask yourself that question. "I want to accomplish something worthwhile in my own life and perhaps in the lives of others. I was born with that as my life purpose. How would I like to fulfill that goal?"

When you are confident of that answer, ask yourself the second question? "Is my money doing that right now? Is the amount I am spending to accomplish that purpose greater than the amount I am spending to accomplish anything else?" If not, what are the percentages? What proportion of your money supports the accomplishment of what your life should accomplish? What proportion of your money supports entertainment, food, creature comforts, items meant to impress people? The percentages will allow you to list in order of importance what you are doing with your life. What are the things in which you invest your life, your time, your energy, your money and your value?

The answer may be revealing, shocking or intimidating. You may feel guilty, which is inappropriate. The truth is that you should live comfortably. You should live a comfortable, healthy life, feeling prosperous and wealthy, without guilt. Simultaneously, you should be able to know that the bulk of your money is causing results that are meaningful.

Many will think, "Yes, of course I would like to do something great, something worthwhile. But I can't afford it. I have to take care of security first. I have to make sure I have some money in the bank, some property, some way to prepare for my old age. Those things are more important."

People who look apprehensively toward the future in terms of income, housing, health, current events, economical conditions, world politics, world war, earth changes or whatever are actively creating thoughts of insecurity and fear. And they will experience the result of what they create.

On the other hand, those who trust that at any given moment, "I am where I feel I ought to be, doing what I feel I ought to be doing, and nothing else matters. The rest will take care of itself," are actively creating for themselves a secure future.

It is not Pollyanna to have faith in life. It is not naive to trust that your life is secure while you are busy doing what you came to this planet to do.

A law of prosperity says, "If you are doing something that should be done, the universe will provide the means to finance it – and you." Get busy with what is meaningful. Get busy with your reason for being here, and what you need will automatically come to you.

Look at our culture and our planet and find things that ought to be done. Find things that you believe need to be done to make a positive difference. Then give your life to doing those things instead of doing things that will make money for you.

You can work for a difference, or you can work for money. If you work for money, it will manipulate you. Just look at almost every aspect of our modern culture for evidence of that, from politics and the government, to big business, to merchandising, to Hollywood, to the church. People who are working for money are controlled by money. People who attempt to accumulate and hoard money interrupt the flow of economic vitality. For the health of our society, a circulation of money through our culture is more important than its accumulation.

If you work for healthy, positive change on the planet rather than money, you will have what you need to survive. If you give your life to something that ought to be done to make a difference, someone is going to support you for it. It is almost impossible to become the champion of a cause without someone becoming enamored and deciding to get behind you because people love heroes. Instead of your objective being to work for money, make your objective to contribute what you have of value to producing positive change.

WHAT IS SECURITY?

There is only one security that is valid and consistent. The only valid security comes from knowing the value of who you are, the value of what you can do, and the value of what you have to give.

Your value is a cause. Therefore it is consistent and does not change. And it is not subject to loss of money, whatever form that might take.

Your security for whatever happens in life is within you. It is not dependent on your expertise, your talent, your ability, your education. Your security is beyond those things. You have within you something that the world wants, something that is valuable to share, and you need to discover exactly what that is. Whatever challenges this society faces, whatever you have within you that others want will be your security.

Some people think that if they have enough statements of value hoarded somewhere, they have something of value saved. If all that were taken away, the truth is they would still have the same value that they had before it was taken away. No one can take anything from you except symbols of value. If you lose all your money to a burglar, you have not lost anything of value. Nothing of value can be taken from you. Your statements, your symbols, your indications of what you value can be lost, but your true value is inherent within you, and it cannot be banked. When people give or pay you money, they are stating the value of something they have received from you or they are telling you what value you are to them, which indicates how much value you have made of yourself to that person.

When someone says, "I want to take your workshop for free. You should just give it to me because that is the spiritual thing to do," I know what value they have placed upon the experience. And I know exactly how much value they will get from it.

A person will receive exactly the value that they are willing to recognize in something, nothing more. Anything else would be a violation of universal law. If an individual believes that a workshop, a book, something found at a yard sale, something put into a shopping bag by mistake, or something that a good friend is selling is not worth paying for, then that item will remain worthless to that individual.

WHAT IS BALANCE OF VALUE?

The harmony that produces prosperity occurs when the value given equals or exceeds the value received, and when the giving and the receiving are done freely without coercion or pressure, but with love and appreciation. Our world economic crisis has resulted in part from a collective attitude of individuals seeking to get more for less and something for nothing. It is a commonly accepted belief, though out of balance with universal law, that we must try to get as much as we can and get away with paying as little as possible in exchange for goods and services.

This universe is tenacious of equilibrium, which means that it always seeks balance. In other words, it is impossible to get a bargain. Every time you find something that costs less than you think it is worth, and you buy it for less than you believe its value to be, you will find a way to pay for the rest of it. Always. Before long, your wallet may be stolen, or you may be taken advantage of by someone else charging too much. In some way, you will find a way to pay for what you got as a bargain, what you perceive that you got away with. Or else the item that you got as a bargain will break or wear out more quickly than it should. In that way, it will prove to be worth no more than you paid for it.

Life balances itself. If you want something, you should pay for it, pay for it generously and be delighted to do so. If you want something to be worth great value to you, pay an enormous amount for it. If you believe that you received more value than the amount you paid, pay more. Pay for it again and again, and you will receive that value again and again.

When making a purchase from a person who you think is making a financial killing off you because what you are buying is overpriced and not worth it, you are likely to experience resentment within yourself for several reasons. First, he is making a killing, and you are not. Second, the item is overpriced. Third, you must have it, so you are a captive audience. And fourth, you do not want to spend your money anyway.

If you ever buy anything under those circumstances with those feelings, you will automatically experience a lack of prosperity, because you are not loving yourself or that person and you are not respecting the laws of exchange. You are not allowing things the freedom to move to and from you with ease.

Over the years, people who have insisted on taking courses and workshops without charge, or who did not pay a fair amount in donation, rarely grasped the information. They sat through the experience, but they did not get the message. Other people who not only paid for the workshop, but took responsibility for sponsoring it and spent their own money to create the possibility for others, received an enormous value out of the experience every time. They caused a vacuum into which energy could come.

People have tried everything to avoid paying for workshops. Some have said, "Jesus didn't charge for his teachings." Anyone who makes such a statement has not studied the Bible thoroughly. Jesus did not settle for a few dollars. He said, "It's your life, or nothing. Leave your family, your home, your job. Drop everything else and give me your life, or forget it." (Mark 1:17-18) That was the tuition

Jesus charged for the course he taught. He said, "Forget the symbols. Leave them at home. You won't need them. We're not going to symbolize money in this class. We're going to use direct experience." That means exchanging real value, which is the investment of your whole self, who you are. When that happens, you are paying reality instead of symbols, the value itself instead of the symbol of the value.

There are many ways of expressing value other than the exchange of symbols. In our modern culture, money is usually involved in any exchange, but not necessarily. Anyone can express value by communicating value, which means taking action. Giving action means giving an investment of self. As you take the value away from the symbol and put it back into the reality, you will discover that the true value lies within yourself.

There is a woman from Houston who has taken several workshops including one on prosperity. She listened to these ideas about money and began to feel nervous. She was seventy years old with quite a bit of money in savings accounts. Finally, she jumped up in the middle of a class and said, "Now, Paul, I hear what you're saying, but I also keep reading about old people eating cat food out of cans, and I don't want to end up like that." That was her rationale for saving her money in the bank.

I reminded her that at different times in history, the economy of this country had collapsed. In less than twenty-four hours, money that was very valuable became meaningless scraps of paper, no longer symbolizing the value of the previous day. "If your security is in your bank account," I said, "you're in trouble because you're really not secure." Then I told her, "I happen to know that you won't ever eat cat food from cans, not because you've got money in the bank, but because you're feisty. You've got energy and determination. You're resourceful, and clever, and stubborn. If money were suddenly worth nothing tomorrow and your savings accounts were empty, you would be fine. You would be drawing on your talents to take care of yourself."

Suddenly, it was as though a light bulb came on inside her. "By God, you're right! My money is not my security. I'm my security!" In that moment of realization, she took what isn't away from money and gave credit to herself for what is. Her money symbolized value, and she was the value that it symbolized. And the value that she is was far greater than what she had in the bank. She was worth even more than her money symbolized. That is true of most people, but until you know that, you will not have the symbols that match your value.

WHAT IS YOUR PERSONAL VALUE?

You are valuable, very valuable. If you accumulate the accurate representation of your value, it will be a lot of money. Every one of you, when focused and applied, is worth millions. If you do not have millions to show for yourself, I assert that you have a wrong relationship with money. You are still maintaining that money is where value lies, and you are not noticing that what is of real value is being suppressed within you as if it were worth nothing. You are racing around, trying to accumulate more and more pieces of paper, while keeping your true security locked up, hidden away. Is that sensible?

If you want to have money, express your value. If you begin to express the value that you are while making yourself valuable to others, money will come. By trying to hoard your symbols of value, you are really saying, "Nothing in life is worthwhile. I won't release my symbols of value. There is nothing in the world valuable enough for me to give up my money. I won't communicate the values that I recognize in the world. I want to hang onto the symbols I have in case I ever need to give statements of value for something that I don't have." And you call that security.

To create real security, you need to recognize your true value. Begin to think of your body, your mind, your personality, your talents, your determination and resourcefulness, your stubbornness as spiritual tools – no less spiritual than your soul or whatever you call the container that carries God within you.

YOUR MONEY REFLECTS YOUR BELIEFS

Everything that you do in your life is a spiritual act, from peeling potatoes to kneeling beside your bed. Listen carefully to that.

Everything that you do in your life is a spiritual act. Let that become a part of your belief system.

Begin to feel that every aspect of your life is a spiritual experience. Know that God is manifesting as much through your financial welfare as through your prayer life. They are inseparable. When you are confident of that, your prayer life will be reflected in your financial condition. Your health will be a reflection of your relationship with your source. Your relationships with people will be reflected by your appreciation of the true value of yourself. Your relationship with your alrightness will reflect in every aspect of your life. Nothing, and no one, outside of you can be a part of determining or establishing that relationship. It is your sole responsibility to recognize that.

So instead of seeking confirmation of your alrightness in every relationship and experience for the rest of your life, decide right now to assume that it is already established innately, for all time. Accept that as a fact and never question it again. You are all right just as you are. Nothing has to change. Ever. It is true, so accept it.

By accepting your alrightness, you become able to recognize the alrightness of others as well. It will happen naturally. You will no longer require them to go to great lengths in order for you to discover whether they are all right. You will just know without question that you and they were born with alrightness, and it cannot be otherwise.

What a relief! You can know that everyone in your life is all right. And you can stop the impossible alrightness-challenge you have been subjecting yourself and others to since childhood!

ACCEPTANCE DETERMINES PROSPERITY

Imagine accepting all individuals and all situations in the world just as they are, without wishing they were different. When you love life just as it is, when you accept every aspect of it without wishing it were different, life is what you get. You receive liveliness, and you expand, grow and prosper. Your prosperity manifests in wealth beyond money – wealth in material success, relationships, friends, professional success, love, health, wisdom, peace and happiness.

When you do not approach life with the energy of love and acceptance, when you resist what happens, you get to live in a world of shoulds – judgments imposed upon reality. You get to be angry because everything is not as it should be. Life is not fair.

Forget fairness in the game of life. Life is what it is, and if you welcome that, you get to prosper and grow. If you do not, those aspects of life that you resist and deny will hurt you. You get to live with pain and poverty.

This discussion of prosperity is not about getting what you want out of life. It is about truth. Truth is what is. If, instead of struggling to get what you want out of life, you will begin wanting what you already get out of life, life will work effectively in your best interest. And this universe is designed in such a way that whatever is in your best interest is in the best interest of every other being on the planet. If you are willing to enjoy and appreciate everything in your life, you will be amazingly prosperous. God will supply your every need, far better than you ever dreamed possible.

Repeat often, "I give to all people the right to be exactly as they are. No one has to change a thing for me. I accept life exactly as it is without wishing it were different. I am in harmony with the source of life, and so I accept life as it comes. At the same time, I accept personal responsibility to encourage, uplift and empower the people around me, to create and recreate harmony wherever I see the need."

Life is rich, and the planet is abundant. In conjunction with that, there are people amassing millions who do not "deserve it." If the laws regarding money stated that you have to deserve it to get it, those people would not have any. So drop your belief about needing to deserve money. This planet gives freely and provides sufficiently for all the children of God.

This planet stands ready to provide for you beyond what you can imagine, if only you will let go beliefs about not deserving to receive, about needing to be punished, about needing to experience lack and poverty to be spiritual. The child of God who is not receiving his or her share is the child who is finding an excuse to go without and be unhappy. If you want an excuse to be unhappy, there are plenty. You can always experience a lack if you desire it, but understand that you must desire it. You can only be poor if you believe that is the way you should live.

The real objective of spiritual growth on this plane is to master the laws of this planet. Mastery means that all things work for us, not against us, including money.

The majority of people on this planet work for money. We work for money, which means money is our boss - and money is a tyrannical boss, an exacting demanding master who does not pay well. If you want to go on a pilgrimage, or take a workshop, or go on a retreat, what is the first thing you must do? You have to ask your money if it is all right. Your boss, which is your money, will tell you what you can and cannot do. Your money will tell you whether you can feed that emaciated spiritual body. If your money says, "Well, that's going to put a strain on our lifestyle," you will say, "Well then, I'd better not do it." And so you express your obedience to the god of money.

Prosperity is the experience of reversing that position. Prosperity is the act of causing money to work for you instead of you working for money. How is that accomplished? The first step is to be strong in self-image. Your Father is the wealthiest in the universe, yet you have been taught that "God is not pleased with your extravagance. You should want nothing, live frugally, and deprive yourself because there is not enough. Your God has limitless wealth but wants you to live in poverty. Being spiritual means doing without."

If you believe that, it sounds like your Father has a psychological hang-up! The truth is that *that* God is a concoction of humankind's mind and has nothing to do with your true source.

Your true source created the universe and is the wealthiest being in his creation. The way to compliment him is to live accordingly, to live as if you are the most richly blessed being in his great creation. There is nothing spiritual about being poor or broke. This is an abundant planet, an abundant universe. Your choice is to serve a creative being who makes abundance available for your use, every minute of every day.

BEGIN AT THE BEGINNING

If you want to assure your prosperity, stop worrying about money and do exactly what you know you ought to be doing, whether you have enough money to do it or not.

Where do you start if you are flat broke? The thing to do if you have no money is to look around and discover the genuine needs in your neighborhood and begin meeting one of them. If someone's lawn needs mowing, do it. If someone's house needs repair, see that it gets done. If someone needs advice in an area that is your expertise, make yourself available. If there is a need for volunteers in your community, which there always is, get involved. Look for a way to meet the needs of others instead of concentrating on earning money.

Focusing on a way to make money is a mistake. Most individuals make that mistake and, as a result, receive only part of what is available to them. We have a Protestant work ethic that says, "In order to deserve to live on this planet, I must work." That is not one of God's laws and has nothing to do with the laws of this universe. You do not gain acceptability by being willing to work. If you can get past feeling guilty when you are not busy, your life will become more productive in areas that matter. If you are going to work, do it because it ought to be done.

Stop working for money and decide, "I'm going to give my time, effort, energy and commitment to accomplishing something that ought to be done. I'll work for that, and money will come in abundance." Accomplish something that makes a difference, not because it will bring the most money, but because it needs to be accomplished. If it brings money, wonderful. If it does not, you have still accomplished what you came here to do.

You are prosperous if you are experiencing joy of life. If you are having fun, enjoying life, having a ball, living every moment to its fullest even when there is little money, you are prosperous. Prosperity is synonymous with love and appreciation for life. If you must have money to enjoy life, money has become your god.

YOU HAVE EVERY REASON TO EXPRESS JOY

The traditional work ethic also states that happiness should come only occasionally, in small increments – that it is hedonistic to always enjoy everything. Yet we live on this incredible planet full of wonderful things, where life itself is a miracle and magic abounds in every experience if we want to look for it. It is not likely that God

429

said, "Now get out there and have a really rotten experience sometimes. I don't want you to have too much fun."

This is a wondrous world. And that in itself is a good indication that we are meant to enjoy it and have a ball. Do not feel guilty about enjoying every day of your life no matter what. Dare to flash a smile in the face of misery. Be brave enough to walk down a street full of strangers grinning ear to ear. They may try to lock you up, but someone in your family will come to give sound explanation.

Learn to play again. Learn to feel joy for life. The result will be prosperity in your life. Your health will improve, your bills will get paid, your worries will disappear, other people will enjoy you more, and the planet will transform itself in front of you. Your world will be transformed because it will change from a frightening, demanding place into a joyous, adventurous one.

Cause the people around you to smile, to laugh, to have fun, to love and appreciate themselves, to feel good about themselves. They will likely stop hoarding money and goods, and they will begin to turn loose of things.

Remember that people around the world are starving because people in other parts of the world are insecure. If you can get enough people to feel good about themselves, others will in turn be affected, and the hungry of the world will be fed.

THE WORLD NEEDS MORE JOY

You are not obligated to feel unhappiness here because there is unhappiness elsewhere in the world. It is not even sensible. It only produces two unhappinesses, and one is not serving the other. The world does not need another morose, unhappy, fearful person. The world needs more individuals who can experience and express joy, hopefully causing an epidemic and resulting in a world of happy, secure, loving people.

Too much control of the world's abundance is in the hands of the fearful. The money and goods of this planet are available to everyone. The joyous, loving people of this planet have a specific purpose – to use money to cause specific results in the world, which is their global responsibility. What would happen if the wealth of the world were controlled and directed by loving people? A major conversion! But as long as loving people believe they do not deserve to have a lot of money, the majority of it will remain in the hands of the insecure.

Instead of feeling, "I deserve to be poor," begin feeling, "I deserve to be a master of economy. I should be causing money to flow where it will produce positive results in people's lives. I don't need to gather or hoard it. I don't need to save it. I don't need to pad my world with needless things. I do need to tell money what to do and where to go."

Look for a need in your community that you would like to meet, and then look for a way to meet it. Become involved in the lives of others. Make yourself valuable to someone who has a need, and you will be paid in return for your giving. The source of your payment may not be the person you helped, but someone in the universe will make the payment to you. If you are making yourself valuable to others, money will come to you.

LOVE IS YOUR GREATEST ASSET

Individuals who feel all right about themselves secure their prosperity by automatically assuring others of their alrightness. They become valuable to others for that reason. The world will support people who assure alrightness in others because they are providing something more valuable than food or money.

Security for such people derives from their greatest asset, which is the love they give. It communicates, it supports, it heals, it forms relationships, it builds understanding. Their security is not based on the amount of money they have in the bank, but in knowing that they have gold for bartering that is of value. Their gold is of greater value than the commodities on which currency is based, for love and alrightness will always be more valuable than currency.

YOU ARE GREATER THAN YOUR FINANCIAL ASSETS

The foundation of a prosperous life is love. If you love yourself, if you have a right relationship with yourself, if you feel good about yourself, you will feel and be prosperous. Prosperity has little to do with money, and everything to do with love. People who love and are loved will be wealthy no matter how much available cash they have, while people who have a lot of money and are not loved will experience poverty no matter what else they possess. Love is a power that produces the force that allows you to experience prosperity.

Once you are making yourself valuable by meeting the needs in people's lives, ask your source to meet your needs. Then go ahead and live as if that prayer is being answered. Live your life expecting that your needs will be met, knowing that what you have asked for is coming to you.

The law of precipitation can be stated as simply as this: "Whatsoever thing you ask in prayer, believing, you will receive." (Matthew 21:22) Believing is seeing. Your prayers are powerful because what you believe is, and your reality is your creative responsibility. It is up to you to create the reality that you want, and believing is the first step.

If you are aware of something you need in your life, ask for it assuming that your source who provides you with life has more ways to get it to you than you can figure out. Avoid second-guessing your source, trying to figure out how that thing will come. If you say, "Well, it could come from here. Maybe I should go check that out. But I really wish it would come this way. Or maybe I need to do this to make it happen," you begin limiting the avenues through which it can come. If on the other hand you get on with your life, assuming that what you need will be there when you need it, it will appear.

Remember, if you are doing something that should be done, the universe will provide the means to finance it, and you. Get busy with the next step. Get busy with your reason for being here, and what you need to do that will automatically come to you. You deserve it!

Too often, our relationship with God has been put into a warped perspective for us by a foolish reference to humankind as a lowly worm – a different kind of creature, separate from its source. Enlightened teachers of today tell us that we need to kill our ego, get rid of all thoughts of self. Because of the limitations of words, that becomes an excuse to hate what God created, which is misguided and unfortunate.

You are a being fashioned with infinite care. You are a beautiful individual, a beautiful creation, deserving of a great deal of love.

Can you think of yourself that way? Can you love yourself that much? If you can, you can allow yourself to be prosperous. And just as importantly, you can allow others to be prosperous as well, because their prosperity becomes your prosperity.

When you see a smile on someone's face, when you recognize happiness, when you witness another's success, the same feeling wells up in you as in that individual. That person's prosperous experience becomes yours. Their happiness becomes your happiness, and you prosper together.

ENJOYING ANOTHER'S ENJOYMENT

Your participation in life means noticing how happy another person is and experiencing joy because of it. Love means participating in the lives of others by confirming and affirming what others have and by rejoicing in their having, enjoying their enjoyment.

Then it is no greater to give than to receive. Everyone can experience both. Everyone can experience love personified. Love personified is what occurs between individuals when they share love.

Love is a lifeblood, a vitality that multiplies as it is expressed. You cannot withhold it and grow. If you give it freely, without limitation, without selfishness, without reservation, without condition, without judgment, it expands and prospers.

Money works similarly. If you try to withhold it to make sure that you do not pay too much or give too much, you will seal it, causing pressure and anxiety. When you see yourself as abundant, prosperous, wealthy, generous and limitless, that new image will open the door of prosperity. And vitality will flow into every area of your life, including romance, health and your wallet.

Believing is seeing. See yourself as an unlimited source of lifeblood, life force, life spirit. And give it freely. People who are afraid of not having it will not have it. People who are willing to give it freely will build an image of being generous and prosperous. They will know that "I cannot possibly give you too much of myself, my life, my vitality or my energy, or even my money."

People often warn me about how much I give of myself, my time and my energy. The days and nights are filled with activities, yet I have more energy than anyone around me. I have life, I have energy, I have vitality, and I have plenty more to give. I have barely begun. Those who worry that I am giving too much do not understand what feeds and sustains me. If I were to listen to those warnings and allow myself to worry, the power would become limited. I do not need limitations, nor do you.

The same is true of giving time, money, energy, vitality and caring. They are all expressions of the vitality of life that is love. When it is given without reservation, the water of life flows into you and empowers you to give more. Those who share it have more to give than they can contain. Those who are afraid of sharing it, never have more than a trickle. Those who believe and act as if they have plenty will have plenty.

Always keep in mind that there is a loving, prosperous source of all that you need, present and living. Your only task is to give that presence an excuse to shower you with abundance.

THE NATURE OF PROSPERITY

Prosperity is more than an economic or a financial matter. A prosperous consciousness means living in a state of wholeness without the imbalance that causes lack. Wholeness means making the deliberate, conscious choice to express love instead of fear, abundance instead of lack or limitation, peace instead of conflict, cooperation and creation instead of competition, support instead of criticism, understanding instead of anger, appreciation and joy instead of pessimism.

Prosperity begins with a right relationship with yourself, loving and accepting yourself, knowing how wonderful you are, and knowing that it is all right to acknowledge that. Being alone with yourself becomes pleasant because there is a source of love and beauty within you and you are confident in your own worth.

Many people are habitually unhappy, and they need an excuse to be happy. Even when their experience is wonderful, their happiness is short-lived. They soon find things to gripe about because it is their habit to be unhappy.

Others are habitually happy. When life is terrible, they are unhappy for a while, but eventually they consider, "Why should I be in such a miserable situation and be unhappy too?" Because it is their habit to be happy, they are prosperous people, and they will prosper under any conditions.

People who love and are loved are wealthy, no matter how much money, possessions or success they have. People who have money but lack love experience poverty no matter what else they possess. The power, the energy, the X-factor that allows prosperity is love.

Be an example of love personified. If you have enough love to give away, you will be prosperous.

A PLAN FOR PROSPERITY

What you do for a living should be based on your values rather than making a living. And your investments should make a life for you and others.

Your money should, above all, provide living proof of the value of two things: the presence of living love in your life and the possibility for mastery of your mind. Mastery of your mind includes the possibility of being in charge of your thinking and calling things from formless force into substance, which is called precipitation. With single-mindedness, you can hold an image and impress it upon formless substance – and it must, by universal law, manifest for you.

The basic law of prosperity is that "If you think in ways of prosperity, you will act in ways of prosperity." Acting in the way of prosperity means doing your work so well that it cannot, it is not humanly possible, to do it more effectively. To do that, you have to manage your time well, accomplish your work well, and know without a doubt that you have given your all.

According to universal laws, there are specific steps for managing money. These simple steps form a plan for prosperity. If you will follow this plan exactly as given, with every portion of money that you have and every portion that comes to you in the future, two things will occur: More money will flow into your life, and your money will begin to work for you, instead of you working for money.

The first step is to divide all the money you have, and all that you receive in the future, into tenths. Every dollar should be divided into ten parts, and the parts should be used in specific ways.

THE FIRST TENTH

The specific use of the first tenth is the most magical because it will set the rest of the plan in motion for you. The first tenth is like a priming pump. It starts the movement or flow of energy, which in this case is money.

The first tenth of all that you receive goes to your source. It is the payment of a debt to the source that provided your existence – your body, your mind and mental capacity, your health, your talents and abilities, the skill and even the opportunity to earn the income.

It is not possible, although in most cases assumed, that the result-you, the created-you, could maintain all those aspects of you. Could your personality maintain the systems of your body, the faculties of your mind, the mechanics of breathing and running your daily expression simultaneously? Only the creator-you can keep you alive. And you owe that aspect of you, the God part of you, a debt of gratitude, which is the first tenth.

One of the most important things you can do with your life is to recognize the source of your ability to think, to function, to do all things – not for the sake of the source but for your sake. If you depend on your personality self to get you through life, without paying recognition to the source of all that you are and have, you will cut yourself off from that source. The pump will go unprimed, and the flow will not occur.

There is an age-old principle found in the sacred scriptures of many cultures. It is the recognition and acknowledgement by an individual that life originates from a source other than the conscious self, and that a debt is owed for that gift. Often, the teaching advises a tenth of the individual's income.

SETTING PRIORITIES

The word tithe literally means *one tenth*. The ancient tradition of tithing referred not only to giving one tenth of the product of your labors back to your source of spiritual inspiration. It also meant giving the very best tenth, the first tenth. This action places spiritual nourishment as the first priority in your values, it acknowledges your awareness and appreciation of your source, and it affirms your confidence in your source to continue bringing abundance to you.

To neglect to tithe back to your source is foolish and grievous because of what it reveals about your relationship to your source. When calamity befalls, and it always does, you will have no other recourse but to call on a God whom you have refused to support and refused to recognize as the source of all you receive, the source of your life itself.

God does not depend on your money and does not need to be supported by you. The reason to support your source is for the honesty and validity it brings to your relationship to God. If you plan to call on a divine power other than your conscious self for help at any point in your future, then give recognition and support, just as you would exchange payment for service with anyone else who would provide assistance to you.

TITHING DEMONSTRATES RIGHT RELATIONSHIP

The word tithe has become cliché. It is one thing to give your time and attention to your source by going to church once a week, meditating or praying a few times a week, saying to God, "I want to know you, I want to serve you, so please do this for me." It is easy and cheap.

It is more difficult to give a tenth of everything you receive to your source. But then, what is the value of the gift of life and the ability to sustain it? Giving the first tenth back to your source means you are serious. You are serious that your source is a valid and important facet of your life and that your gratitude is equal to at least a tenth of your income.

Tithing is not something to do because it is nice, helpful or spiritual. Tithing is a cause factor that creates a right relationship between you and your source. Remember that your money cannot lie. It is easy to say, "I believe in God, and I appreciate all my blessings." Are you willing to put your money behind that statement? "I can't afford to tithe," means "God is not where I place my value. These other things are what I value more and what I trust in more. Besides, how could I possibly survive if I gave God a tenth of my income?"

How can you possibly survive if you do not? If you fool yourself into believing, "I can have a relationship with God without giving him my money," you have made it clear that your money is more important than that relationship.

It is not the money that works the magic of priming the pump. It is the recognition that "I cannot live without the source of life and love that dwells within me, and I gladly give back a tenth of all I have so wonderfully received. I would give everything to sustain that relationship. Even a tenth is not sufficient because my love for my source is boundless, as are his blessings in my life." It is that recognition that will result in magic and miracles in your daily life. It is the energy behind the words that will cause results.

FIND AN EXPRESSION OF GOD

How do you give money to your source? The best way is to find those sources of enlightenment that are serving you in your life. Find those things that you can recognize in society where God is at work in people's lives. Find things that are making people happy, causing people to be healed, causing people to learn and be enlightened. Then sponsor them by giving money to them.

Give the first tenth to some source of God's expression. That can be a church or a spiritual organization, if it is the source of your spiritual sustenance and if it is accomplishing what you want your money to support. If it is providing food to your spirit, it is acting as a direct line between you and your source, and it is one of the lines that your source is using to communicate with you.

By giving your first tenth to the support of something that is causing joy or spiritual awareness, something that is making a positive difference in the world, you have taken a step to direct your money toward something that ought to be done. Instead of just accumulating funds and goods and simply supporting your physical existence, you have directed your money toward what you believe your life purpose is. By giving a tenth of your income away to right purpose, your money is already beginning to work for you.

In making the decision "To what should I give my money?" consider this. What ought to happen in the world? What does this world need for its continued growth and well-being? What contribution do I want to make to this planet? Then take a tenth of your money and say, "Go to work for me. Be my contribution to the world. Cause this to happen that I believe is important."

Money is a sacred instrument and a servant. It is alive with the energy of God at work in this plane, and it is meant to do your good works in the world. Relate to your money as if it were alive, take charge of it, and send it out to accomplish a specific purpose. "Go out there and get something done. Go out there and cause people to be happy, to be healed." Go beyond thinking that your money is supporting a good cause. Know that you are sending your money to work by telling it, "Accomplish something and show me some results." Demand to be shown those results.

Avoid giving your money away just for the sake of giving it away. Choose carefully something that you think ought to be accomplished in the world. "If I were going to do something with my life, if I were going to make my life matter for an important purpose, what would I choose to do with my life." Then take the first tenth that gives recognition to your source and use it to support that thing you would choose to do. If you find an individual or a group who is accomplishing what you would choose to do with your life, get behind them with your money and help them to do it.

Then look for the results that your money causes. Your life will begin to matter in a new way that you have carefully and specifically chosen. Your money will work for you to fulfill what you would do with your life. You will be working for what your money is causing, rather than working for your money. Your money will be causing a result in which you believe, and it will be working for you as your servant.

CREATE A PROSPEROUS FEELING

Another reason to give away the first tenth is that you cannot give money away without feeling prosperous, and you cannot feel prosperous without being prosperous. By giving this money away, you will begin to change your image of yourself and your belief about money's power over you. Instead of looking at a stack of bills and thinking, "Oh my God, I can't pay my bills. What am I going to do?" give the first tenth away. You will automatically feel differently about your relationship with money as well as your relationship with your source. Say to your money, "Listen, you can't tell me what to do and how to feel. You can't make me live in a straight jacket of problems. I'm not going to let you have power over me. I'm going to show you and me both that I have power over you. I have the power to give some of you away." That new attitude will make a difference.

People who give money away produce a prosperous feeling in themselves. Those who do not feel prosperous will feel too uncomfortable to give money away. To give, you have to feel able to give. Those who say, "I will give when I feel prosperous enough to give," will never feel prosperous. People who say, "I will give, and because I know I can give, I will feel prosperous," will use that feeling to expand prosperity in every area of their lives.

THE LAW OF TENFOLD RETURN

There is a further reason to give away the first tenth. There is a universal principle called the law of tenfold return. This principle reaches beyond money. It is the same law in effect when one tiny seed results in a stalk that produces enormous amounts of food, a volume much bigger than itself, and produces more seeds that produce vast numbers of stalks, constantly expanding. It is the law of tenfold return. What is planted will produce a volume bigger than its original form. That is the law invoked in the giving of the first tenth to your source of life.

In the Fellowship's history, various people have been in charge of the business aspect of the organization. And over the years, people have sometimes neglected to pay our tithe. During one of these periods, the accountant came into my office, his head hung low, a defeated look on his face. I thought a member of his family had died.

"The Fellowship is in a terrible financial condition." I thought he might cry. "It doesn't look like we'll ever get out of this mess."

I laughed and said, "Let's take a look at the books. Did we pay our tithe this month?"

Looking even more pitiful, he said, "We haven't paid a tithe in two months because we had to pay the bills first."

"For goodness sake," I told him, "Pay our tithe so we can get out of this hole." We owed three thousand dollars in back tithes. We had to begin a special campaign to earn the money to pay it. We did, and in a trip to New York shortly after that, we received gifts that made up the tenfold return. This principle works. It does not fail.

When you give your money away, expect the amount that you are giving to return to you tenfold. Say, "I am giving this money to something that feeds me, and I expect to receive tenfold in return." It may return to you in money, goods, service, love or joy. In whatever form, there will be a tenfold return, prospering you by ten times the value of what you gave away.

When you give money away, it is not your business to find someone who you think deserves it. To do that, you would have to assume that you are a better judge of character than your source who gives equally to the wise and the unwise, the grateful and the ungrateful. A pear tree gives to anyone who will pluck the fruit. You need to give in that same manner.

Your task is only to give, not to make sure that the person is grateful. If, after you give your money, you complain that the person is not grateful or deserving, you gave nothing away. Your wallet is empty but your action had nothing to do with giving. Instead, you tried to exchange money for gratitude. People who attempt tithing, especially to churches or charities, sometimes find that it does not work for them because they attempted to exchange money for gratitude, recognition, control, a particular promise, a plaque on the wall, a front row pew, or a spot in heaven. In all those cases, they did not actually give. Giving means no strings.

I once asked a financial consultant to advise the Fellowship business staff in working more efficiently. This individual agreed to look at our accounting books and give advice. The final assessment was that we were accomplishing impossible tasks with our recorded income. We were planning publication projects, buying property, contributing to the chiropractic college fund of one of our members, running residential and outreach programs, traveling around the world to provide seminars.

"On this amount of money, it can't be done," he said. Then he pointed to a particular sum on one page of the book and asked, "What is this?"

"That's our tithe," I said. One of the first actions taken in setting up the Fellowship, and one continued throughout its almost three-decade history, has been to pay a ten percent tithe on our income to another spiritual organization.

He looked up at me, his eyes tearing, and said, "This changes the whole picture for me. You are this tiny organization with these vast goals. And you're giving your money away! How can you do that?"

"How can we not do that?" I asked him. "How can we not give back to our source of inspiration? And how can we ask our members to tithe if we do not?"

YOU ARE A CO-CREATOR WITH GOD

There are people who say, "You can give money away expecting a return, but nothing will happen. There's no such thing as expecting a tenfold return and making it happen." This is not true.

Combining a feeling of expectancy with an action of tithing results in effectiveness. Florence Scovel Shinn wrote a wonderful book called *Your Word Is Your Wand* in which she states that our word is a powerful magic wand that can transform life. She knew the power of the spoken word to affect both the subconscious and the substance of which this universe is made in order to create tangible change.

We are talking about God in action. Money is God in action. As a co-creator with God, you can tell your money what to do when you send it out to fulfill your purpose, and you can charge it to return to you tenfold.

Money is God in action, like any other energy in this universe that is used to express divinity. Telling your money what to do as you set it in motion is a prayer. It is the spoken word to the universe to respond with its energy according to the laws that are set in motion. What you plant in the universe will produce a tenfold return whether it is money, or healing energy, or kindness, or love. Plant your energy and watch expectantly for the tenfold return, remembering that the root of all produce is love.

THE SECOND TENTH

By following this plan for prosperity so far, you have divided every dollar of your income into tenths, and you have given the first and best tenth to your source. What do you do with the second tenth?

"Bills!" you exclaim. Yes, that is correct – and you should pay them with joy.

As a person of integrity, you need to pay your bills, but here is something new to consider. Every time you pay a bill from now on, consider enclosing with the check a note that expresses your gratitude for the services received, for having a home, for having power and telephone service in your home, for receiving medical services, for the use of a car, for the use of credit.

The point is that it is important that you express an attitude of gratitude in all that you do. It is important that you feel and express gratefulness for all goods and services provided to you. Not because it is important that the other person hear a "Thank you," but because it is vital to your prosperity that you acknowledge, welcome and feel gratitude for what enters your life.

Never pay a bill with a feeling of resentment. Never do anything with a feeling of resentment! Paying a bill with resentment will cause a monetary drain on you, hindering your prosperity. Pay every bill with gladness and rejoicing, feeling that "I am more than able to pay this bill. I am receiving services, and I gladly send energy to other people who make a difference in my life."

If you question the amount of a bill and negotiation has gotten you nowhere, pay the bill with gladness, remembering that you live in a universe that is tenacious of equilibrium. That means that no one can take advantage of you without your source making up the balance on the other side. All things will come to balance. If someone steals something, or if someone charges you too much, avoid becoming upset. That is not the way to effectively spend your energy. Just say, "I'm waiting for the balance to come back in my favor." Then expect it to come. It will do so because that is the nature of this world.

We live in a cause-effect reality, and karma will balance itself. You cannot be scammed. No one can steal from you. No one can take advantage of you. You cannot lose anything that is important to you without the universe returning to you something equally or more valuable than what was taken.

Pay your bills cheerfully and pay them on time. You have no right to pay them resentfully, complaining. You do not have a right to create the hurt and disease in other people's bodies that can be caused by including negativity along with your bill. Anything that goes from your hand to another person's hand can carry your energy to that person, and you have a responsibility to make sure that energy is positive, vital, supportive, loving and healing.

Pay your bills with joy, even if you feel they are not accurate or justified. Pay them with joy and be thankful that you have it to give. However limited the supply appears, be thankful for the opportunities that come with life.

WHO SHOULD YOU PAY FIRST?

It is important to pay your bills, yet there is probably one bill that you have not paid in years, so you might have some catching up to do. You have paid ample money to all the people who supply you with things, food, clothing, utility power, specific services. You have certainly paid the government plenty. Yet you have forgotten to pay the person who has done most in your life, and that is the one to whom you need to make your first payment. The first person you need to pay is you.

Part of all you earn is yours to keep, so you get the second tenth. That is your portion, and yours alone. Pay yourself the second tenth of every dollar you receive, before you pay any other bill or debt. You have worked hard for yourself all your life, harder than anyone else, and you have earned it.

"This goes to me, and I am paying myself because I deserve it. A part of all I earn is mine to keep." You must develop a supportive relationship with yourself that says, "I have a right to keep part of all that I earn and paying me is just as important to my integrity as paying my bills and my debts." Putting off paying yourself until all the other bills are paid, if there is enough money left, means that everyone else in the world is more important to you than you. Paying you first is your first responsibility.

Imagine if you had been paying yourself what you deserve all along. If you had paid yourself a tenth of all the money you have ever earned, imagine how much money you would have now. The figure would be staggering. If you only take this one step in this plan for prosperity, you will automatically become wealthier.

There are several reasons and benefits for taking this step regularly. If you save your tenth, it will accumulate into wealth. Think of the things you could do with that amount and its interest, if you had been paying yourself a tenth of your income all your life.

Another reason to do it is that over time you will develop discipline over your money. You will be telling it what to do instead of it telling you what to do.

If instead, you spend this tenth because you could not avoid it, you could not afford to keep it, then money will be telling you what to do. Your money will be your boss. If you pay yourself one tenth of your income, your relationship to your money will change and you will be in control. That is a first step. But there is more.

USE OF THE SECOND TENTH

You are not going to keep this tenth. Instead, you are going to use this tenth to do two specific things. You are going to use it to do something that you believe in, just as you did with the first tenth, and you are going to send it out to have babies, meaning you are going to invest it. The second tenth, which you have paid to yourself, is going to multiply as it accomplishes what is important to you. It is to be used for specific investment.

You may have to let it accumulate over time until you have enough to invest, but be active while you are waiting. Look for a project that fulfills three qualifications: It must be something that you think ought to be accomplished; it must be something that will make money in order to return your investment and more; and it must be something in which you can share hands-on involvement. In this way, you get to contribute to something you believe in, working shoulder to shoulder with your money, in order to make more money, while causing a particular result.

This is not about watching the stock market, reading the financial pages, hiring a financial advisor, and building a strong investment portfolio. This is not for the purpose of making a lot of money. This is for the purpose of causing results. It is about disciplined use and experiencing yourself as a cause in this world.

This second tenth should accumulate and grow through worthy investments, because ethical people with right intentions should be directing the money of this world's economy toward right results. Using money to cause specific, carefully chosen results in the world is a spiritual responsibility.

TAKING RESPONSIBILITY

The best way to point our world economy, which represents our system of values, in a new direction is for people who have higher values to take responsibility for money and use it to cause specific things to happen. Too many people are working at jobs only to make a living, without taking responsibility for the product of their work. Too many people are investing money for the sole reason of making more money, for accumulating and hoarding wealth.

We need to change that consciousness. Whatever reflects your personal values, that which you believe needs to occur in the world, is what you should choose to do with your time, energy, effort, talent and money. What you do for a living should be based on your values rather than making a living. And your investments should make a life for you and others.

You are in every circumstance responsible for what your money does. If you are investing it, you need to understand how it is being used and take responsibility for that. You cannot escape responsibility for how your money is used. If you own stock in companies that are contributing to the destruction of the planet, you are responsible for that destruction. If so, get hold of your money and send it back out to accomplish right results.

Those of you who live on a fixed income – stop! Never again tell yourself or anyone else that you live on a fixed income. Anyone who is living on a fixed income is violating the laws of prosperity, and a purpose of this second tenth is to open a channel for money to flow into your life.

Choose a worthy project. Ask yourself, "What needs to be done? What has the potential to increase financially by using my money? Where do I want to invest my time, energy, effort, talent and money?"

When you find a project that will satisfy the qualifications of this second tenth, say to those involved, "I want to be a part of what you're doing. I will put my money into what you're doing. And I want an agreement from you that I will have a percentage of the profits that you take in. And I want to contribute my time and energy as well."

The second tenth should always come back to you, and it should come back with children, meaning more of its own kind. If done correctly, this investment will result in a return of the amount you invested, plus more money. When it comes back, do not spend the financial return. Put it into the original pot with your tenth and send it out to work again, causing a right result and bringing a return. Continue that pattern, working with the plan and causing it to be successful. You will reach more people, affect more lives, cause more results, and the money will keep growing.

Here is what can happen, more easily than you think. Over time, that portion of your income may become bigger than your salary. It is possible and likely that you will make more money doing what you believe ought to be done than with the job through which you presently earn your living. Of course, then the question becomes, "Should I keep this job, working for money, or should I be out there doing what I think ought to be done, with money working for me?" You will probably enjoy being faced with that decision. Here is a tip: If you do quit your job, do not quit this plan for prosperity.

Can you lose money with this plan? Probably, but this tenth is designed for investment. You do not depend on it to live. Have you realized yet that, according to this plan for prosperity, you are to live on 80% of your income? You do not have to worry about whether you lose this tenth. If you lose it, you will learn from the experience and know better what to do next time. Remember this, which is more important: If done correctly, meaning the project is really something that ought to happen, it will be successful and so will you.

BEGIN IMMEDIATELY

We have talked about the first and second tenths, and the appropriate use of each. The first tenth is paid to your source. The second tenth is paid to you, and you will use it for investment. Both tenths are going to accomplish things that are important to you, and both are going to bring a return. Neither tenth is money on which you depend to live.

You must live on the other eight tenths, 80% of your income. If you think, "I can't even live on 100% of my income! How am I supposed to live on 80%?" there are some things you need to know.

First, you can live on 80% of your income almost as easily as you can live on all of it. Second, if you follow this plan precisely, you will soon begin to receive more income than you have been receiving. You will have more money because of operating this plan for prosperity, not less. Third, by directing 20% of your income toward right results and using the remaining 80% to support your lifestyle, you take a step in the direction of devoting more and more of your thoughts, activity, time, energy and your being toward higher purpose, until the whole of your inner and outer value is dedicated to realizing good on earth.

If you think you do not have enough money right now to operate this plan, you are wrong. If you are experiencing financial problems, it is even more important that you get started. No one has too little to operate the plan. A dollar can be divided into tenths. If you do not even have a dollar, borrow one and begin immediately. You will see immediate results in your life.

THE THIRD TENTH

It is impossible to give money away without feeling prosperous, and that brings us to the third tenth. This one is optional. It is only for the purpose of helping others. There are no qualifications, so you can give to any cause or person you choose. This tenth is for the daring and the confident who know that it is truly impossible to out-give God.

The thing to do with this tenth is to plant it. You plant money by thinking of it as a seed with the potential to result in a stalk that produces enormous amounts of food, a volume much bigger than its original form. What is planted will produce. You can give away any amount of money to whomever you want to give it, and claim a tenfold return on it within a specific time period. That amount will return to you tenfold. Try it and see the results.

FOLLOWING DIVINE UNIVERSAL LAWS

People who are living according to divine universal laws will not be affected by financial problems. When people apply the laws properly, their finances will take care of themselves. Living according to these laws means working in harmony with this universe at all levels, and the result is prosperity in every area of life.

Setting aside the first and second tenths of every dollar you receive for the specific purposes stated will cause you to work in harmony with the universe. It will allow you to take control of your money, to make your money work for you for a change. It will allow you to send your money out as your contribution to this planet, and it will allow you to become prosperous through the application of the law of tenfold return. It will demonstrate your priorities of your source, yourself and others as important in your life.

Perhaps most important, it will cause you to allow your source to affect your life in ways that are discernible and measurable. You will be a witness to its direct movement in your life. Your creator can take care of you in beautiful and substantial ways that you have not even imagined, if you will stop trying to handle everything yourself. You can become prosperous by making your money work for you. And while you are busy using your money to improve the planet, your source can take better care of you than you can.

If you have a need, do not focus on and confirm the lack. Say to your source, "Take care of that," and get on with the business of making a difference in the world. Stop begging for dollars to pay for this and that.

What you really want is life and love. Ask to be an expression of love. Align yourself with the source of life that gives life, love, health, wealth, happiness, growth and anything you could possibly want. Praying for dollars is like begging a God who does not hear well to do something he does not want to do for someone who does not deserve it anyway.

Instead, align your will with living love, whose nature is to give freely. Attune your mind to what you need in your life, knowing that it will be given, knowing that there is an abundance of everything needed, knowing that being alive means being love to others.

THROW OPEN THE DOORS
FROM THE PAUL SOLOMON SOURCE

*T*ithing is not for the purpose of offering support to a church
or organization. Tithing is an act of obedience to a divine
or universal law, which is not an arbitrary law, so that
*energy may be allowed to flow. The law states that you give not only
a tenth part of all that you have to the Father, but that you give the
first part, the best part.*

*You are instructed to give so that you might receive, for it is only
through that manner that you may receive. Those who seek to be
given freely the waters of life fail to understand that, while the water
is given freely, it cannot be received by those who do not also give
freely in return.*

*You have not given when the first fruits already belong to God.
You have only established a relationship, by recognizing what is
already owned by God. This is only giving thanks, only recognizing
ownership. And it is the meaning of the giving of the first fruits.
Returning the best says, "I am allowed to keep that which remains,
only after I have recognized the ownership of all that I have."*

*Recognition of ownership is established by giving the first tenth
to the Lord and to his cause. Then one is allowed to become a
participant in the activities of that cause. It is not an arbitrary
decision. Universal law has declared that to be so.*

*Those who believe that they can receive from a spiritual
organization, which is working in harmony with divine cause,
without giving a tenth part of all they have, will find themselves
disappointed and going away fruitless. It is not in anyone's power to
negate universal law.*

*It is a simple fact that those who give a tenth part of all they
have will receive all that is provided, however much or little that may
be. This is true, wherever and to whomever they give.*

*Then select the manner in which you will give to the Father.
Find that which expresses God and give for the purpose of
establishing your relationship with the Highest, through throwing
open those doors, for the giving of the first fruit is the statement of
the first thought. If you give a tithe out of that which remains when*

bills are paid, where have you put the importance of the Father and spiritual growth in your life?

Be absolutely certain that the universe will return to you in the same manner in which you give. Have you not seen evidence that those who give reluctantly receive so little in return out of such a bounteous storehouse?

You have in your hands a treasure, food to fill the world. Yet even those who work in this storehouse are starving while surrounded with that food. They attempt to gorge themselves with that which is at hand, yet they do not assimilate and grow. Why? They have not opened those doors. They give to God what remains after other considerations, and so they are incapable of taking that which they have not emptied themselves to receive. The giving of the tithe is the opening of the door.

You have not given the first fruit. You have only paid a debt. For the paying of the tithe is the recognition of a debt that is owed. No gift is given until after the first tenth of all that you earn. There are no exceptions to this expression of universal law. It has been established and is at work.

But again, who can out-give God? Do not be threatened, feeling that God would take away from you and leave you with less, having taken your first fruits.

Rather, recognize the opportunity to let God prove what he has asked for opportunity to prove. For he said, "Try me and see if I will not open the windows of heaven and pour out upon thee a blessing thou shalt not be able to receive." (Malachi 3:10)

Then try him by bringing the tithes into the storehouse. See what returns. See if the windows of heaven are opened. See the Law of the Tenth blessed, and know that he will return tenfold a measure, shaken down and still running over.

The science of prosperity is an exact science, mathematically structured and mathematically certain. The Lord will bless him who gives of the first fruit and will return to him tenfold. A tithe that is paid on what remains after other considerations will not bring a tenfold return. Understand the manner in which these laws work, for it is the Law of the First Fruits.

As to application of the principle of seed money, understand that as you begin to give of your abundance, be absolutely certain that you could not stop the return to you, even if you tried. Giving – giving away all that you have – will bring more than any other action toward abundance.

If you gave all the money you have, it would be returned to you tenfold. And thinking you had divested yourself of it, you would find yourself ten times richer. How few can understand this and apply it.

But then, understand this as well: Even if you did not become ten times richer for the giving, you still would have made of your life greater through giving, by causing another to receive. And even if it cost you all you have come to consider precious, even if giving your money away deprived you of what you most desire, it could not deprive you of the giving and its inherent blessing.

It is your responsibility to support and care for one another. But always take responsibility as well, in your caring for one another, to assist each individual to lift himself into prosperity.

Let not your giving be the kind of charity that reinforces and reaffirms the poverty of the one to whom you have extended your caring and sharing. Take responsibility to awaken prosperity consciousness in others so that they may personally prosper. For the abundant source, your Father, owns the cattle on a thousand hills, is wealthy beyond measure, and has no desire that his children should have lack, or want, or limit.

Let prosperity be your vision. Prosperity in all ways, and in all areas. Hold prosperity as a vision, and all that you do, think and say will be effective.

Prosperity is the growing, fulfilling, overflowing of all that is good in this world. Let that be the foundation for the role that you are to play. Go with the sacred words of liberation, peace, prosperity, freedom and attunement to the one who is the source of all.

GRATITUDE

There is one final step, which will work more quickly and effectively than anything else you can do.

There is a promise in the Bible that is written, "Draw nigh to God, and he will draw nigh to you." (James 4:8) This verse speaks of two forces coming together, impelled by something. What is the impelling force that draws the two together? The simple truth is gratitude. Gratefulness.

If you can be grateful in all things, for all things, at all times – constantly grateful to your source for everything in your life, no matter what is happening, no matter what it looks like at the moment, no matter what catastrophe seems to be occurring at the moment – if you can be grateful for all things, in all things, at all times, you will draw nigh unto him and he will draw nigh unto you, until you are brought together, melded together as one.

This may mean discovering a God that is different from the one you have known thus far. If the God you have been relating to is not supportive of you – your past, your future, your accomplishments, your desires, the other people in your life – then you should probably fire that one, because God within you should be supportive of all that you are.

Each human being is an absolutely perfect creation, including weaknesses and congenital defects. Congenital defects, illnesses, weaknesses, disadvantages, disabilities and challenges only exist to point out opportunities to deal with particular issues and lessons for growth, as determined by the soul. So they are a part of the perfection of a life experience.

Every soul is born perfect, with particular strengths and weaknesses. The weaknesses are as perfectly planned as the strengths. And the greater or superconscious mind, which is God within you, knows everything there is to know about all those aspects chosen by the soul.

All you have to do – in order to listen to the superconscious mind and gain insight into the conditions and lessons at hand – is shut up. That means causing all the voices within you to become quiet. Your five senses, as well as your knowings and beliefs and prejudices, all have voices. And they all carry on a chatter in your mind that becomes louder and louder, as they compete contrarily for attention and dominance.

Learning how to quiet all those voices is an absolutely essential first step in spiritual growth. Everything else depends on it – the ability to discipline the senses and appetites and the voices of the body and the conscious mind, to set aside your beliefs and feelings, and to listen, in an eternal attitude of gratitude for everything about you, with no exception. If there are exceptions – things that you resent or dislike about yourself or your life situation – dismiss them. Change your relationship with them until you can be grateful in all things, for all things, at all times.

An attitude of appreciation will draw you close to the part of you that knows everything you will ever need to know about yourself. It will draw you close to your divine source that lives within you.

You have the right to have a good relationship with that higher part of yourself, to enjoy your God within, to have fun in that relationship, free of fear and guilt. Enjoying God is called spiritual recreation. It means being joyfully serious, and seriously joyful. In such a relationship, you ask questions and you listen. You never feel condemned. You always feel loved and forgiven, cherished. And that is the way it ought to be.

If you can experience such a level of appreciation for everything in your life, every moment of your life, living with an attitude of gratitude, then your link with your source will cause you to live life effectively, with prosperity in every area. It will cause you to be supportive to yourself and to everyone around you, at all times. And it will cause you to enjoy life beyond anything you have experienced.

Thank you for letting me share this time with you. I loved being with you.

456

MANY CANDLES ABOUT THE EARTH
FROM THE PAUL SOLOMON SOURCE

I *t is possible for any one of you to become consciously aware that there is always a divine desire inherent within you that impels you toward good, toward God. There is a spirit, or a presence, or a consciousness within each one of you. It causes within every man, woman and child an inherent seed of desire to be what you might call an expression of good, or of God.*

There is inherent within you a portion of yourself that desires to be the best that you can be in all aspects of endeavor. It is a seed of your source that desires to germinate and to bear roots, and boughs, and fruit – to grow and to mature into that possible being, that one you could be, who through complete harmony would be an expression of the highest and the best that you might have potential to express in the earth.

In moments of quiet and peace, there is often a consciousness in your heart of the existence of such a seed. And you desire to feed, to water, to nourish that seed so that it might express. In other times, desperation within you drives you to awaken that seed of consciousness in order to establish a communication between that seed and its source.

It is the nourishment and the awakening of this seed of source that allows and causes the experience known as regeneration, metamorphosis, transformation and the new birth.

The first step in this experience of transformation is a moment of evocation. There are times when you desire to express totally that which is good, that which is unselfishly of God within you. There arises a need in you to express perfect love, harmony and peace.

The dreamer in you dreams of being all that you can potentially be, as an expression on earth of the Divine Creative Principle, the Creative Fiat.

In those times when you experience that desire or quest, those moments are called the evocation of the highest or the divine to be in you and speak through you. You seek the highest that is within you – the creative nature, living love made manifest. You hunger for the true nature of your heart of hearts, where the only desire is to express on earth as a presence that will contribute to life on earth – a light extending from yourself, to burn as a candle in the darkness.

There manifests within each of you a presence that is the seed of your source. When watered by your expression of desire and prayer, there is awakened a need to express your holiness. This is the transforming experience. The seed that is planted in you is fed and watered by the transformation of all else that has been self. As self falls away into insignificance, it becomes like compost to this seed of the divine. The seed, sprouting as it were, reaches for its source, for it is a seed of a tree that is planted in heaven whose boughs, leaves and fruit extend into the earth.

The seed of God in you cries out to its source for the creative awakening spirit, the Divine Fiat. It is the extension of God that allows the spirit of creation itself to germinate that seed in you. And in that moment – when the best and the highest in you, that which is good and of God in you, that kernel or seed of God himself that he has planted in you, begins to awaken – there is the calling toward you of all the beings of the universe.

There exists a Great Cloud of Witnesses, which has been spoken of by the Apostle Paul as those who have gone before you from earth's experience to become the heavenly witnesses of the times when the source of creation reaches its points of love into the hearts and activities of men, to empower life in a man or men, in a woman or women, and even in children, to express themselves in such a way as to lift the entire race a little closer to the perfection of the expression of God on earth.

This Great Cloud of Witnesses surrounds the earth with its presence. These witnesses to the power of God are responsive when any one of you cries out to know the spirit, the presence, the power of God. These witnesses are drawn to the light, which occurs in the moment of evocation of holiness, when self seeks its source so that it may germinate and express its potential of allowing God to live in and through the body. In that moment, the seed becomes active through the intentional evocation of that which is of God, of creativity, of good and growth.

A light is created in dimensions hardly known to you, but which are occupied by this Great Cloud of Witnesses. This light, or spark of light, comes from the intent of one individual to know his source, to discover his creator, to discover the source of love in himself, the source of motivation to turn away from alternate lovers, distractions of the earth that keep the mind bound to things, that allow the mind to be so occupied with things not of God that there is left little room in consciousness for this seed to have that bit of attention that it must have to become activated.

This tiny seed, which is of God, is surrounded by a boundary, born of the insistence of God himself. Your source, your creator, has insisted that this seed be surrounded by a barrier that consists of your own freedom of will, so that you might live your life according to a will that is separated from the natural fruit of this seed of God within you.

In those moments when any man gives up his separate identity, when any woman gives up her will that is separate from the will of the source contained in the seed of God within, when the barrier of self-centeredness and self-interest is pierced in order to explore the presence of light, of love, of goodness within self, when the consciousness is turned in full desire without reservation, when all other things become insignificant in comparison to the discovery of the potential of this seed of God in self, when evocation has occurred, invocation takes place.

The seed of God draws to itself its source of divine nourishment. There is created between the individual being, the human, a living link between the seed and its source. This, in turn, creates a light in dimensions hardly known to you – a light that draws to itself that great host of the angelic kingdom, the Great Cloud of Witnesses. There is drawn that presence that has been described as the spirit of holiness and that presence that has been called the expression of God. There is called ultimately to this flowering of God in a man, the presence, the wisdom and the nature of the divine source itself.

So as we speak, we attempt to explain who we are. We are those in the unseen that are attracted to a prayer, a request, a commitment, a dedication – an emptying of all that is human self, presenting for a moment only that seed of God, with all else of the self lying dormant, unconscious, having given up its own thoughts, which remain contrary to one another because of the nature of the cleft brain of

459

man. And going beyond that mind, the seed of the source opens communication with those gathered here who are all presences, dedicated and committed to that one who has before him the records, the book and the books, as called in The Revelation. These are opened before him – the books giving the thoughts of the source of creation itself in the Creative Fiat when the worlds were spoken into being.

His purpose in so doing is recorded here, and the history of the development of his creation is laid before him here. We, the witnesses, are gathered to be a part of this divine experience, to contribute to it and to bring our strength as witnesses to affirm and confirm to you that it is possible for the mind of man to be influenced and directed by the spirit and presence of God.

We would draw your attention to the prophet Daniel and the manner in which, by entering a sacred sleep, he allowed the communication of divine source to fill him with inspiration of the instruction of that source that he might then be a channel of the guidance of the divine.

This process has ever been available to humankind, and is. We seek not in this moment to describe for you some special gift, something that you would think of as supernatural or psychic in nature. But rather, we present before you that which can happen and does happen when any one among you enters a moment in time when your very heart seeks to know experientially and personally the presence of good and God – the manifest presence of holiness of the universe, available to you, that you might attune to his presence.

The seed in you is awakened through experiences such as this, in moments when you set aside all thoughts and opinions, all appetites and expressions of the body and the mind separated from its source. The seed is awakened as you enter into a time of utter stillness, listening with every part of the self to the expression of the source, listening with a request from the heart – not the mind, but from the very depth of self, the soul, the heart of self – crying out to know its source and to be an expression in perfection of that source so that it may reach itself into earth through you.

That experience of awakening is called by some transformation. Others call it metamorphosis of the human spirit. Others call it the experience of the new birth. All of these link the consciousness of man with its source and produce potentially what has been spoken of through this source and this channel as the Meta-Human. It is the birthright of all humankind to know, to be in tune with, to be an expression of and filled with the presence of the divine to the extent that the limitation of what you can experience and express through human life is not the limitation of human possibility or capacity.

We have attempted to explain that what is occurring in this moment, the words that come and that you record, is not a phenomena for entertaining the fancy, for channeling the words of consciousness of an ancient being who will give his opinions of that which occurs on earth today. We do not purport to be a psychic source speaking through this channel.

We express ourselves only as a response to proper prayer – proper prayer being the setting aside of the self that is a distraction from the perfect inner desire to know God and the crying out sincerely from that heart of self that seeks to know God and asks, "Will you respond through me?"

Our words are a response to that prayer – which is made possible by the setting aside of the limited consciousness of the brain's activity, ideas, prejudices, opinions and beliefs – that there might be produced a clear channel for all that is of God, all that there is of good and living love, to operate the consciousness and speaking mechanism of this one in order to speak words of divine guidance. This should not be more uncommon among you than the practice of the ministers, preachers and priests who claim to speak the words of God before congregations of virtually every religion and creed about your planet.

It is in that spirit that we come before you. If there is a single message that we are commissioned to speak through you and to you, it would be as simple as this. When the voice of God rang forth in the origin of what you know as creation – when the supreme primal voice that was the first stirring of vibration, sound and light manifest in the utter darkness and emptiness before the worlds were – as this sound went out to create light, which is units or quanta of potential energy expressing in darkness, darkness having no resistance to it whatsoever, no power over it in any manner, so there went out one, and only one, original force.

This vibratory force is best likened to the quanta of light called photons, having neither positive nor negative electrical charge yet having the potential to become charged negatively, positively and neutrally. So that if there were in the beginning of time nothing more than light, you must understand from the point of view of your science of physics that that expression alone is sufficient, that all else that is created and manifest is possible from that one expression of the divine. But this divine expression, being a spectrum of vibration, allowed that creation be of both light and sound, and so provided the seeds of the energies you know as electricity and finally magnetism.

That that was sent out originally as light and sound had within it all potential to become gases, liquids and solid matter. And the ability of the light responding to matter in the presence of water gives you an image of all that was necessary for life itself to spring forth from this Creative Fiat.

We would lay a foundation for understanding that surely may be communicated to men, women and children of every race, creed, nation, religion and even science. It is of such consequence that, understood appropriately, it could possibly restructure consciousness and human nature to the extent of creating a science and technology based upon this simple truth that would reawaken earth to its natural productivity and expression of the divine source.

The sending forth of light and vibration by that which we have referred to as the Creative Fiat – which come first as light and sound, then combine and recombine, as positive and negative and neutral particles, resulting from the travel of the photons – there is the basis for all that is created. And the extent of creation might be understood as having come from this force that does not wholly disagree with your current theory called the big bang.

Now we would have you understand that in the sending forth of this energy that is light and which, as you have seen in the combination of the elements through the simple conversion of light into electricity and thus into the building blocks of atomic structure, might then simply by changing rate of vibration and varying combination of the positive, negative and neutral charges, lay the

462

groundwork for atomic structure and thus following molecular structure. And having these, you have the building blocks of the expression that you know as life.

Life itself, having preceded the expression of life, which came through photosynthesis as these energies we have described, combined to form light, color, sound, and then gases, liquids, solids and matter. And light upon matter, combined with water, gave forth photosynthesis and the building blocks of life as you have discovered them to unfold.

We wish to say then that there is the one energy that is life itself in expression. This that we call life also has qualities that in an ancient time were referred to as agape – life that, by its very nature, seeks to expand and to share.

Life that desires to share is known as love.

It was the desire – of this original Creative Fiat to share – that went out in light and sound and all other things. It was its desire – to share itself – that allowed life forms and other expressions to participate in its own liveliness.

Now we wish to make the point clear that there was and is only one primal energy from which all other energies are components, results, expressions of this one. Here is the basis for your unified field, if it be understood: There is not, at the ultimate point of expression, flowing forth of energy and vitality, even in your theory of big bang, a positive and a negative force and counter force.

At the beginning of all that is created, there is more simply a pouring forth of light, which is something that is living, that exists, as evidenced by the fact that it can travel in units called photons, quanta of energy, as compared with its counterpart, darkness.

Darkness exists not. There are no quanta or units of darkness. There are no such expressions of darkness that travel. It does not travel. It has neither substance nor reality in any form other than its appearance to be a point of reference for the existence of light. And so it exists only to that extent.

That extent is the extent of nothing, which allows the fact that something exists to be known. That is its only purpose. And even as we speak of darkness as it, we speak in improper terms, for it is not it. Rather, it simply is not.

If this is true of light and darkness, it is also true of life and death. You can demonstrate for yourself that death is not the annihilation or the disappearance of something that has expressed or lived. You do not know some force or form that you can appropriately identify as death for such does not exist. Experiment as you like, and you will find that you can cause nothing to permanently cease its existence, whether of consciousness, light, plant, animal or any other expression of life. Should you seemingly extinguish it totally, it simply will cease its expression for a time and then return to express itself again.

There is no death. Thus the word serves only the purpose of a point of reference to express a positive. Death is appropriately used only as an expression of the fact that there is something which is, which does exist, which is an opposite of that which does not exist. That which does not exist is called by the name death, but which is a name for something that is not. Yet it serves a purpose in expressing that there is a counterpart that is, which does exist.

May we offer then a third? We have referred to agape as the tendency or the need in that which lives to live more abundantly, to share its life, to share and share and share, in combination and recombination of expression. The force of agape is that force which causes all living things to wish to re-create. Re-creation is the ultimate expression of love. It is the desire in the soul of all that lives to give life and to continue the living of life by spending the life force of itself, for the purpose of giving that life force to something that will continue the expression of its existence.

Love is so inherent in life that life itself might even attempt to extinguish itself, or sacrifice itself, for the purpose of giving new life, to continue the living of life.

Life cannot be caused to cease to exist. If you created of your planet a barren place, totally annihilating the expressions of life upon it, you would find that for a time it would seem to be barren. Perhaps ice would form, and then eventually, begin to melt away. With the melting, a sprig of green would appear in photosynthesis and build the process of ever increasingly complex forms of life again to repopulate this place.

There is no sphere, in all those spheres that you know in the universe, that are without life. The life on these spheres does vary in its expression. On many of them, you would not encounter life with the limitation of your senses, for they are peculiar to your planet. You are not well equipped to interact with life from other spheres.

There is only one force that is in fact real. It is original, creative force. It is logoic or logoidal energy. It is, in the terms of the writer of the Gospel of John, the Living Word. It is the expression of God gone out to reveal itself in many different forms so that the broad spectrum of its expression might be known.

Now we would offer you a prayer that can be understood by adults and children, people across all racial barriers, cultural barriers and religious barriers, which are artificial structures. Let us give this.

It is well that each of you enters into a time when you seek in quietness to confirm and affirm that there is something in you that is good, that is of worth and value. There is something within you that has a desire to express good, to contribute to the world in which you live, to contribute to life itself, to be a participant in co-creation.

When you find that part within yourself, speak to it. Speak without fear that you will not be heard. Speak to the heart for it will hear. It is the very source of your ability to speak, thus it can hear and understand. Speak to the highest, the holiest, the best, the good, the source of love itself within you. Speak to that and say, "Please, you are the most God-like seed of expression within me. Please, will you become activated and grow within me. And will you grow to such an extent that there is pushed out of me all energies that are not you, the good in me."

Would you request that of yourself? This is the first step. Let each of you, man, woman and child, speak to yourself, within yourself, and say to the highest, the best, the holiest, the good in you, the living seed of God in yourself, that which makes you wish to be good and kind, saying, "Please grow in me until everything that I don't feel good about in myself, everything that is not divine, everything that is not loving and kind and creative, everything that is a misuse of my energy and a seed of dis-ease, everything that is of the nature of fear, falls away. Will you grow in me until I am filled with

465

your presence, the presence of life and love, the presence of all that contributes to joy, laughter and wellness? Will you, seed of God in me, seed of holiness, of wholeness, of healing and health, of joy, allow me to want to be kind? Will you continue to grow and occupy my senses and every cell of my body, occupy every part of my being, until I am no longer me, but you, until I am you manifest, holiness and goodness, and there remains nothing of me that is unlike you."

As you pray that simple prayer, reach one step further and say, "Seed of good and God in me, seek your source, your Father, for you are the child of God in me. Child-God in me, seek your Father, that you may be about your Father's business."

You will become so filled with love that you can reach out to make contact with living love, with God alive in the world. You will become an extension of God in the world. In so doing, you create a cord, a spiritual cord of communication, and contact, and healing that allows you to be connected with God, God-connected.

Allow the force of God to flow into you and fill you with his presence and his being. Allow your words to quite automatically be his words. So will your personality become one of strength, of wholeness, of confidence and of love. So you will begin to know yourself in a new way, having confidence in yourself, knowing that you are filled with love and with kindness and with power, a power over which evil has no effect and cannot befriend.

Know that all things that are not of God have no ability to affect that that is of God. And as you are filled with his holiness, you become invulnerable to darkness, death, threat and evil.

Then may we offer this last simple prayer: "I speak this day to the highest, the holiest and the good in me. I speak to that in me that is capable of unconditional love, that in me that is capable of giving life. I say to you, 'Please grow in me until I am filled with you.' And reaching beyond that which I find in myself, I reach to the source of all good in the universe, and I say, 'I want to get to know you better. As your seed grows in me, I reach out to you to be filled with your divine presence, and so become an incarnation of love alive, of life living, and of light shining in this world of darkness.' And I pray that through my communion with the source of creativity, that we may become many candles about the earth creating one great light that allows for the healing of our suffering Mother, the earth.

"We know that those who have attempted to kill, in the minds of men, the Father God, have never succeeded. And those who attempted to crucify the Son of God only multiplied his presence. Now we attempt to crucify the Mother, and in this attempt, we may come closer to accomplishing the death of an expression of God than we ever have in the past.

"Let us then as men, women and children of earth, awaken to the need to soothe the skin of our Mother Earth, to bless her heart with our prayers and our caring, to clear the air which she must breathe of the toxins, which we may through prayer and listening find a way to eliminate from her breath. And may we live on earth, not as parasites upon this great host being, which tolerates our presence and even provides for our needs. But rather than as parasites, Lord, teach us a symbiotic relationship, that earth may become fuller, stronger, manifest more completely, in a healthful, peaceful way, because we have lived gratefully upon her surface and placed ourselves deliberately into symbiotic relationship with her, our Mother host."

We are through with this that might go out to affect, having been blessed by your hands and hearts, the consciousness of those who have ears to hear about this globe. So let it be.

Paul Solomon
1939-1994

Made in the USA
Charleston, SC
01 February 2011